# THE REIGN OF THE PHALLUS

Nude woman carrying a large phallus; caricature of female phallic aggression.

# THE REIGN OF THE PHALLUS

*Sexual Politics in Ancient Athens*

EVA C. KEULS

HARPER & ROW, PUBLISHERS, New York

*Cambridge, Philadelphia, San Francisco, London*
*Mexico City, São Paulo, Singapore, Sydney*

*1817*

FIRST EDITION

*Designer: Sidney Feinberg*

Library of Congress Cataloging in Publication Data

Keuls, Eva C.
    The reign of the phallus.

    Bibliography: p.
    Includes index.
    1. Women—Greece—History. 2. Sex customs—Greece—History. 3. Sex symbolism—History. 4. Phallicism—Greece—History. 5. Athens (Greece)—Politics and government. 6. Greece—Civilization—To 136 B. C.
I. Title.
HQ1134.K48      1985          306.7'0938          83-48793
ISBN 0-06-015300-8          85 86 87 88 89 10 9 8 7 6 5 4 3 2 1
ISBN 0-06-091129-8 (pbk.)          85 86 87 88 89 10 9 8 7 6 5 4 3 2 1

# Contents

*Acknowledgments*     *vii*

Introduction     1

1. Military Expeditions, Protest, Lament, and Scandal     16
2. Attic Mythology: Barren Goddesses, Male Wombs, and the Cult of Rape     33
3. The Phallus and the Box: The World Seen in the Shapes of Human Genitals     65
4. Bearing Children, Watching the House     98
5. Brides of Death, in More Ways Than One     129
6. The Athenian Prostitute: A Good Buy in the Agora     153
7. The Whore with the Golden Heart, the Happy Hooker, and Other Fictions     187
8. Two Kinds of Women: The Splitting of the Female Psyche     204
9. The Sex Appeal of Female Toil     229
10. Easier to Live with Than a Wife: The Concubine     267
11. The Boy Beautiful: Replacing a Woman or Replacing a Son?     274
12. Learning to Be a Man; Learning to Be a Woman     300
13. Sex Among the Barbarians     321
14. Classical Tragedy: Weaving Men's Dream of Sexual Strife     329

15. Sex Antagonism and Women's Rituals                          349
16. Love, Not War: Protest in the Arts and on the Streets       381
    Epilogue                                                    404

    *Notes*                                                     417
    *Bibliography*                                              421
    *Sources of Illustrations*                                  435
    *Index*                                                     443

# Acknowledgments

This book could not have been produced without the support and the facilities of a variety of scholarly institutions. I carried out the basic research for it during a year's residence at the School of Historical Studies of the Institute for Advanced Study in Princeton, New Jersey. Several shorter stays, at the Fondation Hardt pour les Études Classiques in Geneva and at the American Academy in Rome, provided spells of tranquillity and contemplation. The National Endowment for the Humanities and the University of Minnesota granted funds which bought time and helped defray the cost of the illustrations. To all these institutions and their directors and trustees my warmest thanks.

Numerous colleagues, students, and friends have enriched my text with fresh insights and saved me from countless errors and omissions. I cannot enumerate them all here, but my very special gratitude is due to my colleague John P. Sullivan and to my agent Craig Comstock for improvements of the text, and to Duane Bingham for outstanding photograph processing.

Most of the illustrations are of objects dispersed over a large number of collections of antiquities. In many cases the curators have provided photographs free of charge and waived the customary reproduction fees in the interest of historical scholarship. Their graciousness is acknowledged in the Catalogue of Illustrations.

Greek mythology is largely the dragon-fight mythology of a consciousness struggling for independence/from the mother image/and this struggle was decisive for the spiritual importance of Greece.

ERICH NEUMANN, *The Great Mother*

# THE REIGN OF THE PHALLUS

# Introduction

In the case of a society dominated by men who sequester their wives and daughters, denigrate the female role in reproduction, erect monuments to the male genitalia, have sex with the sons of their peers, sponsor public whorehouses, create a mythology of rape, and engage in rampant saber-rattling, it is not inappropriate to refer to a reign of the phallus. Classical Athens was such a society.

The story of phallic rule at the root of Western civilization has been suppressed, as a result of the near-monopoly that men have held in the field of Classics, by neglect of rich pictorial evidence, by prudery and censorship, and by a misguided desire to protect an idealized image of Athens. As a Professor of Classics, I believe that an acknowledgment of the nature of this phallocracy will have the effect, not of disparaging the achievements of Athenian culture but rather of enriching our sense of them, adding yet another level to their meaning. In any case, the evidence cannot any longer be ignored.

Even to propose the concept of a phallocracy in ancient Greece may touch a sensitive nerve. In writing about Greek homosexuality Sir Kenneth Dover declared, "I know of no topic in Classical studies on which a scholar's normal ability to perceive differences and draw inferences is so easily impaired." As this introduction will make clear, Athenian male homosexuality was only one aspect of a larger syndrome which included men's way of relating to boys, wives, courtesans, prostitutes, and other sexual partners, and, in a larger sense, not only to people in Athens, but to other city-states.

First of all, what is "phallocracy"? Literally meaning "power of the phallus," it is a cultural system symbolized by the image of the male reproductive organ in permanent erection, the phallus. It is marked by, but is far more particular than, the dominance of men over women in the public sphere. In historic times, at least, such dominance has been almost universal. Nor does phallocracy refer simply to the worship of the male organ, a practice considered bizarre by most Westerners but common in many parts of the world, especially in conjunction with worship of the female counterpart. Although cultures that revere sexuality are, like others, generally dominated by men, much of their art and rituals presents the phallus as a symbol of generativity and of union with, rather than dominance over, the female. Furthermore, phallocracy does not allude to male dominance solely within a private sphere of sexual activity. Instead, as used in this book, the concept denotes a successful claim by a male elite to general power, buttressed by a display of the phallus less as an organ of union or of mutual pleasure than as a kind of weapon: a spear or war club, and a scepter of sovereignty. In sexual terms, phallocracy takes such forms as rape, disregard of the sexual satisfaction of women, and access to the bodies of prostitutes who are literally enslaved or allowed no other means of support. In the political sphere, it spells imperialism and patriarchal behavior in civic affairs.

In speaking of "the display of the phallus," I am not referring, as Freudians do, to symbols that may remind us of the male organ, such as bananas, sticks, or Freud's own cigar. In Athens no such coding was necessary. As foreigners were astonished to see, Athenian men habitually displayed their genitals, and their city was studded with statues of gods with phalluses happily erect. The painted pottery of the Athenians, perhaps the most widespread of their arts, portrayed almost every imaginable form of sexual activity.

## Painted History

In describing Athenian phallocracy, I rely heavily on pictorial evidence. As a source for history, vase paintings and other figured monuments have the advantage of coming directly from their period, unlike literary texts, which have had to pass through centuries of copying, selection, and censorship to survive into our time. Yet until the very recent past, most studies of Greek sex relations and other aspects of social history have either ignored these artifacts or used them essentially as illustrations of views derived from the written record.

Discovered during an era of sexual repression, "pornographic" Greek vase paintings were, in many cases, locked away in secret museum cabinets. When censorship was sufficiently liberalized, selections of the most sensational pictures were published in books apparently intended less for historians of sexuality or social customs than for devotees of erotica. Now it is time to study all the pictorial evidence for what it can teach us about the sexual politics of Classical Athens, and in particular about phallocracy.

Artifacts have to be studied with circumspection. As art historians have taught us, the interpretation of pictures raises subtle problems. Artists are affected by graphic traditions, the limitations of the techniques available to them, social conventions about what is permissible and interesting to depict, rivalry with other artists, requirements of composition, and other factors. To read a painting as if it were a snapshot would be as naïve as to regard a Greek tragedy as a slice of the life of its audience. Like a piece of writing, a painting can take such forms as fantasy, caricature, slander, or official propaganda. Pictorial conventions have a significance of their own, although it is not always easy to extract it. Why did artists favor certain subjects and treatments, neglecting others? Why do we have a fairly extensive pictorial record of the Athenians' crafts and trades, but not of their political activities, even though they were passionately devoted to these? Why is so much of the subject matter of vase painting mythological, even though it is often clearly intended to convey very concrete patriotic, political, or philosophical notions?

Often the basic meaning of a vase painting is clear and when it is not, we have techniques for concluding that one interpretation is more probable than another. A book intended for the general reader is not the place to explain the intricacies of "reading" pictures, but a comparison of my descriptions with the visual evidence reproduced in these pages will allow readers to intuit many of these procedures and to decide for themselves whether a given vase painting supports the argument in which it figures.

## An Obsessive Fear of Women

One way to grasp the essential nature of a culture is to look at its charter myths. In Athens, the legendary combat of Greek heroes and Amazons held first place in popularity. The legend of these warrior women, who fight men and exclude them from their society, is the mythological archetype of the battle of the sexes and constitutes what Phyllis Chesler has called "The Universal Male Nightmare." From Classical antiquity in its entirety, over eight hundred portrayals of Amazons have survived. Nowhere else were they as numerous as in Athens; representations of Greek heroes stabbing and clubbing Amazons to death could be seen everywhere in painting, in sculpture and in pottery decoration. In Figure 1, a detail of a vase painting, a feisty female warrior identified as the Amazon queen, Hippolyte, aims her spear at the exposed genitals of a naked Greek man, probably Theseus, Athens' national hero. The Amazon on the left aims the blunt end of her spear at the abdomen of another Greek fighter. To a male viewer such scenes seem to say: women threaten our manhood, and need to be subjugated to prevent them from rebelling against us. On this vase, the outcome is in doubt. In most depictions of Greek warriors and Amazons, however, the women are shown being defeated and, often, being slain. Not infrequently, as in our cover illustration, the killer plunges his weapon into his opponent's breast near a nipple, as if to dramatize his assault on her femininity, even though he has to make an unnatural stabbing movement in order to do so.

The motif of the rebellion of the Amazons was the most prominent expression of men's gynophobia, or fear of women. Many other myths—as well as drama, the law, and the practices of everyday life—document the same view of women, as caged tigers waiting for a chance to break out of their confinement and take revenge on the male world.

Regardless of how women would actually have behaved had they no longer been suppressed, this male fear existed as a social reality and formed part of the justification for phallocracy. As in the arguments for perpetual war to defend the integrity of the empire, Athenians apparently feared that any concession to women would lead to a collapse of the social order that men had built. Earlier, we distinguished phallocracy from worship of phallic images as organs of reproduction, and from the many patterns of male rule not symbolized by the phallus. Now we can add another element to the Athenian syndrome: a pervasive fear among men that, if they weakened the tenets of phallocracy, women might rise against them and in some sense destroy them.

The reign of the phallus comprised nearly every aspect of

1. Amazon aiming her spear at the genitals of a Greek warrior.

Athenian life. Once alert to its implications, we can see it reflected in architecture, city planning, medicine and law. In the public sphere of men, buildings were massive and surrounded by phallic pillars, whereas private dwellings, largely the domain of women, were boxlike, enclosed, and modest. In law, we can trace the origins of the syndrome back to Solon, a founder of Athens and a father of its democracy. In the early sixth century B.C. the great legislator not only overhauled the Athenian political system but also instituted many controls over sexual and family life. He originated the principle of the state-controlled and price-controlled brothel, and passed, or singled out for perpetuation, "Draconian" laws for safeguarding the chastity of citizen women, including the notorious statute that a father could sell his daughter into slavery if she lost her virginity before marriage. He also may have instituted the Women's Police (*gynaikonomoi*), not securely attested in Athens until the post-Classical age but probably much older. At any rate, enough domestic legislation goes back to Solon to consider him a codifier of the double standard of sexual morality.

## Women and Slaves

One of the most revealing aspects of Athenian society was the similarity of the positions of women and slaves: a considerable number of references and symbols connect the two categories. The legal term for wife was *damar*, a word derived from a root meaning "to subdue" or "to tame." When the bride arrived at the groom's house, a basket of nuts was poured over her head for good luck, a treatment also extended to newly purchased slaves. This was called the *katachysmata* or "downpourings." Like a slave, a woman had virtually no protection under the law except insofar as she was the property of a man. She was, in fact, not a person under the law. The dominance of male over female was as complete during the period in question as that of master over slave. As a result, the lives of Athenian women have been nearly excluded from the record. The women of the age of eloquence were silenced, and deprived of the form of immortality that Greek men prized above all others: that of leaving a record of their achievements. With unintentional aptness a scholar entitled a recent study of the Periclean age *Men of Athens* (R. Warner, 1973).

But men sat uneasily on the victor's throne. For there was a vital difference between women and slaves in the minds of the men who owned them. Slaves and their agonies could be excluded from one's consciousness, like the sufferings of animals, but women are men's mothers, wives, sisters, and daughters, and the battle of the sexes had to be fought over again in the mind of every male Athenian. Nevertheless, the institution of slavery provides the key to the understanding of the sexual and moral stances of the Athenian Greeks to be described. Without a grasp of its implications, these attitudes would not be comprehensible by the modern mind.

Judged by the ideals of modern Western society, life in the ancient world in general was brutal. Slavery brought the gruesome implications of man's victories over his fellow men into every home. Even so, household and other urban slaves were a privileged elite. What went on in the mines, quarries, and treadmills (with which the masters of comedy constantly threaten their slaves) must largely be filled in from imagination. We have no references to those practices from the Greek age, but from the Roman Imperial period the author Apuleius has left us this description of a treadmill where slaves were punished:

Merciful gods, what wretched mannikins did I see there, their entire skin covered with bluish welts, their backs torn into bloody strips, barely covered with rags, some having only their genitals covered with a piece of cloth, all of them showing everything through their miserable tatters. Their foreheads were branded with letters, their heads half-shorn, their feet stuck in rings. They were hideously pale, the dank vapors of the stinking hole had consumed their eyelashes and diminished their sight. Like wrestlers, who are sprinkled with a fine powder as they fight their bouts, they were blanched with a layer of dirty-white flour. (*Met.* 9, 12)

Some Classicists argue that the ancient Athenians were mild masters to their slaves, thus echoing Aristotle, who wrote of the "customary gentleness of the Athenian people." Such evidence as we have, however, suggests that slavery was more unmitigated in Athens than in many other ancient societies. A telling detail of their customs was the use of an object called a "gulp preventer" (*pausikape*), a wooden collar closing the jaws, which was placed on slaves who handled food to keep them from eating it. The tortures of Tantalus were mirrored in everyday life.

A practice exclusive to Athens among Greek cities (with the possible exception of the Asian city of Miletus) was the routine torture of slaves in legal proceedings. A slave's testimony was admissible in court only if he gave it under torture, a provision that shows contempt for his character and disregard for his well-being. An owner could refuse to surrender his slaves to the opposition for questioning, but this would obviously cast a suspicion of guilt on him. If the slave was permanently injured during torture, the owner was entitled to damages. The state maintained a public torture chamber for legal purposes (*basanisterion*). The interrogations there were a form of popular entertainment: "Whenever someone turns over a slave for torture, a crowd of people gathers to hear what is said," Demosthenes reports. The Athenians were, in fact, inordinately proud of their practice of examination by torture, considering it, as one orator put it, "the justest and most democratic way" (Lycurg. 29).

Sexually, as in all other ways, slaves were at the mercy of their owners. In fact, we will see that slaves, whether owned by public and private brothels or by individuals, provided men's habitual sex outlets, a circumstance which in itself must have generated an equation of sex with domination. Those slaves who were also women carried a double burden of oppression and were the most defenseless members of society.

## The Majesty of the Law

Criminals as well as slaves were treated harshly in Athens. Theft was punishable by death, and a common manner of execution seems to have been a form of crucifixion. Only favored convicts, like Socrates, were granted the more merciful death by poison. The place of execution was an open area outside of the city. Plato mentions a man who left Pyraeus and in the "public place" saw the bodies of executed prisoners lying around (*Rep.* 4, 439e). The victim was stripped naked and fastened to an upright post with clamps, with a heavy iron collar around his neck. This method of execution is probably identical to that of "planking" (*apotympanismos*), mentioned in literature and dramatized in the figures of Prometheus and Andromeda, both of whom were shackled to rocks. Aristophanes makes sport of the practice by having his character Mnesilochos tied to a board for execution in his comedy *Thesmophoriazusai*. In 479 B.C. the Athenians did away with the Persian leader Artayctes by exposing him to the elements, tied to a post (Hdt. 7, 33). Pericles, who crushed an attempt at secession from the Delian League on the part of the inhabitants of Samos in 439, had a number of prisoners tied to stakes in the marketplace of Miletus. He left them there for ten days, after which he had them clubbed to death (Plut., *Per.* 28). Corpses of prisoners executed by "planking" have been found near Athens (Gernet; Flacelière).

As with the later forms of crucifixion, the publicity of the execution was clearly as intentional as the prolonged suffering of the victim. Indeed, the agonies of torture and death must have been familiar to every resident of Athens. In Aeschylus' *Eumenides* Apollo chases the Furies out of his temple, back to the ordinary places of torture and execution, where they belong and which evidently were not unknown to the audience:

> This house is no right place for such as you to
> Cling upon; but where, by judgment given, heads
> Are lopped and eyes gouged out, throats cut, and
> By the spoil of sex, the glory of young boys is
> Defeated, where mutilation lives, and stoning,
> And the long moan of tortured men spiked

Underneath the spine and stuck on pales.
(185–190; trans. H. W. Smyth)

Whether or not a master could legally kill a slave at will is debated, but an owner could certainly inflict everything short of outright death on his property. The mere suspicion of a crime was sufficient cause for execution of a slave, as is revealed in Antiphon's speech *Against the Stepmother*: a slave prostitute, who had been an unwitting accessory to alleged murder, is routinely tortured and executed, apparently without any legal process.

## The Scholarly Response

In the face of evidence for these practices, what has been the response of Classics scholars? At best, they have habitually overlooked or interpreted away the evidence; and all too often they have openly endorsed or at least provided apologies for phallocracy. While one school of thought has been arguing that things were not as bad for women as they might appear, another school has been declaring that women deserved everything they got. Understandably a number of scholars have been drawn into Classics by sympathy for the patriarchal character of Greek life, or by a sense of kinship with Greek male homosexuality. Such scholars have consistently stressed, and endorsed, the phallocratic aspects of Athenian life, while ignoring the strains of feminism and anti-militarism that developed in opposition. Among the visceral misogynists should be counted Friedrich Nietzsche, who began his career as a classical philologist. In his essay "The Greek Woman," he finds it inevitable that an advanced and creative culture should reduce its women to the status of vegetables.

In the 1920s a German professor by the name of Paul Brandt wrote a two-volume social history of Greece, devoting the second volume to sex life. At the time, a work on this subject had to be published under a pseudonym, and Brandt chose that of Hans Licht, presumably to suggest that he was throwing light on an obscure matter. Under the title *Sexual Life in Ancient Greece*, the English translation of the second volume became a best-seller and went through many printings. It still constitutes the most thorough combing of Greek literary texts for allusions to sex, and the German edition also contains many photographs of artifacts, though without critical analysis. In Brandt's view, the Greeks "assigned to woman as a whole the limits which nature had prescribed for them," and also pioneered and acted upon "the modern idea that there are two kinds of women, the mother and the courtesan" (18). Wives were "banished . . . to the seclusion of the woman's chamber" because of their inability to converse with the flair demanded by "highly cultivated Athenians . . . as their daily bread." Women failed as conversationalists because of "their entirely different psychological conditions and their completely different interests" (28).

In making this kind of circular argument, Brandt joined a great tradition extending back to the Athenian men themselves. One first deprives women of education and then excludes them from the political process for being uneducated. One bars them from athletics and then denigrates them for being physically underdeveloped. One teaches them to define their value solely in terms of sexual attractiveness to men, and then scorns them for primping constantly.

Another school of Classicists, rather than defending the Greeks for their polarization of the sexes, denies that it occurred. The groundwork for this view was laid by A. W. Gomme, otherwise a splendid scholar. Gomme argues that the appearance of rebellious and independent female characters in Greek drama proves that actual women enjoyed high status at the time the dramas were written. Many of the plays, however, are set in the distant past— they are half-historical, half-mythological. Some of the heroines can better be regarded as projections of male fears than as realistic portrayals of ordinary women in the fifth century B.C. How would we respond to a critic who sought to describe women of the 1980s through a study of horror films, westerns, and experimental theater?

Apologists for the Athenians display wonderful ingenuity in defense of their idols. For example, L. J. Kuenen-Janssens argues that "women had considerable freedom of action," citing a statute according to which "neither child nor woman may accumulate [or possibly: transact for the value of] more than the price of one medimnus of barley" (Isae. 10, 10). Overlooking the fact that the statute cites a limitation rather than a right, this scholar conjures up a sphere of female capitalism, regardless of our lack of knowledge of even how much barley a medimnus was.

A third school of thought described Athenian women neither as respected and prosperous, nor as unpresentable, but as imperiled by men. Did husbands confine women to the house? Well, that was "protective solicitude," in the words of Donald Richter (7). After all, the streets of Athens were "notoriously unsafe." Besides, there is no doubt in Richter's mind about the "sexual laxity" of Athenian women. "It was because Greek women were in fact so voluble that men reminded them so frequently that 'silence is a woman's glory.'" This view appears to combine the scorn of Brandt with the solicitude of Gomme.

In her brief, but rewarding section on Athenian women of the Classical age, Sarah Pomeroy comments on the dispute over their status, in which "some scholars hold that women were despised and kept in Oriental seclusion, while others contend that they were respected and enjoyed freedom comparable to that of most women through the centuries." She aptly observes that the dispute can in part be traced to the genres of evidence consulted. Scholars who treat the women in Classical tragedy as if they were modeled on contemporaries of the playwrights, uphold the position taken by Gomme. A contrary school prefers to rely upon orations, especially speeches from trials, which yield a more mundane, and far bleaker picture of the lives of women than does drama. Both schools of scholarship have largely failed to exploit the pictorial record, here used as a major resource: the panorama of ideals, myths, fantasies and, above all, scenes of daily life that appears on the tens of thousands of Greek vases, scattered in museums all over Europe and the United States. Over three hundred of these pictures are reproduced in this book.

The failure of historians to recognize the dark side of Attic culture has created an erroneous picture of the difference between the moral climate of Athens and that of her perennial antagonist, Sparta. This city-state is remembered in history as militaristic, aggressive and ruthless. In reality she allowed her women roles of some dignity and freedom, did not practice external military imperialism, and is entitled to the gratitude of the Western world for a sublime act of mercy: after defeating Athens, she spared the city and its population. Had Athens won the Peloponnesian War, Sparta probably would have been eradicated. For that matter of fact, the greater leniency of the Spartans, while largely ignored by scholarship, was recognized by the Athenians themselves. At all times, before, during and after the Peloponnesian War, prominent citizens of Athens, such as Aristophanes, Xenophon and Plato, "spartanized."

## Scope and Aim of This Study

As a Classicist I am committed to the study of Greece, but I hope that many readers will come to this book primarily through an interest in human sexuality, patterns of social dominance, and possibilities of reform, rather than from a background in ancient history. Those who feel that phallocracy remains a problem in modern, more subtle, forms, may wonder about the value of reaching all the way back to ancient Athens instead of confronting the pattern directly in our own society. However, just as a traveler learns about his or her own country through immersion in a foreign culture, so we can sharpen our sense of the present by contrast and comparison with a detailed case history from the past. Classical Athens is historically related to subsequent Western culture, and similar enough to illuminate it, but it is also alien enough to jolt our ordinary sense of reality.

A second reason for studying fifth-century Athens is that, compared with patriarchal industrial societies, its phallocracy, as yet not modified by serious challenges or concealed by prudery and guilt, was severe and crass. The reaction it triggered at the end of the century was correspondingly intense and produced the first anti-militaristic and feminist manifestations on record in the West. Thus, this short span of history provides us with extremes in the realms of the military and sexual ethics which still govern our societies. Classical Athens is a kind of concave mirror in which we can see our own foibles and institutions magnified and distorted.

Since I would like to make this book accessible to the general reader, I must ask my fellow Classicists to overlook explanations not intended for them, and to look instead at new evidence and new argumentation. Artifacts well known to historians of ancient art are reproduced side by side with unpublished vase paintings. Familiar quotations are intermingled with passages from Greek texts not previously cited in contexts of social history. Many readings of vases and literary passages in Greek are new, and my colleagues will recognize them as such.

I leave it to others to explore the thematic links between the phallocracy of Classical Athens and that of other times and places, including our own. Much remains to be done, and I hope that other scholars will address the origins of phallocracy as a distinctive social system, the detailed reinterpretation of Greek tragedy in this light, the links between sexual ethics and public affairs, and the revolts against and modifications of phallic rule (such as occurred after the defeat of Athens in 404 B.C.). For each of these topics this book offers some clues.

## *Outline*

Until the end of the Periclean age, 430 B.C., a pronounced phallicism prevailed in classical Athens, which we will take to mean a combination of male supremacy and the cult of power and violence. Most of the following chapters will point to the phallic elements in a variety of aspects of Athenian life, and argue that the suppression of women, the military expansionism and the harshness in the conduct of civic affairs all sprang from a common aggressive impulse. They will also attempt to show that undercurrents of protest were always present in the city, and that these came to a head in the fateful year of 415 B.C. In that year the Athenians embarked on a rash, ill-planned military expedition against Sicily, which was to break the back of its wealth and power for all time. The event, however, took place over great opposition, which marked the beginning of an overt anti-phallic movement. The year 415, as it were, divided the classical Athenian age into two periods, one marked by extreme phallicism, and one of anti-militaristic reaction. This book begins and ends with the events of that year.

Chapter 1 tells the astonishing course of events of the year 415, and recalls the most puzzling mystery of all of Classical history which they posed, namely: Who was responsible for the scandal which was the Watergate of ancient Athens, the so-called "Mutilation [actually Castration] of the Herms"?

In Chapter 2 we explore the powerful myths that provided a warrant for male supremacy, most of them still popular today. In Chapter 3 we draw a contrast between phallic exposure and female invisibility on the Athenian scene.

The following eight chapters examine the kinds of relations that existed between men and their sexual partners. Thus, Chapters 4 and 5 discuss the status and experience of wives; Chapters 6 and 7 the world of prostitution, including that of the famous courtesans or hetaerai. In Chapter 8, the splitting of the female psyche between these two realms is clarified; and in Chapter 9 the sex appeal of female drudgery is shown. Apart from marriage and prostitution, men had another common way of relating to women: taking a concubine, which might combine the stability of marriage with the sexual primacy of prostitution. After examining concubinage in Chapter 10, we turn to the troubled subject of male homosexuality. Chapter 11 puts forth an original interpretation of Athenian homosexual practices.

In the third part of the book, we turn to a consideration of a cluster of rituals, dramas, and other manifestations which are aspects of, or responses to, phallicism. In Chapter 12 we look at rites and customs of sex role initiation; in Chapter 13, at stories and beliefs about what happens when, in foreign cultures, women are allowed to assert themselves; in Chapter 14 at Classical tragedy as an expression of male fear that domination might fail; and in Chapter 15, at the brilliant and varied forms through which women expressed their frustration at being dominated and sought momentary relief from it.

Finally, in Chapter 16 we return to the subject of the crucial year of 415 B.C., in which the extreme Athenian phallicism had its last spasm, and in which the latent opposition to it erupted in protest, too late to save Athens from disaster and its empire from collapse. It is here that a solution to the historical conundrum of the "Mutilation of the Herms" is proposed.

My focus is on Athenian life, and on the period of the greatest flowering of Attic culture, the Periclean age or *pentekontaetia* (Great Fifty Years) from 480 to 430 B.C. and its immediate aftermath. From this period date most of the vase paintings reproduced, and the greater part of the tragedies discussed. But evidence from other parts of the Classical world and from other periods had to be adduced, notably the Athenian courtroom speeches, a major source for the practical side of life in ancient Greece, which date mainly from the fourth century B.C.

I have identified, either in the text or in the notes, all citations from Greek and Latin literature by the abbreviations used in the Oxford Classical Dictionary, through which they can easily be traced. A few abbreviations are taken from Liddell-Scott-Jones' *Dictionary of the Greek Language.* In the bibliographies to the Introduction, the Chapters and the Epilogue I have listed all works referred to in the text, a few selected important titles, and the most recent work on the topic under discussion known to me, through which the interested reader can find his way to older studies.

The artifacts reproduced are mainly Attic vase paintings; literature on these can be located in J. D. Beazley's *Attic Black-Figure Vase-Painters, Attic Red-Figure Vase-Painters* (Second Edition) and *Paralipomena.*

Unless otherwise indicated, translations of ancient and modern texts are my own.

# 1

# Military Expeditions, Protest, Lament, and Scandal

During the summer of 415 B.C. Athens was shaken by a scandal that roughly coincided with the launching of the boldest Greek military effort since the Trojan War. A group of conspirators, moving throughout the city under cover of night, mutilated statues of the god Hermes. Found in every neighborhood, and in front of private dwellings as well as in public places, these statues had the shape of plain rectangular columns except for two carved features: the head and the erect genitals. When Athens awakened, almost all of these phallic sculptures had been castrated. This highly symbolic crime is remarkable because of the authorities' failure, despite extreme measures, to discover who committed it, and because of the political, social and cultural matrix within which the scandal arose.

Less than a year prior to the mutilation of the herms, Athenian power had sacked the Greek island city of Melos, killed its men, and sent its women and children into slavery, all for the offense of declining to join a military alliance. At about the same time, Athens dispatched a delegation to faraway Sicily, to explore the prospects for asserting power there, the first step along a path of imprudent aggression that soon led to disaster.

In the spring of 415 the playwright Euripides produced *The Trojan Women*, a tragedy that passionately denounced the cruelty and injustice of war. During the same season the Athenian assembly voted, against the advice of a respected statesman and general, to proceed with a major invasion of Sicily, the home of Greek colonies, many of them allied with Sparta. Despite the lack of a clearcut strategic objective, the expedition was launched in the summer.

During the preparations, two cultural events occurred. One was the rampage against the ubiquitous statues of Hermes, already mentioned; and the other, the annual celebration of the festival called the Adonia, in which the city's women lamented the premature death of an exotic god, the gentle lover Adonis.

These events exhibit both the reign of the phallus and certain striking forms of protest, lament and scandal occasioned by it. Thus, they serve to introduce dominant motifs in the sexual politics of ancient Athens.

The military and political sides of these events have always been well known; schools used to teach Greek history from the masterful account provided by Thucydides in *The Peloponnesian War.* However, we would be disappointed if we hoped to find the culture or society of Athens elucidated by Thucydides. For example, he hardly mentions a woman by name in the eight books of his detailed narrative, preferring to focus upon debate, diplomatic initiative, and battle. We would not know from Thucydides that in the season of the debate on the expedition to Sicily, Euripides produced *The Trojan Women*, a portrayal of the way the worst wars end. Nor would we learn, from *The Peloponnesian War*, about the women's festival, the Adonia, a counter-cultural event.

It is the purpose of this chapter to display in action the society whose sexual politics are dissected in the remainder of this book, and also to reconsider the events preceding the decline of Athens from the viewpoint of its women, both the real ones and the ones brought onstage in Euripides' tragedy. Above all, this account is intended to arouse curiosity about links between phallocratic behavior in political and military affairs and the sexual ethics of Athens. In addition, this chapter is meant to pose that unsolved historical conundrum: "Who was responsible for the Mutilation of the Herms?", to which an answer will be proposed later in this book.

## Teaching Melos a Lesson

In 416 Athens was the head of a powerful empire, based largely upon its command of the sea. A few generations earlier, in 480 B.C., the Athenian fleet had defeated the Persian invaders in the straits off the nearby island of Salamis. This victory gave Athens a leading position among the Greek city-states and, with the subsequent defeat of the Persian land forces at Plataea, freed Greece from its attackers. Under the leadership of Athens, a defensive alliance against future Persian expeditions was formed of city-states around the Aegean Sea. Called the Delian League, it kept its treasury on the sacred island of Delos. Before long, in a symbolic move, the Athenians transported the treasury to the temple of Athena on the Acropolis of Athens. The reconstruction of the Parthenon, and other civic buildings damaged during the Persian occupation, was financed from it. In fact, the history of the Delian League reads somewhat like George Orwell's *Animal Farm*. What began as a voluntary alliance created in a common cause, gradually became the empire of its most powerful member. Contributions to the League by its other members, in money and in matériel, became a tribute to Athens, which that state enforced with iron hand. When the great war between Athens and Sparta, the Peloponnesian War, broke out in 430, the League, which had been created in defense against a foreign enemy, was forced to turn against a Greek opponent, a development that placed many of its members in a dilemma of conflicting allegiances. For this and other reasons, several of the smaller city-states attempted to secede from the League, but without success.

Athens gave a dramatic illustration of her power early in the Peloponnesian War, in the year 427. The city of Mytilene, on the island of Lesbos, began to make moves toward a withdrawal from the League. In response, an Athenian garrison occupied the island and sent some of the leaders of the revolt to Athens as prisoners. Not content to have the leaders in custody, the Athenians sent a trireme to Lesbos with the command to destroy the city, with the usual implications of killing the adult males and enslaving the women and children, a treatment commonly extended to enemies, but not to recalcitrant allies. However, after a dramatic debate in the assembly, the Athenians changed their minds and dispatched a second trireme, to cancel the orders. The crew had to row day and night, "taking turns at sleeping and rowing," to catch up with the first ship. It arrived just in time to prevent the sack of the city (Thuc. 3, 36 f.).

By 416 the Athenian mood had hardened. The war with Sparta— which lasted for a total of twenty-seven years, punctuated by peace negotiations, truces, and periods of relative quiet—had already taken a cruel toll. By now the Athenian strategy had turned into an elaborate checkerboard game. In a domain composed of independent city-states, war was as much a matter of building alliances as of fighting battles. In the fateful year of 416 the Athenians decided to bring into their fold the island of Melos, located about one hundred miles from Athens' port city of Piraeus. Although Melos was ethnically related to Sparta, it had maintained neutrality until an earlier attack by the Athenians. What the Athenians sought now, in 416, was to command its allegiance. In Thucydides' account of the negotiations, known as the Melian dialogue, the Athenians offered no justifications for their demand, apart from the observation that the Melians, by submitting, would avoid destruction at the hands of the superior Athenian force already gathered. What the aggressors wanted was tribute, less for its own sake than as a symbol of submission. If Melos were to say no, and to get away with its refusal, the Athenians feared that other reluctant allies might follow the example.

Confident that their Spartan kinsmen would come to their aid, the Melians did refuse, arguing that they meant no harm to Athens, but that they valued the freedom they had enjoyed for seven hundred years. Later in the year an Athenian force destroyed the city. The space given by Thucydides to the Melian incident, and especially the negotiations between the Athenian ambassadors and the rulers of the island, is striking: several comparable atrocities of the war are treated matter-of-factly by the historian. Surely the account reflects the Athenians' belated misgivings about the action, after they had had a taste of defeat and disaster themselves.

## Melos and the Women of Athens

Since the women of Athens were silenced, we have no knowledge of how they responded to this ruthless and unprecedented act of destroying an unoffending Greek state. However, especially in view of subsequent events, we might hazard some guesses.

We do not know in what form the news of the fate of Melos reached Athenian women. But an expeditionary force is composed of husbands, sons, brothers, fathers, lovers, or, in the case of Athens' prostitutes, of customers. Unless the soldiers never spoke of their deeds—hard to imagine in a city devoted to glory—many women would soon know the story; and unless women in Athens were less curious and more reticent than in nearly every other culture about which we know, they talked among themselves about the news.

How would they have felt about the events on Melos? Probably very few had an "opinion" in the modern sense: women did not participate in what the men were pleased to call a democracy; nor does it seem, from the preponderance of what we know, that they were even allowed to contemplate historical and mythological events in the theater. Women were to be seen rather than heard, and seen as little as possible: their place was the inside of a house. For most purposes they did not even have names. Possibly their reaction to the news from Melos was simply relief that so many of the Athenian soldiers returned safely. Possibly it was a feeling that the Melians must have done something terribly wrong. (As a United States citizen said after being told about the massacre at My Lai in the Vietnam war, "It never happened and besides they deserved it.")

We have no record as to where the enslaved women and children of Melos wound up; Thucydides does not mention such matters. A number of them, however, surely must have been sold to Athenian citizens and brought back to the city. Euripides' *The Trojan Women* probably reflects this, as in the scene where the captive Andromache comes onstage with her little son on top of a wagon loaded with the spoils from the sack of Troy (568 f.). In any case, the fate of the women and children of Melos was bound to strike a responsive chord in the hearts of Athenian women.

In the Introduction I pointed to the harshness of the institution of slavery in Athens. Slaves owned by Athenian households had probably for the most part been foreigners. But here were the former citizens of a fellow city-state, a smaller version of what Athens had been before it acquired an empire. The women of Melos spoke a similar language, engaged in the same domestic tasks. Through no provocation of their own, they and the children of Melos were sold into slavery, the implications of which every Athenian woman had before her eyes daily. What is more, at the very time these events were taking place, the leading politicians of Athens were contemplating a far more ambitious military undertaking, the expedition against Sicily, which, if unsuccessful, might expose the women of Athens to the same fate as those of Melos.

## Recalling the Women of Troy

In the spring of 415, shortly after the events just narrated, Euripides presented *The Trojan Women* to his Athenian audience.

Like many an artist since then, trying to deal with controversial policies or to challenge a cultural presupposition, Euripides chose a subject parallel to the current events but set safely in the distant past—much as a Soviet artist might have alluded to Stalin through the figure of Ivan the Terrible. For a Greek in 415, the Trojan War lay even further in the past than Shakespeare does from us, but the legend of the city's capture continued to fascinate the Greeks. Even today, most college graduates have at least heard of the epic told by Homer, of Helen who left Sparta to run away to Troy with the young Paris, of her face that launched a thousand ships, and of the famous "Trojan horse," a Greek contrivance to smuggle soldiers into the besieged city. In 415 Euripides turned his genius to the theme of the sack of Troy and asked not only what happens to the losers of a war, but what can happen to the souls of the victors.

As *The Trojan Women* opens, their city—to quote Richmond Lattimore's translation—"smolders now, fallen before the Argive spears, ruined, sacked, gutted" (8–9). The Greeks, their ships loaded with spoils, await a favorable wind. In the meantime, they allocate among themselves the last of the captive women, including the family of Priam, the defeated king. His widow, Hecuba, is a central figure of the play, along with her daughter, Cassandra, who always speaks the truth but is never believed, and her daughter-in-law, Andromache, widow of the Trojan hero Hector and mother of their son, Astyanax. Waiting to be enslaved, the women can do nothing but give tongue to their grief as they dwell in huts under the city walls blackened by fire. In the play the first words against war and its effects are spoken by gods—first by Poseidon, who complains that "once sad desolation takes hold of a city, the affairs of the gods wither also, and their worship is neglected" (26–27), and then by Athena, who, offended that the Greek hero Ajax has raped Cassandra in Athena's temple, asks Poseidon, as the sea god, to whip up a storm and scatter the returning fleet "so that in the future the Greeks may learn to be in awe of my sacred dominion, and to honor the other gods as well" (85–86). Within two years Euripides' audience had reason to recall these lines as an omen of future disasters. In this scene neither one of the deities condemns rape or enslavement, only the wrecking, neglect, or misuse of temples and, as Poseidon adds, "the hallowed places of the dead."

In Euripides' version, Priam is slain before the action begins, and his grandson, Astyanax, meets his end when the Greeks throw him from the battlements of Troy during the play. Odysseus argues successfully for the death of the boy, to prevent him from some day rebuilding Troy and avenging his father's defeat. When the boy's mother, Andromache, hears Odysseus' argument that "the son of so heroic a father should not be raised" (723), she replies, "May he reap the same harvest from his victory some day." And after speaking to her child for the last time, she declares to his murderers: "Oh, Greeks, who have invented barbarian evils, why do you kill this child, who is guilty of nothing?" (764–65).

This is strong language to offer to an audience whose army has, only a few months before, sent all the children of Melos into slavery, if not to immediate death. As Lattimore observes, "I can hardly understand how the Athenians let [Euripides] present this play at all."

The dialogue between Andromache and the Greek herald who comes to take her child contains startling parallels to the negotiations in 416 between Melos and Athens, the Melian dialogue reported by Thucydides (5, 85 f.). In this debate the Athenians urge submission by claiming that Melos can expect no help from its ally, Sparta; by arguing that there is no shame in yielding gracefully to superior force; and by threatening complete ruin in case of resistance. In Euripides' play, produced the next spring, the kindly Greek herald tells Andromache, "Do not offer resistance to him, but nobly bear your grief. Do not give show of strength or power, for you have none. . . . Therefore do not long for battle, nothing shameful or laughable will you do . . ." (726 f.). He warns that if she offends the Greeks who are about to kill her son, they may even deny him honorable burial. Andromache, nevertheless, in the boldest lines of the entire play, curses not only the Greeks but also, without naming her, the goddess Athena herself: "daughter of Vindictiveness, of Hate, of Murder, of Death, of all the evil that the earth brings forth, I cry it out loud, not of Zeus were you born, may you perish, you pestilence to large numbers of Greeks and barbarians alike."

In *The Trojan Women* we find a critique, less of war in general than of a particular war that was ill-motivated, unnecessarily brutal, and, on the part of the Greeks, expeditionary. The war that caused the intense suffering dramatized by Euripides lacked a proper justification and was fought not to ward off an attack but to project military force into an arena far away. In these respects, *The Trojan Women*, in its first production, not only looked back at the recent events on Melos but also, with astonishing premonition, forecast the fate of Athens' upcoming Sicilian expedition.

Without examining the complexities of Euripides' play, especially in the verbal contest between Hecuba and Helen, we may note that the central characters are women who, through war, have lost everything that a woman can lose except life and self-respect; that the Greek victors are repeatedly denounced for their brutality; and that fortune is shown to be fickle: who conquers today, who rapes and burns, may suffer the same tomorrow. What kind of experience was it, in the spring of 415, to attend this grief-filled tragedy? Athens had lost battles in its long war with Sparta. It had suffered invasion and plague only fifteen years earlier, but as yet, unlike Troy, it had never been defeated.

## Wailing for Adonis

Beginning with Aristophanes' *Lysistrata*, literary sources establish that at least some of the deliberations over and preparations for the Sicilian expedition, possibly even the sailing itself, took place while the women of Athens celebrated the Adonia festival. In Chapter 15 we will have occasion to consider some other religious rituals practiced by Athenian women. The Adonia, however, had unique counter-cultural, even rebellious, aspects, and they were closely connected with the events of the years 416–415.

Our evidence is in considerable part pictorial. Figure 2 shows a bronze mirror lid from Corinth decorated in high relief with a group of three figures. A handsome young man with a nearly clean-shaven face and a kindly smile sits on a chair. With his left arm he clasps a woman who is seated on his lap and is turning her head and shoulders toward him in an affectionate embrace; they are about to kiss. To the right of the pair stands a boy, and on the left side there is a peacock. Do we have here an idyllic and sexy family scene, which could upset all our notions about Greek family life? No—at least not on the literal level of interpretation. Analogies of the scene with other visual evidence reveal that the relief depicts the goddess Aphrodite; her mortal lover, Adonis; and her young acolyte, Eros, who is her son by uncertain paternity.

During the Adonia, Athenian women celebrated the love affair of Aphrodite and Adonis, and reenacted the death and burial of the young lover. Quite possibly the cult of Adonis was the only form of self-expression developed by Athenian women, in response to an

2. Mythological family group: Adonis, Aphrodite, Eros.

emotional need of their own, and not dictated by the voice of male authority; everything in the cult of Adonis spelled protest against the existing order. The figure of the kind, even timid, young lover in the Classical Greek context was, as it were, a counter-cultural male sex symbol, the antipode of the male model canonized by society and embodied by Heracles and Theseus, brawny, aggressive strong-men.

There are numerous variant myths about Adonis' birth, life, and death, but all include striking elements of "illegitimacy." Adonis is an Oriental: he is variously identified as Semitic, Syrian, Phoenician, and Cypriot. He is the product of female seduction and incest. His mother, Myrrha (Myrtle Tree) after rejecting several arranged marriages, seduced her own father and became pregnant by him. The gods changed her into a tree, out of which Adonis was born. The youth is beautiful even at an early age, and both men and women become enamored of him. As a lover, Adonis is timid and has to be seduced. Aphrodite woos him, not with threats of violence, as she courted Aeneas' father, Anchises, but gently. Adonis is potent, even excessively potent, but not fertile.

In what appears to be the most widespread version of his death, Adonis is killed by a boar, symbol of aggressive masculinity. In this mythological confrontation of two concepts of masculinity, the boar pierces Adonis' thigh or groin and destroys his genitals. The goddess Aphrodite mourns him excessively, and so did the women of Athens during the festival. In the course of this festival the women moved to the roofs of their houses, in itself an act of rebellion, and spent the night in the open amid flowerpots especially set up and filled with plants for the occasion—the so-called Gardens of Adonis. Broken, with jagged edges, the pots were filled with various herbs and vegetables. The fragrant plants probably had erotic associations; the myrrh was at the same time a reminder of Adonis' mother. The lettuce, a standard ingredient, perhaps spelled death and impotence, as suggested by Detienne (1972, 68); it could have referred to the killing of Adonis. From the roofs the women loudly bewailed Adonis' death, invoking his name and chanting dirges. "Woe, woe Adonis" and "Beat your breast for Adonis" were the ritual laments for the hero, if we can believe the magistrate in Aristophanes' *Lysistrata* (389–98). This character, quite rightly, considers the Adonia a ritual of rebellion against the social order. The lusty lamentations must have been audible throughout the city, especially since the festival took place during the dead heat of summer, when most of the population was likely to be out of doors. The most public of all women's festivals in Athens, it must have created a very special rebellious atmosphere in the city.

After the lamentation from the roofs, the women carried an effigy of Adonis around the city and "buried" it in the sea. Figure 3 shows Adonis, surrounded by an Eros, Aphrodite, and adoring women, in a late-fifth-century vase painting that fully brings out the soft and tender nature of the boy. Aphrodite strokes one of his nipples, a gesture denoting seduction. Although alive, the figure of

Adonis recalls the description in the fifteenth *Idyll* of Theocritus: "Resplendent Adonis lies on his silvery bier; The first down is covering his cheeks, Adonis thrice beloved, cherished even in Acheron [the underworld]" (84–86). Numerous vase paintings from the fourth century B.C. depict the ritual of women climbing to the roofs of their houses with the Gardens (Figure 4 and 5). The winged Erotes who are usually present in these scenes place them in a half-real, half-mythological setting.

3. The beautiful Adonis and amorous women.

In Figure 6 we see the Garden of Adonis transformed in what may be termed a motif of interior decoration in the Roman age: it is featured on the walls of a bedroom from Boscoreale, near Pompeii, which has been restored and set up in The Metropolitan Museum of Art in New York. The Etruscans adopted Adonis, along with many other Greek mythological motifs, and the amorous pair of Aphrodite and the youth, who is named Atunis in Etruscan, appears on a number of engraved mirrors (Figure 7). Note the affectionate pose of the lovers, which, however, to the Etruscan mentality was not as "rebellious" as it was to the Greek.

5. The Adonia: Eros
himself participates.

4.
The Adonia: preparations
for the ritual on the roof
to the sound of music.

6.
The "Garden of Adonis" as
a decorative motif (from
the area of Pompeii).

7. Atunis, the Etruscan Adonis, embracing Aphrodite.

The Adonia must be seen against the marital patterns of ancient Athens, to be described in the following chapters. In bemoaning the death of Adonis, Athenian women lamented their own, loveless lives. And in doing so, they created an alternative male sex symbol, which was to change Western notions of what constitutes the essence of the male lover, at least for the purposes of fiction. Adonis became the archetype of the gentle, timid young lover of later Greek comedy and its Latin adaptations, the comic young man in love who needs the machinations of his "cunning slave" to help him reach consummation of his erotic desires. Adonis is the model for the young male lovers of the Greek prose romances, such as *Daphnis and Chloe,* and *Cleitophon and Leucippe*—lovers who are passionately devoted to their mates, but less brave and enterprising than their female counterparts. Adonis is the reason that the romantic lead in opera is normally sung by the tenor and not by the more "masculine" baritone or bass. He is the spiritual ancestor of Romeo and of Rudolph Valentino.

Adonis, we are led to believe, made women have orgasms,

8. Craftsman chiseling a herm.

9. Phallic humor: herms in conversation.

10. Phallic satire: a bird perched on the phallus of a herm.

whereas Heracles, who "deflowered fifty virgins in one week," did not. The word for the myrtle, which played such an important part in the ritual, also stands for the female genitalia, and that for myrtle berry (*to myrton*) denotes the clitoris, the female instrument of sexual pleasure. Through the Adonia women voiced a claim to an active role in sex relations. Aristophanes, whose play *Lysistrata* was heavily inspired by the Adonia, was well aware of this. In fact, he has one of his characters phrase for the first time the feminist slogan "Up from Under." Lysistrata, in order to bolster the courage of her female co-conspirators, dreams up a fake oracle, foretelling the victory of the lowly over the proud; "Does that mean that we women shall lie on top?" asks an unnamed woman (773).

This was the festival that the women of Athens celebrated, within earshot of the entire city, during part of the ominous events of the summer of 415.

## *Living in the Company of Women: The Herms of Athens*

Chapter 3 will amply illustrate the ubiquity of the erect phallus in the public life of Athens. The women of the city, however, were cut off from most civic functions and largely confined to their homes. For them the most familiar phallic images were the statues of the god Hermes which regularly stood in the courtyards and doorways of private houses. As shown in Figures 8, 9, and 10, herms consisted of busts of the bearded Hermes, set upon smooth stone pillars out of which protruded, at groin level, more or less realistic and erect genitalia. Figure 8 shows a sculptor carefully chiseling the final details of a smaller herm. The evident caution with which he moves around the erect penis underscores the vulnerability of that part of the statue. Figure 9 appears to contain a joke on the homey familiarity of these statues: the painter has placed three of them in a group as if in conversation. Figure 10 is a caricature; a large bird, perched on an enormously extended phallus, kisses the Hermes head on the mouth.

Such statues were present in Athens by the hundreds, not only in the private but also in the public areas of the city. To the women of Athens they must have been a constant reminder of the phallic powers that governed their lives.

## Waking Up to Scandal

Sometime in the summer of 415 during the final preparations for the expedition to Sicily, possibly on its eve, an incident occurred that threw Athens into turmoil, elicited grave charges against one of the commanders of the expeditionary force, and caused numerous respectable citizens to be arrested on the word of informers speaking under a grant of pardon. One morning, as early risers passed the herms outside their houses or along their street, they noticed that somebody had hacked at the front of the statues, which consisted, as I have explained, of a face above and a phallus below. At first, each person may have thought the statue he saw had been damaged by accident or by a casual prankster or drunk; but as word spread that herms had been mutilated all over the city, fears of a conspiracy arose. Although some scholars maintain that the mutilation was directed at the heads of the statues, the more obvious, vulnerable, and outrageous target was the phallus. In Chapter 16 we will look at evidence, from sources other than Thucydides, that the phallus was the primary target of the herm choppers.

Hermes was, among other things, the god of travelers, and the sacrilege inflicted on his image cast an evil spell on the expedition about to be launched. The emotional impact of the scandal is difficult to reconstruct, and was perhaps best evoked by the historian Grote:

> If we could imagine the excitement of a Spanish or Italian town on finding that all the images of the Virgin had been defaced during the same night, we should have a parallel, though a very inadequate parallel for what was now felt at Athens, where religious associations and persons were far more intimately allied with all civil acts and with all proceedings of every-day life. . . . To the Athenians, when they went forth on the following morning, each man seeing the divine guardian at his doorway dishonored and defaced . . . , it would seem that the town had become as it were godless. (VII, 168)

Nobody has discovered who mutilated the herms. In spite of accusations, confessions, and convictions, Thucydides makes clear his own doubt that the real culprits were found or their motives understood. What goal could justify the risk of discovery? Who was in a position to effect the mutilations? In a later chapter I will attempt to answer these questions, presenting the least unlikely suspects until now and supporting the hypothesis with previously overlooked evidence.

What happened in 415 was that, although nobody could prove the identity of the mutilators, informers talked about other sacrilegious acts, especially private parties during which the Eleusinian mysteries were allegedly burlesqued. Among those implicated in the latter charge was Alcibiades, leader of the pro-war party and one of the commanders of the expedition then being prepared. Although he requested an immediate investigation, before going off to Sicily, his political enemies had the trial delayed so that Alcibiades had to leave with the charge hanging over him—somewhat as if a United States general had been accused of ridiculing the Constitution and then had been sent to command the forces in Vietnam.

The castration of the herms was an act of protest against the extreme phallocratic atmosphere that pervaded Athens, and against its current manifestation, the expedition to Sicily. Unlike public events, such as battles or debates, the attack against the herms took place throughout the neighborhoods of Athens, and its results were observed even by those who had to stay close to home. Thus the mutilators, like the women on their roofs during the festival of Adonis, acted in the public sphere while remaining adjacent to domestic space. It is hard to imagine a more exactly targeted or more widely visible form of protest against the reign of the phallus. In order to grasp the nature of this syndrome, which provoked such an extreme and bizarre reaction, we shall turn next to the myths of Athens, which perhaps codify attitudes and tendencies better than any other historical source.

# 2

# Attic Mythology: Barren Goddesses, Male Wombs, and the Cult of Rape

> It is not the mother who is the parent of the child, although she is so called; she is merely nursemaid to the newly planted fetus. He who mounts is the one who gives birth; she, a stranger to a stranger, merely preserves the seed if god does not destroy it. And I'll give you proof of my argument: there can be fatherhood without a mother.
> —Aeschylus, *Eumenides* (658–63): Apollo speaking

A strong sense of national identity began to emerge in Athens in the sixth century B.C., the age that saw the creation of the first comprehensive Greek legal code, by Solon, and the first major public building program, by the tyrant Peisistratus and his sons. Attic chauvinism crystallized fully after the battle of Salamis in 480 B.C., whereby Athens became the heroine of the Greek world and, in time, the mistress of a powerful and profitable empire, the Delian League.

Predictably, this sudden rise to power of a relative newcomer in the family of Greek city-states was accompanied by the formation of a nationally oriented body of myths. Among the chauvinistic statements which the Attic myths made were that of the antiquity of the Athenian people; that of their great contributions to the prehistoric heroic feats of the Greek people, such as the Trojan expedition; and that of their "autochthony": the Athenians claimed, in myth and directly, to have had, alone among Greek ethnic units, continuous roots in their native soil of Attica, and to have avoided the upheavals and large-scale migrations of the generations following the Trojan War.

What was not so predictable in the new national mythology was the overriding phallocratic element. To be sure, the slaughter of animals and of human enemies is a standard component of national myths, since ethnic identity ultimately rests in the victory over rival tribes and over the animal kingdom. However, no mythology so teems with tales of male supremacy as does the Attic. Athenian mythological phallicism takes various forms. There are the countless stories of the clubbing, stabbing, and strangling to death of sundry animals and monsters of fantasy; second, there are the manifold tales of rape, a theme in which no other mythology has been as rich as the Attic. The mythological rape is generally that of a mortal female by a male divinity or hero, although homosexual and reverse variants occur. A third category of typically Athenian motifs consists of tales of goddesses who could not or would not bear children, and of stories of male motherhood, in which offspring are born from parts of the male anatomy or directly from the male semen.

An especially characteristic theme in Athenian mythology, next to the motif of rape, is the killing or subduing of the rebellious female. The most notable example is the Amazonomachia, or the battle between Greeks and Amazons, which, as we will see, was one of the charter myths, perhaps *the* charter myth of Athenian society, and, in its day, the single theme most often represented on Attic monuments. Wherever an Athenian turned his eyes, he was likely to encounter the effigy of one of his mythological ancestors, stabbing or clubbing an Amazon to death. Because the Amazons are often depicted wearing Oriental garb, the Amazonomachia is widely believed to symbolize the victory of the Greeks over the Persians, or that of the West over the East, but this view does not account for the pronounced element of sex antagonism in the theme.

In Athenian myth and art, the slaughterers of animals and Amazons, as well as the rapist gods, are armed with weapons with phallic associations, such as clubs, swords, and spears—in the case of the rapists often meaningfully aimed at the crotch level of the victim. In fact, the phallic ethos in Classical Athens seems to have been reinforced by what might be termed pictorial propaganda. The most telling aspect of Attic mythological "history" is the intertwining of phallocratic motifs of slaughter, aggression, and rape with patriotic themes.

## The Goddess Athena: The Man-Woman
## with the "Toothed Vagina"

In a charming episode in Book 13 of Homer's *Odyssey*, the goddess Athena encounters Odysseus as he is beginning to explore his native island of Ithaca, where his friends, the Phaeaeceans, have deposited him while he was asleep. Upon awakening, Odysseus, always suspicious and not knowing where he is, first checks his gifts, to make sure his helpers have not taken any of them back; then he starts out cautiously along the shore. The goddess, in disguise, queries him about his adventures and Odysseus spins a fanciful tale of kidnapping, on the assumption that a lie is usually safer than the truth. After hearing him out, Athena reveals herself and smiles at her protégé, saying, "That's why I cannot abandon you when you're out of luck, because you are so handy with words, and shrewd and sensible" (*Od.* 13, 331–32).

The warlike and virginal facets of Athena are already fixed in this pre-Classical phase, but at the same time she is the goddess of the crafts and of craftiness, those survival skills whereby men get by in the world, epitomized by the figure of Odysseus. When we find the goddess ensconced, in the sixth century B.C., as the guardian

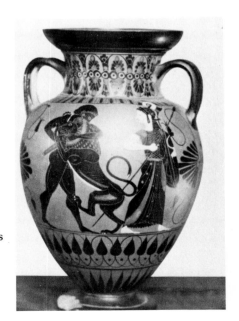

11. Athena as patroness of Heracles (killing the Nemean lion).

divinity of a city newly aware of a national destiny, she has become the patron not so much of complex Homeric heroes such as Odysseus and Achilleus but of that prime exponent of machismo, Heracles. John Boardman (1975) has examined the mythological motifs on Attic black-figure vase paintings to 510 B.C. and, on the basis of a large sampling, has concluded that about 44 percent of them feature stories from the life of Heracles. On most of them Athena is also present. Significantly, Heracles' labors and humiliations, which later, in the Greco-Roman age, make him an exponent of the salvation-through-toil notion, are mostly absent during this phase. Such trials are his cleaning out of the Augean stables and his greatest humiliation of all—helping a woman, Queen Omphale, with domestic chores. Instead, we find him over and over again, under the approving eye of his patroness, killing the Nemean lion (Figure 11) and the Erymanthian boar and, especially, piercing Amazons. One of Heracles' more conspicuous feats, later dramatized by Sophocles in his *Women of Trachis,* was the abduction of Iole, daughter of King Eurytos. While he is the king's guest for dinner, Heracles takes a liking to his daughter, kills his host and the latter's sons, and takes Iole with him as a captive. We see the story depicted in Figure 12 in the characteristic turbulent style of the sixth-century vase painters. Eurytos is trying to restrain Heracles with his bare hands; his sons are fallen all around. On the far right Iole is awaiting her fate.

Eventually Athena goes so far as to wait on Heracles as he rests or banquets. Figure 13 shows the tondo of a cup by the painter Douris, with Athena pouring wine for Heracles; in Figure 14, a late-sixth-century vase, Heracles is at dinner in the presence of Athena. It is curious to contrast the subservient role which the goddess plays in these scenes with the martial character she shows in some of her own adventures. Figure 15 depicts her in one of her feats on the battlefield, the killing of the giant Enkelados.

While the prominence of Heracles reflects the phallic traditions that were developing in sixth-century Athens, as a local hero he had one great drawback: he was a Dorian, and no degree of manipulation could extricate him from his associations with the Doric cities of Sparta, Corinth, and Megara. To be sure, an attempt was made to link him more securely with Athena, through a myth in which the goddess sponsors his deification and personally introduces him to the gods of Olympus. However, as the rivalry between the Dorian

13. Athena waits on Heracles.

12.
Heracles slaughters the men
in Eurytus' household
before abducting his daughter
Iole (on the right).

14. Heracles dining on Mount
Olympus in the presence
of Athena.

15. Athena as monster-slayer
(killing the giant Enkelados).

and the Ionian Greeks became more intense, Heracles became an unsatisfactory national hero, and a native personality, Theseus, came to the fore, to be fashioned into a synthetic Attic Heracles, inheriting the patronage of Athena from his Doric counterpart.

By the mid-fifth century, the image of Athena was stripped of any vestige of femininity. Her most authoritative effigy was the gold-and-ivory statue in the Parthenon, created by Phidias at the height of Athenian power. Although the inner construction of this type of statue is still debated, we have a fairly good idea of its appearance from copies and descriptions (Figure 16). The Athena Parthenos (the Virgin) was, as a late Roman author put it, a "virago," a sexless man-woman who can defend her position in a male world, but only at the expense of her own sexual role.

Athena's image in the Parthenon included a number of anti-female motifs. Her genital area was, as in all images of her, concealed by long robes. Her breasts were covered by the traditional aegis, probably originally a goatskin but in her later effigies a corselet bristling with snakes; scholars of a psychoanalytic bent consider the aegis an expression of the male fear of the *vagina dentata* (toothed vagina) and of castration. On the aegis Athena wore a Medusa head, with similar associations. Indeed, the snakes around the open mouth of the Medusa are suggestive of pubic hair, and the aggressive associations of the image help explain why Athenian women practiced partial depilation of the genital zone (Kilmer, 1982). The aegis with the open-mouthed head is depicted in a number of vase paintings (see Figure 17). The statue's helmet was topped by a sphinx, another monster out of the mythological female bestiary. Figure 18 shows a fifth-century bronze statuette, in which this feature is copied as the helmet's sole ornament. The original Athena Parthenos held a spear in one hand, and her shield, which was one of Phidias' triumphs, in the other. The shield showed on the outside the Amazonomachia, or slaughter of the Amazons by the Greeks, the major symbol of the victory of male over female.

16. The Athena from Varvakion, modeled after the Athena Parthenos in the Parthenon.

17. Athena with the Medusa head and snakes.

According to legend, one of the Amazon killers on the shield was made to look like Pericles, which was possibly an injustice to that leader. The inside of the shield showed the battle of the gods and the giants, a tale in which, as we saw, Athena played a role. On the goddess's sandals the battle of Lapiths (aboriginal Athenians) and centaurs was depicted, a familiar Attic patriotic motif which celebrated the victory of culture over barbarism. The statue's base featured the birth of Pandora, the epitome of the evil female. In mythology Pandora stands for the entire female sex. In the most misogynistic version of her origin (Hesiod, *Works and Days*, 60–69), Zeus orders Hephaestus to create her "of doglike mind and thievish character" as a punishment for man, in retaliation for Prometheus' unauthorized gift of fire to the human race. Since the name Pandora means All Gifts, in an earlier phase she may have actually been a fertility figure.

Athena's birth was as sexless as her mature personality. She was the result of one of Zeus' great feats of male pregnancy and parturition, the other being the god Dionysus. Athena was born, highly symbolically, from her father's head—that is, out of patriar-

18. Athena with owl and sphinx helmet.

19. The birth of Athena out of Zeus' head.

20. Zeus' thigh as womb: the birth of Dionysus.

chal male fantasy (Figure 19). In the most common version of her birth, when Zeus' cerebral pregnancy had come to term, the divine craftsman Hephaestus split Zeus' head open with an ax and out sprang Athena, fully equipped with the armor of militarism. The birth of Athena was represented on the east pediment of the Parthenon, and this alone was sufficient to give the event its status as a charter myth. The sexless birth of Athena makes a worthy complement to that classic tale of uterus envy, the birth of Dionysus, in which the father of gods and men develops a pseudo-womb. Zeus impregnates a mortal woman, Semele; when her pregnancy is well advanced, he destroys her with his thunderbolt, removes the fetus from her body, and sews it into his thigh. From there the young god is born—like Jesus Christ, half-mortal, half-divine. The choice of the thigh for the male womb, instead of the abdomen, probably

reflects the practices of male homosexual life. In Chapter 11 we
will see that the favored mode of homosexual copulation during
the Archaic age of Athens was intercrural—that is, between the
legs; the sexual aggressor ejaculated between the thighs of his lover.
Figure 20 shows the birth of Dionysus on a fifth-century vase
painting; the infant god is emerging from Zeus' thigh, much as
from a womb.

Despite her defeminization, Athena, as reigning divinity of
Athens, had to have some kind of dynastic connection with its early
rulers, so she acquired a pseudo-maternity in the myth of the early
king Erichthonius, whose name, in part from the root *chthon*,
meaning earth, reflects the Athenian claim of autochthony. Hephaestus, enamored of Athena, pursued her; when she defended her
virginity successfully, his seed fell on the ground, and Ge, the earth,
produced Erichthonius, whom she handed to Athena in a box, a
symbol for the womb. The myth of Hephaestus engendering a son
on the earth constitutes in effect another tale of birth without a
mother. I show it here in a stately rendering, now in Munich, from
the middle of the fifth century (Figure 21).

As patroness of the crafts, the goddess was known as Athena
Ergane (Of the Workshop), but in Classical Athens this function
was largely taken over by the god Hephaestus, a humbler figure in
the family of gods, possibly in part because the Athenians developed,
at least in theory, an aristocratic contempt for craftsmanship.
Athena Ergane, however, remained an important deity for women
in her capacity as guardian of the home textile industry, which will
be discussed in Chapter 9.

## Hera and Her Son Hephaestus: The Mockery of the Enthroned Goddess

Of all the Attic myths that reflect the defeminization process, I
can touch on only a few, which seem to have played a particularly
strong part in molding Athenian consciousness. One of these is the
motif of Hephaestus locking his mother, Hera, in her throne, a
burlesque tale that perhaps was dramatically enacted on some
occasions. Hera, Zeus' sister and official consort, had to surrender
many of her sexual and maternal features. She was goddess of
marriage, but her domain was, at least in Athens, encroached upon
by Demeter. She is a mother only peripherally, and of secondary

21. The birth of Erichthonius from the earth and spilled semen.

gods, whom she despises. Her children are Ares, the patron of war, whom even the gods dislike; the minor divinity Hebe, cupbearer to the gods, who loses that function to Zeus' boy lover Ganymede; and Hephaestus, whom she cripples by hurling him down from Mount Olympus. Hephaestus takes revenge on his mother by crafting a chair for her from which she cannot get up. All the other gods plead with him to release her; finally Dionysus succeeds by getting Hephaestus drunk and escorting him back to Olympus on a donkey, surrounded by equally inebriated satyrs. The story is depicted on so many vases that it must have been part of a standard ritual. Quite possibly the comical group was part of the procession which took place before the festival of the Greater Dionysia. In Figures 22 and 23 two vase paintings illustrate the myth, one in black-figure technique and one in red-figure, both conveying the ritual aspect of this motif. As Erich Neumann has shown, the enthroned goddess is a widespread pictorial motif denoting maternal fertility. The myth of the return of Hephaestus represents a diminution of Hera's maternal aspect. Hera, in the Athenian view, was

22. The return of Hephaestus: a mockery of Hera's maternity.

23. The return of Hephaestus, possibly as a stage play.

essentially not a mother but a jealous and malcontent wife, the prototype of the nagging housewife in literature.

The city of Athens did have a visible relic of the Earth Mother cults, namely the Metroön (Temple of the Mother) in the Agora, dedicated to the Asian fertility goddess Cybele. It housed the state archives.

## The Battle of the Greeks and the Amazons

The myth of Classical Athens which, as it were, codified the rule of male over female was that of the Amazonomachia. The lost epic poem *Aithiopis*, one of several composed perhaps in the seventh century B.C. filling in the events of the Trojan War around Homer's *Iliad* and *Odyssey*, is the first known literary rendering of the tale: on the plains outside the Trojan citadel the Greeks defeated a band of exotic warrior women who had come to the aid of the besieged city, and they killed their queen, Penthesileia. Athenian mythology added a whole new element to the story—namely, that of the Amazons invading the Attic homeland and being defeated at the hands of the Attic hero Theseus. This addition had the double effect of tying early Attic history in with the glorious epic past of the Greeks, and of creating a mythological male-female confrontation connected with the origins of Athenian society. The Amazonomachia constitutes the most striking example of the intermingling of the male-sexist and the nationalistic elements in Attic culture. The ubiquity and repetitiousness of the motif in Greek art is astonishing. In addition to the Amazonomachia depicted on the shield of Athena Parthenos, there were pairs of fighting Greeks and Amazons in the western metopes of the Parthenon, of which parts survive. There was a painted Amazonomachia in the Temple of Theseus, and another one in the Stoa Poikile, or Painted Porch, which was decorated by the best fifth-century painters. Scores of surviving vase paintings, which probably to some extent reflect these public monuments, show battle scenes of Greeks and Amazons. In addition, vase painters frequently depicted individual mythological heroes, especially of course Heracles and Theseus, stabbing, slashing, or clubbing Amazons, often hitting them in a breast near a nipple.

Heracles, with his fierce-looking lion's skin and club, made the best pictorial contrast with the usually rather dainty Amazons, and he was accordingly favored by the pottery painters. Out of a large selection, Figures 24, 25, and 26 reproduce three different renderings of the theme, which show how different artists, in different techniques and on a variety of vase shapes, created a repertoire of the slaughter of females. In a number of cases, Heracles' female antagonist is identified by name, most often as Andromache (no relation to the wife of Hector); the name means "man fighter." This name for an Amazon is attested only in the vase paintings.

Figure 27 shows Achilleus slaying the Amazon queen, Penthesileia; the vase was drawn by one of the finest artists in the black-figure technique, Exekias. The tale of Achilleus and Penthesileia is perhaps the most poignant mythological dramatization of male-female antagonism. According to a myth, presumably also told in the *Aithiopis*, Achilleus did kill the Amazon queen, but fell in love with her at the very moment in which he stabbed her—a story which smacks of a love-hate relationship between male and female, and an underlying equation of the penis and the sword. The theme is the subject of one of the most outstanding surviving artifacts from the Classical age, a drinking cup by a painter who is known as the Penthesileia Painter (Figures 28 and 29). The artist, who had

25. Heracles killing an Amazon.

24. Heracles killing an Amazon.

26. Heracles killing an Amazon.

a special gift for squeezing the utmost pathos out of a traditional story (more of his work will be examined later), probably introduced several innovations into the depiction. The Amazon has fallen on her knees before Achilleus and is caressing his breast in a gesture of seduction. Achilleus' sword is piercing her from above; in other words, the hero has stabbed her while she was pleading for mercy, but the magic moment has arrived: there is eye contact between the two and the ardent expression on Achilleus' face indicates that he is responding to the pleading, but too late. The pathos conveyed by this story, if reconstructed according to the clues given by the painter, is intense: the Amazon has had her day on the battlefield, dealing death to men. When she is in danger herself, she falls back on her womanly wiles of seduction. Only after her surrender can Achilleus appreciate her beauty, but the sword, the perennial symbol for male aggression, is already in her breast. On the right, a second Amazon is expiring, also from a chest wound. The warrior on the left, who has just felled her, is coolly walking away from the scene and looking at Achilleus with an expression on his face that seems to say, "What's all the fuss about?"

The Amazonomachia played a peculiar role in Greek consciousness, as the geographer Strabo, who lived in the second century B.C., noted: "The tales surrounding the Amazons have a special place. For in the other instances the mythical and the historical each have their own, clearly separated places" (11, 53). In effect, to the Classical Athenians, the legend of their victory over the rebellious women was both myth and historical reality. The Amazonomachia was regularly included, along with the defeat of the Persians, in the catalogues of glorious deeds in eulogies and funeral orations, by which Athenian patriotism was bolstered, as in Isocrates' *Panegyricus,* or *Praise of Athens* (70). As we shall see in the Epilogue, it cropped up again in later phases of Greek history, as a myth justifying imperialist ambitions.

## Tales of Rape

Rape is the ultimate translation of phallicism into action. Rape is committed not for pleasure or procreation, but in order to enact the principle of domination by means of sex. It is no wonder that the Athenian Greeks were obsessed with it. It is, in fact, one of the most characteristic features of the specifically Attic mythology

27. Achilleus killing the
Amazon Penthesileia.

28. Achilleus kills Penthesileia
as she tries to seduce him.

29. Detail of 28.

which emerges in the beginning of the fifth century B.C. Most typically, a male divinity or hero assaults a mortal woman, but homosexual rape is also fairly frequent, and occasionally a goddess overpowers a mortal man. In no other mythology of which I am aware does rape play a more prominent part. In modern literature about the Greek myths it is customary to refer to the rape stories euphemistically as tales of "dalliance," and "amorous" or "*galant*" adventures of the gods. However, the artifacts, which are for the first phase of this phenomenon our most abundant source of information, make it quite clear that they tell of rape. (Later, a number of these stories acquired a mystical connotation of erotic-religious union with the elements of eternity and were then converted into funerary symbols, but this does not seem to hold true for the fifth century B.C.; in fact, here the story often takes a turn for the worse for the rape victim, as happens in real life.) Despite Greek frankness about sexuality, the consummation of the rapes is never shown, nor are erections: visible sexual excitement is reserved for coarser creatures, such as satyrs and mortals. Instead, the rampaging gods and heroes wield their characteristic attributes as symbolic phalluses, often aimed revealingly at the genital zones of their victims—Zeus, his scepter or his thunderbolt (or both); Poseidon, his trident; and Hermes, his caduceus.

Figure 30, a stem krater now in New York, may be considered characteristic of the type: it shows the gods Hermes and Poseidon out on a sexual rampage in tandem. Their victims here, as far as we know, are anonymous. The women's stereotyped gestures denote protest and leave no doubt that violence is alluded to. The gods are

30. Poseidon and Hermes on a raping expedition together.

discreetly wrapped in cloaks, but their weapons are held in phallic positions and are aimed at the women's crotches.

The master rapist, of course, was Zeus: the catalogue of his conquests became a *topos* of Greek literature, and led to a scurrilous Greek anecdote. A foreigner once came to Athens and asked why the Athenians so often used the exclamation "by Zeus"; the answer: "Because so many of us are." In the literary tradition, Zeus overcomes most of his female victims by trickery: he rapes Leda in the form of a swan, Danaë in the guise of a golden rain, and Alkmene in the persona of her legitimate husband (holding up the dawn for three nights to draw full profit from his scheme), and he does not even hesitate to take on so coarse a disguise as that of a randy satyr for the purpose of violating Antiope. In the pictorial tradition of the mid-fifth century, on the other hand, his excursions are represented mostly through the motif of pursuit. Figures 31 and 32 show him on a Dionysiac drinking cup (kantharos) by the Brygos Painter, in two scenes of rape, one homosexual and one heterosexual, carefully balanced in composition, with that typically Greek bisexual promiscuity. The male victim, without doubt, is Zeus' perennial favorite, Ganymede; the female is anonymous.

One exception to the pursuit formula in the tales of Zeus' amorous conquests is the picture of Europa and Zeus in the shape of a bull, shown in Figure 33. It was drawn by an artist whom we know as the Berlin Painter, who indulged in some humorous dramatic irony with this picture. Europa is cautiously stroking the one horn of the bull that is visible—which has phallic overtones: she clearly considers the animal tame. The coy expression in the bull's eyes tells us something else.

One can only marvel at the candor with which Greek myth fashioned and depicted these tales dramatizing the power of the male over the female. This is especially true of the story of Zeus and Semele, told above, which is virtually a mythological blueprint of the relationship between the sexes in Classical Athens. Translated into societal terms, the male has the power, marries at his choice solely for the purpose of reproduction, deprives the female of credit for genetic motherhood, and destroys her. Figure 34 shows one of several fifth-century illustrations which follow the general pursuit-and-violence scheme; here Zeus aims both his scepter and his thunderbolt at Semele. Scholars have debated whether this scene depicts Zeus' rape of Semele or his destruction of her. I suspect a double allusion may have been intended.

Kaempf-Dimitriadou's recent book, euphemistically entitled *The Love of the Gods in Attic Art of the Fifth Century B.C.*, is a useful catalogue of illustrations of rape. It impresses especially by its numbers: the list contains 395 items, and includes rape by all the major male divinities on Olympus and by one rather obscure goddess, Eos (Dawn), who is known primarily for her aggressive sexual appetites. The author offers no explanation for this explosion of sexual violence on Mount Olympus; instead, she views the tales of rape as a subtle expression of the Athenians' "yearning for the divine" (57).

One of the clues pointing to a specifically Attic element in the theme of rape is its connection with one of the local Athenian foundation legends. The rape myths which contain patriotic elements are those connected with the career of Theseus and the tale of Boreas, the North Wind, who raped Oreithyia. Significantly, several of these myths with an Athenian locale connect the story of the rape with the institution of legitimate marriage, thereby, unlike the other tales of sexual violence, lending a social sanction of sorts to force. Oreithyia was the daughter of Erechtheus, another legendary early king of Athens (the Erechtheum on the Acropolis is named after him), perhaps a mythological double of the Erichthonius mentioned earlier. Oreithyia is forcefully overcome by the fierce and barbaric Boreas, but this was apparently condoned by her father, Erechtheus, and by the goddess Athena, who view the scene in many vase paintings. Unlike most of the non-Attic rape victims, who had to endure one-night stands, Oreithyia settled down in marriage and bore glorious sons, the Boreads Zetes and Kalais. Aeschylus dramatized the story (Fr. 492 Mette), but his play was apparently not very successful, and it was probably the myth's patriotic flavor that made it the most popular rape story in the pictorial arts (Kaempf-Dimitriadou lists 56 vase paintings on the subject).

The most revealing of these paintings occurs in the lower register of the krater reproduced in Figures 35 and 36. In Figure 35 Boreas is grabbing Oreithyia; her parents, on the left, are making gestures of protest but are not interfering. A conspiring attendant with a key in her right hand is already leading the way to the bridal chamber. In the lower register in Figure 36, the "happy resolution" is portrayed: Oreithyia is in the women's quarters of her new abode,

31. Zeus in sexual pursuit of Ganymede.

32. Reverse of 31. Zeus in sexual pursuit of a woman.

33. The Zeus-bull with phallic horn about to abduct Europa.

34a,b. Zeus destroying Semele with his thunderbolt.

with the standard symbolic allusions to spinning and sex (the half-opened door on the right), about which I will have more to say. The upper register of the same krater shows another myth of marriage by rape—namely, the wedding of Peleus and the sea nymph Thetis, also extremely popular in Attic art. Peleus, a mortal man, overcomes the goddess Thetis, who resists his aggression, even though in her defense Thetis changes herself into various monstrous shapes, including that of a snake and that of a lion. That the union was successful despite these ominous beginnings was mythologically established by its offspring: the glorious hero Achilleus. Figure 37 shows one of the more elaborate renderings of the myth of Peleus and Thetis, by the painter Peithinos, with pictorial allusions to the bride's unsuccessful metamorphoses into a snake and a lion.

In view of the Athenians' overriding preoccupation with rape, it is hardly surprising that there was, as I shall elaborate later, an unusual moral and legal tolerance of this offense, as well as notions of violence governing all aspects of the Athenian man's sex life: in his concept of marriage, in the ethos governing his pederastic love life, and even in his relations with prostitutes. The Penthesileia Painter provides us with an original elaboration of sexual violence: Figure 38 shows his rendering of one of the few myths of a mortal molesting a goddess. Tityus, the son of Ge (Earth), had molested the goddess Leto, mother of Artemis and Apollo. Leto, like so many other goddesses, had probably had a more illustrious past as an Earth Mother divinity, but, in her Classical phase, she derived her status mostly from her two powerful children. Apollo kills Tityus, who goes on to have a rather celebrated career as one of the standard sinners punished in Hades. In the Penthesileia Painter's rendering, we see Apollo about to execute the offender. The god's idle left hand clutches his customary executioner's tools, bow and arrows; with his right hand he vigorously swings the more phallic sword, expressing the anger which moves him. Tityus has fallen to his knees and is pleading for quarter; the expression on his face and the position of his left hand, clutching his breast, convey righteous astonishment, a "What have I done wrong?" feeling. The scene must be viewed against the background of the record of sexual aggression of all the gods, including Apollo himself. Tityus has done only one thing wrong: he has used poor judgment in his choice of victim.

35. Marriage as rape. Upper: Peleus rapes Thetis. Lower: Boreas rapes Oreithyia.

36. Reverse of 35. Upper: the rape of Thetis, continued. Lower: Oreithyia before the bridal chamber.

37. Marriage as rape: Peleus forces Thetis to marry him.

## Heracles and His Women

Heracles, the dominant hero of the Athenian Archaic period, who was never completely eclipsed by his native rival, Theseus, was certainly an exponent of male supremacy. We have already noted his career as Amazon killer and abductor. The stealing of the "girdle of the Amazon Hippolyte" was another one of his sexual confrontations which conveyed both sexual and physical victory over the female, inasmuch as the "loosening of the girdle" symbolically denoted sexual surrender. Heracles was involved with numerous other women, and in one exploit deflowered fifty women in one week; yet he never acquired a clear-cut image of a rapist, nor were his adventures depicted in the standard scheme of gods pursuing women. This is probably to be explained by the fact that his career as a lover was tainted, as it were, with attempts at persuasion and with an occasional affectionate relationship. In an unattributed fragment of a fifth-century tragedy, someone asks Heracles, "Did you take your favors by force or after having persuaded the girl?" This is a question which could never have been asked of the Athenian hero Theseus. We even hear of Heracles freeing the girl Hesione, who, like Andromeda, had been exposed on a rock; apparently he did not take sexual advantage of her. He is happily married, at least for a while, to Megara, who bears him children, and to Deianeira, who is featured as his devoted wife in Sophocles' *Women of Trachis*.

## Theseus, Athens' National Hero

If my thesis, that the mythological glorification of sexual violence is particularly intense in the Attic tradition, is correct, we should

38. Apollo kills Tityus for having molested his mother. Tityus' mother Ge on the right.

expect it to be reflected in the career of Athens' national hero, and so it is. The stories surrounding this figure are numerous and varied, and it is not my purpose to repeat material which can be found in any handbook of mythology. However, even a brief look at Theseus' traditional personality reveals an exceptionally large number of stories involving the assertion of power over women.

The mythological personality of Theseus before the era of Athenian hegemony was already somewhat murky: he was the traditional savior of Athens, killing the Cretan Minotaur and relieving the city of its tribute of youths and maidens to the monster. However, his desertion of his Cretan helper, his new wife, Ariadne, on the island of Naxos is an action strangely lacking in even mythological rationale. That the story took a happy turn for Ariadne, who was rescued by Dionysus and became his consort, was not Theseus' doing.

In the Athenian sources about his life, Theseus' father, Aegeus, abandoned his mother, Aethra, after impregnating her. When the boy grew up, his mother revealed to him the "tokens of recognition" which his father had hidden under a stone at the time of his departure. They consisted of a sword and a pair of sandals. In a number of vase paintings the hero is shown drawing his sword against a woman. Some believe that she is his mother, from whom Theseus is trying to exact revenge for his illegitimate birth. Others hold that he is threatening his stepmother, Medea, who had married Aegeus and was trying to do away with her stepson. At any rate, a drawn sword is Theseus' standard attribute, a fitting item for an Athenian national hero.

The killing of the Minotaur, however, remained Theseus' most celebrated exploit; Figure 39 shows it in a beautiful rendering by the painter Aison, who depicts it taking place under the protection of Athena—a version discreetly overlooking the aid given by Ariadne.

To be promoted from his role as a caddish figure of provincial standing to one of major, heroic proportions, Theseus had to be integrated into panhellenic legend, and this was effected in several ways. In a bit of mythological one-upmanship, Theseus, together with his friend Peirithoos, abducted Helen, the later Helen of Troy, before she was married to Menelaos. Theseus had to return her, of course, so the legendary events could take their course. In return for assistance, Theseus helped Peirithoos in his attempt to abduct the queen of the underworld.

39. Athena, Theseus and
the slain Minotaur.

40. Theseus and Heracles as monster-slayers together (Theseus slays
the Minotaur, Heracles the Nemean Lion).

Theseus was assimilated to Heracles in many ways. Figure 40
shows a detail from a cup in the Louvre on which Theseus kills the
Minotaur while Heracles does away with the Nemean lion. Eventually a catalogue of the labors of Theseus was worked out, almost
shamelessly modeled after those of Heracles. If Heracles killed the

Amazon Hippolyte, Theseus carried off the Amazon Antiope, sometimes also called Hippolyte. If Heracles killed the Cretan bull,
Theseus could do no less but kill the bull of Marathon. The labor
of the Erymanthian boar is rendered in the tradition of Theseus
with a small but telling twist: Theseus kills a sow, represented in
vase paintings with prominent dugs, as an image of fecundity
(Chapter 12). Figure 41 shows the killing of the sow together with
the slaying of an unidentified youth, probably the robber Skiron,
who hurled his victims off a cliff. Significantly, the humiliating toils
of Heracles, such as knitting and cleaning, were not assimilated in
the Thesean tradition. On the other hand, Theseus has several more
abductions of unwilling maidens to his name, notably that of a girl
named Korone, which is frequently depicted on vases. In the Attic
version of Theseus' Cretan adventures even the princess Ariadne

41a,b. Theseus killing a youth and the Crommyan sow.

42. Theseus in phallic pursuit of Ariadne.

43. Athena summoning Theseus to abandon the sleeping Ariadne.

was won by him, not through love but by force, as shown in Figure 42.

An early-fifth-century vase painter, of mediocre skill but with an original grasp of his subject matter, captured the essence of Theseus' transformation from a legendary prehistoric adventurer into a national hero in the Attic monster-slaying, woman-dominating tradition. The humble little oil flask in Taranto in Figure 43 shows Theseus and Ariadne on the island of Naxos. The sprite perched on Ariadne's head, who is personified Sleep (Hypnos), communicates that the heroine is soundly asleep, and the blissful expression on her face shows that she is having happy dreams. The source of that happiness, Theseus, is sharing the bed with her, but he has just been awakened by the goddess Athena, who is standing over him in her martial, sexless glory: she is summoning him from the couch of affectionate love to the patriotic career he is to play out under her aegis.

According to Aristotle, the labors of Theseus were extolled in the *Theseid*, presumably an epic poem composed in Athens in the sixth or fifth century B.C. It has not to my knowledge been suggested that this poem could have been the model for the episode in the *Aeneid* of Vergil (Book IV) in which Aeneas abandons his lover Dido at the command of the gods in order to fulfill his destiny as founder of the new city of Rome. (There was, however, no rescue in store for the hapless Dido.) Both Theseus and Aeneas were synthetic heroes, fashioned to bolster a patriotic mythology and to support the imperialistic aspirations of a rising power.

## Other Patriarchal Mythemes

Numerous vase paintings from the early fifth century B.C. combine different motifs of the male-sexist type sketched here, some of them including so many that, like the statue of Athena Parthenos on the Acropolis, they constitute veritable catalogues of sex antagonism myths. Figure 44 shows a wine krater in Geneva, by a painter called the Geneva Painter, after this elaborate if not very artistic vessel. On the upper level a conventional Amazonomachia rages. On the lower level a young man pursues a woman while her attendants flee. Most probably it is Theseus besetting Korone.

Patriotic themes were especially favored for large, flat drinking

44. The mythological conquests of woman. Above: Amazonomachia. Below: hero in phallic pursuit of women.

cups, the oversized version of the wine cup used for private drinking parties. Probably the large ones were intended for use or display at

45. Aglaurus and Herse pursued by the phallus-snake.

46. Same as 45. Demeter and Persephone wait on the new male fertility figure Triptolemos.

47. Same as 45, inside.
Poseidon in sexual
pursuit of Aethra, the
mother of Theseus.

the civic banquets of the Athenians, hence their nationalistic decorations. The cup in Figures 45, 46, and 47 combines a number of
the sex supremacy themes in Attic tradition, especially those most
closely intertwined with the Athenian founding legends. Among
the more easily identifiable motifs, we see in Figure 45 the girls
Aglauros and Herse, the disobedient daughters of the Athenian
founding father King Cecrops. They are being pursued, and will
shortly be driven to death, by a huge serpent, a penis symbol. Figure
46, part of the same vase, depicts a mythological defeminization
motif: it concerns the myth of Demeter and Persephone, which was
the cult legend of the Eleusinian initiation rituals. (We will return
to this myth, as well as to that of Aglauros and Herse, in Chapter
12.) Into the Eleusinian ritual, which was originally an Earth
Mother–fertility religion, the Athenians artificially injected a male
god, the boy Iakchos, later called Triptolemos. Here we see Demeter
and her daughter respectfully attending the young god, about to
depart on a winged chariot to bring the gift of grain to the world.
An enthroned king of Athens pours the parting libation, thus
creating an anachronistic bond between the Eleusinian youth and
the founding fathers of Attica. The flat inside of the cup (Figure 47)
shows yet another patriarchal theme: the god Poseidon, who was
closely tied to the origins of Athens, sexually pursues an anonymous
woman. Most probably she is Aethra, the mother of the Athenian
founding father Theseus. Thus, in the mythological scenario featured
on this cup, rape lies at the very heart of Athenian tradition.

# 3

# The Phallus and the Box: The World Seen in the Shapes of Human Genitals

> What's outside, is man's business, and let no woman give it thought. Let her stay inside and do no mischief.
> —Aeschylus, *Seven Against Thebes* (200–201):
> Eteocles speaking

> ... the nature of women should be completely unknown, except to those who live with them.
> —Plutarch, *Moralia* (217 f.)

In his famous work *Mutterrecht* (Mother Right), J. J. Bachofen first voiced the insight that mankind in the early phases of its social development worshiped the female principle as the source of life, nutrition, and prosperity. Since Bachofen's time, archaeology has confirmed that view a thousand times, unearthing numerous artifacts from man's prehistoric past that show adoration of the female genitalia. There can be little doubt that this uterine worship harks back to a phase in man's history when the male role in reproduction was not recognized, though it probably continued long after paternity was discovered. Bachofen thought that this preoccupation with the female constituted proof of an early matriarchy. He cites a number of Greek myths of female rebellion against male control, such as that of the Amazons, and those of women who murder their husbands and sons, as a vague memory of a society in which women were dominant over men. Bachofen's views no longer find much acceptance as far as the history of the Western world is concerned. We have yet to find the traces of any Mediterranean culture in which women had more power than men. Such a state of affairs is indeed physically unlikely. Power structures are rooted in brute strength. Women, smaller in stature, have always been weakened by menstruation and pregnancies, and decimated by that historical curse of the female sex, death in childbirth.

The Greek mythological obsession with monstrous women and with gynecocracy (literally "women's rule," but more accurately "women getting out of hand") reflects man's irrational fear of the female and his feelings of guilt, not his memory of a vanished world. Bachofen's hypothesis of early matriarchy was not necessary. The Egyptians worshiped animal gods, yet ate meat. The Athenian Greeks adopted a female divinity as patron goddess of their state and worshiped a number of other goddesses besides, yet enslaved their women. The modern world idolizes queens and movie actresses, yet does its best to exploit and repress the female sex.

The Jungian psychologist Erich Neumann wrote the most influential book on the worship of the female in man's prehistoric past, *The Great Mother*, from which the epigraph at the beginning of this book is taken. Neumann sees phallic worship as a reaction in man's development, an attempt to free himself from bondage to the female principle and canonize the penis as the fundamental generator of life. Except in myth, however, men cannot bear children, so they must take possession of the bodies of those who can, their women; hence, violence is at the root in this second phase. Fifth-century Attic culture is an excellent illustration of this process because seldom has the function of "respectable" women been more drastically restricted to childbearing, and seldom did phallic worship coincide so clearly with manifestations of violence, such as militarism, imperialist expansion, and brutality in the conduct of everyday affairs.

The Athenian Greeks were not alone in their cult of the phallus. The idolization of the male genitalia as the source of life and of the immortality of the race was not as widespread as was the worship of the female, but it was by no means confined to Athens or to the Greek world. However, no society on record was more imbued with phallic beliefs and usages and generated a richer set of phallic fantasies. In the *Realenzyklopaedie der klassischen Altertumswissenschaft*, a veritable monument to German industry and erudition, the article "Phallos" covers sixty-eight dense columns of print, jampacked with information on phallic rituals, cults, and beliefs attested for ancient Greece, without the author even pretending to come close to completeness.

There is a great difference in the social effect of female and male genital worship. The early idolization of female reproduction is no proof of matriarchy, but it is likely to have acted as a check on the male control over the female. Phallic worship, on the other hand, reinforced the stranglehold of man over woman, and in its extreme form, as found in fifth-century Athens, virtually destroyed the female sex.

## The Dainty Penis: Male Genital Narcissism

Athenian men displayed their genitals with great pride, at least as long as they were young, a custom which, according to Plato, was ridiculed by the "barbarians" (*Rep.* 452c). That this practice was not confined to the gymnasia and the wrestling arenas but was a feature of daily life is shown in Figure 48, which depicts a reveler coming home drunk from a party with his lyre on his shoulder. His boisterous mood is indicated by the fact that he is banging on the door with his walking stick even though there is a knocker. In something of a reversal of the modern comic cliché of the drunk sneaking home in fear of reprisals, his wife is anxiously approaching the door with an oil lamp in her hand, in fear of what his bluster may bring her.

While it is true that other Greeks also were free of shame in

48. Husband coming home drunk.

regard to male nudity, they did not cultivate the contrast between the male and female to the same extent. In Sparta, for example, women also exercised in the nude, whereas Athenian women were expected in public and even private appearances to be muffled in garments, almost beyond recognition.

As K. J. Dover has shown, the Athenian taste in male genitalia ran to small and taut. Our modern stag party jokes of "well-endowed men" would have been lost on the Athenians. Large sex organs were considered coarse and ugly, and were banished to the domains of abstraction, of caricature, of satyrs, and of barbarians. In the inexhaustible genital vocabulary of Aristophanes, diminutives denoting small penises are used as words of endearment—as, for example, *posthion*, which might be rendered as "little prick."

Even though the Athenians were aware of its hygienic advantages (Hdt. 2, 37) they had a horror of circumcision and of conditions of the penis which resemble it. Figure 49 shows a vase painting of Heracles killing the attendants of the Aethiopian King Busiris (Dover, 1978, R 699). As Dover rightly points out, the artist emphatically contrasted the small, pointed penis of the burly Heracles with the stubby and circumcised genitals of the barbarian attendants. Aristotle, feeling obligated to provide a scientific explanation for this Athenian predilection for small genitals, argued that the small penis is more fertile than the large one, because the seed, while passing through it, has a shorter distance to travel and hence doesn't cool off as much.

The taste for dainty, pointed penises led to a custom evidently practiced only in Attica, and not mentioned by Dover, which is called infibulation. To prevent the foreskin from becoming damaged while exercising in the nude, young athletes tied it down over the glans with a leather string, sometimes tucking up the penis with the same string as well. The knot, or perhaps the resulting bundle, was called *kynodesme*, literally "dog tie" in Greek. Although there has been some debate whether this measure served hygienic or aesthetic purposes, the description in Photius' *Lexicon*, cited in Stephanus' *Thesaurus* (s.v.), gives cosmetic reasons, and I see no reason to doubt this author. The dog knot was the ancient equivalent of the modern jock strap and, like that item of men's clothing, acquired associations of male sexual pride and supremacy.

The wine vessel in Figure 50, painted by Euphronius, shows young athletes in a gymnasium. The youth on the left is just about

49. Elegant and coarse male genitals (Heracles killing the attendants of king Busiris).

50. Youth putting the "dog knot" on his penis.

to put the "dog knot" on his penis, while his little slave boy stands by to help. The youth with the ball in the center may be due for similar treatment, since the sports master with the rod is pointing at his genitals. A scene on the tondo of a drinking cup in Toledo, Ohio (Figure 51), shows an infibulated youth playing the guitar and being accosted sexually from the rear by a mature man. The aggressor's walking stick carries the symbolic phallic charge here.

In the late sixth century B.C., at about the time of the invention of the red-figure technique in pottery, vase painters began to experiment with the representation of the human body frontally and with foreshortening. One of their favorite details was the foot; the other, not surprisingly in view of their genital obsession, was the male reproductive organ. As a result, a compositional stereotype developed of a crouched man facing the viewer with his legs apart, a position which allows the draftsman to apply his skill to both appendages. Figures 52 and 53 are red-figure vase paintings with men in this pose; the one on Figure 53 is probably the god Hephaestus in his smithy. Figure 54 is a famous vase by the Sosias Painter from about 500 B.C.; it depicts Achilleus bandaging his wounded friend Patroclus. The genitals in this case are more successful than the feet, inasmuch as the toes of Patroclus' right foot look somewhat like fingers.

A number of youths in vase paintings strike narcissistic poses. Several, for instance, throw back a cloak to reveal naked rump and genitals. If they were women, we would think of prostitutes displaying their wares. In the case of male characters, we can't always be sure. What are we to make of Apollo and his muse in Figure 55? It is probably best to interpret Apollo's posture in this scene as the artist's expression of the god's youthful beauty.

The humorous painting by the Penthesileia Painter in Figure 56 is easier to read. A delicate youth is in sexual pursuit of a girl. He proudly throws back his cloak to reveal his infibulated genitals, which qualify him as a man, since now he partakes in serious athletics, but disable him for the business at hand. Note especially the contrast between the articulation of the male body and the shapelessness of the girl, whose form is concealed by the drapes of her loose-hanging garments. The scene sums up the Greek conception of physical beauty and sex: the male is the aggressor—the boy is pursuing the girl and reaching for her with his left hand—but it is his physical beauty and his organs which provide the sexual induce-

51. Mature man approaching infibulated youth sexually.

53. More feet and genitals in foreshortening (Hephaestus in his smithy, detail).

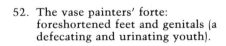

52. The vase painters' forte: foreshortened feet and genitals (a defecating and urinating youth).

54. Achilleus bandaging the wounded Patroclus.

55. Male narcissism: Apollo revealing himself to a seated Muse.

ments. She is "boxed in" beneath her garment.

An amusing small consequence of the Attic preoccupation with male genitals regards the portrayal of children. Where children appear in interior domestic scenes, which they do occasionally, and on funerary monuments, which they do frequently, given the rate of death in childbirth, the child is usually male, and we know he is

56. Amorous youth displaying infibulated genitals.

male because he is naked, and placed so that his genitals show. The preponderance of boys in home scenes should not be construed as evidence of female infanticide, although this was in all probability quite common (Chapter 5), but as an expression of the notion that only the male child counted, and that his genitals constituted his identity.

Figure 57 shows a mythologized interior scene with a mother and two naked boys, perhaps the family of Theseus, since he is represented on the reverse. The boys are carefully placed in such a position that their genitals are visible. Their nudity is not totally unbelievable, since they are old enough to be toilet-trained. In Figure 58 we have a rare family grouping of mother, father, and child. The seated mother hands the baby over to a nurse; with total disregard for her lovely dress, and contrary to what we know about ancient child-rearing practices the mother had held the infant naked on her lap, in order to give the vase painter an opportunity to depict his tiny genitals. On funerary monuments boy babies are also depicted in the nude, with their genital area in view, and we should probably conclude that babies who are bundled up are meant to be girls. We will see several instances of such portrayals in Chapter 5.

In contrast to the proudly paraded dainty penis, the caricature

57. Mother (perhaps Ariadne), nurse and two sons.

58. Mother hands naked infant son to a nurse (the father and a loom are also shown).

59. Caricature of circumcised man, defecating and holding his nose.

in Figure 59 shows a shitting man, about to wipe himself with one hand and holding his nose with the other. His circumcised, droopy penis reaches down almost to his heels.

## The Permanent Erection: The Phallus of Male Imagination

Now that during recent years the secret cabinets of the museums of Naples, Tarquinia, Munich, Boston, and other cities have begun to admit a few privileged scholars and photographers, and a spate of more or less sensational studies of ancient erotic art has come out, it has become clear that the imagination expended on the male organ of reproduction was more whimsical than previously thought, notably in Athens. Phallic bronzes from the fifth century B.C., such as those shown in Figures 60 and 61, had long been prized collectors' items. They belong largely to the category of satyrs and related theatrical creatures, which were long thought to have served to promote fertility. It is now widely recognized that the erect penis is as likely to be defensive or hostile as fertility-promoting. Beyond that recognition, it is difficult to place these phallic bronzes in a culturally significant context, especially since it is often impossible to assign a specific place of origin to them. The phallic Attic vase paintings, on the other hand, which are now becoming known and

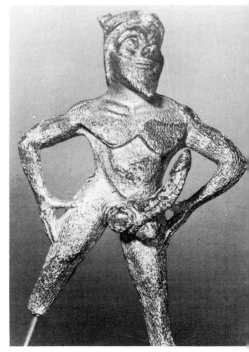

60. Horse-satyr with huge phallus.     61. Satyr with grotesque genitals.

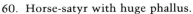

which date mainly from the late sixth and the fifth centuries B.C., show a degree of fantasy which can no longer be explained along anthropological lines of utility. They include double phalluses; phalluses with eyes, whereby they gain a kind of separate, living identity; phallus plants; and an entire bestiary of phallus-shaped animals and creatures with part of their anatomy transformed into phalluses. Only a small sampling can be reproduced here; for further examples the reader is referred to the richly illustrated works by Vorberg, Marcadé, Boardman (1977), Vermeule, and Dover (1978).

In the domain of religion, the phallus belonged primarily to the god Dionysus, whose cult included numerous playful and obscene elements. As a result, in many instances of phallic fantasy it is difficult or impossible to determine whether the intent was humorous or reverent, or conceivably even both. Figure 62 shows a horse with a phallus instead of a head. The two pieces of a somewhat fragmentary drinking cup in Figure 63 feature on one side a bird, whose head has been transformed into a perky-looking phallus, on the other side (not shown) a satyr who is lowering himself onto a phallus stuck into the ground, for his sexual satisfaction, one assumes. A more refined phallic joke is contained in Figure 64, a painting on the inside of a flat drinking cup, or kylix, which usually was decorated by the more skillful artists. The picture shows a boy riding a flying swan. Since the swan is the bird of Apollo (among other divinities), the scene may represent the god carrying off Hyakinthos. The joke, at any rate, is pictorial: the swan's long neck emerges from the boy's groin. The phallic shape is also found as an almost abstract decorative motif in vase painting—as, for instance, on the fragment in Figure 65, where it is combined with a stylized "evil eye," thus showing that its symbolism is one of hostility. No oversized phallic monuments are extant from Classical Athens, such as the huge phalluses on Delos which are still standing today to the delight and puzzlement of modern visitors (Figure 66).

The Athenian regard for the erect penis as the essence of man's being had a peculiar result in the rites of black magic, which the Athenians, even those of the higher classes, were not above practicing. If their studied rhetoric had failed in the courtroom, or they had other unyielding enemies or sexual rivals, they frequently inscribed imprecations against their foes on leaden tablets, so-called curse tablets, which they placed preferentially in the graves of boys: the ghosts of the "premature dead" (*aoroi*) were believed to wander and wreak evil until their natural lifespan had been fulfilled.

63. Phallic fantasy: a bird with phallus head.

62. Phallic fantasy: a horse with phallus head.

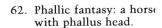

Sometimes the cursor added a voodoo doll of his intended victim, a crude leaden puppet placed in a tiny lead coffin, with its hands tied behind its back, that is, bound for torture and execution. Obviously the cursor hoped to take revenge on his enemy by homeopathic magic. Invariably these voodoo dolls are phallic, surely not because the victim was thought to have an erection under torture, but because his enemy wanted his most significant limb to be vulnerable. The image with oversized genitals in Figure 67 is that of one Mnesimachos and was placed in a child's grave by his unsuccessful opponent in a lawsuit, a legal tactic one would not have surmised from the speeches of Demosthenes.

## The Phallus in Public Cult

The entire Dionysiac religion, and with it both tragedy and comedy, seems to have sprung out of a systematic veneration of the male generative principle. A few illustrations must suffice to underscore the phallic fantasies unfolded in the public adulation of the penis. Figure 68 shows a phallic procession, which is remarkable in that it shows what appear to be men dressed up as satyrs, and a "real" satyr, the one with horse's legs. Figure 69 depicts a winged phallus, which is capped by a three-cornered sacrificial basket as if it were a hat. This may be a satire on the altars topped with phalluses, large numbers of which have been found in the sanctuary of Aphrodite on the north slope of the Acropolis. The festive procession, which enacted the myth of the return of Hephaestus (Chapter 2), also encouraged phallic fantasy. The ass on which Hephaestus rides back to Mount Olympus is regularly depicted with an erection. In the illustration of the group in Figure 70 the phallicness of the animal is underscored by a wine pitcher which dangles from his penis.

If the herms presented the most numerous phallic effigies in the Athenian urban scene, the largest phallus was the one which was carried around the city in the grand and gay parade which preceded the Greater Dionysia, a yearly dramatic festival. (Of course, such phallic processions, or *phallophoriai*, took place in many other Greek cities as well.) Figure 71 shows what appears to be an actual picture of a *phallophoria*, together with one of fiction. Below, a team of men carry a long phallus of rather modest circumference (the real one), while above a satyr, goaded on by a rider, is perched on a more impressive specimen, which is the product of imagination.

## Phallicism in Literature

The comic drama of the Classical age is so steeped in far-fetched genital allusions and imagery that no scholar can hope to decipher it unless armed with complete sexual single-mindedness and a formidable vocabulary of obscenity in ancient Greek. If Philip Roth could read Aristophanes with full understanding he would blush. Classicists teaching Aristophanes tell their students that if they fail to find an obscenity in any one phrase, they probably are not getting the point. Fortunately Henderson's learned book *The Maculate Muse* has opened a number of new perspectives on the pornographic implications of Aristophanic comedy.

## Socrates' Last Words As a Phallic Joke

The dialogues of Plato, which have pleasant and sometimes frivolous social settings, also contain many salacious phallic allusions, some of them not readily apparent to the casual reader. I will give but one example of the intermingling of solemnity and scurrilousness in the dialogues, namely Socrates' mysterious last words, as recorded in Plato's *Phaedo* (118a). It has long puzzled scholars why the philosopher died with the words, "We owe a cock to Asclepius. Pay it and do not forget." It was, in fact, a joke and by our taste a coarse one, understandable only against the background of the consistent portrayal of Socrates as satyr-like in appearance and perpetually randy.

When the time has come, Socrates empties the cup of hemlock and, at the instruction of the jailer, lies down on his back when he feels his legs getting heavy. In a little while the warden inspects Socrates' feet. He pinches one foot, asking the philosopher if he can feel this. Socrates says no. Then the jailer moves his hands up Socrates' legs, observing that the victim is growing stiff and cold. Socrates touches himself, too, and comments that when the stiffness will reach the level of his heart it will be all over. At the very moment when "the region of his lower abdomen" has become cold, or "has come to life" (there is a pun here on the Greek word *psychoo*, which can have both meanings), Socrates uncovers himself—not his head, as is usually understood, but his groin, to show

64. Phallic humor, the swan's neck protruding
from its rider's groin (Apollo as swan
abducting Hyakinthos).

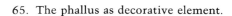

65. The phallus as decorative element.

67. Fifth-century voodoo
doll of Mnesimachos.

66. The monumental
phalluses of Delos.

68. Sixth-century phallic ritual; fantasy and "real" satyrs.

69. A phallic shrine.

70. Phallic procession (the return of Hephaestus); donkey with wine pitcher dangling from his penis.

71. The phallus carried through town.

off an erection, whether from the poison or from the jailer's touch, or both. It is, however, a known fact that men tend to have erections at the moment of death. The rooster was not only a standard offering to Asclepius, but also a conventional homosexual love gift, and Socrates' commandment to render one to the god of health and healing can only be a tribute to his humorously pretended last moment of sexual excitement, as well as a thanks offering for having "healed him of the sickness which is life": the two implications are by no means incompatible.

## The Dildo: Male Fantasies Projected onto Women

How the female psyche developed in Classical Athens under this barrage of verbal and visual phallicism, we can never know, because we have no expressions of the women's sexual idiosyncrasies. If women are, indeed, subject to penis envy, those of Athens may have suffered a massive case of it, but our sources document only male ideas of female sexuality. Since Athens' society had promoted the male organ as the symbol of fertility, parenthood, creativity, and self-defense, it is only natural that Athenian men could not conceive of women otherwise than as obsessed with insatiable lust to fill up their vaginal void with penises, real or artificial. This notion was no more based on inquiry or observation than their belief that the womb travels through the chest of women and that conception takes place during menstruation.

In comedy there are a number of jokes about the use, by women of a respectable class, of self-satisfiers, or dildos, made of leather. They were known as *olisboi*, a word derived from a verb meaning "to glide" or "slip." Such objects must have been manufactured and marketed, but that they were put to the fantastic uses depicted by vase painters is less likely. Since the women using these instruments in vase paintings are usually naked, they may represent hetaerai, or, possibly, they are not intended to belong to any special category but are imaginary figures.

Figure 72 shows three women putting an entire collection of *olisboi* to various uses. In Figure 73 a woman uses two of them; she is moistening one of them in a basin. In Figure 74 a woman is wielding a double *olisbos*, even though she has a perfectly competent satyr at her disposal. The flute player in Figure 75 makes do with an upturned amphora. Figures 76 and 77 show women sporting with baskets full of *olisboi*. Figure 78 shows two girls, one

72. Women putting dildos to various uses.

73. Hetaera with two dildos and a basin.

74. Satyr and naked woman with phallus.

75. Naked flute player satisfying herself with an amphora.

76. Hetaera leaps into basket full of dildos.

77. Girl with phallus bird and basket full of phalluses.

dressed and one naked, dancing around a phallus of monumental proportions.

The distasteful obscenity in Figure 79, showing two men lowering a woman onto a supine male body, was produced by a coarse hand. Figure 80, on the other hand, shows a fine drawing, but a sexual oddity: a woman is simulating *fellatio* with a dildo, presumably made of leather, an unappetizing technique hardly likely to lead to her satisfaction. Evidently these scenes reflect male notions of women's desires. In fact, most of the instances of "penis fever" reproduced here were painted on kylikes, the flat drinking cups used by men and hetaerai at symposia.

That Greek women of all classes suffered considerable sexual frustration is likely; that it found the outlets imagined by men is less so. Female homosexuality and female masturbation, far more probable consequences of the strained relations between the sexes, are infrequently depicted. One dubious case of a woman masturbating is shown in Figure 215. A vase painting often reproduced as featuring women lovers (Figure 151) may in actuality represent one woman perfuming another in preparation for meeting a man. I know of only one scene of women titillating each other sexually, and it is so discreet that its implication has gone unnoticed (Figure 81); one woman is touching another's breast, a stereotyped feature denoting "seduction." This neglect of female homosexuality in art is paralleled in literature. In the Classical age only Plato mentions it. The reference occurs in Aristophanes' parable of the aboriginal "double person" whose severed halves continue to yearn for each other in love, as told in *The Symposium* (191e):

78. Naked and clothed girl dancing around phallus.

79. Obscene fantasy: men lowering woman onto a phallic male figure.

80. Naked woman handling two dildos.

Those women who are cuttings of females do not pay any attention to men, but are attracted to women, and the female homosexuals [*hetairistriai*] are of this breed.

The island of Lesbos, to the ancient Greeks, was not associated with female homoeroticism, but with *fellatio*. Hence the verbs *lesbiazo* and *lesbizo* refer to that practice. The ancient Greek word for "lesbian woman" in our sense was *tribas*, from a root meaning "to rub," but it is not attested for the Classical period.

## The Mate Without Face or Name

The governing principle of a phallocracy is that the human race is essentially male, the female being a mere adjunct, unfortunately required for the purpose of reproduction. The natural consequence of this notion is the elimination of the female from all social processes. In Classical Greece this took many different forms. One of these was the veiling of the female form, which contrasts sharply with the phallic display practiced by men. In Aristophanes' *Lysistrata*, a male fantasy about a women's uprising, the heroine of the play tells a magistrate to be quiet. He answers in indignation, "You accursed creature. Should I be quiet for you, who wears the veil around your head?" (530–31). Women were expected to be muffled into shapeless forms under all but the most intimate circumstances. Whether custom required them to cover their faces as well as their hair is debated. Figure 82 shows a woman covering her mouth with her cloak, in the manner required today in the more orthodox Moslem countries, but this does not appear to have been obligatory. A sixth-century black-figure vase painting (Figure 83) showing Oedipus and the Sphinx in the presence of Theban women is probably more indicative of what Greek men thought women ought to look like in public: the body is entirely wrapped in garments, but the face is exposed.

Inside the home, of course, where women met only their husbands and close relatives, different mores prevailed. I suspect, however, that the prudery which society imposed on women for their rare

81. Lesbian women (South Italian, from about 350 B.C.).

appearances in public was not wholly abandoned at the door of the bridal chamber: the great stress on female nudity in men's associations with prostitutes, documented in Chapter 6, at least suggests that for conjugal sex the wife did not disrobe.

The Greek literary texts constantly reiterate the commandment to women not to be seen or heard, thus reducing them to a state of nonbeing. The most publicized of these passages is Pericles' exhortation to the widows of the first fallen Athenian soldiers in the Peloponnesian War:

> Not to be worse than your natural condition, such as it is, that is your great glory, and greatest is the reputation of that woman about whom there is least talk among men, whether in praise or in censure. (Thucydides 2, 45, 2)

This is an admonition curiously inappropriate for the occasion.

Lycurgus, an orator of the fourth century B.C., recounts that after the Athenian defeat at Chaeronea "respectable women could be seen hovering in their doorways with fear," making inquiries about their men and "bringing shame on themselves by being seen" (40). A number of similar quotations have been previously collected (see especially Gould) and need not be repeated here. What is remarkable in them is not that silence and invisibility were imposed on women, but that men felt the need to repeat these commandments regularly.

A device for diminishing women's sense of identity which was probably superbly effective and which has not attracted much attention is that of depriving women of names. In a fragment of a speech by Hyperides (Fr. 204, also attributed to Solon) the speaker says, "The woman who leaves her house should be of such an age that those who encounter her do not ask whose wife but whose mother she is." He means to espouse the practice of restraining women's appearance in public until their childbearing years are over—indeed, those women who lived until menopause must have welcomed it as a liberation—but he also illustrates the widespread practice of referring to women not by name but by their relation to the men in the family. It is often observed that today's practice of making women assume their husband's names is destructive of their sense of self; the Greeks went considerably further and, insofar as possible, deprived their women of names altogether. Most Greek given names, of men as well as women, were derived from word

82. Veiled woman (the significance of the child in monkey suit is unknown).

83. Oedipus, the sphinx and Theban women.

roots with recognizable meanings, so that they had specific associations; Sophocles, for example, means "glory of wisdom," Aristophanes "displayer of the best," Elpinike "victory of hope." The suppression of women's names meant the elimination also of these associations.

In Book 6 of the *Iliad* Helen observes to Hector that Zeus has inflicted an "evil fate" on herself and Paris, "so that later they may live in the lays of future men" (357–58). This notion of immortality through fame, or even through notoriety, was much cherished by the Greeks, who on the whole had not developed strong views of a corporeal afterlife: the ghosts of the dead in the underworld scenes in the Homeric poems are, in fact, something like an allegory of the memory that people leave of themselves among the living. But in order to be remembered one must have a name, and Greek citizen women were largely doomed to anonymity.

We assume that all girls who were kept by their parents to be raised were given a name, but we cannot be sure of even that. Their names were not recorded in the records of their phratry or tribe, as were those of boy children (Gould 40–41). A boy could claim citizenship only if descended from two citizen parents, and this claim was supported in the records by the name and place of origin of his father and of his maternal grandfather; the name of the mother did not appear. Thus, in public registration, the woman served as a nameless channel for the transmission of citizen standing from her father to her sons.

At home the given names of women were apparently rarely or never used. At least, the extant fragments of Middle and New Comedy, which give a fairly realistic picture of middle-class home life in fourth-century Athens, make it clear that a husband normally addressed his wife as "woman." The Greek word for woman, *gyne*, literally means "childbearer"; a woman beyond childbearing age was normally referred to as "old woman" (*graus*). Thus the narrow function of respectable women was constantly recalled. It would be interesting to know whether in the marriage contract the bride was mentioned by name, or identified as "daughter of so-and-so," or possibly designated as "oldest daughter of so-and-so," but we do not have this information.

In the extant courtroom speeches males are usually listed by name, respectable women nearly always anonymously (Schaps, 1977). For example, one typical passage informs us that

> Aristarchus . . . married the daughter of Xenaenetus of Acharnae, who bore him Cyronides, and Demochares, and my mother and another sister of theirs. (Isae. 10, 4)

Among citizen women the exceptions are mainly old (the grandmother Chaerestrate in Demosthenes, 57, 37, for one) or dead. Hetaerai are frequently identified by names, most of them probably professional ones. In the Pseudo-Demosthenic speech no. 59, the speaker accuses the defendant, a prostitute and former slave, of having passed herself off as a citizen. He hammers his point home by using her name, Neaera, which means "Belly," over and over again.

From a viewpoint of legal expediency this practice had awkward, not to say bizarre, results. Lysias' speech *On the Murder of Eratosthenes* was delivered by one Euphiletus, who had murdered the alleged seducer of his wife. This speech is often cited in studies of daily life in ancient Athens, because it affords a glimpse into the home life of an ordinary citizen of modest means. The seducer had first spotted his quarry at a funeral, that of Euphiletus' mother. Given the demure behavior expected of women in public, it is hardly likely that a first flirtatious spark was struck under the husband's nose, so evidently Euphiletus did not attend himself, a telling detail of the story (1, 18). In the course of the speech we learn a great deal about Euphiletus' life and attitudes: he developed a spirit of trust toward his wife after she had borne him a son, but we are never told the wife's name.

Even stranger are those few cases in which women themselves were defendants. Even then the woman did not appear in court herself, but was represented by her male guardian (*kyrios*). In Antiphon's speech *Against the Stepmother*, a woman is accused of poisoning her husband. The accuser is the deceased man's illegitimate son; the accused is defended by her legitimate sons. Since the speaker does not even hint at a motive, one is left with considerable doubt as to the guilt of the woman. We must assume that if the "stepmother" was found guilty, her conviction and execution were also recorded anonymously. Inasmuch as women were reduced to nameless and faceless quantities, disputes over the legitimacy of marriages, divorces, and births were frequent. Demosthenes accused his childhood guardian, Aphobos, of having faked a divorce and the restitution of his wife's dowry, as a pretext for not paying his debt to the orator (no. 30, *Against Onetor*). Two of Isaeus' speeches (3 and 8) concern arguments over whether or not a certain person had been legally married and had legitimate issue.

No study of the daily living habits of the ancient Athenians can dispense with the description by Xenophon's character Ischomachus of the training of his bride (*Oec.* 7 f.), a document to which we will have repeated recourse. Ischomachus' account of how he made his fourteen-year-old bride an obedient and industrious spouse is an oily tale, full of male condescension, but it gives us rare information about the management of a private home. His bride, although she is the center of the tale, is never named.

In more literary forms of composition the namelessness of women—here perhaps often an unconscious touch—can be equally striking. In the oldest extant tragedy, Aeschylus' *Persians*, produced in 472 B.C., the scene is set in the palace of the Persian royal family at Sousa; King Xerxes is about to return in defeat from the ill-fated last Persian invasion of Greece. Throughout the play Aeschylus, who likes exotic detail, delights in introducing foreign-sounding and in part fictitious names of Persian nobles, such as Amistres and Pharandakes, but the Persian dowager queen, who plays a major part in the proceedings, must speak her lines anonymously: she is merely identified as "mother of Xerxes" or "Queen of the Persians." The name Atossa, which appears in many editions of the play, is an editorial addition.

Herodotus tells the lurid story of the Lydian King Candaules, who is so proud of his wife's beauty that he compels his general, Gyges, to watch her when naked (1, 8). The queen is so incensed at this kind of visual rape that she forces the involuntary Peeping Tom to kill her husband. Gyges does so, marries the queen, and becomes his victim's successor. The queen, the pivot of the plot, is never named.

The attempt to deprive women of immortality through memory was successful: we know next to nothing about the citizen women of fifth- and fourth-century Athens. Despite formidable repression, some women must have broken through to competence somewhere, but the historical record is silent about them. The names of the wives and the mothers of prominent men have also in large part been erased. For many famous personalities of Classical Athens we have no marital record at all; in the case of others we assume that they were married only because they had sons.

## Elpinike

One citizen woman, however, did manage to make a name for herself during the height of the Fifty Golden Years—the only kind possible for a woman, which was a rather shady one. She was Elpinike, daughter of the general Miltiades, the hero of the battle of Marathon. Her paternal half-brother was Cimon, a leading political and military figure in the early years of the Delian League, and she married Callias, also famous as a soldier and diplomat. A leaning toward peace and friendship with Sparta is attested for both her brother and her husband. The historical sources (the principal ones are recorded in Plutarch's *Life of Cimon*) wove a minor web of legend around Elpinike, dramatizing her political influence via these two men. They also, however, told scandalous tales of her sexual cohabitation with her brother, and of a love affair with the painter Polygnotus, who is even reported to have painted her picture in a Trojan scene in a public building (*Life of Cimon* 4, 5). By a fortunate accident we have a surviving portrait of her, conceivably reflecting that by Polygnotus (Figure 84): the seated flutist in this vase painting is identified as our famous lady by an inscription. We cannot know, of course, for what occasion this rare vase painting was made, but in the light of the prevailing mores, the identification of the figure by name was so rare as to constitute an act of social defiance.

## Inner and Outer Space in Greek Architecture

Athenian men spent most of their lives in the open air. Many of the activities which in our society take place indoors were carried out either in open terrain or in unroofed structures. This was true of the political assemblies, all drama, and most of the religious

84. Elpinike playing the flute for dancing girls.

ceremonies and legal procedures. As a result, those buildings which were enclosed took on a special significance in Greek town planning, and their designs reflect their social functions.

The prototype of almost all Greek public architecture was the temple, essentially an oblong, windowless stone box, surrounded on all four sides by a colonnade. The inside of the temple served as housing for the cult statue and the temple treasure, not as the scene of religious ritual, which took place outside the building. The boxlike inner core of the temple has feminine associations, and its shape is echoed in the boxes and chests which in Greek iconography signify women's lives. The outside colonnades form the transition between inner and outer space, and have masculine, not to say phallic, associations. Figure 85 shows the Acropolis of Athens from the southwest side, with the restored Temple of Nike, or Victory, exceptionally designed with a colonnade in front only.

In secular architecture the stoa was a common design, in which the "transitional" colonnade of the temple became the whole build-

85. The entrance to the Acropolis, with the Temple of Nike.

86. The Stoa of Attalus.

ing. The restored Stoa of Attalus in the Athenian Agora, although dating from the second century B.C. and built with columns of an unorthodox, post-Classical shape, gives a good idea of the design and purpose of this type of edifice: it constituted a transition between inner and outer space (Figure 86). Another adaptation of the temple design was the round shrine (tholos), of which the enclosed inner core was circular, surrounded by a round colonnade. The entire public area of Athens consisted of an alternation of enclosed inner spaces and colonnaded semi-open areas.

Curiously, the design of private dwellings featured the exact inverted pattern: in the standard plan a number of rooms were arranged around an inner courtyard, with only one outlet to the street. The archaeological evidence for the use of columns surrounding the inner courtyard of private houses of this period is not secure, but since we will find in the following chapters that a column was used as an iconographic clue in vase painting to identify

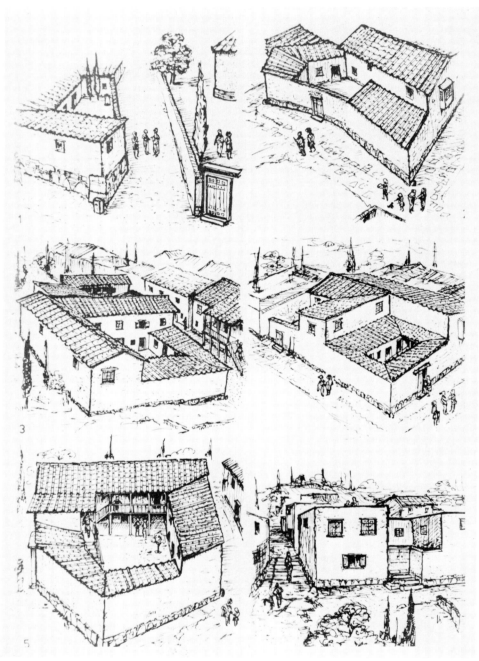

87. Private houses of Athens, as reconstructed by J. E. Jones.

a domestic scene, it is safe to assume that most houses had at least an elementary colonnade inside.

Figure 87 shows some reconstructions of fifth-century houses in the center of Athens, from Wycherley's *The Stones of Athens* (1978). Since the walls have nowhere been preserved up to window level, the windows in these and other reconstructions are entirely conjectural and probably erroneous. Aristotle notes specifically that it was forbidden to have windows looking out onto the street. An equally valid indication of the lack of outside windows may be seen in the practice of throwing out the slop, which, in the absence of a sewerage system, was emptied out into the street; apparently one shouted *existo*—"stand aside"—while emptying buckets and chamber pots (Ar. *Ach.* 616–17). In a fragment by Aristophanes someone is admonished not to pour dirty bath water in the street; significantly the speaker talks of throwing it out the door, not through a window: "Don't pour out the water from footbath or tub through the door" (Fr. 306). Accordingly, we should imagine most private houses as having no outside windows, so that the essential temple plan was, as it were, turned outside in.

We have here anticipated the later discussion of the floorplan of private Greek dwellings to show that even architecture reflected the genital notions concerning the societal roles of men and women. Only this background can explain the contrast between the splendor of the public structures and the modesty of the private houses—a contrast unequaled in any known ancient society.

For the "respectable" classes of Attic society, the anatomical differences between men and women were translated into the shapes of their living spaces: women's reproductive organs are internal and, to the ancients, were mysterious; their outer shape camouflages rather than accentuates them. Men's genitals on the other hand are conspicuous, and expressive of desire and aggression. Analogously, women spent their lives wrapped in veils, nameless, concealing their identity, and locked away in the dark recesses of closed-in homes. Men spent their lives in open areas, in the sunlit spaces of the Agora and other public domains, which were off limits to women except on special occasions. There men displayed their skills and their genitals and indulged their thirst for identity and immortality through fame.

# 4

# Bearing Children, Watching the House

> . . . often I pondered the status of women: we are nothing. As
> small girls in our father's house, we live the most delightful
> life, because ignorance keeps children happy. But when we
> come to the age of maturity and awareness, we are thrust out
> and bartered away, far from the gods of our forefathers and
> parents, some to alien men, some to barbarians, some to good
> homes and some to abusive ones. And after one single joyful
> night of love, we are compelled to praise this arrangement
> and consider ourselves lucky.
> —Sophocles, Fragment 583, from *Tereus*

The above lines from Sophocles' lost play *Tereus* are spoken by the
protagonist's wife, Procne. The plot was taken from the well-known
story of Tereus, who raped his wife's sister, Philomela, and cut out
her tongue to prevent her from revealing his crime. Philomela
reveals the truth by weaving her story into a tapestry, and the two
sisters take revenge on Tereus by killing his and Procne's son, Itys.
It is but one of a number of stories of women's savage revenge, and
one of several in which women murder their own sons in an
impotent rage against their husbands. It took the psychological
genius of a Sophocles to gauge the depth of female despair, which
alone could give rise to such myths.

Procne's complaint of being married off to foreigners and barbarians may reflect mythological times rather than the customs of
Classical Athens, but otherwise her anticipation of marital life
seems correct, including the innuendo of sexual neglect awaiting
the young bride. In a strongly male-dominated society marriage
serves largely as an instrument for the extraction of the services
normally rendered by female to male: sexual satisfaction, childbearing, and cheap labor. The benefits of marriage which may accrue to
the female, such as protection, companionship, and her own sexual

gratification, belong in the somewhat more balanced social structures. Of the three types of services, the Athenian man virtually disregarded the category of sexual pleasure in marriage. The institution of slavery provided him with ample sex outlets, female and male, and he much preferred his hetaerai and pleasure-boys over his wife. The unctuous Ischomachus, whose portrait as a husband Xenophon has given us in the essay *Oeconomicus*, tells his fourteen-year-old bride, "That I'm not suffering any shortage of people to go to bed with, surely should be clear as day even to you" (7, 11). In Xenophon's *Memoirs*, Socrates says to his son Lamprocles, "Surely you don't think that people make babies on account of sexual pleasure, because the streets and the whorehouses are full of persons who will do this service" (2, 2, 4).

Sexual competition from prostitutes and slaves, including those of their households, must have been a common experience for women, and those of Aristophanes' *Parliament of Women* scheme to free themselves of that rivalry (721–24). Nor was the exploitation of women's labor the key to marriage in the Classical age: compared with his modern equivalent—the successful man whose entire existence is propped up by the underpaid services of women, from wives and mistresses to secretaries and laundresses—the Athenian Greek was an amateur in the exploitation of the women of his own class for his material comfort. Attic culture developed a special work ethos for women; the ideal of womanly virtue included "love of toil" (*philergia*) and the best of wives, or, as the case might be, the only tolerable ones in men's minds, were frequently likened to bees. The Greek word for bee, *melissa*, was and still is a favored woman's name. Wives were condemned to a lifetime of labor at spindle and loom, which probably only a few privileged ones could escape, by passing it on to their slaves and hired servants. But the concept of the "helpmeet wife," that most subtle of exploitations, did not exist for the Athenians. An oft-cited statement from the speech *Against Neaera*, which, though not by Demosthenes himself, has come down to us in the body of his writings, brings this out: "We keep hetaerai for pleasure, concubines for the daily care of our body and wives for the bearing of legitimate children and to keep watch over our house" (*Against Neaera* 59, 122). The very restrictions which men put on their wives limited their usefulness; it was the non-citizen concubine (who will be discussed more fully later) to whom it fell to render to men the little services required for their comfort.

There probably never has been a monogamous society in which the role of the wife was more closely restricted to one fundamental function, that of bearing children, or rather we should say, bearing sons, because daughters did not interest an Athenian father. This single-mindedness was brought out, indelicately but accurately, in the standard Athenian wedding formula, which defined matrimony as designed "for the ploughing of legitimate children." The most Draconian, or perhaps we should say "Solonian," laws and practices were applied to safeguard the virginity of unmarried women and the fidelity of those who were married.

The excessive concern over the legitimacy of children accounts for a provision in Athenian law which is strange by our notions. The seduction of a respectable woman was more severely punished than the rape of the same, as the speaker of Lysias' *On the Murder of Eratosthenes* states (49). This is usually explained by noting that seduction is corruption of the mind, but rape, merely of the body. More likely, the difference stems from the fact that rape, being a one-time affair, is less likely to produce bastard offspring.

The Athenian's desire to have legitimate male offspring sprang from several motivations. The one most often cited in modern studies of Greek family life is the need of sons to preserve the clan and to continue the cult of the ancestors and household divinities. But the feeling evidently went deeper: Thucydides makes it clear that, in the Athenian conception, citizens without legitimate sons are not full-fledged members of the community, because no lives of children are at stake when they pass on important decisions (2, 44, 3). It is even possible that a man without male issue was denied a voice in the Senate (Din. 71). An affectionate desire for children was probably furthest from his mind when an Athenian married. In fact, the family structure of his society was designed so as to deprive him of a rewarding relationship with his sons as well as with his daughters (Chapter 11).

## The Dowry

It is one of the ironies of social history that the institution of the dowry is characteristic of the more strongly patriarchal societies: where women are severely repressed, the conditions of marriage such as division of labor, ownership of property, sexual and social freedom, and guardianship of children are in favor of the male. Yet it is in these societies that fathers give dowries to their daughters—that is, in a sense pay a man to take them off their hands. In Classical Athens the dowry was not only customary, but it was a legal requirement for marriage. To be sure, a substantial dowry gave a wife some leverage in her marriage, because in case of divorce it had to be returned, with a hefty 18-percent interest, to her father or other guardian. However, the wife's technical right to divorce in case of maltreatment was largely illusory. For one thing, since she could not initiate legal action, she had to enlist the cooperation of her guardian, who would normally be loath to have her back to marry off a second time.

The dangers of a wife's rebellion may be seen from the story of Alcibiades and his wife, Hipparete. Alcibiades was the most famous playboy of fifth-century Athens, and the personification of phallicism. Hence I will cite his highly checkered career several times. He was of a rich and prominent family, and his wife, Hipparete, brought a handsome dowry into the marriage. Alcibiades offended his wife by bringing hetaerai into their house—that is, into the women's quarters, not into the men's quarters, which was normal (Chapter 6). Hipparete moved in with her brother and brought suit for divorce before the chief magistrate. Alcibiades, who could ill afford to repay the dowry, brought her back home by force and Hipparete died shortly afterwards of an undetermined cause, while her husband was journeying abroad, Plutarch reports reassuringly (*Alc.* 8, 4).

## Marital Law

Greek family law, of which the details are fairly well, though by no means perfectly, known, reveals two profound and abiding concerns: to ensure man's unquestionable paternity of his offspring and to preserve family property. We cannot survey the legal ramifications of marriage here (see the excellent study by A. R. W. Harrison). The rights of women in marriage, however, can be quickly summed up: they had none, except through the intermediary of guardians. In Xenophon's account of a discussion between Ischomachus and Socrates, the former likens wives to slaves and horses, the latter to sheep and horses (*Oec.* 3, 10–11). Women, in fact, were not persons under the law any more than were slaves. They spent their lives being shifted from the tutelage of one man to that of another: their guardians could be fathers, husbands, sons, brothers, or remoter male relatives. They were, in fact, as Aristotle defines the slave, a "living piece of property."

The fourth-century courtroom speeches provide us with ample case histories illustrating men's complete control over women's fates. From Demosthenes' speech *For Phormio* (36) we learn of a husband who in his will instructed his widow to marry a former slave of his, whom he had set free, an arrangement which was not uncommon, as the speech makes clear (29). If such action seems uncharitable, in this case it probably was not: the widow had a son who was twenty-four years old, and hence was probably too old to make a better match.

Demosthenes tells his own family story in the speech *On the Guardianship of Aphobos* (27). Demosthenes' father died while he and his sister were still small children. In his will the father appointed one nephew to marry his widow and another to marry his daughter as soon as she came of age. This scheme did not work out at all: the prospective husband of the mother collected her dowry, but refused to marry or support her. The other nephew refused to marry Demosthenes' sister (66).

If the first concern of the marrying man was to have sons, the secondary thrust of the system was "keeping the money in the family." Marriages of close relatives, such as first cousins, uncles and nieces, and even paternal half-siblings seem to have been common. The desire to preserve family wealth is most clearly illustrated by the legal provisions governing the disposition of estates without male heirs. With the minor exception cited in the Introduction, women could not own property. If a property owner died intestate and without obvious male heirs, his wealth attached itself to a daughter or other female relative who became an *epikleros*, a word usually translated as "heiress," in this case a misnomer. Her nearest male relative had the privilege of marrying her, a provision designed to keep the estate in the family. If she was already married, she was forced to abandon her husband and any children; if the male relative was married, he had the option of divorcing, which he could do at will in any case, or of passing the opportunity on to the male next of kin.

The question arises why the law did not assign the inheritance directly to the male relative, rather than prescribing the cumbersome and surely often traumatic double divorce proceedings. The answer seems to be that the inheritance could not directly fall to a member of a generation older than that of the deceased, so that the hapless "heiress" in such cases not only found herself ruthlessly manipulated, but most likely married off to a much older man. We have a dramatization of this proceeding in the comedy *The Shield* by Menander, one of the newly discovered late-fourth-century "parlor comedies," which, though sentimental and conventional, nevertheless give an accurate portrayal of middle-class social mores in Athens at that time. Davos, a household slave, returns from a battle with a large amount of booty, which his master, believed dead, had accumulated in war. The master's only surviving close relative, his sister, thereby becomes an "heiress." An ancient and greedy uncle claims her as his bride, and would have got her, were it not for a scheme devised by the slave, who is as cunning as he is kind: Davos dangles the prospect of another, even richer, *epikleros* in front of the old miser, who is thus tricked into renouncing his first claim. That such a complicated system for the disposal of estates was bound to lead to abuses is obvious, and "offenses against *epikleroi*" constituted a category of infractions of the law (Dem. 37, 33).

## The Indoctrination of the Bride

Social historians argue that class and caste systems survive because of the tendency of the underprivileged to absorb the ethos and values of the privileged (Gramsci, 600–603). In Chapter 12 I will describe how in Athens the female was indoctrinated by means of cultic ritual. Whether necessary or not, this "moral" upbringing was reinforced by sterner measures, intended to "keep them barefoot and pregnant."

One technique for keeping women physically under control is premature marriage. Athenian women normally married at the age of fourteen or fifteen. Ischomachus' bride was not quite fifteen; Demosthenes' sister was expected to marry at fifteen (29, 43). At that age a girl is malleable and, in many cases, not quite full-grown. What is more, the premature motherhood which is likely to ensue from such a marriage greatly increases the likelihood of death in childbirth, as the ancients well knew (Arist. *Pol.* 1335a 19). Apparently this circumstance bothered only a few of the more enlightened thinkers, who advocated the age of eighteen, which was the normal age for marriage in health-oriented Sparta, or even twenty (Plato, *Rep.* 5, 460e).

Attic authors make no bones about the purpose behind the premature marriage for girls: "Didn't you marry her as young as possible so that she would have seen and heard as little as possible?" Socrates asks Ischomachus (Xen. *Oec.* 3, 12).

The age difference between husband and bride probably did achieve its purpose of making the wife subservient, but it must also have inhibited meaningful conjugal relationships. In a speech by Andocides we learn of a groom who brought home a young bride, but took up with her mother instead, on whom he sired a child (*Myst.* 128). The mother-in-law, perhaps once our Ischomachus' wife, probably was closer to him in years and experience.

Keeping women ignorant was another major component of the techniques of dominance. Women were completely cut off from any kind of formal education; that many, perhaps most, nevertheless learned how to read—by a female educational underground, one supposes—was a source of anxiety to men: "Let a woman not develop her reason, for that would be a terrible thing," the philosopher Democritus said (Fr. 110). A character in a lost play by Menander pronounced the following dictum: "He who teaches letters to his wife is ill-advised: He's giving additional poison to a horrible snake" (Fr. 702 K). The aim was to keep women frozen in their development, so that they would become, as it were, perpetual children, and this attempt may often have been successful. Many vase paintings show grown women engaged in childish, noncompetitive games. As examples I show a charming cup in Brussels (Figure 88), with a woman playing with a top, and a little oil flask (Figure 89), featuring a girl bouncing balls. However, the vase paintings also document women's reading ability: In Figure 90 an ordinary woman is reading a book roll or a writing tablet, although evidently not with ease.

Women were similarly deprived of the next step in education, training in the "arts of the Muses," such as literature and what we call music. A law sometimes attributed to Solon had made such training compulsory for boys, and many vase paintings show them in school receiving instruction. Although the public facilities were reserved for boys, women are shown playing just about every instrument the Greeks used, but especially the cithara. In fact, some dead women seem to have been remembered as muses, because several white-ground oil flasks—vessels produced specifically as minor funerary artifacts—show a muse where one would expect a

88. Woman playing with top.

89. Young woman juggling balls.

90. Interior scene with seated woman reading.

91. Funerary oil flask with
the deceased as Muse.

picture of or a symbol for the deceased (Figure 91). Musical skill
was less threatening to men than reading and writing, and it appears
that many Athenian women, without the benefit of formal instruction, became accomplished musicians.

## The Wedding

The contract between the bride's guardian and the groom constituted the actual marriage: "She who is betrothed by father or
brother or grandfather, [only] she can bear legitimate children," says
Demosthenes (44, 49). The wedding festivities served primarily the
purpose of providing witnesses to the marriage, so that the wife's
legitimate position could never be put in doubt (Dem. 30, 21). For
the young bride it was the acme of her life, as well as the principal
ritual of enculturation for her entry into the world of adults. Two
black-figure oil flasks in The Metropolitan Museum of Art in New
York, a matched pair from about the middle of the sixth century
B.C., give a candid picture of a wedding and of the life awaiting the
new bride (Figures 92 and 93). She is seated with the groom on a
mule cart, traditional for wedding processions, and is about to
arrive at her new home. The gesture she makes, that of lifting a tip
of her garment with the left hand, is sometimes called that of

92a,b. Arrival of the newlyweds at the groom's house.

"unveiling" (*apokalypsis*) and normally points to the nubility, or the sexual surrender, of the woman. It echoes vaguely the attested ritual of "unveiling" in the marriage ceremony, during which the groom officially got a first look at his bride. The "unveiling" probably took place after the signing of the marriage contract. On that occasion the groom gave the bride some presents, called *anakalypteria*, apparently a holdover from an older form of marriage in which the man bought his bride. The groom's mother is awaiting the procession at the entrance, probably an ill-omened presence for the girl-bride. The groom is bearded, indicating that he is probably somewhat older, perhaps about thirty, as was normal for first marriages. Later vase painters of wedding scenes often gloss over customary age differences between bride and groom, by representing the latter unrealistically as a clean-shaven youth. The matching lekythos shows what awaits the bride in her new home: endless labor at spindle and loom.

## The Lock on the Door

In modern societies, within the privacy of the home, the battle of the sexes is frequently fought all over again on the original basis—namely, that of brute physical strength. The widespread problem of battered wives, often accompanied by that of abused children, is ample evidence of this. That men regularly resorted to physical violence against their wives in Classical Athens is not indicated, but then, who would have recorded it if it did take place?

93a,b. Women in the loom room.

One form of physical coercion is, however, documentable, and that is the locking up of women, as was still customary in rural areas of Sicily until not long ago.

Ischomachus states hypocritically that he locked the door of the women's quarters of his house to prevent theft, and to keep the slaves "from making babies without his knowledge" (*Oec. 9, 5*). The lament of Praxagora in Aristophanes' *Thesmophoriazusai* cannot be altogether without basis: ". . . they put seals and bolts on our doors to guard us, and even breed fierce Molossian hounds to keep adulterers at bay" (415–18). What is more, in the iconography of the women's quarters of the private house, the closed door is a standard clue identifying the location. Double doors appear frequently on the low pyxides—boxlike terra-cotta pots especially manufactured for use by women and usually decorated with women's motifs. I show here one such pyxis (Figure 94); we will have occasion

94. Women's quarters with closed double door.

to look at more of them later.

As a result of the strict segregation of men and women, a man's own women's quarters must have been largely unknown territory to him. Since his only interest in his wife was posited in the sons she might bear him, he lived in constant fear of her being "debauched" by another man or of substituting an extraneous boy baby for a girl or dead child she might have borne. The conventions of Middle and New Comedy give some indication of these problems. The birth of an illegitimate child unbeknownst to the head of the household, an event highly improbable under modern social practices, happened frequently in ancient Greek comedy and was not as unlikely as it would seem. Stage convention required that this event be announced to the audience by means of an off-stage cry by the girl during her labor pains.

## The Bitter Joys of Motherhood

Women were trained to define their merit in terms of the motherhood of sons, and to anticipate the considerable likelihood of death in childbirth as a glorious martyrdom. Such joy as they may have had from their children was probably incidental to the system, because the children belonged to the father. The man of the house decided which ones to keep and which ones to "expose," a euphemism for extermination. Since a man married mainly in order to have sons, we may assume that he wanted to raise all healthy boy children; to what extent he practiced female infanticide is a matter of conjecture to which we will return. Only a few vase paintings communicate the charm of motherhood. Figure 95, a shallow-handled dish in Brussels, is one of the rare true genre scenes in Classical Greek art: it shows a baby in a potty seat (one has actually been found in the Athenian Agora), stretching out his arms toward his mother. In Figure 96, a hydria in the British Museum, a servant hands a baby to its mother. Of course it is a boy baby, which we know because it is naked, and as usual the artist has depicted his body at such an angle that his genitals are visible.

The naked male child strutting his budding virility among the robed denizens of the women's quarters was, as it were, a hostage from the powerful and hostile world of men outside, until he was old enough to join them (Figures 97 and 98). The experience may have left him saddled forever with a love-guilt complex, as percep-

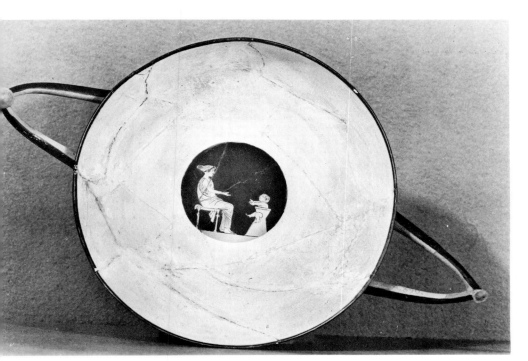

95. Mother with child in potty seat.

tively suggested by Philip Slater in his *The Glory of Hera* and his article of 1974. We get a rare glimpse of a mother-son relationship in Xenophon's *Memoirs*, which purports to be the author's recollections of the life of Socrates. The philosopher's son Lamprocles lodges a kind of "Portnoy's complaint" against his mother, of course not named, but she is the Xanthippe destined to become notorious in the legends surrounding Socrates' life. Lamprocles laments that his mother is unbearably "difficult," but his father defends her as "willing to provide services day and night for the health and education of her son" (2, 2, 5–10). One gets the impression of a possessive and disagreeable mother who binds her sons to her with labor—a stock character still existing in Mediterranean family life.

If the coveted accomplishment of giving birth to sons had a shadow side, mothers surely did not have much joy of their daughters either, even if they were not "exposed." A son to a mother was a temporary guest from an alien sphere; a daughter was earmarked to be transferred to another household to fulfill her role as a procreator. The scenario of the traumatic separation of mother and young daughter was dramatized not only in the fragment from Sophocles quoted at the head of this chapter but also in the *Homeric Hymn to Demeter*, the best evidence we have for the symbolism of the mysteries of Demeter and her daughter, Persephone/Kore, at Eleusis. In the story as told in the hymn, Persephone's father is Zeus, who, however, no longer consorts with her mother, Demeter. At the command of her father, Persephone is snatched away by Hades from a flowery meadow—archetypal symbol of the innocence of nature—to become queen of the underworld. Demeter in grief roams the world in search of her daughter, and finally sits down on a stone, the "laughterless stone," at Eleusis. Local inhabitants temporarily appease her maternal urges by entrusting another child to her, but in the end a compromise is made with the gods, whereby Persephone is restored to her mother for part of every year. A reference to an actual "laughterless stone" was found in an inscription from Eleusis and there can be little doubt that the tale of rape, mourning, and compromise was actually enacted or narrated as part of the mystery ceremonies at Eleusis. If so, it was a clear instance of a ritual of conciliation. The events of premature marriage to an unknown husband at the command of a callous and remote father, and the traumatic separation of mother and daughter closely resemble Athenian wedding practices. No wonder that the mother-and-daughter pair were the divinities most often invoked by women, who alone swore by the "twain goddesses."

Phyllis Chesler cites the myth of Demeter and Kore in the introduction of her well-known book *Women and Madness*. Considering it a celebration of the mother-daughter relationship, she laments that it ceased with the arrival of monotheism (XVIII). Whether the Demeter-Kore model relationship actually fostered affection between mothers and daughters we cannot know. Where geography favored them, cordial relations were probably maintained after the daughter's marriage, and many of the women we see scurrying in and out of the women's quarters in vase paintings may be mothers visiting daughters or vice versa. Many of the separations must have been as final, however, as those between life and Persephone's underworld. (For a parallel between Demeter and the sorrowful motherhood of Niobe, see Chapter 14.)

96. A servant hands a naked boy baby to its mother.

97. Women's quarters with naked boy.

98. Affection between mother and son (or nurse and child).

## Sex in Marriage

Plutarch cites a law attributed to Solon, according to which "a man is obliged to have intercourse with his wife at least three times a month, not for pleasure, to be sure, but for the same reason why cities renew their treatises from time to time" (*Amat.* 769a). It is possible that Plutarch was mistaken and that the law applied not to husbands in general but to those married to "heiresses," as reported by him in his *Life of Solon* (20, 3). We have already seen that these husbands tended to be much older than their wives. In either case, the law bodes ill for the conjugal sex life of Athenians, and the lament of Procne, cited at the head of this chapter, reinforces this impression.

There can be little doubt that citizen women were raised to regard sex as a painful duty, much in the vein of the Victorian counsel to new brides: "Close your eyes and think of England." A passage in Pollux's *Onomasticon* reveals a feature of Athenian weddings not otherwise known. A friend of the bridegroom, called the "doorkeeper" (*thuroros*), had the special task of blocking the door to the bridal chamber when the women of the household wanted to come to the aid of the bride as she was screaming inside (3, 42). While this information gives an exaggerated picture of the agony of defloration, it reflects the awe and fear of sex which was instilled in the young virgin.

For all the Greeks' license in their extramarital sex, there are indications that an ethos of prudery governed activities in the conjugal bedroom. Demosthenes, in his speech *Against Timokrates* (24, 202), accuses Androtion of "selling" his sister—that is, giving her in marriage in exchange for a sum of money, to a foreigner from Corcyra. The foreigner had lodged at Androtion's house and had sneaked a look at the young girl, hence his desire to have her; "I will forego to say in which way," Demosthenes says in disgust. The implication is that the combination of marriage and sexual desire is improper and scandalous.

In vase paintings, even in the privacy of the women's quarters respectable women bare little flesh: they are normally clad in floor-length robes despite the heat of the Mediterranean summer. An iconographic scheme denoting "marital sex" is the loosening of the belt, or girdle, which holds up the overfold of a woman's draped

99. Funerary oil flask, woman loosening robe, woman with alabastron.

100a,b,c. Interior scene with textile worker, a bride(?), woman loosening her belt, woman looking into mirror, woman with oil flask.

dress, or chiton. I show here two instances of this convention (Figures 99 and 100). This symbol, together with the stress on female nudity in hetaera scenes, suggests that for marital intercourse wives did not disrobe.

A revealing passage in Isocrates treats the stripping of women of their clothes as an outrage comparable to rape. The incident concerns renegade Greeks in Asia Minor who abuse the inhabitants of the Greek cities in that area:

> They "shame" [rape] the most beautiful women. The others they strip naked so that those who previously were not to be seen by strangers even fully adorned, are now seen in the nude by many. (*Letter to Archidamas* 10)

In a fragment by Pherekrates, a fifth-century author of comedies, a "bathing fleece" is mentioned, apparently a furry apron which women, while bathing, tied around their middles (Frg. 62 K). If this item has been correctly identified and was in general use, it would seem to indicate that fifth-century Athenian women were not in the habit of undressing completely for their bath, and that those women who are depicted as washing in the nude are always hetaerai or at least non-citizens.

How can we reconcile this puritanical ethos imposed on married women with men's fantasies about women's insatiable lustfulness and penis fever? The two are by no means contradictory, but rather two manifestations of the same mentality. A famous mythological anecdote (Hes. Fr. 179) is told of the prophet Teiresias, who was temporarily changed into a woman; after he took back his male form he was asked whether men or women take more pleasure in sex. His answer: women enjoy intercourse ten times as much as men, or, as another reading will have it, nine times as much. Thereupon Hera struck him blind, and Zeus rewarded him with the gift of prophecy, indicating his approval of this view. In both Old Comedy and vase painting, women's supposed lewdness is a source of never-ending humor. I have already noted the flights of male imagination concerning women's use of an artificial penis, or *olisbos*.

In *Lysistrata*, the women on a sex strike have difficulty sticking to their resolve and are constantly sneaking away from the Acropolis for sex with their husbands. In a fragment of Old Comedy, perhaps also derived from Aristophanes, two women are discussing the possibility of dispensing with their husbands, who "do violence to them" (the word used is *hybrizo*, elsewhere frequently a euphemism for rape). One suggests making do with the well-known substitute, the other complains that the dildo resembles the real organ as the moon resembles the sun: it looks the same but lacks heat.

All in all, it can hardly be doubted that conjugal sex life was unrewarding for both husband and wife. This is not to say that the concept of monogamous, affectionate marriage was completely unknown to the Athenian. Here and there in the literature, but mainly in that of the fourth century, such a notion is expressèd. Xenophon, in *The Symposium* (8, 3), noted, as an oddity it seems, that a certain Nikeratos was in love with his wife and she with him. Plato, while promoting promiscuity in *The Republic* and pederastic attachment in *The Symposium*, formulates an ideal of monogamous marriage in the work of his old age, *Laws* (840d; 841d).

## Marital Sex Symbols in Domestic Scenes

The red-figure technique of pottery making began to replace the black-figure style in Attic pottery production about 530 B.C. Within decades the new style resulted in a technically advanced draftsmanship and the most refined decorations ever applied to terra cotta. Two salient aspects of the new painted vases were the extensive use of pictorial codes and attributes, and the creation of designs with a great deal of dramatic impact; we will look at a number of red-figure vase paintings presenting vignettes in which characters interact with each other in complicated ways—sometimes comic, sometimes tragic.

Scenes from everyday life appear in astonishing numbers in red-figure vase paintings. Although in the past these have been used as illustrations of daily life in Athens, they have barely been studied in detail. The following pages constitute a first attempt at deciphering their code.

Two factors should be borne in mind here. First, each shape of pot had a specific use. The Greeks, with their sense of order and classification, would never put wine in a water pitcher, for example; the decoration of each pot is likely to be connected in some symbolic way with its purpose. Roughly speaking, vessels used for dinner and drinking parties belonged to the domain of men; those having to do with marriage, funerals, and women's labor belonged to the female world.

Second, in contrast to the views of many other scholars, I wish to establish that even those vessels specifically designed for use by women, such as boxes (pyxides), water jugs (hydriai), and "washwater carriers" (loutrophoroi, used both for weddings and funerals), reflect essentially a male conceptual framework; the women's pots were made and decorated by men, notwithstanding the presence of a much-publicized female potter on one hydria (Webster, Figure 17).

In Chapter 9 I will try to prove that visual symbols referring to women's textile manufacturing are intertwined with those relating to marital sex. This conclusion supports my contention that the prevalent ethos governing sexual activity of respectable women was one of duty and obligation, not one of love or joy.

## The Half-Opened Door

If earlier we saw the closed door in vase painting as a symbol of the women's quarters of a private house, a half-opened door affording a glimpse of a bed points to a wife's sexual duties. Figure 101 shows a box, or pyxis, with a pensive lady in front of such a door. Note also the wool-working implements in the scene. Figure 102 shows

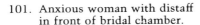

102. The half-opened door on a wedding vase.

101. Anxious woman with distaff in front of bridal chamber.

103. Caricature of woman approaching a half-opened door.

a wedding vase (loutrophoros) in Boston, with the bride, here shown unrealistically as a full-grown woman, approaching the conventional half-opened door to the wedding chamber with raised arms, a gesture denoting fright. In the delightful drawing on the vase sherd in Figure 103, the theme of wedded sex is spoofed: a naked older woman approaches a half-opened door with a torch, striking a pose of eager anticipation. The solemn atmosphere of the other scenes is missing, but this vase was produced in southern Italy in the fourth century B.C. and is imbued with a very different spirit. Indeed, it may represent a scene from a comedy.

## The Oil Flask, or Alabastron

A small oblong bottle with a rounded bottom, which, therefore, cannot stand up but has to be carried on a string, appears as a standard attribute of women in indoor scenes and also on funeral vases. The latter circumstance indicates that notions of merit and service were connected with it. When men carried around oil, they did so in a shorter, rounder bottle, called an aryballos. The alabastron is infrequently shown in scenes featuring hetaerai, but, by the principle which governs iconography, this need not mean that hetaerai did not use them, only that they were not conventionally associated with them. The principal connotation of the alabastron is dutiful conjugal sex, not the purchased variety.

It has often been thought that women used these flasks for oil or unguents, with which to anoint themselves for greater appeal, but that is probably incorrect: they used them to oil their husbands before and after sex, and the communicative signal of the symbol was "dutiful service to the husband." The famous physician Galen in his treatise *On the Conservation of Health* established norms of hygiene for men and recommended oiling the genitals with artfully blended unguents to cure irritation (6, 14, 6) and, especially after sex, to improve skin texture (3, 13, 13). This, without much doubt, is what the resolute lady on the wedding vase in Figure 104 is up to. She is walking toward the conjugal bed chamber, again symbolized by a partially opened door revealing a couch.

The alabastron is also associated with service to men in the comedies of Aristophanes. In his *Acharnians* (1063), Dikaiopolis provides a bridesmaid with very specific instructions as to how the penis of the groom should be anointed, and he demonstrates the technique on an alabastron (for this and other allusions to women oiling men's genitals see Henderson, 120). The phallic shape of the alabastron enhances its potential for sexual jokes.

We have now seen several instances of the alabastron as a symbol connoting conjugal sex, and we will encounter several more, as it is ubiquitous in domestic scenes. Figure 105 shows one example of it in which the connotation of duty is especially brought out: it is a funerary oil flask by the Achilleus Painter, the finest painter of this type of vase. It shows on the left a woman with the oil flask and an unguent vase of a shape known to have served funerary purposes; on the right a woman holds a basket with sacrificial offerings. "Women's dutiful services" are clearly the picture's motif.

## The Wedding Shoes: Symbol of Conjugal Sex?

The Greek lexicon by Hesychius, which preserves many ancient Greek words not elsewhere attested, mentions "bridal shoes" (*nymphides*, s.v.), evidently to be worn by the bride on her wedding day. The wedding slippers appear to be represented on only a single extant vase, the hydria in New York reproduced in Figure 106. It dates from 430 B.C., somewhat later than most of the red-figure vases illustrated here. Without any doubt it shows preparations for a wedding in the women's quarters, although it is not clear whether the bride is the spinning lady on the left or the sedentary one on the right. In my view, the spinster is the bride and the other seated lady is her mother. On the far right a man is approaching (barely visible in the photograph). Eros, the young god of love, hands a pair of pointed slippers to the lady on the right. It might have been difficult to determine the symbolism of the slippers, were it not for the fact that in Baroque painting, especially that of the Dutch

104a,b. Sex and spinning: interior with woolworkers and half-opened door.

school, they appear regularly as a symbol for copulation or for the danger of seduction. If one imagines the motion a person makes when slipping a foot into an open shoe, the origin of this symbolism is not difficult to reconstruct. It would, however, be interesting to know how this pictorial symbol survived through the ages.

## Boxes and Chests

It is astonishing to see, in hundreds of pictures of the women's quarters of private homes, the occupants associated with boxes and chests, well-established symbols for the earth and motherhood. This

105. Women with fillets and oil flask on a funerary vessel.

106. Interior scene with bride spinning and Eros holding wedding slippers.

feature was surely developed by unconscious processes and shows once again that the genre scenes in Greek vase painting are not "realistic" but symbolic.

In Attic mythology the clearest illustration of this symbolism is the myth of Erichthonius, which I mentioned briefly in Chapter 2. In Figure 21 we saw the birth of Erichthonius from the earth, out of Hephaestus' spilled seed. Figure 107 shows the infant Erichthonius emerging from a chest surrounded by snakes, in the presence of Athena; the chest is a substitute for Athena's non-functioning womb.

In indoor scenes women sit on chests, put objects into chests, carry around small boxes, and endlessly remove objects from them or store items in them. To be sure, the Greeks used little furniture, and small belongings seem to have been either hung on walls or stored in chests, but this must have applied to men as well as women. The chests and boxes in paintings of Athenian women reflect on a small scale the uterine boxiness of Greek architecture. Consciously or unconsciously they allude not only to maternity but to the qualities of conservatism and protectiveness thought to accompany it. Two illustrations are show here; others will follow in different contexts. Both examples also include the almost inevitable alabastron. In Figure 108, a seated lady with a chest on her lap holds out a soliciting hand toward a young man with a wreath in his hair. The implications of this scene are by no means clear. Is she lamenting the loss of a breadwinner, since this is a funerary oil flask, or is a worldly transaction taking place?

On the hydria in Figure 109, a vase from a later age, perhaps the end of the fifth century B.C., a naked youth, probably Eros, holds out an alabastron to a lady seated on a chest. Here the meaning is clearly symbolic: the allusion is to forthcoming marriage and motherhood.

## *The Seated Lady: Homey Image of the Enthroned Goddess*

It should by now have become apparent that matrons are frequently represented in a standardized pose, seated in a chair placed sideways and leaning comfortably against its backrest while holding in their hands an object, which may be a wreath; a book roll; a stringed musical instrument, such as a cithara, lyre, or harp; a wreath of flowers; or a necklace. The object may also be an implement of spinning or weaving.

To the several "enthroned matrons" already shown, we may add the lovely seated lyre player in Figure 110, the busy lady spinning in the presence of her husband in Figure 111, and a seated woman holding up her hands in Figure 112. The latter lady probably is a new bride, receiving from the other women of the household the treatment of the "downpourings" (*katachysmata*), the welcoming shower of nuts over the head (see the Introduction).

Are we to conclude that the women depicted led lives of leisure, filling their hours with gracious and creative pastimes? By no means. We are dealing with a symbolic convention. Aristotle does remark that it is unhealthful for women to sit as much as they do (*Gen. An.* 775a 34). Aristotle, however, like other Athenian men, had little insight into the reality of the activities in the women's quarters. There is ample evidence that the typical women's part of the house was a sweatshop, and a labor ethos was instilled in women from childhood on.

Then why all the seated ladies in vase painting? It is most likely that the seated pose, like the omnipresent chest, is yet another symbol of maternity. The enthroned goddess as an archetypal Earth Mother—be she Demeter, Cybele, or Isis—is a well-established visual scheme. As Erich Neumann has put it,

> As mother and earth woman, the Great Mother is the "throne" pure and simple, and, characteristically, the woman's motherliness resides not only in the womb but also in the seated woman's broad expanse of thigh, her lap on which the newborn child sits enthroned. (*The Great Mother*, 98)

The seated lady of the house in *gynaikonitis* scenes, I suggest, is a domestication of the archetypal mother image. Where an "enthroned" woman appears with hetaerai, she is probably to be understood as the madam of the establishment.

## The Frame of Mind of Athenian Wives

From fifth-century Athens we have not a scrap of writing and not a single artifact that can be attributed to a woman. If it is true, as here maintained, that even the pictures of domestic interiors, thought to be "realistic" by many scholars, actually reflect men's conscious and unconscious fantasies, how shall we ever reconstruct the women's frame of mind?

It is clear that the Athenian man, after excluding women from

107. Erichthonius in his box, guarded by a snake, greeting his mother. In front, the wicker lid.

108. Seated woman with chest, and alabastron overhead. Sorrowing over the loss of a breadwinner?

all the significant aspects of public life, felt uneasy about them. As the surviving dramas show, men fantasized hysterically about women rebelling against male supremacy. They peopled their tragic and comic stages with women taking their revenge by slaughtering husbands and sons and defying the social order. The men's mytho-

109. Interior scene with woman seated on chest.

110. Interior scene with seated lyre player.

logical imagery reflects their castration fears: snaky Medusa heads, the jagged aegis of Athena, and a whole cupboardful of female monsters are rightly considered as revealing Greek men's fear of the *vagina dentata*, the emasculating machinery of female revenge.

But what of the reality? We have no evidence for any form of female rebellion, not even on the part of the few somewhat emancipated female figures who have left us a shadowy trace. In fact, in the face of such massive repression, even an internal moral resistance would have required supernatural psychic strength on the part of

111. Seated spinster, servant with chest, and the master of the house.

112. Interior scene; the ritual of "downpouring"?

women. The fifth-century Sophist Antiphon lamented, "Marriage is a big contest for mankind" (Fr. B 49 Diels), but in Athens man had the upper hand as he did in few other ancient societies. With the cards stacked high against her, the Athenian woman probably played a losing game in order to secure a minimally acceptable home existence. For "when a woman is deprived of harmony with her husband, her life henceforth becomes impossible," as the orator Lycurgus remarked. The typical molelike frame of mind of the Athenian woman is probably best summed up in Plato's *Laws*, where he is of two minds. Although he held the female to be generically inferior to the male, the philosopher recommended public education and access to public office for women. Plato's mouthpiece, the "Athenian," argues that women should be admitted to public dining halls and take their meals with men. But immediately the unfeasibility of this proposal is made clear:

> How could one in actuality, without looking ridiculous, try to compel women to expose themselves to public view while eating and drinking? For their kind would endure anything more readily than that. Accustomed as they are to live in concealment and darkness, if one would drag them into the light, they would resist with all their might and be far stronger than the lawgiver. (*Laws* 781c)

Such must have been the mentality of the women in the household, who have been described by Lysias in these words: "who live so properly that they are ashamed to be seen even by members of the household" (3.6).

# 5

# Brides of Death, in More Ways Than One

> There are only two happy days in man's life with a woman:
> The day he marries her and the day he buries her.
> —Hipponax, Fragment 68

> ... I had such grievous fear of marriage as ever befell a
> maiden of Anatolia.
> —Sophocles, *The Women of Trachis* (8–9): Deianeira,
> the wife of Heracles, speaking

People almost everywhere have conceived of the earth as female, since it gives forth the sustenance of life. The earth is also our home after death; in Greek metaphorical language, the tomb is sometimes equated with the womb. Antigone, in Aeschylus' *Seven Against Thebes*, announces her intention to give a proper funeral to her brother's corpse in the following words—"Although a woman, I will devise a grave and a tomb for him, carrying him in the folds of my linen robe, and myself will shroud him" (1037–40)—almost as if she would bury him in her own womb. Cultures which held the "female principle" in honor probably derived some comfort from this symbolism: death is a return to that maternal element from which we have sprung and which will give birth to new life in the cycle of generation. In Classical Athens, however, we find matriarchal ideas of death heavily overlaid with their opposite. The principal surviving Earth Mother figure, the goddess Demeter, whose name probably literally means "Earth Mother," was still the patroness of agrarian and human fertility, but her earlier chthonic associations had almost disappeared. Instead, through her mysteries at Eleusis, she became the source of a more spiritual form of immortality. The death divinities were now male: the king of the underworld was Pluto, or Hades; his consort, Persephone, was merely a part-time companion. Dionysus was another male divinity of afterlife. The escort of souls to the underworld was the god Hermes, and even the ferryman of the barge of the dead was male, the folksy boatsman Charon.

Although the world of death, like that of the living, was male-dominated, the preparations for getting there were assigned to women. The realm of death, like conception and birth, was in the inner recesses of the house, the female space. It shared with the procreative process an occult aspect. All three—conception, birth, and death—required the participation of the female sex, but, like the women themselves, were hidden insofar as possible. I cited previously a small chorus of Greek voices proclaiming that marriage is not for sexual satisfaction, and we will observe the Athenians' striking preference for nongenerative sex—namely, with hetaerai and with men and boys. Related to this distaste for marriage was the Athenians' cultivated ignorance of the female anatomy, especially of the reproductive organs, an ignorance that had disastrous consequences for women's well-being and probably their children's too. The same attitude explains the banishment of death rituals to the women's quarters and the notion that a living woman had, as it were, only a short reprieve from death. As a character in a comedy by the fifth-century playwright Pherecrates observes, "He who bemoans the death of his wife is a fool who doesn't appreciate his good fortune" (Fr. 248a Edmonds). This is not just an expression of that well-established streak of misogyny that characterizes much of ancient Greek culture. This and similar statements reflect a deep-seated and particularly Attic conviction that the proper place for the female, after a stint in the marriage bed, is the graveyard.

## The Bride as Symbolic Victim

Many subtle (and some not so subtle) symbols linked the ritual of marriage with that of death, at least for the bride. As was known to the more perceptive authors, especially Sophocles, the young bride had every reason to anticipate her wedding with fear and not with joy. She had been raised to anticipate marriage as the fulfill-ment of her existence, but with awe: in the vases we saw in the previous chapter (Figures 101, 102) this feeling was expressed both by the half-opened door showing part of a bed and by the bride's stylized gesture of fear. The symbolic equation of the penis with the sword, as in the myth of Achilleus and Penthesileia, must have enhanced this fear. The bride was likewise steeled for the ordeal of childbearing.

It seems that the more any society represses women's activities, the more the wedding ceremony constitutes the bride's day, rather than that of bride and groom together. Marriage is symbolized as the sacrifice of the bride to the system. The purity of the bride is still today expressed by the white wedding gown, just as in Greek antiquity it was expressed by the veiling of the bride. Unseen, she was untouched and pure: like a sacrificial animal she had to be unblemished. It is not without reason that Aristotle likens the first menstrual flow of the pubescent girl to the blood of slaughtered animals. The word *amnion*, from which we have "amniotic fluid," denoted not only the membrane enveloping the foetus, but also a bowl for collecting the animals' blood, another curious tie between the human reproductive function and sacrifice.

The tall, slender jug (loutrophoros) that was the characteristic implement of the bridal ceremony was also used for funerals and, either in its regular terra-cotta version or translated into stone, as a tomb monument (Figure 113). It was used especially to mark the tomb of girls who had died unmarried; their death became symbolized as "marriage to Hades." The masculinization of the underworld

113. Marble nuptial vessel
(*loutrophoros*) as a
tombstone.

and afterlife in Greek mythology greatly fostered this notion. Eventually the concept of dead women as "brides of Hades" became a commonplace of literary symbolism and of funerary imagery. Euripides was especially fond of it: "Ah, my wretched maiden— Why do I speak of maiden? Soon Hades, it seems, will marry her," says Agamemnon, about to sacrifice his daughter Iphigeneia (*IA* 460–61). The corresponding notion, of the death of a man as marriage to Persephone, is occasionally expressed, apparently in imitation of the female pattern. Hence in poetry the underworld is not infrequently referred to as "the bridal chamber of the earth."

The parallels between bridal and funerary imagery prepare us, then, for the depiction, on many sepulchral monuments, of the deceased woman as bride. Figure 114 shows the principal side of a marble oil flask, which surely once served as a grave marker: the woman is both bride and ghost. In Figure 115, on a funerary lekythos the god Hermes, whose hand and caduceus can be seen on the left side, leads the ghost-as-bride to the underworld, with the deceased lady still adjusting her bridal tiara.

## The Actual Sacrifice of Virgins

A number of Greek myths and legends, including several connected with the patriotic traditions of Athens, tell of the sacrifice of "pure virgins" to appease the gods or obtain some favor from them. The rationale of such rites, as of the practice of sacrifice in general, is obscure. If the female is the inferior part of the human race, why sacrifice women? It has been argued that virgin sacrifice consisted of a deception: since the sacrificial person was decked out as a bride, the gods were fooled into believing they were receiving the more valuable offering, in the same way that animals gradually replaced the costlier sacrifice of humans—the ram was substituted for Isaac.

However, in the many tales of children killed in revenge or in *hubris*, the victims are regularly male. In the myths surrounding the Peloponnesian house of Atreus, in which there is a remarkable mortality of children through cannibalism, the victims are always boys. Tantalus makes a stew out of his son, Pelops. He is punished by the gods in appropriately culinary fashion: his appetite is spoiled by an overhanging boulder which threatens to crush him, or, in an alternative version, he is "tantalized" by food and drink which he

114. Woman's figure on a marble funerary vessel: bride or ghost?

115. The deceased as bride on a funerary oil flask.

cannot reach. Tantalus' descendant Atreus takes revenge on his brother, Thyestes, by serving him his own sons for dinner.

When Heracles goes mad, an episode in his checkered existence dramatized by Euripides, he kills his sons. We have already noted two myths of mothers—Procne and Medea—who kill their offspring in revenge against their husbands. The daughters of Minyas, legendary founder of the town of Orchomenes and the ancestor of the "Minyans," behaved in a similar way. In all these cases the victims are male. The reason for this is not hard to find: the murder of girl children would be mythologically ineffectual, since their fate was unimportant. How, then, shall we explain the preference for female virgins in tales of ritual sacrifice?

There can be little doubt that the Greek myths preserve a memory of human sacrifice. Numerous legendary Delphic oracles commanded the sacrifice of a young girl to save families or cities from disasters of one kind or another. Whatever the origin of such practices in prehistoric times, why were myths about them firmly integrated into the nationalistic mythology of Classical Athens, as well as into various local cults, especially those celebrated by women? With their strong element of indoctrination, these myths are the ideological complement to the cult of male aggressiveness, as dramatized in the feats of rape and slaughter by Heracles and Theseus, and in the stories of heterosexual and homosexual rape committed by the gods.

A number of tales of virgin sacrifice are connected with the legendary founding of Athens. Agraulos (or Aglauros) was one of the three daughters of Cecrops who received the baby Erichthonius, born of the Attic soil and the spilled seed of Hephaestus. In one version of her death she voluntarily throws herself from the Acropolis, in response to a Delphic oracle saying that without an act of self-sacrifice the Athenians cannot be victorious in war. In gratitude, the city of Athens dedicated a shrine to Agraulos, in which young Athenian men, upon reaching adulthood, received their arms and took their oath of citizenship. In this shrine and its cult the female ethos of submission and the male ethos of militarism were strikingly juxtaposed.

Another celebrated female martyr, probably of pre-Attic origin, was Iphigeneia, whose cult at the sanctuary at Brauron will concern us in Chapter 12. After Euripides' two successful plays on the myth, *Iphigeneia in Aulis* and *Iphigeneia in Tauris*, her persona bore the playwright's imprint, but we have no reason to think Euripides interfered substantially with her story, if only because she was already a major cult figure. In this archetypal myth of virgin sacrifice, King Agamemnon offends the goddess Artemis by killing one of her deer. The goddess blocks his troops at Aulis until he agrees to sacrifice his own daughter in atonement. In Euripides' version Iphigeneia at first rebels, but in the end goes willingly to her death. We have no Attic visual representation of Euripides' ending, but a south Italian vase painting renders it effectively (Figure 116). The stag hovers over Iphigeneia and will be substituted for her at the last minute, thus bringing about the happy ending of the play, as in older versions of the myth. Note the prominence of the sword, establishing once again the antithesis of armed might and female submission.

116. The willing victim: Iphigeneia about to be sacrificed (after Euripides' *Iphigeneia in Aulis*).

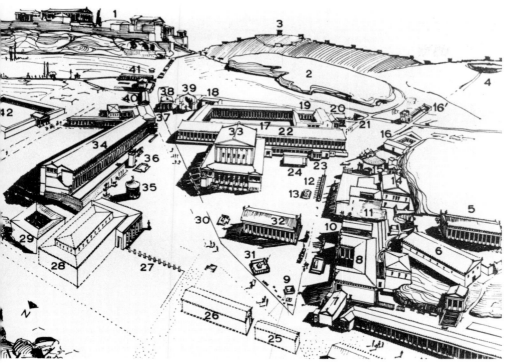

117. Reconstruction of the agora as of 150 A.D. The assumed Leokorion is no. 11.

The myth which probably hammered in the message of female submissiveness to the knife most insistently was that of Leos and his three daughters, because the sacrifice of these girls was commemorated with a shrine erected in the Athenian Agora, called the Leokorion, or "monument to the daughters of Leos" (Figure 117). The Leokorion is mentioned in a number of literary sources (e.g., *Dem.* 54, 7) and was still in evidence in Roman times. Ironically, the area around this monument, erected to the spirit of "respectable" women's submissiveness, was a hangout for prostitutes, as a post-Classical Greek author reports (Alciphron 3, 2, 1). Homer Thompson has identified the remains of a small temple in the Agora as the Leokorion and has suggested, as an explanation for the fifth-century revival of interest in this ancient monument, the possibility that virgin sacrifices were recalled in connection with the terrible plague which befell Athens during the years 430–429. Among the offerings excavated in and around the shrine that Thompson identified as the

Leokorion were a large number of items belonging to the domain of women: loom weights, animal knuckle bones (favorite toys of girls), and infant feeding bottles. Thompson's identification of the monument and his theory concerning the role it played in Classical Athenian life are not accepted by all scholars. Perhaps the implications are hard to swallow for many classicists. At any rate, the Leokorion did perpetuate, all through the Classical age, the memory of the sacrifice of women. If the structure has been correctly identified, the offerings brought to it would indicate that the women of Athens gloried in the notion of self-sacrifice.

A somewhat comical note on virgin sacrifice is sounded in a fragment of Euripides' lost play *Erechtheus*. Praxithea, the wife of Erechtheus, legendary early king of Attica, agrees to accommodate yet another Delphic oracle, which demands the sacrifice of the king's daughters, and even goes one step further: she laments that she has no sons to offer, only daughters, who are "mere apparitions in the city" (Fr. 360, 27). But, as she exclaims in a line full of pathos, "Use, O fellow citizens, the fruit of my labor pains" (50).

## Death in Childbed

The young bride, sequestered in her new home, had to live with the considerable likelihood of death in childbearing. Society glorified such a fate as female martyrdom, analogous to heroic death on the battlefield for men. The equation of the two forms of death apparently was commonplace. Plutarch reports that the Spartans allowed names to be placed only on the tombs of men killed in war and of women who had died in childbirth (*Lyc.* 27). Neither the Spartans nor the Athenians realized the anomaly of equating death incurred in giving life with that resulting from attempts to kill. No serious efforts were ever undertaken to prevent either calamity. On the contrary, at Brauron upper-class Athenian girls were prepared to accept death in childbed as a natural and probable consequence of marriage (Chapter 12). Euripides' Medea correctly espied a vengeful male attitude behind this placid acceptance of women's death (if men die in battle, why shouldn't women have to face a comparable hazard?): "They say of us that we live without danger in our homes, while they contend in war. How badly they reason! I would rather stand three times besides the shield than give birth once" (248–51).

In a fragment of Old Comedy by Theopompus, a speaker comments that the goddess of childbirth, Eilithyia (perhaps meaning "she that comes in need"), is habitually anxious: "But Eilithyia should be forgiven for being constantly in a state of panic about her craft, as a result of the pleading of women" (Fr. 59). We already noted that the Athenians consciously favored child brides because they are easier to train, despite their awareness of the increased danger of death in parturition. Scores of funerary monuments, both tomb steles and the white-ground oil flasks placed in graves, bear melancholy testimony to the many casualties among young mothers. The exact significance of these monuments is somewhat enigmatic: the relationship between the living and the dead on them has been variously interpreted. Where a young woman is shown with an infant, it is clear that she died in childbirth, but whether or not the child survived is open to conjecture. Boys are represented naked, and it seems probable that swaddled infants are always female.

Considering the nature of Athenian sentiment, we may assume that a woman who died in giving birth to a son (Figures 119, 121, 122, and 123) was more likely to receive honorary burial than one who had given birth to a daughter (Figures 118 and 120). However,

119. Mother, male infant, and nurse on tomb stele.

118. Mother and child on a fifth-century tomb stele.

120. Mother and swaddled infant on tomb stele.

121. Mother, slave girl, and small boy on a funerary lekythos.

since we do not have a systematic catalogue of the Attic grave steles, many of which are still unpublished, it is impossible to test this theory. No grown men appear in any of the above funerary images. On many men's monuments no women appear. The Greeks tended to be sexually segregated in death as well as in life.

It is clear that Athenian male society had rung down a curtain of secrecy and disgust over everything that had to do with pregnancy, birth, and death, which they relegated to the sinister domain of their sequestered women. This curtain was not lifted even in the face of medical necessity, as is made clear by a passage in Euripides' *Hippolytus*. Here, the nurse of the heroine, Phaedra, has noticed that her mistress is ailing and is advising her to seek help:

> If you are suffering from one of the unspeakable ills let these women here take care of your ailment. But if your trouble is one that should be referred to males, speak, that this matter may be reported to physicians. (293–96)

In many translations the point of this passage is obscured. The

122. Mother and male infant on a lekythos fragment.

123. Mother, male infant, and nurse (not shown) on a funerary vase.

statement is revealing, especially on account of the word used for "unspeakable" (*aporreta*), which is elsewhere applied to the awesome secrets of the mystery rites and other holy affairs. Gynecological problems, in other words, are taken care of by the women of the household. Male physicians don't deal with such matters. Figure 124 shows a fifth-century Attic relief with a mother giving birth on a birthing stool, assisted by four other women. (The baby's unrealistically small head is just emerging.)

The surviving medical texts from antiquity bear out this principle of leaving routine obstetrical care to midwives and reserving the efforts of trained physicians for instances of disease or extreme complication. What kind of training did midwives receive? In this field the most competent treatise we have from Classical antiquity is the *Gynecology* (or *Gynaicia*) by Soranus, a famous physician who flourished in Rome during the early second century A.D. Soranus gives the qualifications for the "good midwife" (1, 3): for obvious reasons, she must have long, slender fingers, and short fingernails. She must also be free from superstitions and "literate in order to be able to comprehend the art through theory as well." Soranus probably intends that his "good midwife" should study treatises such as his own, but to what knowledge did literacy give access? In Pliny the Elder's encyclopedia of knowledge, *Natural History*, the author repeatedly quotes a Greek midwife by the name of Olympias of Thebes, who had published a handbook on her craft. A midwife brought up on this and similar texts went into the women's quarters armed with the following bits of obstetrical wisdom:

> ... they say that women who eat roast veal together with the herb *aristolochia* [literally "of best birth"] at about the time of conception are sure to give birth to male offspring. (*NH* 28, 254)

> ... for women about to give birth, it is a good thing to have eaten wolf's meat, or if they are already in labor, to have a person sitting near them, who has eaten such. But it would be fatal if that person had come in from the outside. (*ibid.* 247)

> The midwives assure us that uterine bleeding, no matter how abundant, can be arrested by the drinking of goat's urine and by applying dung. (*ibid.* 255)

Even though physicians were at times called in for especially difficult deliveries, in many cases probably too late, Soranus himself

124. Woman giving birth on a birthing stool.

displays that curious ignorance of the reproductive process which indicates that he rarely entered the female domain (4, 7). He upholds the old notion that conception takes place during menstruation: he recommends the days of abating flow for intercourse aimed at conception (1, 36). Even more strangely, he denies the existence of the hymen, an observation which makes one wonder about the physician's own sexual experience (1, 17).

Pliny the Elder gives us yet another sidelight on the hazards of ancient delivery rooms. For babies to be born feet first was considered "against nature" and the boy child so born was thought to be doomed to an unillustrious and calamitous life. By his account, the Caesarean section was aimed at forestalling this disaster, not at saving the lives of mother and child:

> They are born under better auspices if the mother is killed; instances are Scipio Africanus the Elder, and the first of the Caesars [Julius Caesar], who was so called from the killing of his mother's uterus (caeso utero). (NH 7, 47)

In other words, the mother was put to death in order to improve the son's prospects for a successful life.

None of the medical writers sought a cure for death in childbirth. Quite the contrary. Despite the heavy casualties among young mothers, prolonged virginity and failure to conceive were considered harmful, even dangerous, to the health of women by most physicians. Plato, in a passage reflecting medical science, calls childlessness "the source of all kinds of diseases" (Tim. 91). Soranus, on the other hand, considers permanent virginity compatible with good health (29).

In the Greek medical literature we refer to as the "Hippocratic texts"—actually a kind of library of treatises by different authors, spanning several centuries—much of the gynecological information is subsumed under the essay On the Diseases of Women. As this text and others in the collection make clear, the general purpose of ancient gynecology was not to cure the problems and illnesses of women, but to restore their fertility.

The medical negation of the female is evidenced in other ways as well. One of the more sensible and famous among surviving Greek medical treatises is Galen's On the Conservation of Health. It is aimed at the prevention of disease through regimen, rather than cure. It deals entirely with the living habits of men.

## The Female as Feedbag

Aristotle's writings throw a revealing light on Greek medical gynecology of the Classical age. None of them are specifically devoted to medicine, but some of his treatises, especially those on biology, reflect medical knowledge. Aristotle's references are the oldest datable reflection of Greek medicine, since in the Hippocratic corpus and the surviving medical texts by post-Classical physicians, fifth- and fourth-century elements are difficult to sort out from later additions.

Aristotle's remarks on sex and procreation reveal the tendentiousness to which Greek biology and medicine had fallen victim. He sought to prove scientifically not only that the male is superior to the female, but also that the female, despite her nurturing of the fetus during pregnancy, has no genetic input into procreation, thus making the father the only real parent.

The desire of the male to arrogate to himself the procreative function and to reduce the female to a mere incubator is the most fundamental cause of repression and of sex antagonism. This is nowhere better illustrated than in Classical Athenian society. Aristotle's reasoning, set forth in the most detail in his *Generation of Animals*, goes as follows (726 f.). Since the male secretes sperm and the female menstrual blood, conception takes place during menstruation. Since blood is merely nutritious and not procreative, the female has no genetic power, but provides temporary nourishment. It follows logically that the female is merely a male without genitals (728a 18); she is a maimed male, Aristotle says (737a 28–3), anticipating Freud's "penis envy" theory. The bizarre nature of the argument is increased by the observation that scars are passed on genetically from father to child but not from mother to child (721b 30), and that women age sooner. Even the circumstance that women are less likely to grow bald is indicative of their inferiority: they are more "childlike." Among the instances of Aristotle's misogyny parading as science, the nadir is his statement that women have fewer teeth than men (*Hist. An.* 501b). The philosopher Bertrand Russell is rumored to have commented on this passage that "Aristotle would never have made this mistake if he had let his wife open her mouth once in a while."

However, a few other scientific-philosophical underpinnings of the doctrine of male superiority are refuted by Aristotle—for instance, the view that male infants are born from the right testicle of their father and female infants from the left, the ill-omened side. Aristotle also rejects Empedocles' thesis that a hot womb gives birth to a male child and a cold womb to a female child (*Gen. An.* 765a), but that parents who procreate during their prime tend to have male offspring was apparently undisputed doctrine (*ibid.* 766b).

With regard to the denial of women's genetic function, the bad faith of the Greek authors is patent: it is hard to believe that they convinced themselves. Surely they must have observed that some children look like their mothers, or that dark- and fair-skinned parents tend to produce in-between offspring. Aristotle in fact concedes that some children take traits from their mother, but only in case of impaired genetic input from the father (*ibid.* 767b ff.). At least one Athenian institution belies the notion of exclusive male parenthood: under Attic law paternal half-brothers and half-sisters could marry, maternal ones could not. An anecdote preserved by Plutarch also contradicts the principle of "exclusive paternity": Archidamas, a king of Sparta, was fined by his government for marrying a short wife, who would produce "kinglets" instead of kings.

## Female Infanticide

The question whether or not Athenian citizen fathers regularly exposed female infants is being debated with the intensity which such touchy subjects nowadays unleash. We know that the acceptance of a child by its father was not automatic but required an act of will. The killing of the infant was apparently illegal, but nobody doubts that the child could be "exposed," that is, abandoned, with impunity. If the parent wished for the child to survive, he could expose it in a conspicuous place. If recovered by another party, the foundling had slave status, and it seems that there was a lively trade in exposed girl babies for purposes of prostitution. Where else could the armies of slave prostitutes have come from? If the child was deposited in an inhospitable place, "exposure" was tantamount to infanticide, manifesting the same hypocrisy which prompts Creon in Sophocles' *Antigone* to bury his victim alive, rather than incur the pollution of bloodshed by executing her.

There is firm evidence for the exposure of female infants from the post-Classical period. In a fragment of a comedy by the playwright Poseidippus, who wrote in the early third century B.C., it is stated that "Sons are always brought up somehow, even in the poorest family; girls are always exposed, even by the well-off" (Fr. 11 K.). A Greek letter from Hellenistic Egypt, dating from the first century B.C., candidly advocates the exposure of female offspring.

How widely was exposure practiced in Classical Athens? Aristotle states with delicacy that, to eliminate unwanted children "if regular custom hinders exposure," he prefers abortion in early stages of pregnancy over the killing of a larger fetus. He does advocate the exposure of deformed babies (*Pol.* 1335b 20–25). The passage implies that these various acts were all legal, and not uncommon, but that the exposure of normal infants did not have full moral sanction. If children were regularly exposed in Classical Athens, it is a safe assumption that this happened mainly to female offspring, since they required dowries in marriage and were generally considered of little value. A recent article by Donald Engels, arguing that the population of Athens could not have survived the practice of female infanticide does not convince: this argument applies equally to the post-Classical world, in which girls were regularly exposed. It is, however, quite possible that at Athens medical neglect and poor regimen made female infanticide in any considerable numbers superfluous. An observation by Xenophon makes it clear that Athenian women were regularly given food of poorer quality than men (*Lac. Const.* 1, 3–4).

## The Mourning Mother

We hear or see little of the lives of more mature wives, with older children. Socrates' account of Xanthippe's concerns for their son Lamprocles which I cited earlier, was exceptional. When we consider mythology, however, there can be no doubt as to how the Athenian Greeks most clearly perceived the role of the mother of adolescent or adult children: the mother's part was to mourn. The most prominent mythological mourner was, of course, the goddess Demeter, lamenting her ravished daughter, Persephone, or Kore. The mortal manifestation of the sorrowing mother was Niobe, who mourned an equal number of sons and daughters, seven of each in the most celebrated version (Chapter 14).

A whole array of mythological mothers of slain sons brought out the best efforts of some of the most skilled painters. The pietà motif was no innovation on the part of Christian myth makers. Figure 125, a scene from the Trojan cycle of myths, painted by Exekias, depicts the goddess Eos (Dawn) mourning her slain son, Memnon. How clearly the Greek image of the mother mourning her slain son anticipates the Christian motif of the Virgin Mary, mourning over the body of Jesus, may be seen through a comparison

125. Eos mourning her slain son Memnon.

126. The Christian pietà motif: Mary mourning Jesus in a fifteenth-century woodcarving.

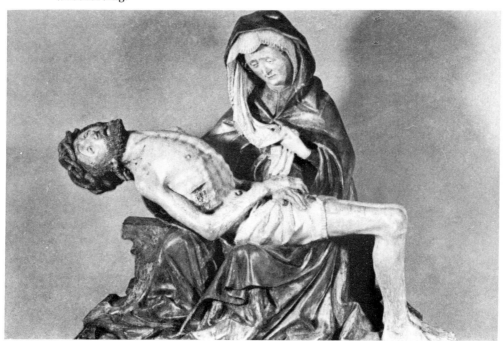

with a fifteenth-century wood carving in the Metropolitan Museum of Art in New York (Figure 126).

In the Trojan cycle of myths, among those who mourned slain sons were Thetis, the mother of Achilleus, and Europa, who had borne Sarpedon to her ravisher, Zeus. Sarpedon fought against the Greeks in the Trojan War. His father, Zeus, wished to save him but did not prevail over the other Olympians, and the hero was killed by Patroclus. However, by command of Zeus, Apollo cleansed the corpse, and had it carried to his homeland, Lycia, by Sleep and Death, so that the hero could be properly mourned and buried by his mother (*Il.* 16, 667 ff.).

The most intricate and poignant illustration of the sorrowing-mother theme was produced by the Penthesileia Painter. Figure 38 shows this artist's rendering of the death of Tityus, to which I already alluded briefly in Chapter 2. Apollo is about to slay his victim, who had offended him by making a pass at his mother, Leto. Tityus' mother, Ge (Earth) is shown on the right. The pathos of this scene lies in its dramatic implications: Tityus' body is turned toward the viewer, and daringly foreshortened. He must have been beseeching someone else just before, perhaps Apollo's mother, Leto, herself. The young god is so angry that he has forsaken his normal executioner's weapon, the bow and arrow, which hang idle in his left hand. Instead he is slashing at Tityus with a drawn sword. Ge has abandoned hope for her son. The vase painter effectively contrasts the mortal motherhood of Ge, which is that of sorrow, with the secure, divine motherhood of Leto.

## The Preparation and Burial of the Dead

The preparation of the bodies of the deceased for burial, a kind of reverse birth, was performed by women. In the Classical age the ritual lamentation over the body also seems to have been performed mainly by women, although seventh-century Attic vases show mixed-gender lamentation choruses. In Figure 127 women perform a dirge over the laid-out corpse of a youth; on the neck of the vase more women are lamenting and tearing out their hair. Significantly, the vessel is the loutrophoros, the same shape of pot used in the wedding ritual. On the lower register of the decoration armed men on horseback are engaging in more virile occupations. Figure 128 shows a detail of another loutrophoros, with the lying-in-state of a female corpse. She is wearing a tiara, which equates the female dead with brides. A woman emphatically characterized as old tends to the body of the deceased. Possibly this feature reflects a law which prohibited women under sixty years of age from taking part in the ceremonial lamentation unless they belonged to the immediate family (Dem. 46, 62). Women, who had few social and emotional outlets, apparently developed a great ardor for funerals. The vase paintings suggest hair tearing, and forehead and breast beating, along with shrieks and ululations. Despite the curtailment of their funerary activities, women were probably made to feel that they were carrying out a necessary and valued social function, and this satisfaction may explain the popularity of sepulchral rituals. Proper burial was a matter of intense concern, to a degree that is hard to imagine in our modern, death-denying society. Antigone's legendary determination to inter her brother's corpse was raised to heroic proportion in both Aeschylus' *Seven Against Thebes* and Sophocles' *Antigone*. The plot of Sophocles' *Ajax* also hinges on whether or not a character will be buried with due honors. One of the motivations behind the strong drive toward the continuation of the hearth, or *oikos*, was the desire to maintain the ancestral tombs, and to have one's own tomb cultivated by future generations.

## The Dead Women of Fifth-Century Athens

From fifth-century Athens we have numerous beautiful grave steles with portraits of women in low relief. Not all of them had died in childbirth. Figure 129 shows a characteristic tombstone of a woman without an infant. When a survey of the entire genre is possible, it may emerge that women are numerically better represented in the fifth-century graveyards of Athens than men. Different conclusions could be and have been drawn from the frequency of these monuments: it could indicate that women died young, since those who did were more likely to have survivors to erect monuments to them, or that women were especially honored during this period, or that the men were more likely to die in war, the women at home. The demographic implications of these tombstones have yet to be studied. At any rate, the pious inference that monuments, even those erected by husbands, imply good marriages is to be rejected as wishful and naïve.

In contrast to the individualization of hetaera portraits, to be

127. Funerary vessel with
women bewailing a
corpse.

128. Deceased woman with bridal tiara

129. Grave stele of Polyxena:
in death she has a name.

stressed in Chapter 6, these sepulchral images lack signs of character. In the ideal Attic conception, "respectable" women were beautiful, elegant, and eternally young, but they were granted as little personality in death as they had in life. Many of the women of Classical Athens, however, after dying acquired something that had been denied them during life—that is, names (Figure 129).

# 6

# The Athenian Prostitute: A Good Buy in the Agora

> You, Solon, saw the city full of young men, under the pressure of a natural need, and going off the track in disreputable ways. So you bought up women and set them up in various places to be used in common, ready and primped for all. So there they stand, all naked, so you don't get fooled, all's there for you to see. Perhaps you don't feel so well, or have some sorrow: the door is open, one obol and in you jump. No prudery, no nonsense, no rejection. You get laid right away, which is what you want, and in any manner you wish. Once you have come out, you tell her to go to hell, she's a stranger to you now.
> —Fragment of a comedy by Philemon, Ath. (13, 569e–f)

> We've come together, a party of men with huge erections, and when we feel sexy, we strike and strangle whom we please.
> —Demosthenes, *Against Conon* (20, 54, 20)

Male and female prostitution was an uncommonly lively trade in Classical Athens and in its harbor, Piraeus. Scholars have lavished a great deal of imagination on this prominent feature of Attic society, in efforts to reconcile it with their ideal views of the Greeks as noble, refined, and gentle. One school of thought glorifies the Greek courtesan, or hetaera—literally, "female companion"—as a free and cultivated spirit, a match for men's wit and education. Here is how the feminist-oriented Wright describes the prostitutes of Athens:

> Often highly educated, it was their business to take part in all men's interests; they were their own mistresses, engaged freely in the political life of Athens, and in many cases exercised very great influence even in affairs of state. (62)

In his study of the sex life in Classical Greece, the French scholar Chevalier de Roton, who published under the pseudonym of Gabriel

Notor, looked at both prostitutes and wives through the rosy mist of his (no doubt tasteful) experience as a French aristocrat and *galant*. In his view the wives of Athens were sensuous odalisques, spending their days perfuming and beautifying themselves in expectation of nights of love with their husbands, and the city's hetaerai were creatures of charm and culture, exercising control over their own lives. Both reconstructions are equally far off the mark.

Another, more conventional, school of classicists has scourged the whores of Athens posthumously as a disease of society, a view upheld with regard to many other societies as well. Puritans always blame the women and not their customers; and even in non-Puritan cultures, prostitution is one of the rare service industries in which the customers regularly denigrate the purveyor. (The only parallel that readily comes to mind is the Hindu untouchable, who had the unenviable task of removing human excretions.) The voluminous literature on the history of prostitution in the Western world teems with pejoratives, and generally represents it as a female cancer which attacks a basically wholesome male civic body. With German being so rich in invective, scholarship in that language has been especially free in the use of such descriptive terms as *Seuche* (contagious disease) and *Laster* (evil of sin). One German scholar, who presumably had looked deeply into the souls of Athenian prostitutes, declared, "One could write volumes on the worthlessness and depravity of these creatures" (Birt, 109). If such an attitude is of questionable validity in the examination of the free practice of prostitution—a trade occasioned by male demand—it is wholly inappropriate to the ancient Greek world, in which most of the prostitutes were slaves, completely deprived of will or choice. In more recent societies, social stigma has been one device for preventing prostitutes and their entrepreneurs from translating their often very profitable business into influence and social status. In Greek society, prostitutes were no threat to the social norms, since they were irrevocably outside them. We know of hardly any women of the citizen class who practiced the trade. (Homosexual prostitution, discussed in Chapter 11, was another matter.) Accordingly, we find few expressions of social censure of the profession. The ownership and exploitation of whores and brothels was a reputable form of business, practiced by citizens of good standing. Theophrastus, for example, lists brothel ownership as an ordinary trade, along with innkeeping and tax collection (*Char.* 6, 5).

### The Guest-Loving Girls of Corinth

The city of Athens and its port, Piraeus, were outdone in liveliness of prostitution only by Corinth, which had been a prosperous center of marine trade since Homeric times. A good deal of anecdotal lore sprang up around the fabled whores of Corinth, who were owned by the sanctuary of Aphrodite; as in many other cities, they were sacred slaves (*hierodules*).

According to Strabo, there were more than a thousand of them, which may be an exaggeration (8, 6, 20). The proverbial saying "Not every man has the luck to sail to Corinth" has been variously interpreted, but it is best taken to mean that such an excursion was both desirable and expensive (*ibid.*). An amusing anecdote, which Strabo probably took from one of the collections of witticisms attributed to prostitutes, tells of a Corinthian courtesan who was reproached for being lazy and refusing to do wool working. In her bawdy reply she punned on the word *histos*, which can refer to anything erectable, including a loom: "Yet such as I am, in this short time I have taken down three looms [erections] already." Figure 130 shows the inside of a Corinthian dish, made in the first half of the sixth century B.C., with two attractive young girls, whose names are inscribed. The plate probably celebrates two of the more popular prostitutes of their day.

130. The Corinthian prostitutes Neuris and Glyka.

In the year 464, a rich Corinthian by the name of Xenophon (no kin to the Attic author) competed for an Olympic prize. He had vowed that, in the case of his victory, he would donate a hundred prostitutes to the sanctuary. He did win, and bought up a hundred young women, who were thus doomed to spend their lives in the triple degradation of being females, slaves, and prostitutes. In honor of Xenophon's good fortune, the poet Pindar composed an ode (*Olympians*, 13) in which nothing is said about the whores; but a fragment of another poem, which was perhaps rejected by the victor, celebrates his sexual largesse. In the appropriately flowery translation of Sir John Sandys it says,

> Guest-loving girls! Servants of Suasion in wealthy Corinth! Ye that burn the golden tears of fresh frankincense, full often soaring upward in your souls unto Aphrodite, the heavenly mother of Loves. She hath granted you, ye girls, blamelessly to cull on lovely couches the blossom of delicate bloom; for under force, all things are fair. (Fr. 130)

We have no knowledge of the conditions prevailing in the brothels of Corinth and Athens, but there is no reason to assume that they were any more commodious than the dark and stinking holes in which Roman whores practiced their trade, and of which Roman authors have left us descriptions. Among the numerous Greek words for "harlot" a common one is "earth striker" (*chamaitype*), which indicates that many girls culled the blossoms of delicate bloom not on lovely couches but on the bare ground. In Pompeii the brothel buildings (*lupanaria*) are equipped with built-in stone beds, which, one presumes, were at least covered with pads or cushions.

## The Story of Neaera

Before turning to the vase paintings, which tell the story of Athenian prostitution best, we can profit by a close look at the extraordinary tale of the courtesan Neaera. Contained in Pseudo-Demosthenes' speech *Against Neaera*, it indubitably derives from the latter part of the fourth century B.C. and provides a uniquely detailed account of life on the fringe of Attic society; we have nothing else remotely like it from any Classical source. Neaera is accused of concealing her true status, which is that of a prostitute and former slave, and passing herself off as a respectable Athenian citizen. The accusers make it clear, however, that their real target is not the woman, but Stephanus, her most recent keeper, who had passed her off as his wife.

Neaera was bought as a little girl, along with six others, by one Nicarete, a freedwoman, who made her living as a brothel keeper. There seems to have been a lively trade in girl babies, most of them probably foundlings. Nicarete had "a good eye for the potential of little children" (18) and was also skilled in training them. She called them her daughters, so as to be able to charge more for them. Soon Neaera was "working with her body" (22), although she had not yet reached the proper age; in other words, she became what Aristophanes (Fr. 141) calls a "not-yet-maiden-harlot" (*hypoparthenos hetaera*). The fact that there was a term for this category of prostitutes shows that the practice was not uncommon. Most Greek dictionaries camouflage this unsavory custom by translating the phrase as "demi-vierge"—that is, a woman who behaves lewdly but preserves her anatomical virginity. The fact that Neaera ate and drank with men is stressed to prove that she was a prostitute (24). The girl must have been extremely desirable, because her owner, Nicarete, moved with her to Corinth, the very home of prostitution, and was able to reap a great deal of profit from her. Rather than pay Nicarete for each visit, two of Neaera's customers decided it was cheaper to purchase her outright for their joint use, as was not uncommon. They paid thirty minas (3000 drachmas). It is difficult to assess the buying power of that sum, but Demosthenes tells of a male slave bought for only two minas (41, 22). Nicarete had made a good investment. When Neaera's new owners decided to get married, they wanted her out of town, and offered her her freedom at only twenty minas, on condition that she would leave Corinth. Whether this was an act of kindness or a reflection of her diminished value is not clear. Neaera was able to raise the money through donations from various lovers. The Athenian Phrynion, who had made the largest contribution, took her back to Athens with him as a free woman.

Phrynion's treatment of Neaera illuminates Athenian sex habits, especially when considered together with a number of vase paintings. He took her to eating and drinking parties with him, and to "revels" (*komoi*), and openly made love to her in the presence of others (33). At one particularly lavish feast, given by one Chabrias, a victor in the Pythian games, Phrynion and Neaera had too much to drink and several men, including some of the host's slaves, had intercourse with her while he was asleep. After that Phrynion treated her churlishly and "did not love her as she thought" (35). As a result Neaera left him, taking along her gifts from Phrynion (clothes, jewelry, and two female slaves), and also some of his property. She set up business in the provincial town of Megara, but did not fare well there, so after a few years she returned to Athens under the protection of a new keeper, the Stephanus who was the adversary of the two prosecutors. Meanwhile Neaera had acquired three children, two sons and a daughter; later in the account (121) a third son is mentioned. Under the guidance of Stephanus, Neaera practiced not only prostitution but also an extortion scheme: blackmailing well-to-do foreign customers, who were made to believe they had committed adultery with an Athenian citizen's wife. According to the prosecution's account, Stephanus and Neaera together not only raised the latter's children, but they passed off her daughter as a legitimate citizen and married her off twice to respectable (if apparently dimwitted) Athenian men. Neaera's old lover Phrynion reappeared on the scene but was easily appeased with the return of his stolen property and the enjoyment of Neaera's favors on alternate days. We don't know what happened to Neaera or Stephanus: if found guilty, she could have been sold back into slavery. Stephanus, if convicted of passing off aliens as his wife and daughter, stood to lose his entire estate and civic rights (52).

## Whores and Hetaerai in Daily Life

The scene of bordello-based whores lined up for inspection by customers, as described in the fragment by Philemon cited at the head of this chapter, is a common feature of organized prostitution. It is also an apt metaphor for all societies in which men control the economic means and hence the bodies of women.

We have no Greek picture of such a line-up, nor any scene that can securely be located inside a brothel or pimp's establishment. The motif of the customer inspecting the merchandise, however, is not wanting in Greek art. In Figure 131 a man peeks under the skirt of a young prostitute. The woman in Figure 132 is displaying her bared body to a mature customer leaning on a stick. The gesture he makes probably indicates that he is trying to get her price down.

If the brothels, bawdyhouses, and independent hookers who

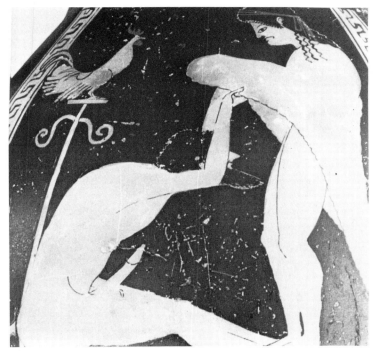

131. Man lifting woman's dress.

132. Prostitute displaying her body and man negotiating.

hunted for customers around the Agora and at the gates of Athens constituted universal features of prostitution, the trade there had social aspects that were unique. In the first place, sex with prostitutes had the kind of sanction it rarely acquires in highly organized societies. Figures 133 and 134 show a late-sixth-century water jar. The belly of the vase shows two youths receiving a music lesson from a seated instructor. The standing figure on the left may be the father, who is seeing how his sons are doing. In Figure 134, the shoulder of the same vase shows two hetaerai reclining on couches, with drinking cups—a typical symposium scene. By juxtaposing illustrations of a schoolroom and a drinking party, this water jug seems to suggest that as the former was to the Athenian boy's intellect, the latter was to his social faculties. In the symposium, a youth probably had his first heterosexual experience, with the help of a slave prostitute. Yet this aspect of the drinking party has been neglected by students of Greek civilization, because it is documented only in vase paintings.

## The Game of Kottabos

The girls in Figure 134 are playing the game called *kottabos,* in which players aim drops of wine from their cups at plates perched on stands, or at the cups of other participants. We don't know the exact rules of the game, but it is clear that the winners normally received sexual favors as prizes. Here the inscription over the heads of the hetaerai reads, "To you, beautiful Euthymides, I dedicate this throw." The joke seems to be that here, for once, the hetaerai, who are young and desirable, have *their* choice of sex partners. In a fragment of Old Comedy there is talk of playing *kottabos* for shoes and drinking cups but also for kisses.

## Sex and the Symposium

The symposium was the most characteristic feature of Athenian sexual and social life. Literally meaning "drinking party," it was a unique gathering, dedicated to a varying blend of eating, drinking, games of all sorts, philosophical discourse, and public sex with prostitutes, concubines, and other men, but never with wives. Demosthenes described this pastime for men as "revelry, sex and drinking" (47, 19). The prostitutes who frequented such gatherings

133. Boys at their music lesson.

134. Shoulder detail of 133. Youthful
hetaerai playing *kottabos*.

135. Ritual group sex.

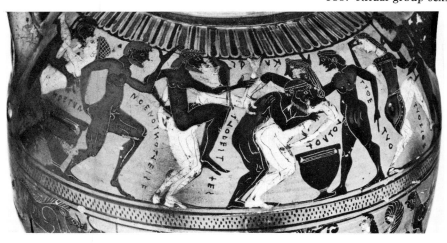

were probably in the main the more refined ones, known as hetaerai.

The origins of the symposium are not clear. A group of vases made in Athens during the Archaic age which are called "Tyrrhenian" (Etruscan), because many of them were found in the part of Italy once inhabited by Etruscans, roughly coinciding with modern Tuscany, show men and women engaging in what appears to be ritual group sex, both homosexual and heterosexual. One example of such a vase is to be seen in Figures 135 and 136. The detail of the copulating heterosexual pair in Figure 136 shows a frontal approach with, as far as one can tell, mutual cooperation. However, the group practices that these vases represent are too obscure and too isolated to provide much food for speculation on their relation to fifth-century usages at Athens.

The private symposium was so characteristic a part of Athenian life that many facets of Greek culture would be incomprehensible if it were not taken into account. The comedy of Aristophanes, for example, displays the same blend of obscenity, lavatory humor, serious and even doctrinaire opinion, and playfulness that characterized the symposium. It is not without cause that Plato brings on the playwright in his dialogue called *The Symposium*. The Platonic dialogues themselves are, in a way, "social comedies," just as much as they are statements of long-pondered philosophy. The fact that hetaerai participated in some of these events gave them a foot in the door of male society, although one may doubt that their status was greatly enhanced by the privilege.

The symposia normally took place in the men's quarters (*andrones*) of private houses. Our knowledge of the layout and appointments of Athenian private homes from the Classical age is limited. In the first place, they were strikingly modest. Second, of course, the modern cities of Athens and Piraeus cover the ancient residential areas. Still, a general pattern has emerged from excavation and reconstruction. The *andron* was essentially a dining room, archaeologically identifiable because it contained raised podiums of plaster or stone on which the dining couches (*klinai*) stood. Men and hetaerai reclined on these for eating and drinking, and the same *klinai* served for sleeping and sex, a domestically economical arrangement. Respectable women also used this type of couch to sleep on, but reclining on them for eating or drinking was apparently taboo for wives and daughters. The dining room was entered through a vestibule, which was directly accessible from the street,

136. Detail of 135: sex without hostility.

so that guests could come and go without disturbing the women's part of the household. Not surprisingly, the *andron* complex was usually the largest and most luxurious part of the house, and often the only one to have floors covered with mosaics. It formed an intermediate zone between the private domain of the household and the public arena of civic buildings and squares where men spent most of their lives. The hetaerai, like the *androines* into which they were invited, were neither quite private nor quite public, and bridged the artificial chasm in men's lives between home and the life of the polis.

A fragment of a comedy by Plato (the playwright, not to be confused with the philosopher) gives some idea of the routine procedure at a symposium (Fr. 72). The dinner is over, and waiters remove the tables and food crumbs and bring in water for washing hands. Now the drinking party begins. While the revelers pour a solemn libation to the gods, a female musician is warming up on the double flute, and slaves set up the *kottabos* equipment. The wine for the guests is mixed with water. While they are getting inebriated, the banqueters sing catchy songs and play *kottabos.* Then the slaves remove the *kottabos* stands, and the party turns to the musical entertainment offered by the flute girl and a harp player.

As the vase paintings make clear, women who were hired for such occasions provided not only sex and music but various other kinds of entertainment as well. The hetaera clad in an animal hide in Figure 137 is dancing to the flute playing of a young man; she may be playing a Maenad. The fourth-century wine krater in Figure 138 shows men at a symposium being entertained by a woman who is either singing or reciting. She wears an elaborately embroidered gown, which suggests that she is giving a kind of stage performance. Quasi-theatrical recitations may well have been part of the symposium life, and this practice might explain why tragedies were

137. Hetaera with *krotala* and
flute-playing youth in *komos.*

remembered over the generations, without, as far as we know, being regularly revived on the public stage.

## The Symposium Cup

The characteristic drinking cup for symposia was the kylix, a shallow, two-handled cup with a short stem (Figure 140). Most of the illustrations we have of symposium practices, and most of the Greek art which by our standards is considered "pornographic," appear on cups of this type. The scenes of copulation and other "obscenities" depicted on symposium cups have led to the view that the Greeks lacked prudery and were free of the censorious restrictions which govern sex life in the Judaeo-Christian tradition. This conclusion, however, is not correct. The moral sphere of the symposium and its figured pottery was one of limited permissiveness, for men only. The utensils for the symposium were probably stored in the men's part of the house, and their decorations clearly were not fashioned for the eyes of women and children.

The great age of kylix production occurred at the end of the sixth century B.C. and in the first decades of the fifth. Several of the finest early red-figure painters, such as Douris and Makron, favored this kind of vase, depicting banquet and sexual encounters, either in a spirit of good-humored satire or with great, even cruel, realism. Some other great artists, such as the Penthesileia Painter, liked the round inside space (tondo) of the kylix, because it is almost flat and lends itself to intricate draftsmanship.

Figure 139 illustrates the lascivious associations of the symposium cup. The vase itself is a kantharos, the drinking cup with tall handles used in the rituals of Dionysus. It features a reclining hetaera, holding up a symposium cup to a mule with a large erection, and offering him not only a sip of wine but her sexual favors as well. Figure 140 shows a kylix with a rather rare scene, hetaerai at a symposium without men. Two of them hold musical instruments, showing, as literary texts also do, that musical entertainment was as much an element of the prostitute's services as sex. Apparently only the lowest level of this complicated hierarchy "worked with the body only": they were the "earth pounders" and the "plodding heifers." The training by which the madam Nicarete increased the value of her girls probably consisted primarily of music and dancing. As a character in a fragment of Old Comedy said, "Already I've

138.
Symposium scene
with woman in
theatrical costume.

139.
Woman offering wine
and sex to a mule.

140.
Banqueting hetaerai with
symposium cups and musical
instruments.

told you of dancers, hetaerai alas young no more; now let me tell you of barely budding flute girls, who in no time for pay make the knees of sailors give way" (Metagenes, Fr. 4). Figures 141 and 142 reproduce a drinking cup by Makron with a favorite theme, hetaerai and their customers negotiating. The scene is painted on the outside

141. Men with money negotiating with hetaerai.

142. Same as 141, other side. Men without money negotiating with hetaerai.

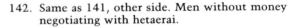

of the rim. The humor here is that the men on one side have the wherewithal: they hold purses in their left hands and flowers in their right. The men on the other side, however, have to make do with persuasion. The one on the right seems successful in establishing credit: his right hand, which also holds a flower, gesticulates and his woman smiles as she holds out a wreath. The man leaning on his walking stick on the left is apparently not as fortunate: he is empty-handed and his lady, while brandishing a flower in his face, has turned away from him and is walking off.

Figures 143 and 144 show a symposium cup portraying four men at a banquet with four naked hetaerai. The striking aspect of this scene is that three mature, bearded men consort with very young, almost boyish-looking, girls, with trim figures and closely cropped hair. The one youth in the party, on the other hand, keeps company with a mature woman of opulent shape, whose hair is caught up in a matronly snood. The portrayal of older prostitutes on drinking cups, sometimes with stark realism, is one of the curious aspects of this type of vase. Greek artists generally did not depict the marks of age in women unless they were of particular significance. The appearance of an aging hetaera in this scene and others has something to tell us. We noted before that the symposium played a part in the sexual indoctrination of the young man. His contact with older prostitutes, here so emphatically brought out, seems to have served to liberate him from any vestige of awe of his mother and the other female authority figures of his childhood, which he might still be carrying around from his early years in the women's quarters.

Figure 145 reveals that the characteristic Greek disregard for physical comfort extended to sexual activity as well: the narrow *kline* apparently was covered by an even narrower cushion, so that the man's knees protrude from it on the sides. Figures 146 and 147 reveal other entertainment customary at symposia. In Figure 146, a cup by the Brygos Painter, a young hetaera called Kallisto—probably a professional name, since it means "most beautiful"—dances as her customer taps out the rhythm on his knee and sings; his flute lies idle in his left hand. In Figure 147 four naked women, artfully arranged around the rim of the kylix, seem to be giving a kind of acrobatic performance.

143. Bearded men feasting with young hetaerai.

144. Same as 143. Youth with older hetaera and bearded man with young one.

## Primping Hetaerai

Hetaerai at their toilette is another favorite motif of the vase painters, sometimes drawn with humor and sometimes seriously. Figure 148 is a satirical treatment of a naked woman. The not very shapely lady, standing at a wash basin, is looking at herself in a hand mirror with satisfaction. Her sagging breasts are propped up with a band, or brassiere. In Figure 149 a hetaera is urinating into a chamber pot. Figure 150 features two hetaerai, presumably preparing themselves for the activities of the evening. One notes the oil flask, or alabastron, in the hands of one, an object of which the sexual connotations have already been observed, although it is far

145. Affectionate, if uncomfortable, sex.

more characteristic of domestic scenes with wives. For the picture in Figure 151, a female homoerotic interpretation has been suggested; more probably, however, it represents one hetaera anointing another.

## The Revelry, or Komos

As fundamental to the symposium as the event itself was the

146. Youthful hetaera and customer
with double flute.

147.
Stylized composition
of naked hetaerai.

148.
Aging hetaera primping.

149.
Hetaera urinating
into chamber pot.

150.
Hetaerai at their
toilette.

151.
Hetaerai at their
toilette.

*komos*, the festive procession of revelers to the drinking party or from one house to another. In Plato's *Symposium* (212) Alcibiades staggers into the dining room drunk, supported by a flute girl and accompanied by other revelers; clearly he is arriving from another symposium. *Komoi*, with and without hetaerai and flute girls, are represented on many vases—most of them, understandably, symposium cups. Frequently participants carry such a kylix in one hand, evidently for a sip along the way. The *komos* was a musical event, involving lyre and flute music and singing, and stylized dance steps. In its coarser forms, it was probably the occasion of the violence with which symposium life is associated.

The revelry on the outside of a cup by the Brygos Painter in Figure 152 could serve as an illustration of the arrival of the drunk Alcibiades. The revelers on the cup by Douris in Figure 153 seem slightly older and more intent on executing graceful dance steps. Where hetaerai are included in the procession, other than the flute girls who were surely also available for sexual purposes, they range from the elegantly attired courtesans on the lovely cup by the Brygos Painter in Figure 154 to the naked and defenseless woman in Figure 155. In the latter, much coarser, scene, the young man on the right carries a wineskin rather than the elegant kylix. He is sexually aroused and accosts the fleeing woman from behind. The man on the left is older and not as fortunate. He carries a stick, which implies, as subsequent illustrations will show, that he will soon brutalize the hetaera and force her to practice *fellatio* on him.

## The Humiliation and Abuse of Prostitutes

It is clear that a form of sexual contact as habitual and free from societal restraint as that between Athenian youths and prostitutes inevitably led to a great variety of human relationships. In the literature and monuments of the age we find evidence for behavior ranging from the coarsest exploitation to affection and mutual accommodation. In the following chapters some of the evidence for a kindly and even amorous rapport between citizens and prostitutes will be cited, but it is obvious that in the relations of Athenians with bought women of all classes the advantage was with the male all the way: his were the privileges of free status, citizenship, money, class, and gender. Male power was such an obvious point that one would not expect the vase painters to stress it in their pictures of

152. Typical revelry with flute girl and hetaerai.

153. A more dignified revelry without women.

154.
Elaborately dressed hetaerai
in revelry.

sexual encounters between men and hetaerai. Yet many vase paintings show the abuse and battering of women, as well as other forms of male supremacist behavior.

Actual copulation of men with hetaerai is frequently represented, especially on the flat inside surface of the kylix. In the greater number of instances, the man has intercourse with his partner from behind, probably with anal penetration, although this is not clear in all instances. The women in such scenes are steadying themselves in a variety of poses requiring practice and some athletic skill, but otherwise the scheme is repetitious. Figures 156, 157, 158, and 159 show four variations on this theme of female submission to penetration from the rear, the first three on drinking cups. The cruder scene on a pitcher in Figure 159, for one, leaves no doubt that anal sex is portrayed. The baskets suspended overhead in Figures 144 and 158 are a standard reference to a dinner party: they allude to the practice of guests bringing a contribution of food to a "pot-luck party" (eranos). Although there is rare reference in literature to prostitutes servicing their clients by "riding" them (keletismos), this position is to my knowledge not shown on Greek vases, in striking contrast to Roman art which depicts it frequently.

The pictures of men making love to hetaerai from the back have led to the view that this was the Athenians' favorite position for heterosexual intercourse. The vase paintings, however, do not necessarily prove this. Most of such scenes occur on the inside of drinking cups. The inside of a cup often portrays the relaxation of the tensions to which the decoration of the outside alludes. The symposium served, at least in part, to develop male supremacist behavior in youths. Intercourse from the rear, and especially anal intercourse, was conceived as humiliating to the recipient, and hence a suitable culmination of initiatory sex.

These attitudes are confirmed by the humble but revealing wine bottle (askos) reproduced in Figure 160. The askos is a translation in terra cotta of a squat leather bottle. On its fairly flat upper surface both sides can be seen at the same time—a natural place for a painter to portray antithetical or complementary themes. In this example we see on each side what appears to be the same man, with a rather large nose, making love to two different women. The one in the lower scene is young and trim: he is making love to her from the front, in the "missionary" position. The prostitute in the upper scene is older; her stomach sags, and she looks toothless. Her

155.
A coarser form of revelry:
men molesting a naked hetaera.

156. Man and prostitute, dorsal sex.

157. Man and cooperative
prostitute, dorsal sex.

158. Man and prostitute, dorsal sex.

159. Man and prostitute, anal sex.

160. Man with younger and with older prostitute: frontal and dorsal sex.

customer is penetrating her from behind, anally. The implication is clear: frontal copulation is the more refined method, reserved for desirable women, whereas sex from behind is less considerate and probably degrading.

A note of censure against anal intercourse in marriage is to be detected in Herodotus, who reports that a certain man had intercourse with his wife "unlawfully" because he did not wish to father children (1, 61). We will return to the animalistic associations of anal sex in connection with male homoerotism in Athens, but I will briefly point here to the motif of sodomy with animals, the topic of several coarse pictorial jokes indirectly implying reproof. Most of these concern the deportment of satyrs. In Figure 161, however, a man is depicted penetrating a startled-looking doe.

Another pictorial way of expressing man's "upper hand" in his relationships with women is the addition to any scene of a money pouch, an iconographic symbol which, in my opinion, has been misunderstood. A money pouch frequently appears in pictures in

161. Man penetrating doe.

which men are bargaining for the services of prostitutes, of which we saw an example on the symposium cup in Figure 141. In the scene of copulation with a prostitute in Figure 162 the money pouch is shown as a peripheral attribute; perhaps it is meant to be hanging on the wall. It establishes, of course, the fact that the man is paying for his sex, but this communication is, in truth, superfluous: no one with any understanding of Greek social customs would suppose that this picture shows a man and his wife. Then why the addition of the money bag? The symbolic value of the pouch in vase painting is that of an "economic phallus"; it underscores the point that the man has the financial power as well as all other forms of supremacy (Chapter 9).

Humiliation of a different kind is depicted in Figure 163, a very curious scene of which the exact interpretation is not certain. It shows a youth in the characteristic symposium pose; the typical food basket is hanging overhead. A youthful hetaera dressed only in a snake bracelet kneels before him and kisses his outstretched hand. On the left stands a young boy with sandal marks on his back: someone has given him a thrashing. Had the hetaera been discovered punishing the young boy for competing with her for the master's sexual attentions? At any rate, she is pleading with her customer for forgiveness.

## The Battering of Prostitutes with Sticks and Sandals

A number of vase paintings show men beating hetaerai with various objects. At least two of these involve older hetaerai who are coerced to perform a sexual service which was apparently regarded as more repugnant than intercourse—namely, *fellatio*. In other cases the reason for the physical violence is not clear, nor is it evident whether the motif of the battering of sex partners was conceived as humorous or satirical. Figure 164 shows a man about to beat an undefending hetaera on the buttocks with a shoe; another man, who approaches from the left, seems to be protesting. In the similar composition in Figure 165 the aggressor is hiding the sandal behind his back and pretends he is about to caress the girl.

Two symposium cups, each of them only partially preserved, illustrate with brutal realism the forcible coercion of resisting hetaerai. Figure 166 shows the surviving portion of a symposium cup by the Pedieus Painter. On the right a plump hetaera is kneeling on the floor. The youth in front of her is thrusting his huge penis into her mouth, wrinkling her cheeks. Another man is copulating with her from behind, as is indicated by a hand shown on her back. The copulator's other hand, perhaps, is meant to be propped against a wall. In the center a woman is lying crosswise over a couch. She is obediently doing service to the penis of the youth in front of her, while a bearded man penetrates her anally from the rear. He is brandishing a shoe or sandal in his right hand to make sure the woman will not interfere with the consummation of this uncomfortable scheme.

The crassest illustration of the motif of men battering prostitutes into submission to their specific desires comes from the hand of the Brygos Painter. The symposium cup in Florence illustrated in Figures 167–170 features several scenes of men coercing women with violence. On the more fragmentary side in Figure 170 a hetaera, again rather plump, is bending over; a man behind her holds her by the hair with one hand and beats her with a sandal with the other; evidently she had refused to practice *fellatio* on the prancing man in front of her. The other side of the cup, Figure 167,

162. Customer and prostitute: a money pouch hanging on the wall.

is better preserved. The grouping on the left (detail in Figure 168) consists of a standing man with a huge erection, a hetaera stooping to reach for his penis with her mouth, and a bearded man copulating with her anally. The woman's close-cropped hair indicates that she is a slave. Her body is lumpy and sagging, and the manner in which she bends over conveys the stiffness of middle age. In the fragmentary scene on the far right a man has lifted a girl off the ground; her legs are slung over his shoulder. A piece of a flute case can be made out; this figure is probably a young flute player, hence the greater agility. The clothed man on the far right holds an oil lamp, indicating the scene is set at night. As shown in detail in Figure 169, the kneeling woman in the center is the most pathetic female figure in Classical art published so far. Heavy-set, she has a lovely but matronly face and the short haircut of a slave, topped by a banqueter's wreath. She is crouching on the ground; a garlanded, bearded man with a large erection is approaching her from the front, trying to thrust his penis into her mouth. The garment he holds in his left hand is probably hers: perhaps he has just stripped it off. With his right hand he brandishes a stick. The hetaera looks startled, and is making pleading gestures with both hands. It appears unlikely, however, that she will be able to hold out much longer.

The Florence cup most clearly illustrates the aspect of symposium life that I have interpreted as the "defeat of the mother image." Did the Brygos Painter, one of the most skilled artists of his time, create it in a spirit of criticism, or was he merely being realistic? I would not presume to say, but as shown by the passage from Demosthenes at the head of this chapter, sexual violence was an integral part of the symposium and Athenian society had a high degree of tolerance for it. One of the hazards of prostitution in general is the potential abuse by the customers to which the women are exposed. The Athenian slave hetaerai, on hire by the hour or by the night from their pimps and brothel keepers, obviously had no defense whatsoever. Even Neaera, it will be remembered, despite the presence of her protector Phrynion, was raped by a number of men during a symposium.

163. Boy with sandal markings and prostitute kissing man's hand. Scene of rivalry?

164. Man about to beat prostitute. Man on left protests.

165. Man with concealed stick approaching prostitute.

166. Man coerces older prostitutes to practice fellatio and submit to anal sex at the same time.

167. Man and older prostitutes.

168.
Detail of 167: compliant prostitute practicing fellatio as another man penetrates her dorsally.

169.
Detail of 167: man threatening disobedient prostitute with a stick.

170. Same as 167, other side. Men battering bent-over prostitute.

# 7

# The Whore with the Golden Heart, the Happy Hooker, and Other Fictions

> . . . meeting a hetaera who lived in a neighbor's house he fell
> in love with her. She was a citizen, but without guardian or
> relatives. A character of gold she had, full of goodness, a real
> companion.
> —Fragment of the comedy *The Waterjug* by Antiphanes (212)

The orator Lysias fell in love with the slave prostitute Metaneira, who, like Neaera in Chapter 6, was in the stable of the brothel keeper Nicarete. Wishing to give the girl a lasting present that would not fall into the hands of her owner, Lysias had her initiated in the Eleusinian mysteries even though, in order to do so, he had to make travel and lodging arrangements for Nicarete and Neaera as well: the shrewd madam apparently did not let her best investments out of sight for long. In the last chapter we saw that Neaera, too, had a paramour and enlisted the good will of several of her other keepers. Relations in which the man had some feeling for a hetaera were likely to lead to common-law marriage or concubinage. In fact, many Athenian men seem to have wound up later in life with such an arrangement. By cruel irony, this relation, the most likely to be based on something resembling harmony and mutual affection, was also the one in which the powerhold of man over woman was the most absolute (Chapter 10).

A vast amount of anecdotal and literary lore developed around the careers of prostitutes and their variegated relationships with men. Of course, these stories tell us more about the psychology of the men who developed and transmitted them than about the actuality of prostitutes' lives. A rich anthology of men's views of Athenian whores is contained in the thirteenth book of Athenaeus'

*Deipnosophistai* (a title sometimes translated as *Doctors at Dinner* and sometimes as *Table Talk*). The fictitious occasion for the recital of these quotations and anecdotes was, of course, a symposium. Numerous titles of works on women (mainly on prostitutes) and many quotations from Classical stage plays now lost have been preserved in this late work, so we owe its author a debt of gratitude.

## The Affectionate Prostitute

Prostitution is sordid business at best. It makes for unhealthful working hours, it exposes women to disease, unwanted pregnancies, and the violence of men, and it involves a great deal of simulation of feelings. Where it is the only independent profession open to women, it can afford them the dignity of controlling their own destiny, and it has acquired a certain glamour for that reason among some feminists. It can, however, hardly be said to be naturally conducive to kindness or generosity, or to be in any way civilizing in its effect. Yet the whore with the noble character is a cliché of modern literature and dramatic arts. *Irma la Douce, Madame Rosa*, and *The World of Suzie Wong* are a few recent instances of the sentimentalization of mercenary sex. The stereotype can be traced back to Classical Greece, at least as far as the fourth-century playwright Menander, and perhaps further.

Although customers at times become attached to prostitutes, the institution does not provide much opportunity for selection on the part of the women: simulation is part of their craft. The Roman playwright Plautus, who was far from sentimental, did not have much use for brothel keepers and created in his plays some stark scenes of the brutalization of slave prostitutes by their owners (see, for example, his *Pseudolus*, 1, 2). In his *Asinaria* a mother, who is prostituting her daughter, says to the girl, "You must pretend that you are in love; for if you really loved, you would think of your lover and not of yourself" (1, 1). Fifth-century vase painters, on the other hand, not infrequently conveyed the impression of mutual attraction or even tenderness between customer and prostitute, notions far removed from the formal and stylized interaction of men and women in domestic scenes. Figure 171 is a celebrated vase painting by the Brygos Painter. A young slave hetaera is tenderly holding the head of a youth who is vomiting, presumably from too much drinking. Though she is fully dressed, she was a participant

171.
Young hetaera comforts
vomiting customer.

172. Kindly prostitute and older customer.

in the symposium, since her hair is garlanded. A cup painted by the artist Onesimos gives a sympathetic picture of a rather homely hetaera (Figure 172): she is still clothed, and her chunky outline is unglamorous. She has entertained her customer with lyre music; the instrument is lying on the ground on the left. She is about to untie her belt in order to bed down with her customer, who is also long beyond the age of beauty. The hetaera has a kindly, smiling face, and the entire picture suggests a civilized arrangement. In Figure 173 a girl is about to serve a customer who is seated on a chair in a condition of obvious readiness. The youth and woman are making eye contact, the vase painters' iconographic scheme denoting "emotional relationship."

The exchange of kisses and embraces is also not uncommon,

173.
Prostitute and customer
as amorous pair.

indicating that at least a certain display of affection was part of hetaera life. One painter even had a predeliction for such scenes, and therefore has acquired the name Kiss Painter. On the inside of this artist's name cup a man and a girl are about to kiss (Figure 174). Although the hetaera is small of build, she has reached puberty; the representation of the prepubescent prostitutes attested in literature was apparently too crass for the vase painters, as was the realistic portrayal of the barely pubescent brides.

An unusual grouping is featured on the water jug in Figures 175 and 176. In the center a youth is meeting with a young girl. She greets him with a warm embrace, while he is "feeling her up." On the left stands another youth: his cloak and walking stick indicate that he, too, has just arrived from outside. In front of him stands a mature woman. To the right of the embracing couple another matronly figure holds a small hand loom in her left hand; the decoration of this vase is one of many that combine elements of prostitution with those of textile working. All three supernumerary figures watch the embracing couple; apparently the scene represents the cordial reception of a regular customer, not an encounter of a bride and groom, as experts have thought. How far this behavior is removed from notions of what is proper matrimonial conduct may be seen in Plutarch's essay *Precepts for Conjugal Life:* "it is shameful to embrace and kiss and caress each other in the presence of others" (*Mor.* 139e).

## The Noble Prostitute on the Stage

Most of the painted pottery with hetaerai scenes was produced during the late sixth and the early fifth centuries B.C. The spirit of satire displayed by the artists of this age reappeared in the dramatic arts of the later fifth century. All the plays from that period in which a hetaera was the main heroine are lost. From the hetaera figures in Aristophanes (and the fragments of other Old and Middle Comedy plays) we can surmise, however, that these works did not sentimentalize prostitutes, but satirized them for an obvious repertoire of vices: greed, bibulousness, and insatiable lust.

Sentimentalization is first clearly attested in the New Comedy of Menander, in which the savage bite of satire has given way to the gentle mocking of minor human vices. In *The Woman of Samos,* of which we now have a nearly complete text, the Samian heroine,

174.
Prostitute and customer in
affectionate embrace.

named Chrysis (Goldie, a typical hetaera name), is a former prostitute, now free and kept as a concubine by a wealthy man. During
an absence of her lover she bears a baby, which dies. Since the
young master of the household has raped a neighbor's daughter,
there is an unwanted male infant born at about the same time, so a
substitution is made. Chrysis is confident that her lover, Demeas,
will let her keep the boy, but when she finds out that she is
mistaken, she prefers being thrown out into the street rather than
abandoning the child. Figure 177 shows how long this sentimental
story was popular: it is a mosaic from the sixth century (A.D.) found
on the island of Lesbos in recent years. Menander's Woman of
Samos, dressed for the street, clutches the baby. The characters on
her left are identified by the inscription as a cook and Demeas, her
unappreciative lover.

Another play by Menander, *The Arbitration*, features a hetaera
by the name of Habrotonon, which means "sounder of mellow
tones," who is a slave and again the noblest character in the story.
It is through Habrotonon's kindly machinations that the highly
improbable happy ending comes about (see Chapter 14 for the new
sexual morals governing Menander's plots). As Ovid said of the

175. The welcoming of a customer.

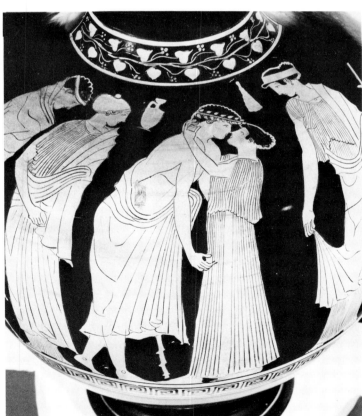

176.
Detail of 175: girl
greeting customer as
he "feels her up."

playwright, whose works were popular in the Greco-Roman world until the very demise of Classical culture, "No play of the cheerful Menander is without love." Under the conventions of New Comedy, hetaerai are a great deal more loving than respectable women. Menander himself was "romantically linked" with a hetaera called Glykera (Sweetie), also a characteristic name for a prostitute.

Making heroines of hetaerai may perhaps best be seen in the legend of the prostitute Leaena (Lioness), which arose in post-Classical times but became attached to the stories surrounding the early history of Athens. Harmodius and Aristogeiton, a pair of Athenian male homosexual lovers of the sixth century B.C., were honored in the city as "tyrant slayers" and liberation heroes; a copy of a statuary group of the two young men is now proudly owned by the archaeological museum in Naples. The two youths were credited with slaying one of the last two tyrants of Athens, Hipparchus, who was actually a rather enlightened ruler; the slaying seems to have occurred in reality during a sordid homosexual brawl. Improbably, Leaena became known as the mistress of Aristogeiton: according to the late legend she was taken prisoner after the slaying, and she cut off her own tongue to prevent herself from revealing under torture the names of the conspirators in the assassination. In her honor the Athenians erected a statue of a lioness on the Acropolis.

## The Courtesan: Refinement and Prosperity?

The Athenian Greeks developed a reputation among the Romans and in later Western culture for having raised prostitution to a unique level of refinement. The keys to this alleged achievement were said to be the education and grooming of the woman, and her ability to translate her charms into a high enough economic status so that she could feel autonomous. The name "hetaera" has come to refer to this ideal. Athenaeus wrote about "hetaerai who had a sense of self-respect, who took care to get an education and set time aside for learning" (583 f.), and in the post-Classical Mediterranean world there is at least some evidence for women of this type. The Hellenistic age was one of monarchy, with vast amounts of wealth and power concentrated in the hands of rulers. Via their men, a number of women managed to attain wealth, influence, and sometimes even power, with or without the benefit of marriage.

177. Menander's noble prostitute Chrysis clutching her baby
(late Roman mosaic on Lesbos).

Hellenistic monarchs patronized the fine arts, and as a result the
successful painters and sculptors of the age, such as Apelles and
Praxiteles, were able to amass fortunes, part of which they lavished
on courtesans. But what about fifth-century Athens, a society given
to vast spending on public projects but frugality in domestic arrangements? In fact, the city supervisors (*astynomoi*) had as one of
their specific functions the task of preventing prostitutes or their
owners from charging too much. A brothel tax, evidently strictly
enforced, threw a further financial burden on the operation. During
the period of their youth, when their services were most in demand
and most highly paid, prostitutes were likely to be slaves; the

proceeds of their charms went to their owners, as did any sales price they might bring. By the time a *porne* could buy her freedom or wangle it out of accommodating lovers, her best years most probably were behind her.

Yet the legend of the wealthy courtesan arose early. In a play by Eupolis (Old Comedy), a young man reproaches the hetaera Myrrhina: "I have squandered my patrimony on you" (Fr. 44). Significantly, however, much of the lore in fifth- and fourth-century literature about opulent and proud hetaerai concerns those practicing elsewhere than in Athens. Aristophanes alludes to the wealth of a famous courtesan by the name of Lais, who was born in Sicily but plied her trade in Corinth (*Plout.* 179). It will be remembered that Neaera, too, had her best times in Corinth; in Athens she had to resort to extortion schemes to keep the money coming in. In fact, if one scratches through the later layers of legend, it becomes apparent that the only manner in which a prostitute in Classical Athens could aspire to modest financial autonomy was by becoming an entrepreneur in the trade and stocking up on young slave girls. Such owners were known as *pornoboskoi*, literally "harlot herders" (from *bous*, ox; the parallel *geroboskos*, "caretaker of the old," originally may have had a similar unpleasant connotation). *Pornoboskoi* bought girls small and raised them for prostitution. We saw that this scheme worked for Nicarete, who had an "eye for budding beauty."

In the speech *Against Athenogenes* by the orator Hyperides (3), we learn of another shrewd female panderer and former prostitute. She was called Antigone—a name that she adopted, one suspects, as a symbol of emancipation. The speaker, who was enamored of one of Antigone's slave boys and wanted to buy him, was duped by not reading the fine print in his purchase agreement. In an earlier negotiation Antigone had managed to collect a reward of 300 drachmas for her services, in order to acquire a "child prostitute" (*paidiske*).

In Isaeus 6, *On the Estate of Philoktemon*, we can follow the career of yet another prostitute with survival skills. Euktemon, a well-to-do citizen, operated several brothels staffed with slaves, a perfectly respectable line of business. A purchased girl with the apt name of Alke (Strength) was exploited in one of these as long as she was young enough. Many in the audience might have "known" her, the speaker observes. Euktemon must have freed her at some point, because he did not claim as his property the two sons she eventually bore. When Alke became too old for the general public, she still appealed to Euktemon. He put her in charge of another brothel, located in the Potters' Quarter (Kerameikos) of Athens, evidently closer to his home. Soon he began to go there more often than necessary to collect his profits. Eventually he moved in with Alke altogether, abandoning his wife and children, and he lived out the rest of his ninety-six years there. He even tried fraudulently to legitimize Alke's eldest son.

In Xenophon's *Memoirs* of the life of Socrates, the philosopher visits the establishment of a successful madam (*Mem.* 3, 11). Surely this encounter was essentially historical, and the lady, by the name of Theodote, must have been a real-life personality. It is one more of the tales of Socrates' sympathetic and understanding attitude toward women. Socrates visits Theodote as a customer, but does not turn to sex until after a spirited conversation with the lady. As he enters the house, Socrates sees that

> . . . she herself is beautifully adorned, and that her mother is there, well-dressed and well attended to, and there are many beautiful servant girls, and they too show absolutely no sign of neglect, and in general the entire household is abundantly outfitted. (3, 11, 4)

That the "servant girls" do more than serve and are, in fact, prostitutes is made clear when Socrates agrees to have sex with Theodote, "unless you have a sweeter thing than you inside" (11, 18).

Socrates does not specify the civil status of Theodote. If she was a citizen, which was not likely, she would have had at least a technical guardian (*kyrios*), and if she was an alien, she would have needed a citizen "overseer" (*prostates*), but, in the picture drawn by Xenophon, there is no man in sight. In a society which afforded so little status to women, it must have been nearly impossible for them to function economically without some kind of male protection. Athenaeus (591 f.) tells us that the actor Satyros, who flourished about the middle of the fourth century B.C., sponged off the hetaera Pamphile, but we should probably think more of a pimping arrangement than of a courtesan affording herself a gigolo. Athenaeus also mentions a member of the Areopagus court (that is, of high-class standing) as a parasite of the courtesan Phryne, but this must have been an arrangement of a later date. Phryne was the fabled mistress of the late-fourth-century sculptor Praxiteles.

## The Legendary Aspasia

Probably the best-known hetaera of the Classical age was Aspasia, who was a free immigrant from Miletus. In Athens she undoubtedly started as a prostitute. The comedians call her a *porne*, or harlot, one of the more disparaging among the many Greek terms for prostitute. Aspasia means "Welcomer" or "Gladhander" and may have been a professional hetaera name. In addition, she appears to have traded in prostitutes. Athenaeus reports of Aspasia that she "imported large numbers of beautiful women, and all of Greece was filled with her little harlots" (569 f.). Undoubtedly this statement is hyperbolic, but it must have had a grain of truth in it, because Aristophanes, in his *Acharnians*, refers to Aspasia's whores in a spoof of the many traditional stories in which raped women are the causes of wars:

> Some young men, drunk with kottabos games, go to Megara and steal the whore Simaitha, then the Megareans, furious as fighting cocks with grief, take revenge by stealing two of Aspasia's whores. And so, over three strumpets, the beginning of war set in for all Greeks. (524–29)

Aspasia, by all accounts, was an exceptional person, but it appears that she acquired her fame or notoriety more by intelligence, and the protection of Socrates, than by sex appeal and womanly wiles. Plutarch, in his *Life of Pericles*, does not stress her beauty but reports that she had grace and cleverness, as well as "handsome looks." Athenaeus calls Aspasia a "Socratic," and a marginal notation on the *Acharnians* records that "Aspasia was the specialist in sophistic learning and teacher of speechwriting to Pericles. Later she also became his wife" (although not in legitimate Athenian marriage, of course).

Plato's dialogue *Menexenus* gives a fictionalized account of Socrates' relationship with Aspasia. Here the philosopher is also a pupil of Aspasia. Socrates relates how she outlined a funeral oration to him, partly off-the-cuff, but partly from memory, "because it seemed to me that she had composed the funeral speech which Pericles delivered, and that she glued together a few of the leftovers from it" (236b). Socrates had learned the new speech by heart and was all but flogged by his instructor, Aspasia, whenever he forgot a line (236c). In this bit of playful banter, Plato is poking gentle fun at Socrates' admiration for women. Yet there must have been some truth to the contention that Aspasia gave guidance and instruction to Pericles. So, in fact, the great hetaera of legend wound up more like a behind-the-scenes "help-meet wife" than a freewheeling courtesan.

What Pericles did for Aspasia was not fundamentally different from what Phrynion did for Neaera: he gave her the unofficial status of common-law wife (*pallake*), and, since as a non-citizen she was free of many of the social restraints circumscribing the lives of legitimate wives, she could move in the world of men, just as Neaera attended symposia and revels while enjoying her lover's protection. Such arrangements were common in Athens. Apparently what startled men was not Aspasia's appearance in their world, but the fact that she had the poise and wit to hold her own among them.

Shortly before Pericles' death of the plague in the year 429, Aspasia was tried for impiety and acquitted. According to one source she later "married" a sheep breeder. One may surmise that the practical streak in her make-up, discernible in her earlier life, helped her through the pitfalls of old age.

## The Witty Hetaera

Without doubt Aspasia became an articulate and cultivated woman, but the "refined hetaera" for which she later became the byword was probably a fabrication of the male mind, at least for the Classical age. In the post-Classical era witticisms attributed to prostitutes were assiduously collected—many are quoted by Athenaeus—but they do not glow with sophistication. They are for the most part male-generated jokes, hinging on puns and sexual innuendos. In the previous chapter we noted a *bon mot* in Strabo, attributed to a Corinthian whore who lost no time in taking down three looming erections. In general, however, these jokes do not translate well, because the play on words has to be explained. For example, the Greek word for "old woman" (*graus*) is, somewhat cruelly, also used for the skin on boiled milk. When the legendary hetaeara Glykera brings the playwright Menander some boiled milk and he refuses it, she retorts: "Get rid of the upper part and use what's below" (Ath. 585c). To Aspasia's credit, no such feeble jokes are attributed to her.

What social function was served by the elaborate collection of puns of this quality? It appears that Athenian men were at pains to construct an image of witty, prosperous hetaerai in order to gloss over the fact that their principal sex outlets were debased and uneducated slaves, who were at the mercy of their profit-hungry owners, and who were almost certain to end their lives in misery.

## Negative Images

In the comedy of the fifth and the early fourth centuries, prostitutes fare no worse than wives, homosexual men, gluttons, or anybody else, and the catalogue of vices imputed to them is predictable. A fragment by the fourth-century playwright Alexis of Thurii is of special interest, however; it provides a catalogue of the tricks whereby an artful madam prepares her novice slave prostitutes for business, including elevator shoes and false buttocks to satisfy customers partial to women's rear ends (Fr. 98). They must have charming manners, too:

> Does she have healthy teeth? By force she's kept laughing, so that the customers see what a dainty mouth she has. If she doesn't like to laugh, she must spend the day indoors, with a twig of myrrh upright between her lips, just like the goats' heads displayed in this way at the butcher shops so that the customers will buy them. That way in time she smiles whether she likes it or not.

What the Greeks objected to most in prostitutes was the fact that they grew old. And, in truth, their chances of aging gracefully must have been minimal. The Attic state, though socialized in other respects, did not, as far as we know, provide financial support or protection to needy women in old age, except via their male relatives (*pace* Pomeroy, p. 91). How prostitutes survived after even their coarsest customers were no longer willing to pay for their services is hard to imagine. To turn once again to the comedy of Menander, in *The Woman of Samos* the concubine Chrysis is expelled from Demeas' house and has no choice except to return to her previous status as a prostitute. Here is how her lover describes her fate, in a passage which is all the more poignant because the character Demeas is generally portrayed as a decent, well-motivated type: "Whores like you, Chrysis, make a mere ten drachmas running from dinner to dinner and drinking without restraint until they die of it; or, if they don't find a quick and ready death, they starve slowly" (392–96). Menander, although sentimental, was not bereft of a streak of stark realism.

We have already seen a number of vase paintings in Chapter 6 in which the artist dramatized the role of the aging hetaera, and the progressive humiliation to which she had to submit. Evidently painters were more aware than authors of the circumstance that youth is a great equalizer of social differences and that in old age the effects of underprivilege are magnified. The Pistoxenos Painter expressed this awareness, perhaps unwittingly, when he decorated the upright drinking cup (skyphos) reproduced in Figures 178 and 179. It represents a mythological scene, with Heracles and his brother, Iphicles, taking music lessons from their teacher, Linus. On one side Iphicles, the mortal brother, is taking his lesson like a good boy, watching intently how his master fingers the strings; a lyre of another type hangs on the wall. On the reverse side Heracles arrives, late for school but cockily confident, although as yet he does not have his club and lion's skin. His aged nurse behind him carries his lyre. In the story, Heracles kills Linus with the teacher's lyre when the latter tries to punish him. The instrument on the wall is probably an allusion to that outcome. Both Linus and the nurse are old, but Linus still has a function in society and a position of authority over his pupil. The nurse, who has deep wrinkles even on her right arm, has an expression of abject servility on her face. For the true pathos of old age, however, we have to await the realism of the Hellenistic age, as in the famous "old woman with wine jug," a textbook example of post-Classical genre art; the woman is thought to represent an old prostitute clutching a wine jug, "her last lover," to her abdomen (Figure 180).

For the authors of comedy, old prostitutes were an easy, much too easy, target. Aristophanes spoofs them at length, but mainly in his later plays, in which his satire is directed toward the pathetic rather than the evil. The three old whores of his comedy *The Parliament of Women* are not among his better creations. Here's a description of one:

> But you, your eyebrows' hairiness
> With tweezers you've attacked.
> You've filled your faces' cracks with white
> Where time has roughly hacked,
> Until you look a plaster corpse,
> Death's whore, in fact.

In *Ploutos,* a youth has been sponging off an old whore for food and handouts, comes into money and returns to his mistress with a torch to have a good look at her:

> O gods of old! Poseidon of the Main!
> What countless wrinkles does her face contain!

When the youth and another character engage in a bet on the number of teeth left in the hag's mouth, it turns out she has only one.

178. The old male teacher Linus and his pupil Iphicles.

179. Reverse of 178: the old nursemaid
(with her ward Heracles).

180. Old prostitute (?) clutching her "last lover," the wine jug. Hellenistic statue.

CHAPTER

# 8

# Two Kinds of Women: The Splitting
# of the Female Psyche

> . . . often we used to talk [at symposia] about married women
> and prostitutes.
> —Athenaeus 555b

> It's no wonder that in every town there is a shrine to Aphrodite
> the Harlot, but one to the wife is not to be found in all of
> Greece.
> —Philetaeros, Fragment (5)

> The husband of a virtuous but unaccommodating wife should
> say to himself: "It is not possible for me to consort with the
> same woman as I would with a wife and as I would with a
> hetaera."
> —Phocion, a prominent fourth-century statesman, as quoted
> by Plutarch, *Moralia* (142c)

The famous double standard of sexual behavior has striking statistical
consequences. If we disregard for the moment homosexual practices,
whenever a man has sex, so does a woman. If the sexual conduct of
the respectable woman is restricted to marital intercourse, while
the corresponding male is permitted to be promiscuous, it must of
necessity follow that the female population is divided sharply into
two classes: those who have limited sexual contacts in the course
of a lifetime, probably far less than their physical nature could
accommodate, and those who have sex in great abundance, far more
than they could possibly experience in a meaningful way. The last
category, of course, consists largely of prostitutes. In Attic society,
this basically unhappy pattern must have been aggravated by two
circumstances: the social ethos did not encourage—on the contrary,
it discouraged—marital sex, and, as a result of female infanticide
and the high incidence of death in childbirth, the male population

far outnumbered the female except after periods of especially costly wars.

The resulting frequency of contact with bought sex partners goes a long way to explain not only the Athenian preoccupation with hetaera life but also the social and moral sanction given to prostitution. In later Western societies the double standard also prevailed, but prostitution was concealed and treated as the sewer side of society. In Classical Athens the rift between the notions of sex for procreation and sex for pleasure and release, between Demeter and Aphrodite, was so complete that it left its marks on almost all facets of organized society. Did the Athenians also develop the corresponding notion, still strongly represented in the modern world, that these two functions, of childbearing and of sex for its own sake, represent two antipodes of the feminine character—in other words, that there are natural-born mothers and natural-born whores? We saw in the Introduction that a commentator as recent as Paul Brandt, alias Hans Licht, praised the Greeks because they had "discovered" this important truth about female psychology. In this view, the male soul normally combines the two urges of sex and procreation, incompatible in the female psyche. I know of no statement in Greek literature to this effect, but the monuments make it likely that in the male Athenian view this division of the female sex was introduced by nature herself.

## The Fragmentation of the Female in Myth

Chapter 2 already pointed to the desexualization of most goddesses except Aphrodite, and the parceling out of the female functions to various divinities. Thus these roles became distinct, as if they were incompatible within the same person. Hera, Zeus' sister and official consort, had her maternal role undercut by a variety of mythological mechanisms; Demeter was all mother, but no longer wife, and she was a mourning mother at that; Athena was the man-goddess, sexless in birth and in life, wearing the Gorgon's head, the symbolic *vagina dentata*, on her breast. Artemis was also a virgin, and at the same time the goddess of childbirth, thus propagating the notion that mothers should be chaste. The sexual functions of woman were concentrated in the various manifestations of Aphrodite, but especially the personae called Aphrodite Pandemos (Of All the People), and Aphrodite Hetaera (Harlot), who was neither wife nor mother. In Chapter 12 I will try to show how, through the cults of these various goddesses, fragmentation was perpetuated. In contrast, male divinities combined features of the father, the husband, and the lover, whether heterosexual or homosexual, in one personality.

The motif of the Judgment of Paris shows that the principle of fragmenting the female was present in Greek mythology long before Attic civilization reached its zenith. The Trojan youth Paris serves as judge in a beauty contest of the three principal Greek goddesses and is bribed by Aphrodite, with the promise of Helen's love, to award her the first prize. Had the myth been born in Classical Athens, the three rival goddesses probably would have been Demeter the Mother, Hera the Wife, and Aphrodite the Mistress. In the inherited version, popular in Attic art, however, the competing symbols of femininity are Hera the Matron, Athena the Sexless One, and Aphrodite the Sensualist. Figures 181 and 182 give a charming rendition of the Judgment of Paris by the Penthesileia Painter, on a woman's box (*pyxis*). This vessel represents one of the painter's rare departures from his favorite one, the male-oriented symposium cup; it seems to indicate that he considered this motif relevant to women's self-concept. On the left in Figure 181 we see the coy Aphrodite flirting with her son, Eros, confident of victory. To her right Athena and Hera stand glowering at each other. Athena is dolled up for the occasion with a handsome bonnet, and holds her customary helmet in her hand. Then comes the herald Hermes (in Figure 182), who is leading the three of them to the judgment. Paris is portrayed as a young rustic. The figure behind him is probably his father, Priam. In typical Attic fashion Eros and Paris are both identified as "The Beautiful Boy."

## The Heavy Hand of the Law

To keep the categories of whore and mother strictly separate, and to keep both types of women under firm control, Attic society instituted a rigorous system of offices and laws, many of them evidently going back to Solon, the father of the Athenian state and of democracy. Prostitutes who had slave status were automatically subject to the unfathomable horrors of that institution, which included abuse by their owners, torture, random execution, and sale at any time to the highest bidder (or even to joint buyers). It will

181a,b.
The judgment of Paris: Aphrodite with Eros,
Athena, and Hera.

182.
Same as 181: Hermes,
Paris, and Priam.

be recalled that Neaera was bought for joint use by two men, and several other such cases are documented in courtroom speeches. If slaves were emancipated, which seems to have been the case with a number of older prostitutes, they were still bound to their former owners by certain rules and could readily be sold back into slavery for such offenses as owing money to their former masters. If they were aliens, they were without any civic rights altogether and thus subject to expulsion from the city.

The finances of prostitutes were controlled by the city magistrates (astynomoi). These officials had a variety of functions, but it is striking that Aristotle, in his Constitution of Athens, lists the price control of prostitutes first among these:

> . . . there are ten astynomoi. Of these five operate in the Piraeus and five in the city. And they see to it that the girl flute, harp and cithara players do not charge more than two drachmas for their services. (Ath. Pol., 51, 2)

The players of these musical instruments are the hetaerai whom men hired for revels, symposia, and sex. From a speech by Hyperides we learn of two men who were indicted for hiring out flute girls for a higher price than the law allowed (3, 4). There was a brothel tax (pornikon telos), collected by a special category of tax gatherers (pornotelonai), who, for obvious reasons, were not very popular. Their title, in fact, seems to have been a common insult, which turns up, for example, in a small catalogue of curses in Old Comedy: "Accursed from birth, brothel-tax collectors, Megarians, scoundrels, parricides" (Philonides, Fr. 5).

On the side of the respectable women, rigorous laws were enacted to prevent the unmarried from being seduced and the married from committing adultery. Solon, who is perhaps most remembered for abolishing slavery through debt, passed a law to the effect that a man could not sell his daughters or sisters, except in case of premarital intercourse. If a man caught an adulterer in the act with his wife, he could kill him with impunity, as is clear from Lysias' speech On the Murder of Eratosthenes. If adultery was determined in court, the culprit was turned over to the injured party, who could "do with him as he pleased, but without dagger" (Dem. 59, 66): evidently he could batter his rival but not kill him. Husbands of adulterous wives not only were entitled to a divorce, but it was actually unlawful for them to stay married, and the ex-wives were barred from all public rituals. If they were seen to attend any of these, anybody could inflict all punishment on them save death (Dem. 59, 86–87). In other words, they were fair game for any kind of abuse. Aeschines, in *Against Timarchus* (1, 183), gives more detail of what their punishment might entail: they were not allowed to adorn themselves, and anyone could strip off their clothes and kick them, but not maim or kill them. Intermediaries in adulterous love affairs, both male and female, could also be punished, Aeschines reveals.

In praise of enforced chastity, Aeschines cites the hoary legend of an Athenian father who, upon finding that his daughter had been "corrupted," walled her up in a deserted house together with a horse (the significance of the animal is obscure). The remains of this building were, according to the speaker, still venerated in Athens and referred to as *The Horse and the Maiden* (*ibid.*, 182).

The behavior of citizen women was supervised by the Women's Police, the *gynaikonomoi* (there was also a corresponding Children's Police). Aristotle makes it clear that the principal function of these officers was to restrict the movements of women. The Women's Police is well attested in Athens for the Hellenistic period, and as far back into the classical era as Aristotle. This author deemed that neither institution belonged in a democracy, which view has led scholars to assume that he knew them from some Greek state other than Athens. The philosopher, however, is judgmental in the matter, stating once that it is impossible to prevent the women of the poor from going out, and once that it is unfair to do so "because the poor need to use their wives and children as attendants on account of their lack of slaves" (*Pol.* 1300a; 1323a). This polemic by no means indicates that the Women's Police had always been unknown at Athens; in fact it suggests the contrary. That the institution goes back to Solon is merely a hypothesis based on the general character of his laws. Although our knowledge of actual Solonian legislation is far from complete, and many statutes later attributed to the founding father actually were of much later date, we know that his laws reached into every home, including its bedrooms, and into every aspect of daily and family life. Plutarch records that Solon "also enacted a law concerning damage caused by quadrupeds, in which he ruled that a dog who had bitten someone had to be surrendered, tied with a leash of three cubit length" (*Solon*, 24e–f). A legislator who was concerned with the length of dogs' leashes and who set up state-controlled brothels might well have instituted a system for policing the virtue of respectable women as well.

## The Division of the Athenian Home

Division of the private house into a women's part (*gynaikonitis*) and a men's part was characteristic of Athens and of at least some other towns of ancient Greece. Vitruvius, in his description of the Classical Greek house, further distinguishes the "men's quarters" (*andronitis*) from the "men's room" (*andron*), which was part of the former and synonymous with the dining, or symposium, room. The men's room was so called, says Vitruvius, "because women do not go there" (6, 7, 5). Figure 183 shows the floor plan of a house in the center of Athens, one of the rare instances of a fifth-century dwelling there of which the floor plan has been determined. It includes one room (no. 12) with an outlet to the street; presumably it was a shop, a common feature of many Greek houses. The main complex has only one entrance; rooms 10 and 11 have easy access from the entrance, and may therefore constitute the men's quarters, although they are not, as they normally were, the largest rooms in the house. Figure 184 shows the floor plan of two fifth-century houses in Olynthus, the only site where extensive residential areas of the Classical age have been excavated. These areas were laid out in regular blocks, and a somewhat homogeneous style of homes was developed. The rooms euphemistically identified as "réception" were the men's quarters. Each consists of an anteroom leading to the larger dining room, in which podiums for the dining couches were found. In both houses the men's quarters have privileged communication with the sole entrance to the house. The stippling in the plan indicates that this part of the house was paved with pebble mosaic, whereas in the rest of the house no traces of floor covering were unearthed.

The gulf between these two divisions of the house was deeply experienced by the Greeks. Plato, observing that "the breast houses baser and nobler parts, separated by the diaphragm" (*Tim.* 69c), likens these parts to the segregated women's and men's quarters of the private house—the former, naturally, corresponding to the cruder part of the soul.

The philosopher Antisthenes uses a different metaphor: "going from Athens to Sparta is like going from the *gynaikonitis* to the

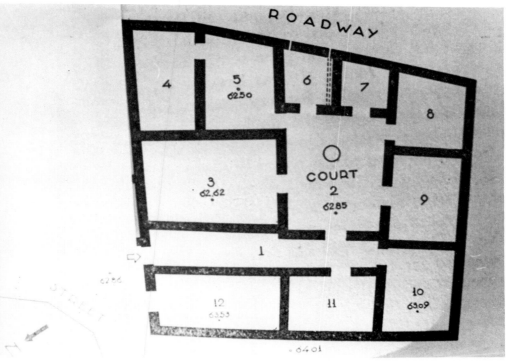

183. Floorplan of a fifth-century Athenian house; men's quarters have easy access to the street.

184. Floorplans of fifth-century houses in Olynthus. Men's quarters have mosaics and privileged entrances.

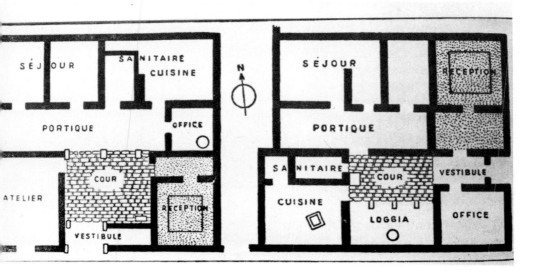

men's quarters" (Theon, *Prog.* 215), presumably from a place of indulgence to one of virtues. From Lysias' speech *On the Murder of Eratosthenes,* we learn of a house in which the men's and the women's rooms were on different floors. The speaker, one Euphiletus, who had killed his wife's seducer, owned a two-story house. Originally the women's quarters were upstairs and the men's area downstairs. However, after the birth of a baby boy, the arrangements were reversed, perhaps because the ground floor had a water supply for the bathing of the child. The wife now spent her nights downstairs and as a result was an easy prey for her seducer. The speech confirms what vase paintings suggest about conjugal life— namely, that husband and wife did not normally spend the night together, but used the narrow couch (*kline*) only for the purpose of intercourse; no sleeping arrangements large enough to accommodate two persons are represented in vase painting. Xenophon, moreover, mentions separate sets of bedding (*stromata*) for the men's and the women's quarters (*Oec.* 9, 6).

Although the men's dining room (*andron*) and the women's quarters were probably in most cases separated only by some walls and a bit of courtyard, they represented two distinct zones of social activity. In one domain respectable women were sequestered, while in the other, the *andron,* men enjoyed the company of hetaerai. Prostitution occurred in many settings but it was at the symposia, held in private homes, where hetaerai left their strongest mark on society, literature, and the fine arts. Figure 185 shows a typical symposium scene. Two men with drinking cups are cozily reclining on couches with hetaerai; the figure in the center sings to the accompaniment of a flutist. Figures 186 and 187, on the other hand, illustrate the conjugal side of the Greek household. In Figure 186 a wife is eating and drinking by herself in the women's quarters. A distaff, symbol of domestic industry, hangs behind her on the wall. She is bent over and appears to reach eagerly for the food. Her drink is awaiting her in a straight cup (skyphos); the flat symposium cup (kylix) was not used by wives. Figure 187 features a similar scene, which includes a youth, perhaps the woman's son. He watches her eat, with a drinking cup in his hand. Presumably he is saving his appetite for the dinner party to come in the men's quarters.

Whereas the women of the household did not share meals and parties with their men, the female staff was responsible for their

185. A typical symposium scene: sex and entertainment in the men's quarters.

preparation. Ischomachus was prosperous enough to have a hired or purchased female housekeeper, under the supervision of his wife: "We have made that woman manager of our establishment who seemed to be the most competent in matters of the stomach, of wine and of sleep and of the get-togethers of men" (*Oec.* 9, 11). The word for "get-together" (*synousia*) can refer to any kind of party, but also to sexual intercourse. The ambiguity is appropriate here, because symposia is what Ischomachus is talking about. In less opulent households the wives themselves must have organized the drinking parties and revels of their husbands, withdrawing before the arrival of guests and hetaerai.

186.
Wife eating and drinking
by herself in the women's
quarters.

187.
Woman eating alone
as youth watches.

By way of contrast Figure 188, a domestic picture from a century later, reveals different family habits. It is a scene from a late-fourth-century Attic comedy, which probably reflects the new marital ethos of that age fairly accurately. The master and mistress of a household are enjoying a snack together from a large tray of dainties. What is more, the inscriptions reveal that the woman has a name, even if it is ironical: despite her cavernous mouth and the large wart on her nose she is called Charis (Grace). The counter-heroic master is Philotimides (Lover of Honor), and the nearly bald slave sneaking away with a stolen cake is Xanthias (Blondie). The stage door on the left is half open, a symbol which may be a holdover from the fifth-century convention of the semi-opened door and bed, which alluded to the couple's sex life. For all its burlesquing of the family, the shared snack and the giving of a name to the wife reveal a new conception of married life.

In the imagined world of the afterlife, wives were remembered by name, but even there they did not recline with their husbands on dining couches, as they did on contemporary Etruscan monuments; in the Athenian afterlife they sit at the foot end and wait on their men, in a kind of banquet of the dead. Figures 189 and 190 (the latter perhaps not Attic, but from Thebes) illustrate this continuation of servility after death.

By and large, there can be little doubt that in the choice between wife and whore, the Athenian man preferred the latter, as indicated by the fragment from the comedian Philetaeros at the head of this chapter. The author's name, in fact, which could mean "Friend Lover" as well as "Hetaera Lover," probably means the latter and may be a nickname. At least, a certain lasciviousness is evident from other fragments as well: "The most beautiful way to die is in the middle of intercourse" (Fr. 6, 2).

## *The Antithesis on Monuments*

Inevitably this deep split in men's minds between two female sex partners—the wife with whom he mated, reluctantly, for the sake of offspring, and his hetaera, who was at his command for the purpose of sex—left its mark on the fine arts. According to Pliny, the late Classical sculptor Praxiteles created a statuary group consisting of a weeping housewife and a merry hetaera (*NH* 34, 70). No other memory of this work survives, but its description by Pliny

188.
Husband and wife snacking together: domestic scene from a fourth-century comedy.

189.
Banquet of the dead. Family scene on a funerary relief.

190.
Banquet of the dead. The wife waits on her husband.

is of some interest because it reveals, once again, the notion cultivated by the ancients that the prostitutes had a happy lot. Personally, I think that the housewife was likely to fare a little better, at least in the long run.

From the fifth century B.C. we have documentation of the hetaera-housewife antithesis in the form of one of the most cele-brated surviving Greek monuments, the so-called Ludovisi throne (probably in fact an altar), shown in Figures 191, 192, and 193. The central panel (Figure 191) depicts the birth of Aphrodite. She is arising, fully grown, from the sea and is being dried off by attendants. The two side panels of the monument dramatize the two traditional roles of women, as two separate manifestations of Aphrodite. On the left panel a chastely veiled figure is engaged in a sacral action; she is taking something, perhaps a first fruit or some other offering, from a bowl and placing it in a burner on a stand. Undoubtedly she stands for the dutiful housewife, bearing the stamp of Aphrodite's more respectable facet, that of Aphrodite Ourania, the Heavenly One. On the right panel a naked woman is playing the double flute. She is a hetaera and represents Aphrodite the Harlot. To emphasize his juxtaposition of the side figures, the artist has shown them in analogous poses, reclining on the same type of cushion. It may be taken as a token of the continuity of Classical Greek tastes that the hetaera panel of this well-known monument is more frequently reproduced than that of the pious wife.

By far the richest source of pictorial information about the sexual and social attitudes of the fifth century is the symposium cups, or kylikes, of which we have seen a number already.

## Reading a Symposium Cup

The most common scheme of decoration of these vases consists of two main parts: a band of standing or seated figures around the outside rim, and a more intricate composition in the bottom of the inside (tondo). In most cups these two parts are conceptually related, even when they are done by different hands. In order to grasp the jests created through this relationship, we must visualize the kylix in use. When the cup is full it is held in the hand and the outside decoration is plain for all to see. This is especially true in the use of the kylix in the *kottabos* game, of which Figure 194 is a famous example, a detail from wall paintings in the Tomb of the Diver at

Paestum, near Naples (the tomb dates from 480 B.C.). However, only the user of a cup gets to see the inside of the kylix, and only when he has emptied it. Not infrequently, the outside features a riotous revel, or a party, or negotiations with hetaerai, while the inside depicts, somewhat ruefully, the dire consequences of the exuberance, or presents some other antithesis.

To clarify the principle of the decorations on many symposium cups, one must look at the complete scenario of a few examples. Figure 171 shows the inside of a cup, now in Würzburg, by the Brygos Painter, with a youth vomiting and a young slave girl giving him tender attention. Figure 195, the outer decoration of the same cup, portrays a happy and drunken *komos.* The message is clear: revels are fun but one pays for them the next day with a hangover.

A cup by Peithinos, now in Berlin (Figures 196, 197, and 37), mixes genre painting and mythological scenes, but is nevertheless held together by one thought. The outside decoration features a number of groupings of pederastic lovers and of men with hetaerai. The detail in Figure 196 depicts men and boys courting. Figure 197 shows another detail of the outside decoration, namely, a man conversing with an elegant hetaera. The outside scheme spells "extramarital love." The theme in the tondo (Figure 37) presents the myth of Peleus and Thetis, the parents of Achilleus. It is one of the few stories of a mortal man marrying an immortal woman. In the myth, Thetis is reluctant and changes herself into a variety of shapes, but in vain—she must succumb to forcible marriage. The lion and the snake in the drawing refer to her unsuccessful metamorphoses; her immortal status is indicated by her tall stature. The total program of the kylix contrasts extra-marital sex, based on negotiation and free will, with marital sex based on compulsion.

A kylix in Ferrara will concern us again in Chapter 11, because it illuminates Greek notions about pederastic love. I show it here inside and out to demonstrate the tying together of decorative motifs into a conceptually coherent scheme (Figures 198–200). The inside of this kylix was painted by the Penthesileia Painter, the outside by a competent but less talented hand. The part of the rim in Figure 198 shows a riding master with a stick and his young pupils; on the other half (Figure 199) there are four more boys, a horse, and another older man. The latter is propositioning the youth in front of him, who makes a gesture of protest. Several inscriptions state, "The boy is beautiful." The magnificent drawing on the inside

191. Ludovisi throne. Aphrodite arises from the waves.

192. Ludovisi throne. The dutiful
wife (Aphrodite Ourania?).

193. Ludovisi throne. Aphrodite the Harlot.

194.
A *kottabos* player
with poised cup.

195. Same as 194, outside: the party.

196. Men and male lovers.

197. Same as 196, other side of rim: men negotiating with hetaerai.

shows Zeus about to rape the lovely youth Ganymede. The total program contrasts the pursuit of youthful male beauty on a mortal plane with that in the domain of mythology.

The cup in Figures 201–203, entirely decorated by the Penthesileia Painter, presents a vignette which might be entitled "too little cash." In Figure 201 three youths confront hetaerai. The one on the right seems to expose himself, evidently to dramatize the urgency of his need. Only one has money, and he holds up his purse, not to a woman but to his companion, as if to say, "Don't you know you have to pay for sex?" On the other half of the rim, in Figure 202, one youth, also without a pouch, proudly departs. The paunchy, older man on the right does have money: it is shown suspended behind him. His woman, nevertheless, walks away from him, pointing at his genitals, which are not shown but should be imagined as relaxed. Her gesture conveys, "For the service *you* require, you don't offer enough." In the tondo the problem has been resolved at least for one young man: he has had his sex, as the couch on the right indicates, evidently on credit, and he is walking away. His anxious hetaera seems to say, "When *will* I get paid?"

This excursus on the iconography of drinking cups has, I hope, served to establish the programmatic nature of these decorations, and the great variety of jokes and pleasantries about everyday sexual life in which the vase painters indulged. Only against this background can one grasp the impact of schemes that contrast the prostitute and the housewife. The inside, or tondo, is especially appropriate for the "housewife" side of the antithesis, because of its general connotation of "the party is over."

In Chapter 6 I discussed the outside of the stunning symposium cup by Makron which is now in the Toledo Museum of Art in Ohio. It shows the favorite theme of men bargaining with hetaerai with a subtle, humorous twist: on the one side the men have money, on the other side their wit must carry the day. Figure 141 reproduces the half of the outside band with men offering money to hetaerai. In Figure 204 we see the tondo of the same cup: it features a stately, handsomely gowned woman pouring a libation onto an altar, surely in a household. The three-cornered basket is a standard sacrificial implement. Behind her stands an incense burner. Clearly this serene figure represents the dutiful wife, keeper of the hearth. When the user of this cup had drained it to the last dregs, he saw a picture of a wife in her most matronly and virtuous guise, a reminder of the other sphere of his relations with women. Many similar messages can be culled from vase paintings through the study of juxtaposed motifs.

A last example of the hetaera-housewife antithesis is provided by the two sides of a much humbler vase, a pitcher (pelike), in Figures 205 and 206. The same man holds up a purse on each side, but to two different women. In Figure 205 the woman looks stern, even though she carries a flower; in front of her there is a wool-working basket. The woman on the other side (Figure 206) is more gracious; she has a wreath in her hair and also holds a flower in one hand. If my reading is correct, the pelike juxtaposes a man with his wife and the same man with a hetaera. In each case the money pouch indicates that he "holds the purse strings"; the following chapter will present evidence that this iconographic symbol connotes an "economic phallus."

The polarization of the female between whore and housewife, nowhere more pronounced than in Classical Athens, has left palpable traces in modern society. Despite a liberalized climate, most professions and trades that are hospitable to women are extensions of the Hera and Aphrodite principles: lower-level schoolteaching, nursing, and secretarial work are extensions of the patronage of Hera; acting, entertainment, any form of show business, serving at tables and on airplanes, fashion designing, and the manufacture of cosmetics fall under the sway of Aphrodite the Harlot.

198. Youths and horse master on the outside.

199. Same as 198, other side of rim: man makes sexual overtures to boy

200. Same as 198, inside: Zeus pursuing Ganymede.

201. Men with and without money negotiating with hetaerai.

202. Same as 201, other half of outside: more negotiations with hetaerai.

203. Same as 201, inside: youth leaving hetaera after sex?

204. Same as 141, inside: respectable lady bringing offerings at house altar.

205.
Money and sex at home: wife with flower and work basket.

206.
Same as 205, reverse: money and sex away from home. Same man with walking stick and a hetaera.

# 9

# The Sex Appeal of Female Toil

> [There are] the conjugal bedroom, the women's room, the loom room, the spinning room, and the corn-grinding room, not to call it by its unpleasant name of treadmill.
> —Pollux, *Onomastikon* (1, 80)

> At that time [in the good old days] no one had a Manes or Setis as slave, but the women themselves had to do all the chores in the house; they got up at dawn to grind the wheat, so that the village resounded with the sound of their milling.
> —Fragment of the comedy *The Savages* by Pherekrates (10)

Herodotus (5, 12) tells a story of two men from Paeonia in northern Greece who tried to enlist the favor of the Persian king Darius by bringing him their sister, a woman "tall and beautiful" who was also a prodigious worker: she could simultaneously carry a full water jug on her head, lead a horse by the reins, and spin flax as she went along. Herodotus' vision of this improbable wonder woman conveys what men in his society wanted from women: sex and labor. In philosophical terms, Aristotle expressed the same notion with surprising candor:

> The specific virtues of women with respect to their body are beauty and height, and with respect to their soul prudence [*sophrosyne*] and love of labor [*philergia*] without servility. (*Rhet.* 1361a)

For the philosopher the corresponding virtues of the male are prudence and "manliness" (*andria*), a character trait which he does not define exactly, but which clearly has nothing to do with hard work.

## Leisure and Labor: Male and Female Work Ethics

As the above citation from Aristotle shows, the Attic Greeks developed separate work ethics for men and for women. For women idleness was not only immoral, it was also unhealthful and conducive to difficult childbirth, according to Aristotle (*Gen. An.* 776a 34). Male Athenians, on the other hand, developed an aristocratic contempt for manual labor. Even the arts and crafts ranked very low in their esteem: they were scorned as lowly (*banausic*) activities, which Attic Greeks regarded as "slavery." In reality, a number of Athenians must have worked hard in the various arts and trades, but at least during the most prosperous period in Athenian history, many of the crafts were practiced not by citizens but by slaves, metics (resident aliens), and foreigners. Pseudo-Xenophon, in the essay *The Athenian Constitution*, observes that "the city is in need of metics on account of the large number of crafts and in order to man its fleet" (1, 12).

In Plato's ideal state no citizen, or even any male slave of a citizen, should engage in any of the trades and crafts (*Laws* 846d). Aristotle did not extend such privileges to slaves, but did recommend that all male citizens be exempt from soiling their hands with wage-earning work (*Pol.* 1337b). This glorification of gentlemanly leisure is characteristic of Athens, and far less so of the non-Attic Greek tradition. The gruff Boeotian poet Hesiod certainly considered labor praiseworthy, or at least unavoidable: "Both gods and men pursue with wrath the one who lives in idleness, image of the stingless drones consuming the fruit of the toil of bees, eating without working" (*Op.* 303–6). The ethnic hero of the Dorian Greeks, Heracles, was not exclusively a monster-slayer and rapist: his various ordeals also included arduous, humiliating toil, whereby his soul was ennobled. In contrast, Heracles' Attic twin, Theseus, did not take on elements of toil as part of his persona.

Attic and non-Attic peoples disagreed about the moral desirability of labor for men, but traditions throughout Greece regarded women's labor as a moral good. In the Homeric poems weaving is done not only by Penelope, the exponent of domestic virtues, but also by Circe and Calypso, who are superhuman and immortal. (They use golden looms, however.)

From an Aegean poet by the name of Semonides we have fragments of a poem entitled *On Women*, apparently an interminable, according to some satirical, tirade against women. All categories of women are criticized and hatefully likened to various animals. The only "good" women are those who resemble the industrious bee (lines 83–93). This comparison to the bee was a commonplace of misogynistic literature; it is also found in a fragment by the poet Phokylides (Fr. 2 Diehl) and in the portrait of the "good wife" in Xenophon's *Oeconomicus* (7, 32; 38).

Although Greek women were urged to remain as busy as bees in the home, the moment they performed any work for pay they met with social disapproval and might even be classed with prostitutes. The poet Anacreon of Megara spoke scornfully of "that foul Artemon who made a disreputable living, consorting with bread-women and voluntary male whores." It is to the sexual connotations of female labor that we must now turn.

## Women's Tasks

From literary sources, especially courtroom speeches and the comedy of Aristophanes, we learn that the women of Athens did at times perform a variety of labors for pay or profit. The same sources, however, make clear that such transactions took place outside, or on the fringes of, respectable society. According to Demosthenes (57, 45), some citizen women became wetnurses, laborers, and grape pickers for wages in times of duress. They were free women who were forced by circumstance to perform what Demosthenes calls "the chores of slaves." Women sold practically everything in the marketplace, but especially foodstuffs. In *Lysistrata* Aristophanes in jest makes up the word "seed-market-cereal-and-vegetable vendors" (457), using the female gender. By selling merchandise women tarnished their standing as ladies of class; the mother of Euripides, according to Aristophanes, sold vegetables in the market, and the comic poet never tires of poking fun at the "greengrocer's son." Whether such vendors usually operated on their own account or merely sold the products of their husbands' labor or estate is not clear. The women of Athens did not regularly work the fields or perform any of the "outside" labors, as Xenophon puts it (*Oec.* 7, 22); their domain was the "indoors." As a result, a pale complexion was considered the mark of class, respectability, and beauty; as a make-up foundation women used white lead, which must have given them a rather ghostly appearance. In vase painting this taste for paleness led to the convention of depicting the exposed flesh of women as white, and that of men in varying shades of brown. Some female professions, such as matchmaking, midwifery, and professional mourning, were probably practiced mainly by post-menopausal women, who were free from many of the social restrictions affecting wives of childbearing age.

Two female labors were not only sanctioned but even glorified by Attic society: textile working and water carrying. These two chores, it will be recalled, were included in the labors performed simultaneously, and with superhuman athletic skill, by Herodotus' fantasy woman from Paeonia. The canonical roles of wool and flax making and of water carrying as female occupations were nearly universal in the ancient Mediterranean world. The practice of fetching water in jugs went out of fashion, at least in the urban areas, as the Romans created more advanced forms of water supply, including their aqueducts. The home textile industry, on the other hand, has had a continual history; it still survives in such altered forms as home carpet knotting, and industrial sewing and knitting under the putting-out system.

In Athens, too, not all of the products of women's toil at the loom wound up on their own backs and those of their families. Like other labors and like prostitution, textile working provided an income of the last resort for women fallen on hard times. The fillets, or headbands, which the Greeks donned for religious events may have been a common marketable item produced for sale. A lady in a comedy by Aristophanes complains that Euripides, by denying the existence of the gods, is depriving her of her livelihood: "For my husband died on Cyprus, leaving me with five small children, whom I was barely able to feed by weaving fillets and selling them in the Myrtle Market" (*Thesm.* 446–48). In "better" circles women surely did not market the goods themselves but left the financial transactions to their men, and this principle may well lie behind many instances of men with money purses in scenes of textile working. We even have a literary description of this practice. In Xenophon's *Memoirs of Socrates,* we learn of a man by the name of Aristarchus, who finds himself the reluctant guardian of a group of female relatives who have been left without male support. Aristarchus is unable to feed this enlarged household and, on Socrates' advice, he buys wool and sets up a home sweatshop: "And when you have arranged things so that they are busily at work," says Socrates, "you will appreciate them, seeing that they are useful to you, and they will love you when they notice that you are pleased with them" (2, 7, 9). Evidently the plan worked, but the women were not quite as docile as Socrates predicted: their guardian reports their complaint that he alone of the household "ate the bread of idleness" (12).

In Greek culture we find these two traditional occupations of women, water carrying and textile working, deeply embedded in the religious-mythological thinking of the age and in men's consciousness of women. Numerous religious cults featured water-carrying rituals (*hydrophoriai*), most of them performed by women. The traditional vessel for carrying water was the hydria, a big-bellied vase with three handles, two on the sides for lifting it when full and one at the neck for picking it up when empty. When filled, a typical Greek hydria weighed about sixty pounds, so there was no concession to the "weaker sex" here. As is still the custom in Italy, Greece, and Turkey, women carried such loads on their heads, supported by a twisted kerchief known as the porter's knot. Men are only rarely shown carrying water pots, and when they do, they carry them not on their heads but on their shoulders, as in one of the sculpted friezes from the Parthenon (Figure 207). The exact ritual here represented is not known. It could be a reference to a water-pouring rite at the Eleusinian mysteries which was performed by men. Why the practice of carrying burdens on the head was regularly regarded as appropriate for women but not for men is one of the minor mysteries of the history of civilization.

In a number of myths, women carrying water or pouring it onto the ground are thereby transformed into figures of fertility and blessing, canonized, as it were, through their patient toil. The fifty daughters of Danaus, the mythological byword for the mass uprising of women against the male order, were purified of the murders of their husbands through a water-carrying ordeal, and transformed into benevolent water nymphs (see my history of the motif: Keuls, 1974).

The myths and rituals surrounding women's textile processing reflect, on the one hand, the perception of spinning and weaving as a major element in the enculturation of the female, a kind of initiation second in importance only to that of marriage, and, on the other hand, man's awe and fear of his incarcerated female, who, though defeated and exploited, holds ineluctable powers over his life and soul. Woven garments feature heavily in myths of female rebellion. In Aeschylus' Orestes story, Clytemnestra entangles Agamemnon in his robes before killing him (A. *Aga.*, 1383). It is no tribute to her housekeeping that in the sequel, *The Libation Bearers*,

207. Parthenon frieze: the male way of carrying waterpots.

after Orestes has grown up to avenge his father, the bloodied garment is still around and her son bemoans it (981). Medea takes revenge on her unfaithful husband, Iason, by sending a poisoned robe to her rival, Iason's new wife-to-be.

The superman hero Heracles also dies a death-by-textile: his wife, Deianeira, unwittingly causes his death by sending him a poisoned garment, thinking it is steeped in a love potion. The very thread of men's lives is allotted, spun, and snipped by women, the Moirai. Perhaps the most telling of the textile myths is that of Arachne (Spider), told by Ovid after Greek sources (*Met.* 6, 5–145). The girl Arachne had not only the hubris of vying with Athena in domestic skill but also the imprudence to depict in her tapestry the deceitful dalliances of gods with mortals, a topic understandably offensive to the virgin goddess on several scores. Athena struck the hapless girl with a weaving shuttle and Arachne, in fear, tried to hang herself, the inevitably textilic mode of suicide for Athenian women; Athena saved Arachne by turning her into a spider in the nick of time. The image of the spider spinning away in dark recesses is not only an apt metaphor for the lives of Athenian women during the height of Attic civilization; it also reflects the Athenian man's fear of the web of treachery being woven for him at home. In Aeschylus' *Agamemnon* the chorus laments over the body of their slain king: "There you lie, gasping out your life in unholy death, ensnared in that spider's web" (1493–94).

In sexual matters, fantasies of fear are rarely far removed from fantasies of lust, and this holds true for the home textile industry in Classical Athens. Sex and textiles were closely intertwined in the Greek male consciousness. Before documenting this contention with vase paintings, I should like to make some observations on the chore of water carrying as it appears on Greek monuments, because this labor has a social parallel with that of textile making, but also differs from it. Both involve the exploitation of women as a source of cheap labor, but the societal consequences of each were different, in fact opposite: home textile working was and, in some parts of the world, still is a mechanism for the restriction of women to private quarters. In Rome, for example, under the moral rehabilitation program of the Emperor Augustus, an attempt was made to drive women back to the loom. The Emperor even spread the improbable propaganda that his Empress, the formidable Livia, wove his togas for him. The fetching of water from a public well or fountain, on the other hand, brings women out of the seclusion of the home into the public areas and makes them cross social boundaries, a circumstance of which the vase painters were fully aware.

## Rape at the Well

Scenes of women fetching water in jugs from fountain houses are represented on scores of Attic vases, most of them water jugs themselves; the majority of them are in the black-figure technique. In the latter part of the sixth century B.C., during the "tyranny" of Peisistratos and his sons—actually a benign if autocratic rule—a number of public fountain houses were constructed in the center of Athens; one of them was known as the "Nine Springs Fountain"

(*Enneakrounos*). Scholars have connected the appearance in vase painting of groups of women at fountains with this innovation, and they are undoubtedly correct. There is, however, a deeper significance in these scenes than simply appreciation for a public facility: we know from excavations that, to accommodate the public structures of the Peisistratids, a number of private houses in the center of Athens were torn down and smaller, presumably family-owned, wells were filled in. In other words, a function that had previously taken place in the privacy of the courtyard was now transferred to the public zone, with social and sexual consequences perhaps not anticipated by Peisistratus' city planners.

Figure 208 is a basic rendering of the water-carrying scheme; the woman in the center, in exception to custom, carries her full hydria in her arms rather than on her head. In the scene on the hydria in Figure 209 the artist has stressed the social aspect of the occasion: the women who arrive at the fountain and those who leave it with full water pots gesticulate in passing—that is, they converse. In Figure 210 we get another glimpse of the social interaction at the fountain. This hydria shows a double-headed fountain house with mature women and young girls at work. One mother has brought her little son, who is perched on her right hand in an improbable position. The little girl on the right has abandoned her water pot under the spout and is playing with a ball, apparently to the dismay of her mother on the left, who seems to be admonishing her; the double standard of work ethics applied to children as well as adults.

Not all social interaction in fountain scenes is quite so innocent: a number of them show scenes of sexual molestation of the women by men. The water-carrying ritual provided an outstanding opportunity for male aggression; it was one of the rare occasions on which women were unchaperoned, and the bulky water jugs rendered them defenseless.

The picture on the hydria in Figure 211 was perhaps intended to be merely funny: it shows two women and two men—if we judge by their simple loincloths, they are slaves—at a fountain house with four heads. The inner spouts have the customary lion's heads, the outer fountains are in the shape of mule's heads. The woman and the slave on the right are gesticulating; it seems that the slave has elbowed the woman out of her rightful place at the lion's-head fountain and she has to make do with the mule's-head spout. Whatever the exact social status of the women, their fairly

208. Women at fountain house.

209. Social interaction at the fountain house.

210. The naughty girl playing ball at the fountain house instead of fetching water.

elaborate gowns and hairdos indicate a higher class than that of the male water fetchers, yet it is the women who are displaced. In the comparable scene in Figure 212 the aggression is clearly of a sexual kind. A slave with ugly knobby knees molests a woman who is just arriving at the fountain, by touching her breast. Her raised arm indicates protest.

A full vignette of the theme of molestation at the well can be seen on a hydria, now in Detroit, by the Pig Painter (Figure 213). It dates from the early fifth century B.C. and constitutes one of the rare instances of a group scene at a fountain house in the red-figure technique. On the far left a man sneaks up behind a woman with an empty pot on her head. She pushes the man away with her right hand and raises the left in protest. In the center, another woman has put her water pitcher on the ground to keep a would-be lover at bay. She gesticulates with her left hand; it appears that she is trying to dissuade her accoster with words. Behind her a third water carrier approaches with a full hydria on her head. She is turning around to give warning to the woman who is busy filling her hydria and who, probably because of the noise of the running water, is not yet aware of what is going on. It is characteristic of fifth-century vase painting that the topic of sexual aggression is treated with charm and light-hearted humor.

Who exactly were all these women at the various wells of Athens? They are too fancily dressed to be slaves. A passage in the lexicon by Pollux records a memory that in Athens the wives of alien residents used to fetch water for pay (3, 55); some of the women in the vase paintings may indeed be metics, but surely not all of them. In Aristophanes' Lysistrata the chorus of women citizens laments the difficulty in obtaining water to quench the fire on the Acropolis started by their antagonists; their description parallels the vase paintings:

> At last I'm here, barely could I fill my hydria from the spring at dawn, on account of the crowd and the noise and clatter of jugs. I snatched mine away, jostled as I was by slaves and scoundrels. (327–31)

We are, of course, in the land of fantasy, and the water fetching may in itself be part of the women's comic rebellion. Nevertheless, the passage seems to indicate that the use of public fountain houses by citizen women was not completely unthinkable in the latter part of the fifth century B.C. Most likely, occasions for respectable

211. Women and slaves
at fountain house.

212.
Slave molesting woman
at fountain house.

women to fetch water at public (or other visible) places were rare and furtive enough to give rise to male erotic fantasies. Two fifth-century water-fetching pictures reveal such a Peeping Tom mentality. In Figure 214 (a krater, or wine-mixing vessel), two satyrs in their customary state of sexual excitement are harassing a girl who is drawing water from a rustic-looking pump. Figure 215, a vase painting applied to the shoulder of a hydria, shows a more intricate scene. On the left a girl approaches a low fountain with a jug to fill; on the right another girl has placed her pot under a second spout. She has taken off her clothes, which hang overhead, and she sits on the ground masturbating. A man stands between the two girls in a contorted position. Having turned his back on the naked girl, he looks at the new arrival with a startled expression. It appears the couple has been caught having sex at the well, and the frustrated girl is completing the action by herself.

There are a number of Greek myths in which women are raped at or abducted from a well, but the myth of Poseidon and Amymone may be considered the mythological codification of the theme. In Chapter 2 we noted that the rape of Amymone was one of the many myths of sexual violence by the gods which became popular in the early fifth century. After the rape the god shows Amymone a well, which was subsequently named after her, in compensation for her lost virginity. Thus the story had what the Greeks regarded as a happy ending. To illustrate the transformation of this tale of rape into one of blessing, Figure 216 shows it in a fifth-century Attic rendering. Poseidon is wielding his particular phallic weapon, the trident, in the customary aggressive manner. Amymone is fleeing, but she also makes the stereotyped gesture of *apokalypsis* which spells sexual surrender. Figure 217, on the other hand, shows a south Italian picture of the myth from the fourth century B.C.: by now all traces of violence are gone, and Poseidon and Amymone are metaphors for the mortal bride and groom. The other side of the same vase, in fact, idealizes a mortal couple (Figure 218).

## Wool and Sex in Vase Painting

Illustrations of textile processing in private houses are found only sporadically in black-figure pottery, but have survived by the hundreds from the great period of Attic red-figure production. It has often been stated that such pictures provide realistic glimpses

213. Molestation at the well: men harassing women sexually.

214. Satyrs molesting a woman at water pump.

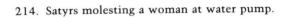

215.
Scene at fountain: masturbating woman, startled man, and new arrival.

216. Poseidon about to rape the water carrier Amymone.

217. Poseidon and Amymone: the happy ending.

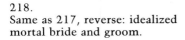

218.
Same as 217, reverse: idealized
mortal bride and groom.

of daily life in the women's quarters of ordinary homes. This view, in my opinion, is erroneous. The men of Athens cultivated their ignorance about the realities of life in the *gynaikonitis* no less than they did about the functioning of the female body. I have already noted their belief that conception takes place during menstruation. Aristotle assures us that menstruation tends to take place during the waning moon, presumably in all women at the same time (*Hist. An.* 581a 35). The combination of these two delusions, if taken seriously, should have caused a monthly stampede of husbands to their wives' quarters. The illustrations of domestic life in vase paintings are equally far removed from reality. In highly symbolic form, they express male-generated notions and fantasies about life in the "other," the female, world. When men do appear in the *gynaikonitis* in a vase painting, they are frequently shown with a walking stick, as if they were making a visit to an alien realm. Occasionally they are wreathed for a dinner they will soon enjoy in the men's quarters.

The symbolic style of rendering interior scenes came in with the red-figure technique during the late Archaic age. What gives these new indoor scenes a particularly unrealistic aspect is that sometimes the graphic form is more meaningful than the object depicted; the symbolic associations attached themselves more to the form than to what is represented. The first indication of what may be termed "the priority of form over function" is the confusion in the *gynaikonitis* of two objects of similar form but diverse use—namely, the hand mirror and the distaff. The distaff is a short staff around which raw wool is wound so as to form a ball. In hand spinning, the spinster draws the wool from the ball and twists it into thread with her fingers. A drop spindle may be attached to the end of the thread to stretch it and make the twisting process faster. Not infrequently, it appears that the wool on the distaff has been carded or prespun, into something like crude threads or roves, which sometimes may be discerned in the illustrations. The hand mirrors commonly used by Athenian ladies were small and round, and attached to a handle. Since mirrors are often depicted at an angle, and distaffs may be anywhere from round and full to nearly empty and cylindrical, the two objects in vase painting look remarkably alike. Figure 148 shows the humorous portrait of a hetaera contemplating her sagging breasts in a mirror. Figure 219 depicts a lady at her spinning, twisting thread from a half-full distaff. A man, doubtless her husband, stands in front of her, like Xenophon's Ischomachus,

219. The distaff: interior scene with woman spinning.

checking up on the progress of labor in the household. His walking stick suggests that he is merely visiting from the outside world of men. The little boy with hoop and stick, also idle, makes it clear that we are in the women's quarters. The oil flask in Figure 220 has an ambiguous object hanging on the wall. From its shape it could be taken for a mirror, but the fuzzy bits of wool around its periphery show that it is a distaff. On the small amphora in Figure 221, the pose of the lady stroking her curly hair indicates that she is admiring her beauty in a mirror. The painting in Figure 222, on the other hand, is not very well articulated, and it is impossible to say whether the lady is holding a mirror or a distaff. Were the painters of these pictures careless, or did the users of pottery in fifth-century Athens have a keener eye than we for the subtle differences in iconography? Neither is likely. It is more probable that the confusion was intentional: for the painter, both forms conveyed the same meaning, feminine grace and charm. Clearly the interchangeability of two objects so dissimilar in purpose reflects a male-centered symbolism, because from the women's point of view the arduous task of spinning and the pleasures of leisurely primping must have had next to nothing in common.

The other instance of form over verisimilitude may be seen in illustrations of weaving. The elaborate stand-up loom which we saw on the lekythos by the Amasis Painter in Figure 93a appears in the red-figure technique in only a few cases. The picture of the mourning Penelope with her son, Telemachus, in Figure 223 is an example. She sits in front of the woven tapestry which, according to the familiar story, she is going to unravel during the night in order to stall her suitors. Instead of showing a large loom, a number of *gynaikonitis* scenes depict women with what may be a small hand loom or perhaps a tapestry loom (or, as some call it, an embroidery frame)—in any case, a luxury implement, not designed for the serious manufacture of cloth. As Pomeroy has recently pointed out, the pose of women holding the hand loom often echoes that of women playing the lyre. Chapter 4 pointed to the stereotype of the seated lady with an object as a vague and probably unconscious memory of the enthroned mother goddess. Figure 100a shows such a seated lady with a hand loom. It is a detail of the decoration of a kalathos, one of the rare work baskets in terra cotta that have been found.

Does the abandonment of the large stand-up loom by the vase

painters of the fifth century indicate that women no longer engaged in weaving in their homes? Certainly not. Plato mentions male weavers, and some industrial textile production was carried out by men in craft workshops, but there is ample literary evidence that the weaving of fabrics for clothing continued to be performed within the family, and loom weights have been found in large numbers in private dwellings of the fifth and fourth centuries. Why, then, do looms almost disappear from vase painting, whereas spindles

220.
The distaff on the wall;
woman folding garment.

221. The mirror: a lady
looking at herself.

222. Mirror or distaff?

223. Penelope at her loom, with son Telemachus.

and wool baskets are depicted in large numbers? Apparently the kalathos, the distaff, the spindle, and the dainty hand loom acquired sexual and social associations compatible with the family ethic of Classical Athens, whereas the loom did not.

## Symbols of Domestic Virtues

Inevitably, both the water jug and the textile-working implements (especially the work basket and the distaff) became symbols, not only of women's lives but also of the virtues of industry and submissiveness that society cultivated in women. The English word "spinster" is a last vestige of these associations. Spinning yarn by hand, before the invention of the spinning wheel, was an enormously laborious task, but only a few illustrations in vase painting bring out the labor involved. Figures 224 and 225 show a shallow pyxis or box, with openings dividing its drum into three parts. The panels of the side walls show three women in the *gynaikonitis*. In Figure 224 the woman is seated on a low stool; in her right hand she holds a spindle, in the left a spool on which she is winding thread. The work basket at her feet is full. In Figure 225 a second spinster is hand spinning from a distaff; a third woman is resting on a bed with her eyes open. Though fully dressed, the latter woman has taken off her sandals, one of which is shown on the floor. The oil flask on the wall perhaps indicates that she is relying more on sex appeal than spinning to please her husband. It would appear that the second spinster is reporting the idler to someone.

Wool-working implements become so strongly associated with female domesticity that they often appear on the white-ground oil flasks that were used as funerary offerings. In this context the work basket presents a last accolade to a deceased wife, as it did later on Roman tombs: "she stayed home and made wool" (*domi mansit, lanam fecit*). Figure 226 shows such an oil flask, from about 480 B.C., with a lady in the "matronly pose" piling yarn or ribbons into a work basket. Occasionally the basket itself may have been used as a tomb monument, commemorating the deceased woman's skill at spinning; at least on the south Italian hydria reproduced in Figure 227, the kalathos is depicted in this way.

## Athena of the Loom Room

We have already had many occasions to look at Athena, patron goddess of the city of Athens, the archetype of the virago, or man-woman. Figure 228 shows her once again, in a detail from a vase now in Cleveland, in which the painter has particularly brought out her masculine build by giving her the arm musculature of a prize fighter. Throughout the Greek world, Athena was also the goddess of crafts; in this capacity she was known as Athena of the Workshop (Ergane). In Athens, however, patronage of the male crafts was largely assumed by the craftsman god Hephaestus, leaving Ergane to oversee the home textile industry. Even within this industry, this

224. Spinning as hard work.

225a,b.
Same as 224: another spinster
and a lazy lady.

226. The work basket as funerary symbol.

227. The work basket as funerary monument.

goddess discouraged women from its more creative aspects. In the myth of Arachne, Athena suppressed Arachne's weaving, the more skilled part of wool working, in which Greek women must have reached considerable artistry. What she allowed was spinning, the more mechanical part. Accordingly, Athena Ergane was regularly portrayed with a spindle, but seldom with weaving implements (Figure 229). No image of Ergane with spindle survives from Attica. Conceivably the same mythological censorship of women's weaving skills is responsible for the disappearance of the loom from fifth-century Attic vases. The four-drachma coin from Asia Minor in Figure 230 shows the goddess with a spindle in one hand and a spear in the other, signifying her two domains.

A pictorial oddity, which to my knowledge is not attested for territorial Greece, but is frequently found in the Greek sites in Italy, is a picture of the owl of Athena spinning wool out of a work

228. Athena as warrior with
male physique.

229. Athena Ergane holding spindle.

230.
Athena Ergane with spindle
and spear on a coin from
Asia Minor.

basket, imprinted on mold-made terra-cotta loom weights. Figure 231 shows such an object (reproduced in drawing rather than as a photograph, since its relief is too low to be captured on film).

## Marital Sex and Spinning

The qualities of industry, obsequiousness, and fear and awe of the male which society fostered in women not only served male convenience but became sources of the sex appeal of women. Numerous domestic scenes combine elements of spinning and sex. Figure 232 shows the inside of a cup by the great painter Douris. It features two ladies with work baskets in the women's quarters. One is seated and is carding wool over her bare leg, which is propped on a little stand. The other is not working but is making the flirtatious gesture of lifting the tip of her dress, the *apokalypsis* which we have already encountered. Behind her is a couch (*kline*). In other words, there is more to this scene than wool working; the gesture and the *kline* both allude discreetly to sexual activity as well. We already saw part of the outside decoration of this cup in Figure 153, which shows an elegant and stately *komos* of men without any women. As usual, there is a playful tie between the outside and the inside themes of the cup: the men at their revels, without the customary female companions, anticipate the sexual delights of the home. The scene in Figure 233 is similar to that on the Douris cup, but the allusions are not so clearly discernible here.

The lascivious aspect of this carding scene is suggested mainly by its occurrence on a kylix.

We know that for the carding of fibers women used a protective knee cover, but this is very rarely shown in vase painting. There are, however, a few examples of these terra-cotta knee protectors, decorated with motifs either of wool working or of marriage, which apparently were favorite bridal gifts. Figure 234 shows such a knee cover, decorated with a wedding scene: the bride is identified by an inscription as Alcestis, the mythological byword for the self-sacrificing bride; as in the play by Euripides named after her, she is willing to die for her husband when nobody else will. In the illustration, which makes no reference to her sacrifice, she leans comfortably against her wedding bed, in the half-opened door, the traditional symbol of conjugal sex. If the vessel itself, with its associations of hard labor in the loom room, already ties the role of the wife to values of industry and submission, the decoration goes one step further and mythologizes the conjugal norms for women. The remainder of the scheme alludes to two other unfortunate

231.
Terra cotta loom weight with Athena's owl spinning wool out of a work basket.

2.32. Wool and sex: woman carding wool and woman making flirtatious gesture. Couch.

brides, Thetis (partially shown) and Harmonia (not shown). Thetis we have met before: she was the immortal sea nymph whom the mortal suitor Peleus married by brute force. The union produced the glorious hero Achilleus, whose early death Thetis had all eternity to mourn. Her poignant role as the anxious mother in the *Iliad* is difficult to forget. Harmonia (Harmony) is depicted on the reverse, enthroned as bride and surrounded by divinities and allegories.

The daughter of Ares and Aphrodite, she married Cadmos, the legendary founder of Thebes. The wedding took place on the Acropolis of that city, in the presence of the gods, who showered the bride with wedding presents. But the gift from the groom, the "necklace of Harmonia," stirred up so much greed that it was the cause of endless strife and acts of disloyalty, including the betrayal of a husband by his wife. The myth of Harmonia dramatized a standard vice in the catalogue of women's traditional shortcomings—

233. Wool and sex: woman with distaff and woman carding wool. Oil flask.

namely, addiction to finery. This knee cover was a beautiful and, no doubt, expensive wedding gift, but one with melancholy implications, because of the ethos under which the bride was to spend the rest of her life.

Figure 235 is a black-figure alabastron (with all the sexual associations of this phallus-shaped oil flask); it depicts two handsomely gowned ladies with distaffs, ribbons, and wool baskets. A narrow column defines the indoor setting of the scene. Two inscriptions read *kale*, "she is beautiful." Concepts of beauty, sex, and women's industry are intertwined in this simple but graceful decoration.

These vase paintings, as well as others reproduced earlier, document the blending of imagery derived from women's labors with that alluding to their erotic appeal. The female qualities of industry, obedience, and fear of their husbands, which surely at first were cultivated for purposes other than sex appeal, wound up being sensuously attractive to men.

It is only one step from such fantasies, about female obeisance to the male, to thoughts of rape. In one of the Roman legends surrounding the origins of the Roman Republic, the brutish Sextus Tarquinius, relative of the early legendary kings of Rome, rapes the lovely and virtuous Lucretia, not only because of her beauty, but because she had been found late at night, industriously spinning away with her handmaidens. As Livy put it, Tarquinius "was

234. Knee cover for carding wool, with a bride ("Alcestis") at the bedroom door.

235a,b.
The phallic alabastron: woolworking
women and two inscriptions
"she is beautiful."

aroused by the vision of her beauty and her virtue both" (1, 57). In the melodramatic account, Lucretia kills herself from shame.

In Attic iconography there is an instance of the "rape of virtue" in the motif of Poseidon and Aethra. This lady, the mother of Athens' national hero Theseus, was one of several victims of the sea god's raping ardor. In vase paintings of the pursuit (Figure 236), Aethra regularly carries a wool-working basket. Conceivably this indicates that in the version presented here she was already the wife of Aegeus. In any case, the scheme illustrates the sex appeal of domestic virtue. If we recall the motif of Poseidon raping Amymone the water carrier, we observe the god, who was prominent in the Athenian founding legends, being sexually aroused by exponents of the two standard categories of domestic labor.

## Spinning Hetaerai

Oddly enough, even though wool-working implements were symbols of wifely qualities, they were also shown in the context of the hetaerai and their customers. Figure 237 reproduces such a scene on the outside of a symposium cup. The two couples are doubtless the familiar "youths negotiating with hetaerai." In the center sits a lady holding a distaff in one hand and a spindle in the other. In the chapter on hetaera life, several illustrations showed textile-working implements in the domain of prostitution. What is the significance of these "spinning hetaerai"? According to one theory, accepted by several experts on ancient art (Rodenwaldt, 1933), the spinning activities are an affectation on the part of the prostitutes or their owners: by equipping themselves with the symbols of respectability, they could wring higher fees out of their customers. The theory is ingenious, and it evokes shades of the sexual fantasies enacted by the prostitutes in Genet's play *The Balcony*, who are trained to cater to their customers' quirks in a variety of disguises. In my native city of Amsterdam, now the whoring capital of the Western world, one can observe prostitutes in their show windows, dressed in exotic disguises, such as hula dancers and geisha girls, but also done up as frumpy Dutch house-wives in aprons. However, in fifth-century Attica such charades are not only unattested but unlikely. Despite the erotic fantasies about domestic life which the vase paintings document, it would seem that an Athenian man would rather see his wife disguised as a

236. Poseidon in pursuit of Aethra
with wool basket.

hetaera than his companion for the evening masquerading as his
wife. It is true that Neaera's owner Nicarete passed off her slave
prostitutes as her daughters for higher profits. Nicarete, however,
was by no means "respectable," but a former prostitute herself. In
fact, the view that wool-working implements denote only matrimonial virtue cannot be defended: too many vase paintings combine
symbols of textile working with those of prostitution. The implements point to the quality of industry (*philergia*), which men found
sexually appealing in *all* women, whether they belonged to the
category of citizen women or to that of prostitutes.

## The Money Pouch in Male Hands

The money purse as a pictorial stereotype presents another problem for scholars. It occurs frequently when men are negotiating with hetaerai. But what are we to make of scenes in which a man offers a purse to a seemingly virtuous woman engaged in wool working? Figure 238 offers one such instance, on an oil flask by the Pan Painter; there a young man holds out a purse to a seated lady who is busy spinning. Behind the youth a slave girl (not shown) bustles about near a wool-working basket. Is the youth trying to woo the seated woman away from wool working to the more profitable trade of prostitution, as some scholars think? This is, indeed, probable, but the interpretation cannot explain all scenes in which men hold up purses to women.

In Figure 239 a stern woman, sitting in a colonnade, is approached by three males, a determined looking boy, a somewhat diffident man and a youth. It has been suggested that the latter are father and son, on a family expedition to the neighborhood brothel—the small boy would be the madam's attendant or son in this reading (D. Williams 1982). However, the woman is characterized as the "disagreeable matron" and the colonnade suggests the inner part of a private residence, not an entrance from the street, and hence we probably have a vignette of family life here, perhaps a henpecked husband trying to appease his wife with money.

What, then, is the meaning of the pouch? As a symbolic image it has some striking peculiarities. It is usually shown in the hands of men or hanging on the wall in a male context. Typically, the persons to whom it is offered seem strikingly unaware of its presence. Although the symbol refers to money, it is rarely shown in scenes alluding to the exchange of cash for merchandise (see the Notes for a recently discovered instance). On an early red-figure cup, to be sure, a youth holding a pouch ogles three vases, and perhaps he is contemplating a purchase, but even here no money changes hands and no seller is in sight (Figure 240). Instead, the pouch is nearly always depicted in scenes where the money governs a human relationship, between homosexual lover and handsome boy, between hetaera and customer, or between husband and wife. In the latter case it signifies that even where the wife produces a

237. Men negotiating with hetaerai; woman
(a madam?) with distaff and spindle.

238.
Man offering purse to seated
spinster (barely shown). Wooing
her away from respectability?

239.
Family scene: wife with distaff and oil flask, young son, father with money, older son with sponge and strygil.

marketable product, it is the husband who controls the purse strings. This must also be the implication in one isolated instance in which a man holds up a purse to a seated woman lyre player (Figure 241).

Pictorially the purse is, as it were, an economic phallus; this impression is conveyed not only by its shape but also by the manner in which the man stretches it out in front of him in the most characteristic instances of the symbol. In Figure 242, for example, a man is following a woman who is leaving the scene but who turns around toward him, making a gesture of protest. The picture could be entitled "rape by money."

By way of contrast, Figure 243 shows a comic vignette of home life, which also deals with money, but in which no pouch appears, since it would have had to be depicted empty. In the center stands a stern matron with a sunken mouth: she is portrayed as toothless, a probably all too realistic feature of middle age in antiquity. She holds up an empty distaff. Her husband, on the left, is making an apologetic gesture which says, "But I have no money." Their young son on the right tries to conciliate them.

The symbol of the money purse appears in its most schematic form in Figure 244. On the left a young woman, characterized as a slave by her short-cropped hair, is leaving the scene balancing an empty water jug on her head. The object in her left hand is probably

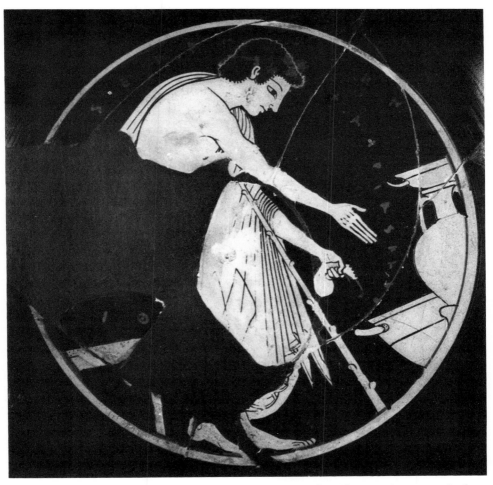

240. Youth with purse in a potter's shop.

the porter's knot on which she will place the filled jug when she returns. She is making a gesture of dismay. The next figure is a man leaning on a walking stick and clutching a purse in his right hand. He is looking toward the far right. In the center a young woman on a chair is busy spinning yarn from a distaff. More wool (or possibly a bonnet) is hanging overhead. On the right stands a woman holding a belt in both hands. Behind her a hand loom can be seen. The man is looking at the standing woman, not at the seated lady. What does this configuration tell us? The gesture of the loosened girdle is an iconographic stereotype implying sexual surrender; if the female figure on the right is taken to represent this association, the bearded man with money finds himself in the presence of three women, who embody the characteristic three services rendered by female to male in ancient Athens—namely, water carrying, wool working, and sex. Another interpretation of this vase painting would have the man trying to woo away the seated woman from virtue to sex, but this reading does not adequately account for the other two figures, nor for the fact that the man is not looking at the spinster but at the woman with the loosened clothes.

As a symbol, the money pouch reinforced man's awareness of the victory of male over female, which formed the psychological basis of his existence. If his physical victory over woman was illustrated for him on numerous civic monuments in the portrayals of the Amazonomachia, and his domestic supremacy was enacted daily in the home through the ethic of labor for women and leisure for men, his economic powerhold found graphic expression in the image of the money pouch.

241. Woman lyre player and man with money pouch.

242. Man and hetaera arguing over money.

243. Husband and wife arguing: she complains that she is out of wool.

244. Water-carrying, spinning and sex, and a man
with money to buy these services.

# *10*

# Easier to Live with Than a Wife:
# The Concubine

> We keep hetaerai for pleasure, concubines for the daily care
> of our bodies, and wives for the bearing of legitimate children
> and to keep faithful watch over our house.
> —Pseudo-Demosthenes, *Against Neaera* (122)

> Isn't a hetaera easier to live with than a wife? Yes, far more,
> and for good reason. For the wife under law can keep her
> home even though she has contempt for it. But the harlot
> knows that she must buy her man with the way she treats
> him, or take off and find another.
> —Fragment of the comedy *Athamas* by Amphis

The above quotation from the speech *Against Neaera* is almost
invariably found in studies of Athenian social life, inasmuch as it
states, with unabashed frankness, the view of women as servants to
men, and also because it documents the moral and legal sanction
extended to prostitution in Attica. Little attention, however, is paid
to the middle category in the speaker's enumeration, the concubine,
who is responsible for "the daily care of men's bodies." If men
could satisfy their sexual needs with prostitutes without incurring
social censure, and if they had indoctrinated their wives in the
virtues of meekness and industry, why did they require the further
services of concubines? For apparently many men, especially later
in life, wound up in such habitual extramarital relationships.

## The Sexual Career of the Perfect Gentleman

The model Athenian gentleman, the "beautiful and good" (*kalos
kagathos*), probably started his sexual experimentation in youth as
the "beloved" of a mature man, who would copulate with him and

offer social and intellectual favors. The youth was introduced to heterosexual intercourse at a symposium, where he could develop a supremacist stance by making slave prostitutes submit to dorsal sex. The practice of humiliating and battering older prostitutes at drinking parties helped him to overcome the lingering mother image in his soul. Soon he began going to brothels and private pimps to rent a succession of prostitutes, with whom he engaged in revels and symposia. Society afforded him a long rope of tolerance; promiscuity, group sex, drinking, and violent "pranks" were standard ingredients of this phase. When no longer very young, our hero brought home a child bride whom he had not previously met. His new wife entered his home, cowed and terrorized, both by the separation from her own family and the overdramatized prospect of defloration. If she survived the hazards of teenage motherhood, she probably developed, as a mature woman, feelings of frustration and hostility against her husband. By then our hero was a full-fledged member of the male community and was probably taking his turn as a lover of boys—getting even, in a way, for the humiliations of his own youth. With the onset of middle or old age he began to yearn for more tender attentions, regular companionship, and personal care; at that time, he would take a concubine (*pallake*). With her he entered into an informal, essentially monogamous, quasi-marriage of undetermined duration, in which he held all the power.

His wife, though restricted in her movements, had enjoyed at least some protection and legal recourse, especially if she was of a prominent family and still had her relatives' support. With the help of a male relative she could turn to the city magistrate and put forward the charge of "ill treatment" (*kakosis*). She could sue for divorce for cause and reclaim her dowry, thus making life difficult for her husband, especially if he had invested the dowry. The prostitute, too, had a measure of protection: her pimp or owner regarded her body as an investment. In contrast, the concubine had neither safeguard, and, once installed, was at the mercy of her keeper. The attractiveness of the arrangement to the man was enhanced by her freedom to entertain his guests and accompany him to other hosts' parties: both Aspasia and Neaera had social contacts with men other than their lovers, which legal wives could not have. In all probability most concubines were former prostitutes, and not subject to social censure. The Greek word *pallake* has no precise legal meaning and can refer to women living in non-legalized relationships whether they had slave, free, or freedwoman status. It is evident from the courtroom speeches that even citizen women who had lost the support of their families occasionally entered into such irregular arrangements.

## The Slave Concubine

With regard to female slaves offered by their owners for sexual purposes, men who had money had every conceivable option. They could visit brothels for quick sexual release, rent the more desirable prostitutes and slave entertainers for a night or for a party, lease them for longer periods, or buy them outright. Not infrequently, as we have seen, men pooled their money to buy a slave prostitute for joint use.

It also must have been common for men to have habitual sexual relationships with female slaves who had grown up in their households; but this form of concubinage would only rarely result in any documentation. We should probably assume that slave women, if they were lucky, might derive some benefit from their charms if they succeeded in interesting their owners in something more than casual copulation. However, the one account we have of the fate of a slave concubine illustrates the horrible pitfalls along the path of this career. The story is told in Antiphon's speech *Against the Stepmother*, and there is no reason to doubt its veracity, since the *pallake*'s fate is peripheral to the issue. The speech was cited in Chapter 3 as an example of the "namelessness" of Athenian women; neither the accused, the "stepmother," nor the slave concubine has a name. The accused and her deceased husband, the alleged murder victim, had frequently extended hospitality to a friend by the name of Philoneos and to his unnamed concubine, who was obviously his slave. Philoneos had tired of the woman sexually and intended to turn her over to a brothel for exploitation—not selling her but keeping her there for revenue, an arrangement which to my knowledge is not elsewhere attested. If the girl was not a seasoned prostitute, her terror at this prospect can only be imagined.

At the same time the head of the household had also developed a roving eye, and his wife, the "stepmother," approached the *pallake* with a proposition: during a dinner party the girl was to serve the two men a love potion that would restore their desire for their respective mates. As usual, the slave concubine, but not the wife, feasted with the men. According to the accusation, the potion was poisonous. Believing it to be a harmless aphrodisiac, the slave administered the philter, and both men died—Philoneos immediately, and the husband after an illness of twenty days. The slave was arrested, routinely tortured for information by wracking on the wheel, and executed without trial. Although the accuser represents the slave as acting in innocence, he nevertheless considered that she was treated "as she deserved" (1, 20). If sympathy for slaves had been conceivable in Athenian culture, it would have been to the accuser's advantage to dramatize the way that the defendant had tricked the slave into administering a poison; but the jury evidently was not susceptible to feelings of indignation on behalf of so humble a creature.

A much less serious hazard of the slave concubine was that of being caught in the middle of that curious and typically Athenian institution, an exchange of estates (antidosis). Wealthy Athenians were obliged, by way of contribution to the city, to finance public events and utilities, some of them extremely costly. A private person might, for example, be called upon to underwrite a performance of a tragedy or to outfit a warship. If a subject of this form of taxation felt unjustly treated, and believed that another citizen had more ample means, he could challenge this person to take over his contribution. The challenged citizen in turn could counter this unwelcome invitation by proposing a complete exchange of estates. In such a case, the entire property of the two citizens, including their slaves, had to be exchanged—a drastic, but probably effective, means of preventing tax evasion.

A confusing and somewhat lurid story concerning the fate of a prostitute in such a case is set forth in Lysias' speech On the Wound (4). The plaintiff and the defendant had agreed upon an exchange of their properties, an arrangement that was afterwards annulled. A slave concubine who had been part of one of the estates thus changed bed fellows twice; evidently both men liked her services and they decided to use her jointly, after making some kind of financial settlement to that effect. The plaintiff, it seems, was keeping the woman to himself without making the corresponding monetary adjustment with the other owner, thus causing the dispute. Although this speech may in fact have been composed for training purposes, rather than for an actual law suit, it nonetheless documents social mores.

Surviving courtroom speeches reveal several cases of men buying women to serve as their concubines. As Plutarch said,

> Isn't it true that respectable women have the reputation of being hostile and insufferable, with their severity and eagle-beaked faces? They call them Furies because they are always nagging their husbands. And when one's legitimate wife becomes intolerable, isn't it best to take a companion like Abrotonon of Thrace or Bacchis of Miletus, without any form of engagement? You just buy them outright and scatter a few nuts over their head. (*Amat.* 753d)

The "scattered nuts" are a reference to the ritual of the "down-pourings" (*katachysmata*), used upon the arrival of both brides and new slaves. Bringing a purchased concubine into the women's quarters when a legitimate wife was already there was, however, marginal behavior. In Demosthenes' speech *For Phormio*, part of the scurrilous picture drawn of the defendant is that he had "married off one hetaera and bought another one free," even though he had a wife (36, 45). If the wife was in a position to protest, she would have cause to do so. Alcibiades' wife, for instance, did lodge a complaint.

By and large the fate of those slaves who had sexual contact with their owners, although not enviable, was probably better than that of the many who had no such opportunity to ingratiate themselves.

## The Free Concubine

The amusing comedy by Félicien Marceau, *La Bonne Soupe*, was produced under the title *The Good Soup* on Broadway, but perhaps should have been called *The Gravy Train* in English. In this play the prostitute heroine decides she is too good for walking the streets and looks for a man to keep her. Her method entails first determining the man's financial eligibility by testing the quality of his socks, and then simulating desire and sexual fulfillment with abundant groans.

In the same way, for many of the free prostitutes of Athens hooking a prosperous older man with a need of "care for his body" must have been the only hope of escaping misery in their declining years. Many succeeded, for, as a character in a fifth-century comedy by Susarion said, "Woman's an ill, but, fellow townsmen, still/No house can be a home without such ill" (Fr. 3; trans. John Maxwell Edmonds). If a free prostitute or other alien managed to win the affection of a prominent man, she had the possibility of living a comfortable life. Pericles' Aspasia apparently fared well through her relationship with the city's leader. Neaera enjoyed many amenities while she was the *pallake* of Phrynion. In Demosthenes (53, 55) an accused man is said to have bought the freedom of a hetaera, and taken her into his house; this relatively fortunate woman "had much gold jewelry and beautiful clothes and was going out in brilliant fashion." The orator Isocrates installed Lagisca as his concubine, and Sophocles too is said to have had an illegitimate wife on whom he fathered children. Late sources name two wives of Socrates, not only the notorious Xanthippe, but also one Myrto. If this account is genuine, Myrto was probably a concubine.

According to post-Classical sources, Athens during the Peloponnesian War passed a law that legitimized the offspring of men and their concubines, even if the fathers also had citizen wives. This information is highly suspect (Flacelière, *Daily Life*, 74). Nevertheless, some men deliberately sired children on their concubines. The offspring of these unions, while not endowed with full citizenship, did not lack some civic status. Official "bastard lists" were kept; and outside the city of Athens a special gymnasium, called Cynosarges and held sacred to Heracles, was constructed for the special use of those who were not of pure Athenian blood (Dem. 23, 213).

Since no records of female citizens were kept, it seems highly likely that a few women managed to wheedle their way into legitimate standing, with or without the connivance of their men. Neaera's daughter, Phano, after all, managed to hook two Athenian citizens as husbands, one of whom became a king-archon.

But for most, the path of concubinage was slippery. Demosthenes' speech *Against Aristogiton* (25, 56–8) contains the account of a free alien woman named Zobia, who had housed the defendant after he had broken jail, and later had given him clothes and money for his escape out of town. Eventually she claimed some recompense from him. In return he accused her of defaulting on taxes and dragged her before the "sales room of the alien registry." If found guilty of tax arrears, she would have been sold into slavery.

The legal position of common-law wives was pitiable. No laws to protect the well-being or the interests of concubines *per se* are known. A curious statute, however, referred to in Lysias' speech *On the Murder of Eratosthenes* (31), gave a man the right to kill anyone copulating with his *pallake* if caught in the act, but only if he was keeping the woman for the purpose of having children. In other words, the law protected not the woman but her keeper's interest in her.

On losing her lover's affection and financial support, a concubine had no other resort than to return to a life of prostitution, as we saw in the fictitious but realistic case of Chrysis, the "Woman of Samos," in Menander's comedy of that name.

# 11

# The Boy Beautiful: Replacing
# a Woman or Replacing a Son?

> You hate women profoundly and therefore you are now turning to boys.
> —Fragment of the comedy *The See-alls* by Cratinus (152 K)
>
> Boys are beautiful too, for as long a time as they look like women.
> —The hetaera Glycera, as quoted by Athenaeus (605d)

No aspect of Athenian culture has been as controversial as its widespread practice of male homosexuality. For centuries historians have tried to justify these habits, explain them, or explain them away. In the past a number of scholars were drawn to the study of ancient Greece in part by a sense of identification with its homo-erotism. The Roman Emperor Hadrian, a philosopher of sorts, should probably be counted among these. Sometimes, perhaps, Athenian men would not have recognized themselves in the studies of these scholars—a comment not on the sincerity of the latter, only on the accuracy of their identification. Heterosexual classicists of a puritanical bent have castigated the Greeks for their homosex-uality, and even excised evidence of homosexual practices from the record. Only recently have some more rational studies of the phenomenon appeared without preconceived opinions on sexual morality. Foremost among them is Sir Kenneth Dover's recent book, which treats the history of sex life as the various efforts of people to reach orgasm in the best ways they can. It is indeed refreshing when an eminent scholar in a somewhat dry field of learning writes freely on "anal penetration" and "intercrural copulation" (between the thighs). The reader who wishes to learn more about the homo-sexual mating habits of the Greeks would be well advised to consult Dover's study.

It is a common opinion of Dover and others that the peculiarity of Athenian social behavior was not that Athenian men practiced homosexuality—among what people has it not occurred at some times?—but that the Athenians sanctioned it and even glorified it as a useful institution. In contrast to this familiar argument, I will try to show that, although male homosexuality was widely practiced, in the Classical period it was, at the most, only half-heartedly condoned.

One standard explanation of Greek homosexuality is that it represented an escape from the female. As shown by the two epigraphs at the head of this chapter, some Greeks considered handsome young boy lovers a substitute for women. Indeed, neither their cowed or vicious wives at home nor the calculating hetaerai of their symposium nights can have been very satisfying sex partners in the long run. The need to escape from the rasping effect of male-female antagonism must have been just as much a factor in the phenomenon of Greek homosexuality as it is in modern society. Yet the theory of the escape from the dreaded and despised female only skims the surface; it fails to reach the depths of the phenomenon.

If the primary impulse had been to replace a heterosexual relationship, corroded by alienation and hostility, with a nobler one, where sex could be mingled with friendship and intellectual stimulation, the ideal partnership would have been that between two men of comparable age, status, and educational level. Instead, the homosexual connection favored by the Greeks was not so much homoerotic as pederastic; the archetypal relationship was between a mature man at the height of his sexual power and need and a young, erotically undeveloped boy just before puberty. The standard Greek nomenclature gives the older, aggressive partner the title of the "lover" (*erastes*) and the young, passive male that of the "beloved" (*eromenos*). This pattern parallels the rituals of initiation of the young into adult society and thus has pedagogic overtones, as has long been stressed in a number of studies (Bethe, Brelich, Bremmer). However, the evidence for homosexual practices as part of initiation points more strongly to the Dorian Greeks than to those of Attica.

## Anal Sex as an Initiation Ritual

The penis can serve not only as an instrument of pleasure and impregnation but also as a weapon of intimidation. In many cultures intercourse is sometimes practiced as an act of aggression. Rape, for example, springs less from a desire for sexual release than from a drive for revenge. The rapist is "getting even," with a particular woman, with the female sex, or with the world in general. If frontal sex has this aspect, the same is even more true for intercourse from behind, especially anal penetration. In Athens men preferred the rear-end approach with hetaerai, especially the older and lowlier ones. Anal sex is charged with aggression and domination: the submitting partner is in a helpless position, penetration can be painful, and opportunity for the gratification of the passive participant is limited.

Such a pattern seems to follow the scenario of initiation rites and other *rites de passage*. In order to enter adult society, the novice undergoes certain ordeals of humiliation, toil, and submission to his elders. By subordinating his needs and desires to those of the older initiates, he learns to take his place in the power hierarchy of organized society. In time he will live to inflict the same humiliations on the next generation of novices. Pederastic anal sex constitutes a perfect initiatory rite of submission to the desires of the established class, at least for young boys; in the case of girls, the factor of later reciprocity is missing. Anthropologists have found such rituals among many primitive peoples, usually surrounded by secrecy. In a famous article, E. Bethe has provided evidence for such practices among several of the Dorian Greek cultures, most specifically the Dorians of Crete. F. E. Williams has made a careful study of such customs among the Papuans and he cites parallels among other peoples.

Pederastic sex as a rite of transition is sharply distinct from adult homoerotic relations. In fact, while submission to anal sex may serve as a way of enculturating the young male, adult male homosexuality constitutes a rebellion against the social order. A mutual sex relationship between two adult men of approximately the same age and social standing negates the use of sex as the underpinning of a power structure, be it that of man over wife, man over prostitute, or adult male over young boy. It is probably for that reason, and not because it is "unnatural," or breaks the link between sex and procreation, that true male homosexuality is almost universally censured, as in the case of Classical Athens.

The use of male pederastic rituals as a mechanism of initiation has two types of consequences, both of them considered socially undesirable in most cultures. One of them is adult male homosexual pair-bonding, which runs contrary to the standard social organization. The other pitfall is the rise of male homosexual prostitution: after all, when the young boy learns that his good looks provide gratification and invite social favors, he is only one step away from exacting such favors by prostituting himself.

In the Classic Athenian relationship between "lover" and "beloved," some overtones of ritual initiation through pederastic sex remain. However, what is far more striking in Athenian homosexual behavior is the pseudo-parental behavior of the "lovers" in the sixth century B.C. and, second, the stringent legal and moral prohibitions, adopted in the fifth and fourth centuries, against the two outgrowths of this pattern—adult male homosexuality and homosexual prostitution.

## Ganymede: Boy-Love in the Sixth Century B.C.

For this formative century in Attic cultural history our best evidence is vase paintings: those in the black-figure technique, and those in the red-figure technique, introduced about 530 B.C. Early Attic vase paintings with pederastic scenes reveal certain elements that are not at all compatible with an initiation scenario of humiliation. First of all, the "lover" approaches his "beloved" frontally, and copulation, when it is shown, takes place intercrurally. The youth is courted with gifts; these hardly suggest humiliation. In some cases the youth is shown with what may be termed a "puerile erection"; evidently the vase painters wanted to show that the passive partner does derive some pleasure from the contact, even without active participation. A second striking aspect of the homosexual scenes is the frequent showing of an affectionate, almost tender, relationship between a mature man and a male child before puberty, which is sexual but has overtones of a father-son rapport.

A number of the black-figure homosexual scenes clearly represent a ritual occasion. A recurrent motif is that of several adult men dancing around a youth and titillating him sexually on the genitals but also on the chin (Figures 245 and 246). In both cases the passive youth is a young adult and his teasers are mature adults; the main differentiating symbol is the beard on the older men. In Figure 245 the man on the right carries the love gift, which traditionally is an animal, dead or alive; in this case it is a live young deer. Presumably the animal is to be consumed at the end of the ritual. In Figure 247 a similar scene is reduced to the key figures, and again we see the stylized gestures of the touching of chin and genitals. Figure 248 shows a more humorous treatment of the same motif, on the inside of a symposium cup, which, as usual, provides the place for a playful treatment of conventional themes. Here the age difference between "lover" and "beloved" is more pronounced, which may account for the fact that two gift animals are shown, probably a dead hare and a dead fox. The tender youth seems startled by his randy suitor, and makes a gesture of protest.

In Figures 249 and 250, two sides of an amphora, there are similar treatments of courting scenes, in which copulation is included. In the center in each case an adult man is copulating intercrurally with a youth, who, by his stance, does not indicate any participation but who does have a moderate erection. Each scene also includes an "odd man out," with no partner, who stands to the right of the fornicating couple.

The ritualized aspect of this type of behavior may perhaps best be seen on an amphora now in Paris (Figure 251). It contains six figures. The youth and the lover stand in the center; again, the older man is touching the boy's genitals with one hand and stroking his chin with the other. On either side of the pair stands another naked man, but beyond these there are two clothed figures, who are, one would assume, functionaries of the ritual rather than participants in it.

The most curious of the homosexual mating scenes on vases are those in which the boy is childlike and the "lover" is characterized as somewhat older than the bearded young adults in the ritual scenes examined earlier; in terms of age, they could be father and son. The boy in such scenes is not reacting sexually but rather expressing childlike affection for his older partner. Much later, Plato was to make a distinction between the "desire" (eros) of the lover and the "affection" (philia) of the beloved (Phdr. 255d), which approximately parallels the relationship suggested by these vase paintings. Figures 252 and 253 show two sides of an upright drinking cup (skyphos). It is striking that in the scene reproduced

245. Ritual pederastic behavior: the touching of chin and genitals.

246.
More stylized caresses.

247.
Another pair of "lover"
and "beloved."

248. The "beloved" protests.

249.
Homosexual group sex;
intercrural copulation
and the odd man out.

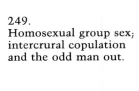

250.
Same as 249, reverse:
homosexual couples
and the odd man out.

in Figure 252 a traditional gesture is reversed, and the boy strokes his mature lover on the chin while the man's left arm rests on the boy's shoulder. On the reverse a similar (or perhaps the same) pair go one step further: the boy jumps enthusiastically into the arms of his lover, who pulls the boy toward him.

In red-figure vase painting the difference in age between lover and beloved is less routinely represented. On a cup by Peithinos (Figure 196) most of the traditional beards are gone, and we must rely on poses and gestures, especially the fondling of the passive partner's genitals, to confirm who is the active and who is the passive partner. Two of the younger participants react sexually. The courtship scene on the inside of the red-figure cup in Figure 254, on the other hand, has a paternal flavor: the lover is bearded, the "beloved" is a mere child and responds affectionately rather than erotically. It is clear from these vase paintings that in the Archaic age of Attic civilization, homosexual behavior was tinged with notions of courtship and mutual affection. The sexual approach was generally frontal and copulation took place between the thighs.

251. Pederastic ritual with overseers.

252. Pederastic sex with father-son overtones.

253. Same as 252, reverse: the "beloved" responds to the "lover."

254. Mature man with responsive child lover. On the wall a sponge and
scraper (strygil).

In several fragments of early Attic literature, in which reference
is made to male homosexual love, there is mention of "thighs,"
which has sometimes been taken as a euphemism for "buttocks."
For example, a poetry fragment by Solon reads as follows: "when
in the delightful flower of youth one learns to love a boy, yearning
for thighs and sweet mouth" (Fr. 25 Diehl). The vase paintings
make it clear that the reference is to intercrural sex. To judge by
Archaic art, anal intercourse was then not associated with reputable
male homoerotic behavior, but with coarser forms of sex, such as
those practiced by satyrs.

The painters' convention of the "juvenile erection" was also a
way of elevating the homosexual relationship to a plane where there
was some degree of mutual satisfaction. Recognition of this conven-

tion helps to solve a small iconographic puzzle. In Figure 255 a seated man is about to whip a small boy named Leagros, a celebrated beauty. For what offense? The penis provides the answer: it is at half-mast, and the boy's hand has just been removed from it. In other words, he was caught masturbating. Censure of adult mastur- bation is conveyed by the scene in Figure 256, where the perpetrators are portrayed as gross, and a defecating dog under the handle adds a scurrilous note.

Devereux has pointed to the striking absence in Attic society of significant father-son relationships. Indeed, by creating a sharp division between home and community life, and strongly favoring the latter, the Athenian male deprived himself of the affectionate side of fatherhood. In Plato's dialogue *Laches*, the character Lysim- achus confesses his inadequacy as a father of sons:

> . . . they and we, and all those who engage in the affairs of their cities, . . . when it comes to their sons and other concerns as well, they neglect their private affairs and arrange them carelessly. (180b)

The "lover-beloved" relationship, at least in part, filled that void. As Devereux has put it:

> The Greek father usually failed to counsel his son; instead, he counseled another man's son, in whom he was erotically interested. As for the boy, who needed an effective father to model himself upon, he had to rely on his *erastes*, who also served as a father surrogate. (78)

## The Myth of Zeus and Ganymede as an Archetype

We saw in Chapter 2 that the male gods in the Olympian divine family have promiscuous tastes and engage in heterosexual as well as homosexual rape of, and love affairs with, many gods and mortals. The standard homosexual paradigm, however, was Zeus' rape of the beautiful boy Ganymede, which was a favorite theme of artists and underwent many transformations through the centuries. While Zeus adopts colorful disguises to go after the mortal women who strike his roving eye—at least, in the literary accounts of his love life—his conquest of Ganymede took place in his own shape until the post-Classical period. In myth, homosexual rape was usually more profitable for the victim than the heterosexual variety: Zeus abducted Ganymede to Mount Olympus, where the youth became his immortal cupbearer, replacing the undistinguished Hebe.

255.
Leagros caught
masturbating.

256. Coarse scene: group masturbation
and a defecating dog.

In vase painting, the standard attributes of Ganymede are a rooster—a conventional homosexual love gift—and a hoop and stick that serve to underline his boyish innocence, as in Figure 257. The best-known representation of Zeus and Ganymede is the statuary group dating from about 480 B.C. in Olympia (Figure 258). Here the boy is depicted as tiny and childlike, and Zeus clasps him to his body in the manner of a father collecting an unruly child.

Figure 200 shows Zeus and Ganymede by the Penthesileia Painter. The artist has compressed a great deal of drama into his theme, without fundamentally departing from the traditional schemes of his craft. In this painting Ganymede is not a child, but a handsome and athletic youth. He is running away, as the story requires. In the confusion, his cloak is sliding off his left arm, and the conventional

rooster, which Ganymede has been clutching, is crowing anxiously—
a touch typical of the Penthesileia Painter. Zeus has dropped both
his thunderbolt and his scepter. Ganymede is reaching out for the
latter as it drops to the ground, but his pursuer restrains his hand.
Lover and beloved look deeply into each other's eyes, signifying
that, despite Ganymede's flight, an emotional tie is already developing.

In the Hellenistic tradition, Zeus ravished the youth not in
human form but in the shape of an eagle, a conceit both more
discreet and more sensuous. Figure 259, a terra-cotta statuary group
from Myrrhina in Turkey, dating from the second century B.C.,
shows Ganymede in the later, effeminate, conception, clutched by
the eagle who is clinging to the boy's back in a suggestive position.
Clearly the parental overtones of the Zeus and Ganymede myth of
an earlier age had by then been forgotten.

## Uneasiness over Pederasty in Classical Athens

By the time Athens entered the period of her greatest power in
480 B.C., male homosexual practices were undoubtedly common
and socially tolerated, but were they sanctioned? The age of pederastic innocence was over and a certain anxiety about the subject can
be traced in art and literature. The misgivings expressed over male
homosexuality usually concern either homosexual prostitution or
the possibility of homoerotic relations between peers.

If we consider the supposed glorification of homosexuality, it
appears that surprisingly little was made of it in tragedy. No
surviving tragedy deals with a homoerotic relationship, although
Aeschylus wrote a trilogy on the Achilleus story, in which that
hero's friendship with Patroclus was represented as sexual. In the
Homeric account of the Trojan War, in contrast, nothing indicates
such a sexual rapport between the heroes. In keeping with the
Athenian ethos Aeschylus had to make one the "lover" and the
other the "beloved" even though the relationship involved two full-
grown warriors. He assigned the active role to Achilleus. In the
course of one play of the trilogy, *The Myrmidons*, Patroclus dies
and Achilleus laments as follows over the corpse of his slain
comrade: "You didn't respect the awesome ritual of our thighs, you
most ungrateful for our many kisses" (Fr. 228 Mette). The reference
to thighs makes it clear that the playwright is alluding to the "more

257. Zeus in sexual pursuit of the boy Ganymede.

refined," intercrural, sex, depicted in the Archaic vase paintings, and we should therefore imagine a relationship involving a mutual exchange of sex and affection.

Later authors quibbled over who was the "lover" and who was the "beloved" in the relationship between Achilleus and Patroclus:

> Aeschylus talks nonsense when he says that Achilleus was in love with Patroclus, because he was not only more beautiful than Patroclus, but also the most beautiful of all the other heroes. He was, moreover, still beardless and younger by far, as Homer says. (Plato, *Symp.* 180a 4)

The pictorial tradition apparently sided with Plato and not with Aeschylus, because in the famous vase painting of Achilleus tending his wounded friend, Patroclus is the one with the beard (Figure 54). The argument over the sex-role division between the legendary heroes is revealing, because it shows that a homosexual relationship of equals was out of the bounds of sexual morality. Aeschylus' Achilleus trilogy was successful enough to be spoofed at length by Aristophanes in the *Frogs*, many years later, but other tragic playwrights, as far as we know, shied away from themes of adult homosexual love. The only major dramatization of pederasty appears to have had a strong critical streak. It concerns the rape of the boy Chrysippus by Laius, king of Thebes and father of Oedipus. Laius has sometimes been called the "inventor of pederasty," and, since the abduction of Chrysippus is the prelude to the various disasters that befell the house of Laius in later generations, the implication of censure is clear. Laius fell in love with the youthful Chrysippus, the son of Pelops, and abducted him. An oracle foretold that Laius, in punishment for this act of rape, would sire a son who would kill him and marry his own mother—Laius' wife, Iocasta. To forestall this, Laius decided not to have intercourse with his wife, but he was carried away one night when he came home drunk. The result was the birth of a son, the ill-fated Oedipus, and so began the chain of incest and other crimes which extended over several generations of the dynasty.

Euripides wrote a play on the Chrysippus story, produced in 409, in which, apparently, the young boy killed himself out of shame—which is yet more evidence of reproof. Pictorially the Chrysippus motif is best known from Italiot vase paintings. Figure 260 shows an elaborate Apulian illustration of the story, probably based on Euripides, although surely not depicting an actual stage

258.
Zeus with a childlike
Ganymede.

259.
Effeminate Ganymede with
Zeus-eagle in suggestive
position.

scene. Laius is whipping the horses on and is clutching the child, who stretches out his arms toward his father, Pelops. The figures in the upper register, mostly divinities, are peripheral to the story; the old man on the far right may be the child's slave supervisor (*paedagogos*), a stock character of Euripidean plays. The tragedy and the scene from it illustrated here contrasted the erotic infatuation of Laius unfavorably with the "legitimate" paternal affection of Pelops for Chrysippus. The demise of Laius by the hand of his own son must have been represented as fitting punishment.

## Censure of Adult Homosexual Behavior

Regardless of actual behavior patterns, anal copulation between males was equated with sex between two adults, not between a mature man and a young boy, and it was obviously not approved. The comedy of Aristophanes, which is rich in obscene and scatological invective, abounds in abusive terms alluding to anal sex. "Wide-assed" (*euryproktos*) was one of the more common insults in Greek, expanded by Aristophanes into "with gaping ass hole" (*chaunoproktos*). The politician Cleisthenes was evidently known as a passive homosexual, and Aristophanes never tires of making fun of his effeminate ways and hospitable rear end. The concept of anal penetration as demeaning and humiliating is perhaps best seen in what may be termed the "radish treatment." A male adulterer could be punished by having a large radish stuck up his rectum, symbolizing, no doubt, the penis of the injured husband. As a further insult the adulterer was subject to having his pubic hair singed off, whereby he was made to look like a woman. The orator Demosthenes, who had a speech impediment, was known as Batalos, which means "stutterer" but can also be construed as "asshole." His perennial antagonist, Aeschines, is not too refined to play on the double meaning of this nickname (2, 99).

Aristophanes' rival, the playwright Agathon, apparently continued homosexual relationships long after he had passed adolescence. Aristophanes derided him for these leanings, by representing him as effeminate and given to male prostitution. In the beginning of his *Thesmophoriazusai* an old man states that he does not know who Agathon is. The character Euripides in the play says, "Surely you have screwed him, but that doesn't mean you know him" (35). The implication is that the old man had copulated with Agathon anally, and hence had not seen his face.

260.
Laius abducting the boy
Chrysippus (probably based
on Euripides).

261. Persian captive submitting to anal penetration by a Greek(?).

The red-figure vase paintings, which mostly date from an earlier age than the comedy of Aristophanes, also present anal sex as humiliating. The odd scene on the two sides of the pitcher in Figure 261 is unparalleled. On the left a nearly naked man rushes forward, holding his erect penis. On the right a soldier in Persian clothes and gear offers his buttocks to the approaching aggressor, while raising his hands in distress. The vase's publisher (Schauenburg, 1975) has argued well that the contemplated anal penetration is the victor's revenge on a defeated enemy.

In the domain of satyrs and their sex life (sketched in more detail in Chapter 15), anything goes. These creatures of fantasy, or the humans who enacted them on certain ritual occasions, embody men's lower urges; they know no sexual taboos. Figure 262 shows a scene of intricately copulating satyrs: one is penetrating, anally it seems, an upside-down colleague. On the far right a satyr is even about to mount an unsuspecting sphinx from the rear. *Fellatio* is also part of the entertainment.

Given these derogatory associations of anal penetration, one may safely assume that in most cases where it takes place between ordinary adult males, it implies male prostitution. This is clearly the case in the scene depicted in Figure 263, even though the customer and the male prostitute appear to be of roughly the same age. A youth is about to mount another, who is seated on a chair. On the right a mature man and a woman are leaning on a cottage door, watching the scene in what is surely a male brothel. The pose of the love makers is remarkably similar to that of the heterosexual lovers in Figure 173, where a naked hetaera mounts a seated customer. For a discreet pictorial allusion to the anal approach, we may recall Figure 51, in which a man is about to embrace an infibulated young lyre player from behind.

Most scenes of homosexual contact in the red-figure technique resemble pictures in which men cavort with hetaerai; not infrequently, heterosexual and homosexual contacts are balanced out, as on the pitcher of which the front and the back are shown in Figures 264 and 265. In Figure 264 a youth is on a revel with a hetaera: she is playing castanets, he a flute. On the other side a bearded man is making intercrural love with a youth in the familiar scheme. The strange tree trunk overgrown with ivy points to a rustic setting. A second youth sits on the ground in a dejected pose; perhaps he is the man's slave, jealous of his master's attentions to another. The

262. Satyrs engaged in varieties of copulation.

263. A homosexual brothel with customer about to be serviced. The owners look on.

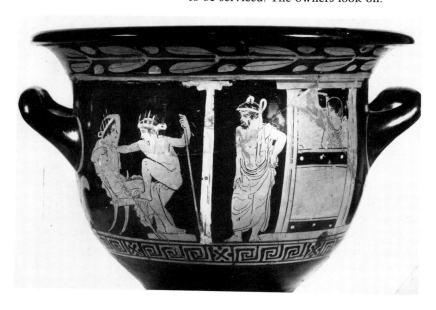

264. Youth and hetaera
in a *komos*.

265. Same as 264, reverse:
man copulating intercrurally
with youth.

cup tondo by the hand of Douris in Figure 266 makes the mercenary aspects of such relations even more explicit: here a mature man approaches a seated boy with a money purse.

## The Protection of Boys Against Homosexual Seduction

As Dover has aptly observed (1978, 88 f.), the same kind of two-faced morality must have governed homosexual seduction that controls heterosexual relations in most societies: pursuit and seduction are sanctioned, the yielding to seduction is not. Athens went to great lengths to protect its handsome young sons from men preying on their beauty; stringent measures were built into the legal system to prevent boys from falling into prostitution. However, since love gifts and social favors were part of the pederastic pattern, it must have been difficult to determine exactly at which point prostitution began.

In late-fifth-century comedy the practice of homosexual prostitution is taken for granted. In a fragment from a play by Theopompus, a speaking part is given to Mount Lykabettus, the spectacular mountain that stands in the center of present-day Athens, but was probably on the outskirts in Classical times: "Beside me, young men too far advanced in years give themselves to their coevals" (Fr. 29). The word here used for "young man," the Greek *meirakion*, refers to a person older than an ephebus and younger than a mature man, hence in his early twenties. The statement, which seems to imply censure, probably refers to male prostitution, perhaps in a brothel, perhaps at a known place of assignation. The divergence from sanctioned pattern, however, involves primarily the age.

The fourth-century speeches provide much detail on pederastic behavior and its mercenary aspects. The principal sources of information are Aeschines' speech *Against Timarchus* (1) and Demosthenes' *Against Androtion* (22), but some other speeches offer amusing glimpses. In the courtroom, evidently, charges of male prostitution flew hard and fast, on how much evidence we cannot know. Perhaps this accusation was frequently made in part because it is difficult to disprove. In Greek, the vocabulary of male prostitution largely parallels that of the female variety, although some words, including the verb *hetaireo*, "to be a prostitute," and the noun *hetairesis*, "prostitution," as far as we know were applied only to men.

In a number of cases the accused, like the playwright Agathon, probably had been known to engage in adult homosexual practice with coevals, and the charge of "prostitution" was a slanderous embroidery on what was merely disreputable. However, the fact that laws had been passed repressing various forms of prostitution shows that they must not have been uncommon. From Demosthenes' speech we learn that persons convicted of male prostitution could not enter the temples (73), make speeches, or initiate official proceedings (30). The defendant in the case, Androtion, had accused another male of prostitution (61). From Aeschines' speech *Against Timarchus* we learn of some of the measures taken in Athens to

266. Men negotiating the price of sex with a boy. On the wall a travel bundle.

protect young boys from seduction. Schools were open only during daylight hours. Youths older than the schoolboys, and male adults other than teachers and family, were barred from the schools. Instructors directing the boys' participation in public festivals had to be over forty years old, this age apparently being considered a watershed from the viewpoint of sexual ardor. Aristotle gives the same minimum age for the producers of boys' choruses, doubtless to protect the virtue of the participants. Men who prostituted their sons were subject to prosecution, as were their customers. Prostituted sons were later relieved of the obligation of supporting their fathers (but not of burying them) (13). In the account given, the accused, Timarchus, had catholic sexual tastes: his homosexual revels included flute girls and hetaerai (75), and he spent 20 minas on the courtesan Philoxene (115). On his own sexual morality, the speaker gives contradictory evidence: he confesses to having experienced homosexual love (136), arguing that it is only the acceptance of money for sex and the association with uncultivated men that are shameful. Later on in the speech, however, he expresses the by now widespread notion that homoerotic love is "contrary to nature" (185) and that those who facilitate such behavior, the notorious "pimps" (*pornoboskoi*), are despicable (188). In the case of strangers and alien residents, however, he does not object (195).

An amusing incident is related in Lysias' speech *Defense Against Simon* (3). The case involved the mutual assault of two litigants, the speaker and his accuser, Simon, over the sexual use of a boy by the name of Theodotus, with whom both were in love. Simon claimed that he had bought the boy's favors with a gift of 300 drachmas (22). The speaker, too, had "done well by the boy" (5) and evidently taken him home. Simon became so frustrated that, one night, in a state of drunkenness, he broke into the speaker's house to recover the object of his passion. Probably looking for his rival, he forced his way into the women's quarters, where, as the latter says melodramatically, "reside my sister and my female cousins, who live so virtuously that they are ashamed to be seen even by the male members of the household" (6). Inevitably a frightful brawl ensued.

## A Propensity for Prostitution

The above outline of the homosexual ethos in Athens shows that it underwent a fundamental change between the Archaic and the

Classical ages. The archetypal homosexual relationship was that between a childlike or pubescent boy and a mature man. The contact had strong paternal overtones, and it involved affectionate response from the child partner and mild sexual response from the pubescent partner. The original image of the ideal "beloved" did not include any feminine traits. In general, the sexual approach was frontal and the copulation intracrural.

The period when this pattern took shape was the Archaic age of Athens, before the greatest flowering of Attic culture. During the fifth and fourth centuries this pattern became compromised and led to male prostitution by citizens and to adult male love affairs; both of these practices were consistently stigmatized as socially unacceptable. Anal sex, generally associated with obscenity and coarse behavior, was the common form of these discredited types of homosexual contact.

Plato's speculations on the ideal homosexual relationship in his *Symposium* are far too involved to be discussed here in detail. Plato stresses throughout the pedagogic aspects of homosexual bonds. The philosopher never married, and he is not known to have had any children; he may well have played Zeus to a number of Ganymedes in his life. Yet he does express misgivings about the sexual side of such relationships. In his last dialogue, *Laws*, he goes so far as to imply that homosexual activity is contrary to nature (841d) and, surprisingly, he extolls the virtues of monogamous, affectionate marriage (839b).

Summing up this examination of homosexual practices, one must conclude that the striking feature of Athenian mores is not the glorification of pederasty but the extraordinary propensity for prostitution, both heterosexual and homosexual.

# *12*

# Learning to Be a Man,
# Learning to Be a Woman

> When he is seven a peasant boy is given a small stick to tend
> a flock of sheep. At fifteen he gets a larger stick and looks
> after cows. When he comes of age, he owns a revolver and
> bosses women.
> —Corsican saying

> Let us, citizens all, start a speech in praise of the city. It's
> right that I should do so, because it raised me in the enjoyment
> of its splendor. For at barely seven years of age, I carried the
> Sacred Vessels; then, at ten, I ground the corn for the leader
> of the rituals. And then, wearing the saffron robe, I was a
> Little Bear for Artemis of Brauron. And later, grown into a
> beautiful girl, I carried the Baskets, wearing a necklace of figs.
> So isn't it obvious that I owe the city praise and good advice?
> —Aristophanes, *Lysistrata* (637–47): the chorus of citizen
> women speaking

In Classical Greece, as in other ancient societies, cult rituals were
observed in bewildering number and variety. Every major function
of life was associated with one or more patron divinities and a body
of myths and rituals. Our own distinction between the "sacred"
and the "profane," the realm of the church and that of the street,
would hardly have been intelligible to ancient Greeks. In turn, we
cannot hope to comprehend their world unless we realize that all
its processes of life and thought were intertwined with mystical-
religious notions. Students of the past, for several hundreds of years
now, have looked for a theory, a single key, that would open the
door to the understanding of the nature and purpose of religious
ritual in pagan societies. An older theory saw in ritual primarily an
immediate pragmatic purpose: ritual was aimed, according to this
school of thought, at promoting the fertility of the earth and the

human race, at producing rain, at pacifying the gods or forestalling disaster. More recent anthropology has stressed the role of ritual in perpetuating social values and behaviorial norms, or its psychic merits, such as helping people to live with the contradictions and problems of life. Man wants to live but must die; and to survive he must kill. He wants order and justice in his society, but is himself full of greed and aggression. Only one thing is certain in the confusing study of myth and ritual, and the underlying meanings: no cult practices survive long unless they respond to a deep-seated social or emotional need.

One would expect that in the city-state of Athens, where the polarization of the sexes was pronounced and rigidly enforced, ritual would reflect this split; indeed, this is the case. In fact, hardly anywhere else can an element of social propaganda be so easily isolated as in some Attic ritual customs. It is only because Athenian history has thus far been studied almost exclusively from a male viewpoint that this aspect of Athens' religious life has not been clearly recognized. This male bias, of course, is not necessarily related to the sex of the scholar.

Rituals of social significance are best considered under two headings: initiation and release, or escape (for the latter see Chapter 15). Initiation and puberty rites follow a basic pattern widely attested among the most diverse peoples: the young undergo certain trials and humiliations which, in telescoped form, symbolize the hardships of life. They perform odious tasks and subordinate their wishes to those of their elders. Usually they die symbolically and are reborn, sometimes through a process of imitation of physical birth, and are then ceremoniously welcomed as full-fledged members of the adult community. Initiation in mystery religions follows a similar scenario, except that here the process is not tied to a specific stage of life but can take place at any age, and the symbolic death and rebirth scheme is more elaborate. There is probably not a society on earth that does not perpetuate customs with vestiges of initiation.

If the purpose of the initiation rites is didactic, to indoctrinate the younger generation with the values of the older so that society can continue, rituals of release tend to protect social patterns by providing a temporary and controlled escape from them. The most common means of serving this purpose is role reversal, which is almost as widely attested as initiation. Under the controlled conditions of the ritual, the suppressed and the powerless and the doomed may step out of the framework of social restrictions and the limitations of existence. The slave may whip his master, the woman may go out and conduct business, man may play god, and son may boss father.

In Athenian cultic life both ritual patterns can easily be found, and both tend primarily to reinforce the notion of the "otherness" of women and to bolster the power of male over female.

## Education for Men, Religion for Women

The enculturation of male and female children in Classical Athens followed entirely different lines. For most purposes the male child was removed from the women's quarters, probably at about age six. It would be interesting to know exactly at which age his second "weaning" took place and he began to take his meals with the men of the household rather than with the women. He was educated professionally outside the home, took his training in sports at the public *palaestrai* and *gymnasia*, and eventually received military training in an official establishment.

Women, on the other hand, were deprived of secular education, except what they might pick up from the "female underground" in their own and neighboring homes. It was through myths and cults that women were inducted into the culture. Religious events, along with funerals, furnished them with the only opportunity to participate in the public life of the community. It is no wonder that there seem to have been more rituals for women than for men.

## The Festival of Pitchers

Probably because of the Athenians' highly developed educational system for boys, no rituals for men are known which follow a clear-cut initiatory pattern. Youths did, however, participate in various rituals in which they were confronted with a role model for male behavior. Almost invariably, the role model was Athens' national hero Theseus, even in the case of rites that appear to have prehistoric origins. I can cite here only one example of the overlaying of older rituals with Thesean motifs. The festival of the Carrying of the Grape Clusters (*oschophoria*) was held in the fall, to celebrate the grape harvest, basically a Dionysian occasion. Young men carried the clusters in a procession, the first two of them dressed as women. Transvestite rites were practiced in the Dionysiac religion. However, Plutarch records, as a commonly accepted explanation of the procession, that it constituted a memory of the tribute of youths and maidens demanded by the Cretan Minotaur, a tribute from which Theseus had delivered the city of Athens. Theseus, this according to illogical exegesis, had substituted boys for two of the girls, before doing away with both the tribute and the Minotaur.

Several other public rituals for men had similar veneers of Theseus worship. Since they reflect sexual attitudes only indirectly, we will not dwell on them. However, one ceremony of male indoctrination serves well to illustrate the behavioral norms for the male and has left clear traces in vase painting. It was called the Festival of the Pitchers (*choes*) and was part of the festival of Anthesteria, celebrated in the spring during the Anthesterion ("flower month") and marking the first sampling of the wine harvest of the previous year. The second day of this apparently rowdy festival was set aside for boys, who were allowed to participate in the drinking, the carousing, and the play-acting that were part of it. They did so from the age of three on. A special miniature version of the wine pitcher with trefoil mouth was made for the children, which presumably they took home as a souvenir afterwards. Many of these little pitchers have been found. Most of them are of modest workmanship, but they form a charming documentation of the lives and aspirations of Athenian boys.

On some pitchers boys are depicted playing games, accompanied by their pet dogs, cats, and birds. Their favorite toy seems to have been a pull cart, either a small roller or one big enough for a child to ride in (Figure 267). On most, however, the children are shown in activities preparing them for the specifically male functions in their future lives. On a number of them boys old enough to walk are crawling. Evidently for the smaller participants crawling races were held, preparing them for the competitive athletics awaiting them. Figure 268 features two plump little boys, one crawling, the other holding out a branch, perhaps the prize for victory in the race. Older boys graduated to more heroic contests. In Figure 269 a winged victory crowns a boy on horseback. The panathenaic amphora on the column behind him points to greater honors awaiting him as an adult. The white head band identifies the boy as a participant in the Anthesteria. Boys learned to play satyr in the course of the

267. Boys with toy carts
and grapes.

268. A crawling contest
for little boys.

269. Anthesteria boy as
victor in a horse race.

ritual, with the help of tied-on satyr tails and "bald caps" (Figure 270). In Figure 271 older boys sneak up on a sleeping Maenad, probably in a stage skit. Figure 272 features Anthesteria boys acting out a drunken revel (*komos*) under torchlight.

Male values are conveyed in a comical way by the unique pitcher reproduced in Figure 273. It features a skinny girl, with an anxious expression on her face, dressed up in martial Athena gear—helmet, shield, and spear. Under the watchful eye of an instructor, she tries out a dance step. It is a parody of the war dance of Athena (*pyrrhiche*; see below). The object prominently displayed on the wall is a bull's penis, with which schoolmasters chastised their pupils. Here it serves as a humorous symbol of male authority.

It is clear that through the Festival of the Pitchers Athenian boys were imbued from an early age with the norms of competitiveness and male privilege. In this connection we may recall the pitcher shown earlier, in Figure 48, with the boisterous man coming home drunk, probably from the Anthesteria, as his anxious wife awaits him.

## Female Indoctrination Rituals

The meaning of many of the arcane religious rites of Athens was probably already lost to fifth-century Athenians themselves, and reconstructing their social purpose from our vague and often contradictory sources is difficult. Nevertheless, at least for the better-known rituals practiced by women a certain pattern emerges: young girls learned the virtues of chastity, submission, and labor, as well as the acceptance of motherhood, including its hazards, while adult women were offered a release from the anxieties provoked by their sequestered lives.

Some initiatory rituals for girls served a double purpose: not only did they promote socially desirable qualities in female children, but, being restricted to or associated with the best families, they also tended to instill a sense of class privilege. The quotation from *Lysistrata* at the head of this chapter refers to the principal social rites performed by Athenian girls. The speaker is proud of her status as a citizen woman of upper-class standing, as reflected in the honorific services she has rendered as a child. As in most male-dominated societies, an elite group of women was given a stake in the status quo; members of a potential protest group were thus disarmed as rebels. Almost any state of degradation is bearable as long as the victim has an even lowlier category to look down upon.

## Behavior Models in the Cult of Athena

The figure of the goddess Athena as Guardian of the City, with her huge repertory of myths, rituals, and pictorial attributes, embodied virtually all Attic social values and behavioral norms for both men and women. During the yearly panathenaic festivals, her peculiar male-patriarchal ethos was celebrated and dramatized. On her male, or martial, side, the most spectacular event may have been the dancing of a wild war dance (*pyrrhiche*, or pyrrhic dance) by armed dancers in her honor; a contingent of girls in "Athena outfits" may have participated in this ritual (Figure 273). The staging of this war dance was a compulsory public service (*leitourgia*), financed by rich members of the community (Lys. 21, 1; 4).

On the female side, motherhood could hardly play a fundamental role in the cult of Athena, the sexless virago. We have seen how she became the ethnic mother of Attica, without benefit of copulation, by lifting from the ground Erichthonius, who was born of Hephaestus' seed, spilled on the earth as he pursued her. Athena's cult laid special stress upon the other two socially promoted virtues for women, chastity and hard work. The Parthenon on the Acropolis housed the formidable statue of Athena Parthenos (the Virgin), adorned with male supremacy themes, such as those of Pandora and of the Amazons. The manifestation of the goddess more intimately connected with local concerns was Athena Polias (Of the City), venerated in a humbler, wooden, image which stood in the open on the Acropolis. The panathenaic procession in honor of the goddess, which is depicted in the partially surviving friezes of the Parthenon, took place once a year, and once every four years it included the offering of a new robe (*peplos*) to the statue of Athena Polias.

The robe was, of course, made by Athenian women; these women were called *ergastinai* (a derivation from Athena Ergane (Of the workshop). The robe was decorated with the motif of the battle of the Gods and Giants, an appropriately masculine theme, glorifying the battlefield prowess of Athena, who herself had slain one of the monsters.

How many women toiled at this no doubt splendid garment is not known, but, as the rather confusing sources tell us, the official

270.
Boy in Silenus cap and
satyr tail for a wine cup.

271. Boy satyrs sneak up
on sleeping Maenad.

272. Acting out a revel.

makers of the peplos were two or four girls from noble families, between seven and eleven years of age, known as the *arrhephoroi*, the "bearers of the sacred objects." Obviously this was a purely honorific function, since the girls were both too young and too few in number to produce the peplos. The social effect was to give prestige to the humble tasks of spinning and weaving and to reinforce a female class hierarchy.

The *arrhephoroi* had another function, dimly recalled in a late source (Paus. 1, 27, 3–4): in a nighttime ritual they carried on their heads baskets filled with sacred and secret objects, as they passed through an underground passage to a hallowed shrine of Aphrodite in the Garden. They brought something else, equally veiled in mystery, upon their return. As Burkert has suggested, this ritual probably echoed the Athenian foundation myth of the daughters of Cecrops, which followed the miraculous birth of Erichthonius. After Athena delivered Erichthonius from the earth, she placed him in a basket or chest—that is, in a symbolic womb—and turned him over to the three daughters of the reigning King Cecrops: Pandrosos, Aglauros, and Herse (see Chapter 2). The girls were instructed not

273. Diffident girl in Athena garb
dances the pyrrhic dance. Trainer.
On the wall a bull's penis.

to open the chest. Aglauros and Herse disobeyed. Inside they saw
not only the baby Erichthonius but also a snake, in some versions
two. The snake leaped out of the chest and pursued the two
disobedient girls, who in fright hurled themselves off one of the
slopes of the Acropolis and died. Earlier, in Figure 45, we saw an

illustration of the pursuit of the girls by the snake, in a context of other Attic-chauvinistic themes.

The genital associations of this strange tale are unmistakable, since "mystical chests" often have snakes in them, and the lifting of the cover off the phallic snake has a later echo in the ritual of the "unveiling of the phallus," although this is not attested for the Classical Greek age. Figure 274 shows the best-known representation of this ritual, in the frieze of the Villa of the Mysteries at Pompeii, dating from the first century B.C. Here the initiate, perhaps a bride, as many scholars claim, is removing a cloth from a phallus large enough to instill awe in even the most intrepid female. The myth of the opening of the basket with Erichthonius in it would seem to dramatize the mysteries of sex and birth, and the need for chastity and innocence in young girls, to protect them against profanation.

Allusions to textile working also abound in this web of charter myths. Athena had wiped some of the spilled semen of Hephaestus off her legs with a tuft of wool. Pandrosos, the obedient sister, according to a late source, had been the first "to make woolen garments for men, together with her sisters." As in vase paintings of seated matrons with distaffs and spindles, so in myth: despite phallic domination, respect for the female as life-giving and nurturing crept back into human consciousness via the manufacture of textiles. Denied biological parenthood, Athena and other mythological women regained a claim to maternity through the imagery of wool working.

The four honorary weavers of Athena's peplos lived for a while in the Arrhephoroi House on the Acropolis, of which archaeologists believe they have identified traces to the west of the surviving Erechtheum. Nearby stood the separate shrines of Pandrosos and Aglauros. As we have already seen, at the latter the young men of Athens were sworn in as recruits, thus beginning the most sex-role stereotyped phase of their lives, that of soldiery.

## Chastity, Motherhood, and Death

In the rituals of Athena the young girl learned the virtue of labor at spindle and loom; in the cult of Artemis she was indoctrinated in the norms of chastity and motherhood, a fateful combination of duties that restricted women's sexuality to the function of child-bearing. Although Artemis, like Athena a virgin, had made a creed out of nonsexuality, she was at the same time the patroness of

274. The unveiling of the phallus. Fresco from the Pompeian Villa of the Mysteries.

women in childbirth. In the sanctuary of Artemis at Brauron, on the coast some twenty miles from Athens, little girls selected from leading families did service to the goddess sometime between the ages of five and ten. Artemis' little acolytes were called Bears and were clad in saffron-colored robes to suggest a bearskin. The story behind this practice is instructive for the values which it was meant to communicate. One of Artemis' virgin nymphs was called Kallisto (Most Beautiful). A variant of the same name, Kalliste, was an epithet for Artemis herself, so that the nymph was in fact another persona of the goddess. Kallisto was raped by Zeus, and, in punishment for this breach of her vows of chastity, Artemis changed her into a she-bear.

The myth of Kallisto enjoyed something like charter status at Athens, since the famous painter Polygnotus painted the motif in the porch built by the Athenians at Delphi, and a sculpture of it by an artist of the name of Deinomenos stood on the Acropolis. No Attic representation of Kallisto survives, but Figure 275 shows an Italiot vase painting of the nymph sitting dejectedly on a rock. The child on the right may be the fruit of the seduction. Kallisto looks with horror at her left arm, which is being transformed into a hairy paw with claws for fingers. Her right ear has already taken on animal form. Her short tunic and the spears beside her refer to her past as a huntress for Artemis. A fragment of a similar scene in Figure 276, also south Italian, likewise includes the child, who must have played a role in the story. The priestesses of Artemis at Brauron may have acted out the fate of Kallisto, the Bear Woman, because some of the pot fragments found there show what appear to be adult figures wearing bear's masks (Figure 277).

If the vase paintings found on the site are a reliable indication of what went on there, the little girls of Brauron during their residence there not only commemorated Kallisto by donning the saffron robes, but they also held what one scholar has called "sacred races," perhaps in honor of both Kallisto and Artemis. They did so in an unorthodox abbreviated costume, recalling that of Artemis the Huntress, or sometimes, even more remarkably, wearing nothing at all. The feminist Plato advocates foot-racing and other athletics for girls up to the time of marriage—before puberty in the nude and thereafter in "suitable attire" (*Laws* 833d). He may have had Brauron in mind. The poorly preserved fragment in Figure 278 shows a procession of girls in short tunics proceeding toward an

275. Kallisto changing into a bear.

276. Kallisto with bear's
ears and paw.

altar. In the fragment of Figure 279 naked girls of different ages are running. The one on the far right is clearly prepubescent. The figure ahead of her, on the other hand, is a developing young woman; hence it is unlikely that a competitive race is illustrated here. The deer and the two dogs in the lower register suggest that the girls are hunting. Figure 280 shows yet another costume. The left figure on this pottery fragment, also found on the site of Brauron, wears a kind of bikini, and she holds castanets or rattles (*krotala*) in both hands. She is confronting a mature woman in conventional dress (perhaps her mother?). The "bikini" of this young lady shows a remarkable resemblance to that worn by a group of women in a highly popular mosaic in Piazza Armerina, Sicily, the so-called bikini mosaic (Figure 281). The latter scene, which dates from the later Roman Empire, is often said to show how "modern" the Romans were. It would seem, however, that these sportive ladies are not engaging freely in athletics, but taking part in a ritual derived from that of the Greek Artemis. One would imagine that in the ritual, as in Euripides' *Hippolytus*, hunting and sports were equated with sexual abstinence.

Other pottery found on the site of the sanctuary, most of it in

277. Priestess in bear's mask(?).

278.
Procession of bear girls
to an altar.

279. Nude girls hunting.

fragments, makes clear that other female values were not forgotten in this intensive training program. Figure 282 shows a young woman at a water fountain, dressed in a diaphanous, speckled robe, probably the Bear dress; she may be playing Amymone—on a similar scene from Brauron part of that name survives—or she may be an anonymous water carrier. The outside rim of the same vessel, Figure 283, celebrates the customary companion theme to that of water carrying—namely, textile working. The half beginning to the right of the double doors represents "ritual textile working," since the two chairs in this scene are covered with cloths or hides, and one woman wears the diaphanous, speckled garment, here apparently a short tunic over a longer one. In the middle of this scene a foot is propped up on a stand for the carding of wool over the knee. The other half of the rim may be taken as the actual domestic wool working that awaits the girl at home. This half includes the closed door, the familiar symbol of the women's quarters. This reading of the paintings must, of course, remain hypothetical, because of the incompleteness of the dish, but if it is correct, it implies that the Little Bears were indoctrinated in the ethic of hard work for women for which water carrying and wool working were symbolic, as well as in the merits of chastity.

Surprisingly, no direct reference to Kallisto, either inscriptional or pictorial, has been found at Brauron. The reason for this is probably that the priestess of Artemis venerated at this particular sanctuary was Iphigeneia, famous through Euripides' two plays *Iphigeneia in Aulis* and *Iphigeneia in Tauris*, and their many later adaptations. Tradition had it that Iphigeneia was buried at Brauron or nearby, and her tomb was venerated there. Apparently, as the focus of local mythological lore, she had supplanted Kallisto.

It is, in fact, from Euripides' *Iphigeneia in Tauris* that we have the best evidence for yet another moral value that was drilled into the Little Bears—bravery in the face of death in childbirth. At the end of the play the goddess Athena comes in as *dea ex machina:* she sets everything right, dispatches the heroes of the play on a safe return journey to Attica, and gives instructions about what to do when they get there (1435 f.). To Iphigeneia she says approximately (the exact reading of the lines is disputed),

> On you, Iphigeneia, I lay the command to bear the temple key around the sacred steps at Brauron for the goddess [Artemis]. There, too, will you be buried after your death, and they will set up for you a memorial

280. Girl in "bikini," with clappers.

281. Bikini girls in the mosaic at Piazza Armerina, Sicily.

of robes, delicately woven garments, which women leave behind in their homes in lifecrushing childbirth.

The passage, surely an allusion to an actual custom, makes it clear that at Brauron certain garments of women who had died in childbirth were dedicated to Artemis and displayed in the sanctuary.

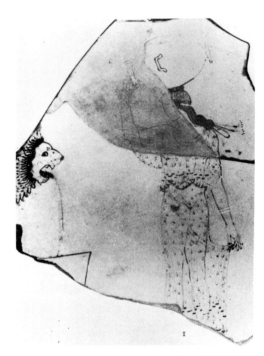

282.
Girl water carrier at fountain. Amymone?

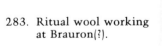

283. Ritual wool working at Brauron(?).

284. Portraits of girls found
at Brauron.

285. Naked boy and clothed girl:
children's statues at Brauron.

286. Greek killing an Amazon. A knee cover
fragment from Brauron.

Perhaps they were the clothes the bride had brought as part of her dowry and not had a chance to wear, and which thus symbolized the lost portion of her life. Indeed, inscriptions accompanying dedications of garments have been found on the site. Thus, the cult of Artemis at Brauron helped to propagate the patriarchal belief that the agony and danger of childbirth were woman's natural fate and therefore not to be relieved. The risk of death in childbed evidently was held up to the little girls of Brauron as a heroic part of their mission in the world. In gratitude for such useful instruction, the families of the Little Bears set up statues or portrait heads of them in the sanctuary—of which many have been found, charming effigies of girls of different ages, usually smiling (Figure 284). A few statues of boys, naked of course, have also been found (Figure 285), showing that sex segregation for children was not as drastic as that for adults.

Not even that old machismo chestnut, the battle of the Greeks and the Amazons, was forgotten at Brauron: a fragment of a black-figure vase painting found on the site shows a warrior spearing an Amazon (Figure 286). Are they Achilleus and Penthesileia? The vessel on which this scene was painted belongs to the woman's domain: it is an *epinetron*, the terra-cotta cap that protected the knee during the carding of wool, and the didactic intent of this tale of male victory is unmistakable here.

The ancient Greek lexikon of Harpokration defines the verb "to be a bear" (*arkteusai*) as "being made sacred to Artemis . . . before the wedding, said of virgins," a paraphrase that brings out the prenuptial function of the rituals. The cult of Artemis Brauronia (and some other, analogous, rites of Artemis) may well have been the most effective way of instilling in females the ethos that male society required of them. Surely it was the most complete; its repertoire covers the full span of tales and symbols that spelled subordination.

# *13*

# Sex Among the Barbarians

> Permissiveness towards women is harmful to the purposes of
> the community and to the happiness of the state . . . for they
> live without restraint in every kind of indulgence and luxury.
> —Aristotle, *Politics* (1269b 12–23)
>
> For there [in Egypt] the men sit at home and weave and their
> wives are constantly engaged out of doors in providing the
> food for sustenance of life.
> —Sophocles, *Oedipus at Colonus* (339–41)

The Athenians cultivated some strange ideas about the mating
habits of other societies, both Greek and "barbarian." Until recently
these reports have been considered sound historical documentation,
but it has now become clear that they are largely the product of
unchecked fantasy and tell us much more about their authors than
about the peoples described. Greek "ethnography," in fact, can be
understood only in the context of the desires and fears of those
who composed it.

## Fear of Gynecocracy

Many passages in Greek literature reveal an underlying fear of
women getting out of hand, and taking control over their men and
their own lives. Evidently the Athenian Greeks perceived their
wives and daughters as caged animals, temporarily subdued but
ready to strike out if given the slightest chance.

In the politics of Aristotle, the word "gynecocracy" (meaning
literally "women's rule") refers not to anything like political matriarchy but rather to women getting out of control or breaking
through the walls of restriction that have been erected around them.
The frequent equation or comparison of women with slaves likewise

suggests an irrational fear of the former. Aristotle, in his *Poetics* (15, 3), finds himself on the horns of a dilemma. Since he requires of tragedies that their characters be "good," what is the playwright going to do with the women and the slaves in his plots? The answer is that he should make them "good" within the limitations of their natural inferiority: "All that is relative to each category. To be sure, woman has quality and so does a slave, although it should be said that of these two the former is inferior, and the latter wholly contemptible."

In legal matters the Athenian gynophobia is best evidenced by a peculiar quirk of Attic law. Under a statute attributed to Solon and perhaps really initiated by him, virtually any legal action undertaken by a man was invalid if it could be shown to have been conceived "under the influence of a woman" or "through the persuasion of a woman." From Demosthenes (46, 16) we learn that a man who follows the advice of a woman is legally "incompetent" (*akyros*), as are the sick, the drugged, or those diminished by senility, madness, or some other affliction. In Isaeus' speech *On the Inheritance of Menecles* a person who had acted "under the influence of a woman" was legally classified in the same category as the "insane" (*paraphron*, 20). Such a charge, like that of male prostitution, is extremely difficult to prove or disprove, especially when, as in Menecles' case, the alleged henpecked weakling is dead. That the charge was taken seriously in legal proceedings, however, is indicated by the fact that in 404 B.C., under the Rule of the Thirty, the statute was abolished for the purpose of donations of property.

Fear of being poisoned by women was apparently another obsession of Athenian men. We have already outlined the not so convincing accusation in Antiphon's speech *Against the Stepmother*, which led to the torture-killing of a female slave on a charge of poisoning, and possibly to the execution of the accused as well. The speeches in the corpus of Demosthenes reveal several instances of women being put to death for poisoning and sorcery. Evidently these cases had stirred up considerable notoriety. A woman by the name of Ninos was executed for supplying love potions to young men (Scholion to Dem. 19, 281). An accused sorceress from the island of Lemnos was exterminated "with her entire clan" (Ps.-Dem. 25, 79–80).

## Gynecocracy in Myth

There will be more to say about the mythological tales of women who got out of hand in Chapter 14, on sex antagonism in tragedy, because most of these myths have come down to us through playwrights. Examining a myth for its underlying meaning is hazardous business, because each story has been transmitted in many variants; one easily falls into the temptation of selecting that version which best suits one's own theory, a common fault among anthropologists and other scholars. At the risk of incurring criticism for the same shortcoming, I will sketch the general characteristics of the large body of myths in which women rebel against the order of their society or their family. What these myths convey is that men who kill are either heroes or the victims of an unkindly destiny, whereas women who kill are monsters. The Gorgons, who turn men to stone, are horrifying creatures with hairdos of crawling snakes; Perseus, who decapitates the Gorgon Medusa, is a sunny hero. Clytemnestra, who kills Agamemnon, is evil. Orestes, who kills Clytemnestra, is virtuous, most clearly so in Homer's *Odyssey*, where the dubious implications of Orestes' matricide are not broached. No act of killing on the part of a woman is glorified by myth; there is no Greek equivalent to the story of Judith and Holofernes.

Most mythological women rebels do not try to subject or rule men; they just kill them, usually within the family, in the bridal chamber or some other place within the private house. The fifty daughters of Danaüs kill their husbands during the bridal night following the mass wedding; the women of Lemnos, commemorated in what was apparently an obsessive myth with Athenian Greeks, kill all the men on their island, presumably in their homes. Only the divine sorceress Circe holds men in domestic subjection, but she has to turn them into swine in order to do so. These and many other legends represent female rebellion against male power as that of the furious animal, striking out blindly and ultimately without success, against whatever male the women can reach from their restriction in a private domain. The only major exception to the mythological "caged tiger" pattern is the legend of the Amazons, who confront male authority on the battlefield.

Typically, in the myths of collective uprising against the male order, there is one strike breaker who is mythologically glorified as embodying "real" female virtue. A rebel against the rebellious, she sides with the values of the male world. In the Danaïd myth, one of the sisters, Hypermestra, spares her new husband, Lynceus—in one version because she fell in love with him, in another because he spared her virginity, an oversight apparently considered a favor. In the tale of the slaughter of the Lemnians by their women, one daughter, Hypsipyle, spared her father, Thoas, out of filial piety. In the case of the Amazons, one of their leaders, Antiope, allowed herself to be captured by Theseus and became a dutiful wife and mother.

Apart from these legends of mythological spoilsports, there is little evidence in Greek myth of what are traditionally considered the "female" qualities of protectiveness, nurture, and conciliation. Antigone's care for her aged and blind father, Oedipus, in Sophocles' *Oedipus at Colonus* is a rare exception, found in the domain of conscious fiction. In the Greek mythological panorama, there is no kindly biblical Ruth, protecting and nurturing her widowed mother-in-law, Naomi. There are no Sabine women conciliating their husbands with their fathers and thus preventing war between Romans and Sabines. There is no Coriolanus, dissuaded from attacking his native city by his aged mother. The role of Greek mythological mothers, as we have seen in Chapter 5, is mainly to mourn their children.

The Athenians' views of sex relations in societies other than their own must be seen in the light of their own irrational fears of women who step out of line. Their ethnography serves to demonstrate that the only alternative to restrictive male-dominated marriage was complete promiscuity and gynecocracy.

These dangers lurked not only among the barbarians, but even more threateningly within the Greek world itself. A prime example was the Dorian family of city-states, which included Athens' perennial antagonist Sparta and her daughter city Taras in southern Italy (later Tarentum and now Taranto). Aristotle seems to think that the city of Sparta, where women had freer positions in society than in Athens, was virtually, or in danger of becoming, a gynecocracy: "For what difference is there between a rule of women and a state in which women rule the rulers?" (*Pol.* I, 1269b 12). Especially scurrilous myths attached themselves to the Dorian colony Taras, which became the wealthiest Greek city abroad. According to a tradition attributed to the fourth-century Greek historian Ephoros and preserved in Strabo (6, 3, 3), the original colonizers were called the Partheniai (offspring of virgins or unmarried women). They had been sired during one of the wars of the Spartans against the surrounding Messenians, as a result of a decree whereby the young Spartan soldiers were ordered to return from the battlefield and "all of them to sleep with all the girls" in order to replenish the population. In an even more scandalous legend, the Spartan women slept with their slaves during the absence of their men in battle.

## Topsy-Turvy Worlds

At about the same time the Athenian Greeks were at the height of their prosperity, the Etruscans flourished in central Italy. The Etruscans appear to have been the earliest people in Western history who allowed the women some dignity in marriage, and they may have been the originators of the "matronage" system. Here, however, is what the late-fourth-century Greek historian Theopompus has to say about the Etruscans:

> . . . it is customary among Etruscans to share their wives. These take excellent care of their bodies and exercise frequently, sometimes with men and sometimes with each other. For to them it is not shameful to be seen in the nude. And they take their meals, not beside their own husbands, but side by side with any men who happen to be present and they drink to the health of whomever they want. They are good drinkers, and also very good looking. The Etruscans raise all the children who are born, even though they do not know who the father is in each case. And these live in the same style as the persons who reared them, having drinking parties all the time and having intercourse with all the women. Among the Etruscans there is nothing shameful about doing things in public or even having things done to them, for that, too, is the custom of their country. And so far removed are they from prudery that when the master of the house is making love and someone calls for him, they openly say that he is having such-and-such done to him, shamelessly calling the act by its name. (Athenaeus 12, 517d–f)

This strange account is not only blatantly untrue, it also displays an astonishing prudery. On closer examination, what Theopompus is really communicating is that the Etruscans do the same things the Greeks do, except they do it with each other's wives instead of with hetaerai, and hence they produce technically legitimate children of uncertain paternity.

The account springs from a naïve "ethnography," in which the customs of other peoples are described in terms of their differences from one's own, following the principle of the "topsy-turvy world." The original creator of that device was evidently the "father of history," Herodotus, who was not an Athenian but an Ionian Greek from Halicarnassus. However, he wrote during the middle of the fifth century, while Athens was at her height, and his stories reflect Attic values. In his accounts of the lives and customs of "barbarians," he pays special attention to their marriage and mating patterns, naturally enough, since these are at the core of social organization. His descriptions tend to support the notions that Greek women are better off than the wives of barbarians, and that the only alternative to the rigidly guarded Attic style of marriage is complete sexual license and promiscuity. The classic topsy-turvy passage in Herodotus is his comment on life in Egypt, which was echoed by Sophocles in the epigraph at the head of this chapter:

> The Egyptians . . . established all their customs and laws so as to be the reverse of those of all other peoples. Among them the women do the marketing and selling, and the men stay home and weave. Whereas the others push the weaving shuttle upwards, they push it downward. The men carry their loads on their heads and their women carry them on their shoulders. And women urinate standing, and men sitting. (2, 35)

Even more suspect than these schematic reversals is Herodotus' report on the customs of a Thracian tribe named the Trausi:

> The relatives of a newborn child sit around it and mourn for it, recounting all the human sufferings which it will have to endure once it has been born. But the deceased they convey to the earth with jokes and merriment, commenting that he is freed of so many evils and in perfect happiness. (5, 4)

A particularly revealing passage in Herodotus' *History* concerns some Athenian settlers in the Ionian part of Asia Minor (1, 146). These immigrants married Carian women, after having put their parents to death. In revenge, the women vowed never to take meals with their husbands and not to call them by their names. Of course, these "punishments" are exactly the restrictions which every Athenian husband inflicted on his wife.

In describing the sexual mores of barbarians, Herodotus tends to show either the state of subjugation or the promiscuity of their women. The Crestoneans, a Thracian tribe, practice polygamy, and when a man dies his widows compete for the honor of being slaughtered on his tomb (5, 5). The Persians, too, are polygamous, having many wives in addition to their concubines (1, 135). The Thracians in general allow their unmarried girls to have intercourse with as many men as they wish, but they do guard their wives (5, 6).

Among several of the peoples Herodotus mentions, women of citizen class are subjected to prostitution. The young women of Lydia must earn their dowries by prostitution (1, 93). The Babylonians have "the foulest of customs": every woman must once in her life act as a prostitute of Aphrodite and offer herself to a stranger for sex outside the goddess' temple. The ugly ones may have to wait as long as four years before someone takes them up on their offer, Herodotus reports sympathetically (1, 199). Many other peoples are wildly promiscuous. Among the Nasamones of Libya everybody sleeps with the bride at the wedding party (4, 172). Among another people women took pride in having slept with many men, and placed a ring around an ankle for every "conquest" (4, 176).

Such passages, which at least in part can be proved to be false (Pembroke, 1967), constitute, in fact, a reaffirmation of the right to enforce strict control over women in the family and after marriage. The "ethnographic" passages in Herodotus seemed to have served as models for later Greek authors. Thus Xenophon reports from his travels that an Asian people called the Mossynoeci tried to copulate with the Greek camp followers in public. "For they do in a group what other people do alone" and vice versa (*Anab.* 5, 4, 34). Much later Apollonius of Rhodes expands on Xenophon with regard to the Mossynoeci: "They have no reverence for marriage, but like pigs raised for food, not a bit embarassed by onlookers, they have intercourse with women on the ground in promiscuous love" (*Arg.* 2, 1023–25).

In the *Arguments and Counter-Arguments* (*Dissoi Logoi*), a Sophist tract from the late fifth century B.C., it is brought out that among the Macedonians girls may sleep with lovers before they are married. On the Persians this text goes further than Herodotus: it maintains that they sleep with their mothers, sisters, and daughters (11, 12).

These passages on the wild mating habits of "barbarian" peoples are surely only to be taken as a kind of "defense by contrast" of Athenian patterns; they define, in fact, promiscuity as the only alternative to the restrictive Attic form of marriage, ruled by the double standard of sexual morals. Interestingly, Plato seems to have come to the same conclusion, but in a positive vein: in the Utopia blueprinted by Socrates in *The Republic*, mating is to be anonymous, and each generation is to be the collective parent of the next—in other words, the nuclear family is to be abolished (461b). It is not clear how serious Plato was in promoting this system, and he certainly did not bother to work out its practical details. We have already seen that in his last work he spoke in favor of affectionate, monogamous marriage, in his time obviously a far more revolutionary view than his advocacy of promiscuity (*Laws* 839b).

# *14*

# Classical Tragedy: Weaving Men's Dream of Sexual Strife

> The Door of Death I open found
> And the Worm weaving in the Ground.
> Thou'rt my Mother from the Womb
> Wife, Sister, Daughter to the Tomb
> Weaving to Dreams the Sexual strife
> And weeping over the Web of Life.
> —William Blake, "For the Sexes:
> The Gates of Paradise," 45–50

> Mother, I beseech you, do not send after me the maidens with the bloodshot eyes and the snake faces. Help, they are here, they are leaping at me.
> —Euripides, *Orestes* (255–57): Orestes hallucinating after killing his mother

> What sins did [Euripides] not lay at our doorsteps? Where did he not slander us? In a word, wherever he can find an audience, actors and a chorus, he calls us adulterers, man-crazy, drunks, traitors, and gossips, altogether unwholesome, a curse on men. No sooner do they come home from the theater, than they start acting suspicious, and scouring the house, to see whether there is a lover hidden somewhere.
> —Aristophanes, *Thesmophoriazusai*, 388–97

The creative genius of Attic culture during the Fifty Golden Years is undeniable: in both sculpture and architecture the Athenians reached unequaled pinnacles. The art of Western painting, as a technically sophisticated and dramatically expressive medium, may be said to have been born there. Whether one holds the same high opinion of Athenian literature of the epoch depends almost entirely on one's assessment of its principal literary creation, tragedy, for the epic was defunct, except for what appear to have been feeble imitations of Homer. Lyric poetry, which for some critics was the finest Greek literary product, was essentially a non-Attic phenomenon belonging to the Archaic age. Attic prose as an art form had to await a later period.

At the height of their political and military power the Athenian Greeks created tragedy, allowing it to overshadow all other forms of literature, and they watched it for days on end during several annual festivals. Later, in the fourth century B.C., the Greek colony of Taras may have developed a similar mania for the theater, but otherwise no analogous phenomenon is known from the ancient world.

Our impressions of Classical tragedy are largely based on guesswork: we have the texts of thirty-two plays out of an estimated total produced of about one thousand; there survive a few meager fragments of others, and there are some rather hypothetical theories concerning the music, staging, and production of tragic drama. Extant texts were mutilated in transmission, and the factors which have determined survival or loss have been erratic. Undaunted by this paucity of materials, scholars have written more about tragedy than about any other Greek literary genre, and have indulged in great subjectivity in their modes of interpretation. With regard to tragedy few things can be said with certainty. One of these is that it reveals a virtually insatiable appetite for tales of madness, disaster, and heinous crime arising out of intense conflict. Another is that most of this conflict took place within sexual and familial relationships, rather than between the individual and society or between man and the gods.

## Did Women Attend the Theater?

Whether or not fifth-century women were allowed to attend the theater has been debated almost as vehemently as the general question of the social roles of the sexes; it is almost as if deprivation of entertainment was thought to be the worst hardship suffered by the female population. It has been maintained variously that women were allowed to view tragedy but not comedy, that hetaerai could attend the theater but respectable women could not, and that women were admitted but had to sit in the back rows. In truth, there is no solid proof in the matter, and internal evidence from the plays provides most of the food for speculation.

Sandbach (1977, 155) argues that women probably did attend fifth-century comedy because of the following passage in *The Peace* by Aristophanes. Trygaios instructs his slave to throw some barley into the audience (the Greek word for barley, *krithe,* also means penis). The slave reports the job accomplished (964–67):

> Slave: "Of all the spectators present there isn't one who did not get any barley."
> Trygaios: "The women didn't get any."
> Slave: "But the men will give them some tonight."

Obviously, this passage could indicate that women were present in the audience, that they were *not* present in the audience, or that they were present but had to sit in the back, too far away to catch the barley.

The late H. D. F. Kitto, an amiable English classicist, applied a conventional double standard of behavior to both Greek and English social life:

> Hetaerai were adventuresses who had said No to the serious business of life. Of course they amused men. "But my dear fellow, one doesn't marry a woman like that!" (235)

His lengthy discussion of women in the theater—he maintains they did attend—is actually an apology for Athenian men. Kitto even observes patronizingly that Athenian women went to "see plays which we should certainly not allow our women to see" (234). Apart from a little evidence drawn from the fourth and not the fifth century B.C., he relies on passages such as the following from *Frogs* (1050 f.). Here the character Aeschylus attacks Euripides for bringing embarrassment to the women of Athens with his plots of adulterous passions:

> Full many a noble dame, the wife of a noble citizen, hemlock took
> Unable the shame and sin of your Bellerophon
> scenes to brook. (1050–51, trans. B. B. Rogers)

Another "proof" adduced by Kitto is a canard related in a post-Classical biography of Aeschylus to the effect that the chorus of Furies in *The Eumenides* looked so frightful that "boys died of fright and women had miscarriages" (Kitto, 233). Against such arguments one might point to the citation from Aristophanes'

*Thesmophoriazusai* quoted at the head of this chapter, about men's behavior when they return from the performance of a tragedy: their sudden suspicions would make no sense if their wives had also been in the theater. Then there is the reference in the same play to the "lock on the door" of the women's quarters, noted in Chapter 4. The complaint of the chorus of women (784 f.) is even more revealing. They report that their husbands forbid them from going out, or even from peeping out.

Even if some women did attend performances, this would not alter the fact that tragedy was essentially a man's affair. Men wrote, staged, and acted the plays, including the numerous female parts and choruses. Men composed and performed the accompanying music. There is no stranger spectacle that we can reconstruct from public life in ancient Athens than these day-long gatherings of men in the theater. In life, men had reduced their women to shadowy creatures, cut off from most forms of social intercourse, their numbers thinned by childbirth, their health undermined by disregard for their medical and nutritional needs. On the stage, these men impersonated, out of the dimly remembered ancestral past, powerful, fearsome women, driven by superhuman passions: a Clytemnestra exulting over the slain bodies of her husband and Cassandra; an Antigone braving death in her defiance of the law; an Agave coming onstage brandishing the severed head of her son on a stick—all impersonated by men. Murder, incest, rape, cannibalism, all the horrors of the mythological past were trotted out to view, as men munched their fruit, the ancient equivalent of popcorn (Ar. *NE* 1175b). After the performances, according to the Aristophanic speaker quoted at the head of this chapter, the men went home and looked under the furniture for their wives' supposed lovers.

Men's feelings about their mothers, wives, and daughters, which for the purposes of everyday life they had banished from their consciousness, gushed forth on the tragic stage of Athens, producing an effect that was at the same time sublime and ridiculous. It is small wonder that ancient tragedy has been the prime source material for scholars with a psychological bent. And it is no coincidence that tragedy flourished at the expense of other forms of literature during the fifty years when suppression of women was strongest and polarization of the sexes the greatest. Comedy, of course, came onto the scene somewhat later and had its greatest flowering during the last decades of the century, the period of the Peloponnesian War.

## Sex Antagonism and Stage Settings

The preoccupation of the playwrights with male-female interaction created a peculiar problem with regard to stage design. Almost all civic and political activities of the Athenian Greeks took place in the open. In fact, the removal of the decision-making process from the palaces of kings and rulers to the open assembly places was a significant step in the formation of Athenian democracy. As a result, by a convention which was upheld until the end of Classical antiquity, stage action, too, takes place out of doors, most often in front of public or private buildings. However, the outdoors is also the male domain, as distinct from the world of women, which is constantly defined as the indoors. How was a playwright to dramatize female action, which by long tradition was defined as taking place inside, and especially those acts of domestic rebellion with which he was obsessed?

Athenian stage designers solved this problem by creating a literal mode of transportation between the indoors and outdoors, namely the "roll-out platform" (*eccyclema*), a unique Attic invention. This device on wheels or rollers allowed the producer to display an interior scene without interfering with the basic outdoor setting of the play. A characteristic use of this stage machine occurs in Aeschylus' *Agamemnon.* The murder of the king and his consort, Cassandra, takes place offstage: Agamemnon's dying screams are heard by the chorus and by the audience. After the killing, the interior scene, with Clytemnestra and the corpses of her victims, is rolled out into view.

Aristophanes gives us a delightful spoof of the symbolic function of the *eccyclema,* that of bridging the abyss between the female and the male spheres. In *Thesmophoriazusai* the character Euripides aims to infiltrate the ritual "City of Women" of the festival after which the play is named. Since he looks too masculine himself, he calls for help from the poet Agathon, constantly derided for his effeminate manners and acquiescence in anal sex. Agathon is rolled out on the *eccyclema,* dressed in a gorgeous woman's gown and wielding such androgynous gear as a hand mirror combined with a sword (134 f.).

## The Glorious Past: The Subject Matter of Greek Tragedy

Almost all the plots of Greek tragedy were taken from the body of myths transmitted from heroic ancestors of the Bronze Age— namely, the Mycenaeans, whose civilization fell into an abrupt decline, from uncertain causes, about 1100 B.C. The Homeric poems deal with the legends of that age, although it is believed that the *Iliad* and the *Odyssey* were actually composed several centuries later, out of orally transmitted material. Apart from mythology, Greeks of the Classical age knew very little about Mycenaean culture. Today, thanks to excavation and the decipherment of the "Linear B" script, we know much more about the Bronze Age of Greece than they did. In fact, the very haziness of the period seems to have contributed to its appeal.

Thucydides, in his sweeping outline of Greek prehistory, the so-called archaeology that precedes his account of the Peloponnesian War, throws up his hands:

> Concerning the events before [the Peloponnesian War] and those even older, it is impossible to determine anything for certain because of the lapse of time. However, after I extended my inquiries as far back as possible, I determined from such evidence as I could trust, that nothing really big happened, either in respect to wars or in other matters. (1, 1, 2)

The tragedians rarely took legends from the Homeric poems, perhaps because these had acquired a "biblical" aura of authority, and were regarded as history. Instead, they favored stories from other epic poems, now lost, which were based upon the same body of myths.

The legendary story material that the Greeks inherited from their Bronze Age ancestors centered on the traditional men's occupations: battles and conquests; the expedition against Troy and the siege and destruction of that city; and struggles for power within the ruling dynasties of the Mycenaean kingdoms, such as Sparta, Thebes, and Mycenae. The fabled women of the period—Helen, Clytemnestra, Iocasta, Antigone, and so many others—have developed personalities, such as would be virtually unknown in Classical Attica. Even so, they play essentially subordinate if somewhat liberated roles.

In Classical tragedy they were modeled into fierce protagonists of the eternal clash between male and female. Clytemnestra, in the

Homeric account, personified a more or less banal tale of a woman who takes a lover during her husband's prolonged absence; when, against probability, he does return, she and her lover plot the husband's destruction in order to escape punishment. It was probably Aeschylus who first made her the symbol of female uprising against male power. In earlier legends, Euripides' Medea had been a sorceress and a schemer. In her tragic persona she became the perpetrator of that ultimate act of impotent rage against male supremacy—the murder of her own masculine offspring.

This raw material of premolded female characters was necessary to the purposes of Greek tragedy—just how necessary may be seen from the fate of the few plays which dealt with current themes. The playwright Phrynichus (an older contemporary of Aeschylus) composed several plays on the subject of the Persian invasion of Greece. In one of these he described a recent event, the capture of the Asiatic Greek city of Miletus by the Persians in 494 B.C. The audience was so overcome with emotion from the memory of the suffering of their kinsmen that they fined the hapless playwright a thousand drachmas and banned any further productions of the drama (Hdt. 6, 21). It is a telling story, because it demonstrates the rejection of historical realism by Greek theater goers: the audience wanted to escape its own time and circumstances.

The wars between the Greeks and the Persians, nevertheless, might have been a likely subject for tragedy, because the Athenians always perceived them as something like latter-day continuations of the fabled Trojan War, the war of wars, and they took on legendary qualities as soon as they were ended. Yet as far as we know, only one more play was composed on the subject, namely Aeschylus' *Persians*, produced in 472 by the young Pericles.

This tragedy is set in the palace of the Persian kings at Sousa, at the time of the return of the armies of Xerxes from the unsuccessful last expedition against Greece. Evidently Aeschylus could not conceive of a play without some male-female interaction, because into what would have been an all-male proceeding by both Greek and Persian norms, he introduced a female character, Xerxes' mother and widow of the late King Darius. He creates her, however, not after the women from the Trojan legends but in an Athenian mold. The Persian dowager queen is a ninny. Even though her late husband as well as her son have launched expeditions against Greece, she asks naïvely where Athens is located (231). When the defeated

Xerxes arrives on the scene, instead of consoling him she dashes offstage to fetch him clean clothes, possibly because the same actor plays both roles, but this display of female servility seems rather unregal. After Aeschylus' *Persians* no more attempts were made to give tragedy a contemporary cachet: it was again relegated to the comfortably hazy background of myth.

The forced introduction of a female personality into a setting, however, is fairly frequent. Among extant plays the only one that is completely devoid of male-female interaction is Sophocles' *Philoctetes*. A case in point is Aeschylus' *Seven Against Thebes.* Here the two sons of Oedipus and Iocasta fight over the control of the city of Thebes. Eteocles defends the city, Polynices attacks it with a band of allies. Polynices never appears on stage. Instead, the siege and, at the end, the mutual killings of the two brothers are described by messengers. Whatever may have gone on before, the proceedings onstage, which could hardly be called a plot, do not provide any natural scope for male-female antagonism. Yet Aeschylus injects such a factor by making the chorus female: it consists of the women of Thebes. Like nearly all tragic choruses, they mean well, but are too timid to take action. In this case, they lament, display anxiety, and bring sacrifice to the gods to sway them in favor of the defenders. One would hardly expect them to do anything else, yet Eteocles lashes out at them in one of the most misogynistic tirades in tragedy:

> You insupportable creatures, I ask you, is this the best, is this for the city's safety, is this enheartening for our beleaguered army, to have you falling at the images of the city's gods crying and howling, an object of hatred for all temperate souls? Neither in evils nor in fair good luck may I share a dwelling with the tribe of women. (181–87; trans. David Grene)

Why this improbable chorus of women on the battlements of Thebes and why this barely motivated hostility on the part of the young leader, if sexual conflict was not felt to be at the heart of tragedy?

We cannot, of course, follow here this intricate strand of antagonism which is woven through most tragedies, but must restrict ourselves to some observations on the more frequently recurring themes.

## *Women Killing Men*

The Athenian preoccupation with legendary tales of wives murdering their husbands was nothing short of obsessive. Clytemnestra

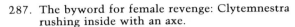

287. The byword for female revenge: Clytemnestra rushing inside with an axe.

always remained the most prominent single exponent of this motif, whereas her son and killer, Orestes in drama, embodied a tragic conflict of motivations. In vase paintings Clytemnestra frequently appears running with an ax toward a closed door (Figure 287). The actual scene behind this pictorial motif is probably her attempt to save the life of her lover, Aegisthus, from attack by Orestes, rather than her assault on Agamemnon. Either way, she was the symbol of violent female revolt against male authority.

Mythological mass murder of husbands was committed by two groups of women. The fifty Danaïds were forced to marry their cousins against their will, and they murdered them in the bridal bed in a blood wedding. The Lemnian women were cursed by Aphrodite with an evil odor that turned their husbands against them; in response, the women killed all the men of their island and established a manless society.

Of Aeschylus' Danaïd tetralogy only the first play, *The Suppliants*, survives. With the subsequent two tragedies missing, it is impossible to establish the drift of Aeschylus' poetic thought for certain, but it appears, surprisingly, that he represented the brides' rebellion against their suitors in a favorable, or at least apologetic, light. The women never explain clearly what is wrong with their potential husbands, only, and this over and over again, that they are being forced into the marriage (Keuls, 1974). The theme of the murderous Danaïds was one of the most, perhaps the most, widely dramatized motifs in Greek culture.

The tale of the Lemnian women had a more completely unredeemed association of female evil. Sophocles wrote a tragedy on the theme, the contents of which are unknown. But a passage in Aeschylus' *Libation Bearers* reveals the relative standing of this myth among others about criminal women. It occurs in a catalogue of female misdeeds delivered by the chorus:

> Of all these crimes the Lemnian is foremost in legend, lamented as despicable by the people. Someone gave evil itself the very name of Lemnian sin. When once a breed of mortals is hateful to the gods, it goes dishonored. For no one holds in awe what is displeasing to the gods. Which of these tales I collect is not worthy to be told? (631–38)

While the tragedians and their audiences revealed a great taste for motifs of female aggression, they ignored, for the most part, the tales of male violence against females, which were also abundant in the inherited pool of legends. Or at least, they did until the end of the fifth century, when the Athenians' own agonies, experienced during the great war with Sparta, aroused Attic sensitivity about the suffering of the innocent. The legends of the Trojan cycle included such events as the slaughter of Iphigeneia by her father Agamemnon, the sacrifice of Polyxena on the tomb of Achilleus to pacify his ghost, the rape of the Trojan priestess Cassandra by Ajax, and the killing of the Amazon queen, Penthesileia, by Achilleus. Defenseless males also fared quite badly, as in the slaying of the ancient Trojan King Priam while he sought refuge at an altar, and the brutal slaughter of Hector's small son, Astyanax, who was hurled from the Trojan battlements. Such tales had to await Euripides to find full dramatization on the stage. In this respect, the tragedians of the earlier fifth century differed greatly from the pictorial artists, who from the very beginning of the ascendancy of Athens were prone to use the mythological heritage of the Greeks to express compassion for the victims of violence.

## Enter the Rapists, Olympian and Mortal

Chapter 2 illustrated the sudden popularity in fifth-century Athens of stories of mortal women raped by gods, as manifested in the vase paintings. It would be remarkable if these motifs were not reflected in tragedy, and, indeed, they were. The fragments and titles of lost plays abound in references to Europa, Antiope, Semele, and many other victims of the sexual treachery of the gods, but, whether by design or an accident of history, none of the plays centered on rape motifs has been preserved, possibly because of censorship by monastic Christian scribes.

To be sure, in Aeschylus' *Prometheus Bound* one of the parade of visitors to the chained hero is Io, who is among the mythological females who fall victim not only to the lust of Zeus but also to the vengeance of his consort, Hera; in other words, Io is the embodiment of women's "double jeopardy." In Aeschylus' treatment, however, the stress is less on the rape than on the victim's punishment, which serves as an occasion to take the audience on an imaginary sight-seeing tour of the Mediterranean world, following in the footsteps, or perhaps hoof tracks, of the unfortunate fugitive, who has been changed into a cow.

Aeschylus was especially renowned for his satyr plays. The satyr play was the fourth component of a dramatic tetralogy, and followed the presentation of three tragedies as a kind of comic dessert. Its basic formula, to the best of our knowledge, entailed the dramatization of a myth, acted out by the nonsatyric characters in earnest fashion, into which the satyrs injected themselves with their customary behavior of making obscene jokes and indulging in sexual molestation. This genre is obviously hospitable to rape stories. Aeschylus' satyr play *Amymone,* which followed his Danaïd trilogy, featured the motif of molestation at the well, Amymone's rape by Poseidon. In Aeschylus' satyr play *The Net Draggers (Diktyoulkoi),* of which fragments survive, a chorus of satyrs evidently behaved in their habitual fashion towards Danaë, the victim of rape by Zeus, whom they dragged out of the sea in a chest, together with her infant son, Perseus.

Sophocles does not seem to have been greatly attracted by the rape motif, but he displays the characteristic Athenian blind spot toward sexual violence in his extant play *The Women of Trachis,* which deals with the notorious sexual exploits of Heracles. In this play the hero is married to his last wife, Deianeira, who is beyond her prime and, considering her husband's sexual habits, has every reason to fear the loss of his affection. During a visit in Oechalia, Heracles lusts after Iole, the daughter of his host (Figure 12). Heracles' tactics of courtship are to murder the entire family of Iole and take her home, together with some other women, as his slaves. Thus Deianeira faces the usual plight of Athenian wives, that of sharing her husband's attentions with a young slave. Iole is a silent character in the play. If Deianeira is "noble," because she does not take revenge on the helpless Iole, she is also gullible, for in her anxiety she recalls, from the days when her sexual fortunes were more prosperous and she was Heracles' young bride, that the centaur Nessos had tried to rape her. Heracles shot Nessos, and just before dying the beast advised the young woman to preserve some of his blood, which, he claimed, could serve as a love potion. In a coarser and more plausible version of the myth, Deianeira keeps the centaur's spilled semen. The frustrated wife dips a robe into the blood and sends it to her philandering husband. The garment turns out to be poisoned, and the hero dies an agonizing death, committing himself voluntarily to the funeral pyre while still alive. Instead of feeling relief, Deianeira commits suicide.

Even Euripides, despite some compassionate stances, did not fundamentally challenge the axiom that women are the legitimate prey of the powerful and the superhuman. The protagonist of his extant play *Ion* is the fruit of Apollo's rape of Creusa, one of the several ill-fated daughters of Cecrops. Creusa is twice victimized by power, since she is subsequently given in marriage to a foreigner in return for military aid. She is the "reward for his spear" (298). She does not seem to mind the marriage, but there is a note of rebellion in her against the violence of Apollo: "Oh, wretched women, victims of the daring of the gods! Where shall we find justice if we perish by the injustice of the powerful?" (252–54). In the end, however, Athena, sent by Apollo and speaking for him, sets everything right by reuniting mother and son and inducing Creusa's husband to accept Ion as his own son. As Athena says smugly, "Apollo managed everything beautifully" (1595).

Two of Euripides' once successful but lost tragedies dealt with rapes committed by Zeus. But perhaps his love affair with Alkmene should more properly be called seduction, since he won her consent by disguising himself as her husband, Amphitryon. Alkmene, yet another imperceptive rape victim, did not suspect anything, even though the god held up the dawn for three days to prolong his night of love. This small, lascivious feature of the Alkmene myth is revealing about the sexual pattern which underlies the rape stories. Zeus, after all, could have come back another night. But the divinities of the Greeks, in their sexual contact with mortal women, were one-time hitters, as rapists generally are. When the real Amphitryon came home after a long absence and found his wife illegitimately pregnant, he intended to burn her alive, but Zeus quenched the pyre with a downpour of rain. The theme has obvious humorous potential, and the Roman author Plautus, in his play *Amphitryon*, as well as several later comedians, made comic capital out of it. Quite possibly, Euripides, too, dealt with it in a light vein. At least a south Italian vase painting, based on his play, indicates as much (Figure 288). Alkmene, perhaps depicted as pregnant, sits on the pyre while Amphitryon and a helper are setting fire to it. From above, personified clouds are pouring water at the command of Zeus, shown in the upper left. The female in the upper right is identified by an inscription as Dawn, and refers to Zeus' technique for prolonging his sexual pleasure.

Euripides' most daring dramatization of rape was probably his *Antiope*, in which Zeus violated his victim in the guise of a satyr. This element was probably not invented by Euripides. On the neck

288.
The rape victim Alkmene saved
by Zeus (after Euripides' *Alkmene*).

289.
Zeus in satyr disguise
pursuing Antiope(?).

of a donkey-head drinking cup (rhyton) by Douris dating from about 460 B.C. (Figure 289), we see a rather dignified satyr pursuing a woman. He wears the regal skin of a large panther and he has no erection. Satyrs in such scenes of pursuit are usually depicted in a state of sexual excitement, but gods are not. Hence we most probably have here a scene of Zeus in satyr garb besetting Antiope, well before the time of Euripides' production. Nevertheless, to feature the supreme god in the guise of a satyr must have been a bold piece of writing. I know of no other illustrations of the rape scene in Classical Greek art, but another theme from Euripides' *Antiope* became a fairly popular pictorial motif. Antiope, as the result of the rape, gives birth to twin sons, Amphion and Zethos, later to win fame as founders of Thebes. Antiope falls in bondage to an evil woman named Dirce. After the twins grow up they trace their mother and avenge her by causing Dirce to be trampled to death by a bull. The bull is another incarnation of Zeus and, as the painter of the scene in Figure 290 has conveyed, the execution of Dirce is yet another form of rape by the phallic powers of the gods (note the huge testicles on the bull).

In contrast to the morality of seduction and abandonment behind the tragedians' treatment of rape, New Comedy, which is in many ways more the descendant of tragedy than of Old Comedy, takes a different position. Since the new genre does not deal with myth, but uses realistic middle-class settings, it presents mortal rapists. Menander's *Arbitration* has already been examined in connection with the motif of the whore with the heart of gold. The play, which was greatly admired in antiquity, offers a new view of rape. The romantic hero, Charisius, has raped a girl by the name of Pamphila. As so often in comedy, the event has taken place during a nightly religious ritual for women, and rapist and victim have not seen each other's faces. By a far-fetched coincidence possible only on the stage, the two characters marry each other shortly thereafter. When Pamphila bears a child too soon after the wedding, she exposes it (note the segregation of husband and wife in the home which this plot presupposes). However, a slave betrays Pamphila to Charisius, and he abandons his wife, although he is still in love with her. Eventually the truth comes out, as usual on the stage, via the "tokens of recognition" exposed with the infant. Interestingly, Charisius recants and rejects the double standard of sex morality even before he realizes that Pamphila's baby is also his own (894–

99 ed. Sandbach). In other words, he would have accepted a reconciliation even if his wife had lost her virginity to another man. Fortunately, for the sensibilities of the audience, this sordid compromise was not necessary.

In Menander's *Woman of Samos* the romantic hero, Moschion, has raped the girl next door, but, inasmuch as he is eager to marry her, his standing as a proper young man is untarnished. These stage conventions of the Hellenistic age are still rooted in a smiling condonement of violence. It is still assumed that a perfectly nice man, especially in the ardor of youth, commits rape once in a while, but at least the onus of guilt is removed from the victim. The ethos of New Comedy also incorporates the idea of "reparatory marriage": the principle that the offense of rape is annulled if the perpetrator subsequently marries the victim. In Mediterranean countries this concept has governed both sexual morality and the law until recently. Menander's plots, in fact, recall a famous case which was tried in Italy in 1965. A nineteen-year-old Sicilian girl by the name of Franca Viola was raped by a young man to whom she had once been engaged. When he was brought to trial, he pleaded guilty, but offered to marry the girl. To his consternation, and surely to that of her family as well, the young woman refused and the rapist was sentenced to eleven years' imprisonment. Unfortunately, the heroic girl probably did herself even more damage than her assailant.

## The Plight of Women Dramatized

As the treatment of rape stories on the tragic stage showed, the Classical Greeks were blind to that perennial jeopardy of women— finding their bodies in constant demand but facing severe reprisals from male society if they yielded to that demand in any other than a male-sanctioned manner. The weakness of women's social position in marriage, on the other hand, found some sympathy with the playwrights. If my interpretations are correct, Aeschylus' Danaïd trilogy dramatized the cruelty of arranged marriages, and Sophocles' *Tereus*, the double standard of sex morality for husband and wife. Euripides' *Medea* surely challenges the right of the husband to repudiate his wife at will.

One play stood by itself: it dramatized what may be termed the pietà motif, or that of the sorrowing mother, so characteristic of societies in which woman is defined almost exclusively in terms of

290. Dirce trampled by the Zeus-bull
(after Euripides' *Antiope*).

motherhood, at the expense of other family and social functions.
The play is Aeschylus' *Niobe*, which in antiquity may have been his
most famous one, since it was widely quoted until long into the
period of the Roman Empire. The following remarks are based on
my own reconstruction of this tragedy (Keuls, 1978), and the reader
is forewarned that they are speculative in nature. Like most popular

myths, the Niobe story has many variants, but there are a few common elements. Niobe has many children—twelve, fourteen, or twenty in the various sources—and boasts of her fertility to the goddess Leto, who has borne only two, the twin divinities Apollo and Artemis. Leto then sends her twins, who often function as executioners, to kill all of Niobe's offspring in punishment with bow and arrow. Apollo shoots the sons, Artemis the daughters. Thereupon Niobe weeps until she is turned into stone. A rock formation near the West Coast of Asia Minor, which resembled a weeping woman, seems to have been a visual catalyst for this last element of the story, but the petrification of Niobe also, of course, has a symbolical side: with her children slain, Niobe no longer has feelings; her heart has turned to stone.

For his Beckett-like dramatization of the myth, Aeschylus chose a version of it in which Niobe's husband, Amphion, after the shooting of the children, assaults the temple of Apollo and is also killed. The effect of this device is to remove much of the guilt of arrogance from Niobe, since, after all, she has done nothing but boast, whereas her husband has violently rebelled against a god. At the opening of the play Niobe sits in silent mourning on top of her children's tomb (not her husband's). For a substantial portion of the dialogue she says nothing, a device spoofed by Aristophanes in his *Frogs* (911–13). There is hardly any plot to the play. First, Niobe's mother comes to persuade her to give up her grief; then her father, Tantalus, tries. Both plead in vain. When Niobe finally breaks her silence, she does so only to moan and weep, probably again over her children and not her husband. In the end she pleads with Zeus to put an end to her misery and to turn her into stone. Zeus sends his messenger, Hermes, to announce that her wish will be granted, and that in afterlife she will be reunited with her children. The play, then, is nothing but a long dirge on the sorrows of motherhood. Why were ancient audiences so touched by it?

Niobe, as an agonizing heap of misery atop the tomb, with bystanders trying to distract her from her sorrow, was so reminiscent of the goddess Demeter mourning the lost Persephone atop the "laughterless stone" that contemporary viewers can hardly have missed the analogy. No Attic illustrations of the scene are extant, but Figure 291 shows an Apulian vase painting based on Aeschylus' *Niobe*. Niobe's father on the left and her mother on the right make pleading gestures. A poorly preserved fifth-century oil flask decorated

291.
Niobe bemoaning her slain
children on a stage tomb (after
Aeschylus' *Niobe*).

292.
Mourning woman on altar, with
attendants, one carrying
a baby. Demeter on the
"laughterless stone"?

in relief (Figure 292) perhaps shows Demeter, mourning atop her stone, while the women of Eleusis try to console her.

In Aeschylus' Demeter-like Niobe, the archetypal female raised to define her identity solely in terms of motherhood, but destined to lose her children, many an Athenian would have recognized the women of his family, even, perhaps, his own mother.

## Tragedy as Catharsis

Bennett Simon in his discussion of tragedy observes that "madness is theater gone berserk" (92), a statement that places Greek tragedy at just one remove from clinical insanity. The ancient Greeks themselves, while not going as far as Simon, certainly did consider tragedy a mechanism for emotional relief, or, as they put it, the catharsis of unwanted passions. Aristotle in his famous discussion of the function of tragedy in his *Poetics* defines it as the "catharsis of pity and fear and similar emotions" (1149b 28). Other authors have articulated a kind of *Schadenfreude* theory—namely, that the audience experienced pleasure through its opportunity to watch the heroic sufferings of others enacted on the stage:

> Man is an animal that's born to toil,
> Whose life brings with it many a pain and grief,
> And these are ways he's found to win relief:
> His mind, beguiled to view another's woes,
> Forgets its own, is cheered, and wiser grows.
> Think first what tragedy can do for us.
> The poor man, once he learns that Telephus
> Was poorer, puts a limit to his craving.
> (Timocles, Fr. 6; trans. John Maxwell Edmonds)

Or, as Plato put it derisively, "When one of the writers of tragedy puts on stage one of the heroes overcome by sorrow and stretching out his laments over a long soliloquy, . . . you know full well that we enjoy it" (*Rep.* 605c–d). Nothing is said in these passages about the release of sexual antagonism. Yet, if we judge by the subject matter of the extant plays and fragments, the problems of family relations were of the greatest interest to the tragedians and their audiences, and the emotions purged by drama must have been primarily those ensuing from the alienation of the sexes.

CHAPTER

# 15

## Sex Antagonism and Women's Rituals

> These gifts does he [Dionysus] hold out: the revelries of dancing bands, laughter to the sound of the flute and relief from daily cares, when the sparkling wine flows at the banquets of the gods, and, at the festivals of men, the mixing bowl spreads sleep among the ivy-garlanded carousers.
> —Euripides, *The Bacchae* (379–86): the chorus of Maenads

> In sum, we have good reason to believe that both the hysteria described in Greek literature and the group ecstasy of Dionysiac rituals served to express and potentially to redress a certain imbalance in the relationships between men and women.
> —Bennett Simon, *Mind and Madness in Ancient Greece* (255)

Because many pagan rites are seemingly remote from the customs and concerns of everyday life, they have often been studied in isolation from the patterns of the society in which they were practiced. This fallacy is less seductive to students of the past with psychiatric training, like Dr. Bennett Simon, than to literary and historical scholars. Few classicists have been prepared to acknowledge the connection between Greek rituals, especially those of Dionysus, and the social structure, characterized here as the reign of the phallus.

Of the different ways of looking at religious rites and their associated story material, viewing them as mechanisms for psychic relief is one of the more recent. According to this school of thought, participants in the ritual are allowed to let off steam and relieve what might otherwise be unbearable anxieties provoked by repression and restriction. The order of society is strengthened by an occasional flirtation with its opposite—disorder and its various manifestations, such as obscenity, promiscuity on the part of women, and irreverence toward what is normally sacred. Various social theorists use terms such as "rites of binary opposition," "symbolic inversion," and "ceremonial contrary behavior." The core theory relevant to ancient Athens is best expressed by the term "rites of rebellion," coined by the British anthropologist Max Gluckman (1954). The phrase "rites of rebellion" is, of course an oxymoron, a contradiction in terms: a rite is controlled behavior, whereas real rebellion constitutes a leap over the fence. Such rituals provide the intoxication of temporally limited freedom from social restraint, so that the participants will be the more pliable the remainder of the time.

This socioanthropological perspective of the study of human ritual life is now fairly common, but it has been applied primarily to as yet unwesternized African tribes, to native American peoples who have preserved some of their tribal cultures, to Australian aborigines, and to other "primitive" societies. To impute to our revered Greeks such sordid pragmatism might seem sacrilegious. Ever since Nietzsche, it has been customary to view the Classical Greek as wavering between two poles of personality, the Apollonian and the Dionysiac, or, as some would now say, the left and right hemispheres of his brain. His Apollonian side looks at the cosmos with the cold glance of intellect, his Dionysiac side yearns for ecstasy and the rapture of artistic creation. This scheme does not leave much room for the practicalities of everyday life, but the Greeks themselves were well aware of the more mundane side of their cults. As the quotation from Euripides at the head of this chapter shows, the Greeks knew that one of the functions of ritual celebration is to release frustrations and pent-up energies and so help people get through life from one day to the next. Many other lines delivered by the chorus of Maenads in the same play stress this point.

If there is any truth to this view of religion, one would expect Classical Athens to have been rife with rites of rebellion providing relief from the antagonism between the sexes. This is indeed the case: male-female conflict seems to lie at the core not only of Athenian tragedies, but also of many religious rituals. Since women bore the brunt of repression, one would anticipate more relief mechanisms for them than for men and this, too, seems to be the case. As we saw in Chapter 12, the social and religious rituals practiced by men were aimed primarily at developing in them the desired qualities of "manliness," at molding them in the image of the rapist and monster-slaying national Attic hero Theseus. The ritual "relief mechanisms" for Athenian women were even more colorful, not to say bizarre, than those of their initiation.

## Demeter at Eleusis: Mournful Motherhood

The chorus of Maenads in Euripides' *Bacchae* invoke the Earth Mother even before their own patron god, Dionysus:

> Two things, young man, come first in the lives of people. First there is the goddess Demeter, or Earth, by whichever name you wish to call her. She nourishes us mortals even in time of drought. (274–78)

The second, of course, is Dionysus, with his gift of wine, "the sole remedy of our sorrows."

The cult of Demeter at Eleusis was the most universal of all Greek religions; it was open to men and women, free and enslaved, from all Greece. In the Roman age senators and emperors participated in it, and, as late as the fifth century A.D., the Emperor Julian the Apostate tried to revive its mysteries.

The sanctuary at Eleusis was originally non-Attic. The Athenians established control over it only in the seventh century B.C., and were never able fully to eradicate the maternal nature of its cult and symbolism. The secret proceedings took place indoors, in the sanctuary hall (*telesterion*). This was a unique feature of the ritual, at least in the Classical period, and was in itself a guarantee of maternal associations. During the period of Attic control over the sanctuary, a deliberate attempt was made to reduce the Earth Mother symbolism of the cult, in accordance with the pattern of the "defeminization" of myths. A new male object of worship was introduced, the boy Iakchos, later called Triptolemos. In the new version of the Eleusinian myth, Demeter gives the secret of agriculture to Iakchos/Triptolemos, who, Prometheus-like, passes it on to men and thus becomes a male fertility figure. The artificial addition of a male divinity to the cult at Eleusis was part of the new patriarchal mythology that accompanied Athens' rise to power. Figure 293 shows a relevant scene, with Demeter and Persephone waiting on the newly invented, departing god and thereby being diminished, as Athena was diminished by serving Heracles. Despite vigorous promotion and the collaboration of some of Athens' finest artists—the drinking cup in the illustration here is by the gifted painter Makron—the cult of Iakchos/Triptolemos never caught on. Eleusis continued to be the domain of the "twain goddesses," Demeter and Persephone, and the Eleusinian cult motif most frequently invoked was that of Demeter searching and sorrowing for her lost daughter.

293.
Defeminization at Eleusis:
Demeter and Persephone
waiting on Triptolemos.

Demeter the Earth Mother was celebrated also in another major ritual, this one for women only—namely, the Thesmophoria, a festival that combined elements of a fertility cult with those of a rite of rebellion.

## The Thesmophoria: Symbolic Copulation in the Pit

During this colorful festival, which lasted for three days during the month of Pyanopsion (late fall), the women of Athens were allowed to break through many of the restrictions that normally governed their lives. They moved out of their houses to an area at the foot of the Acropolis near the place of assembly (*pnyx*), into the very heart of the men's part of the city. The Thesmophoria were not as democratic as the Eleusinian rituals, and slaves were excluded; although Lucian implies that hetaerai could be admitted, that was probably not true in the Classical age. Camped in huts decorated with greenery, the women played at being free. The opening ritual, called the "uprising" (*anodos*), was peculiarly unappetizing. On the first day of the festival, selected women descended into pits where pigs had previously been left to die. Their job was to bring up the decaying remains of the animals and place them on altars, together with seed corn. Some sources speak of snakes frequenting the pits, a likely phenomenon considering the free food, and others of facsimiles of male genitalia thrown in after the pigs. Since the pig is a consistent metaphor for the female reproductive parts, and the snake has phallic associations, a symbolic copulation took place in the pits. On the second day of the festival the women fasted, lamenting the sorrows of Demeter, and on the third day they celebrated Demeter Kalligeneia (Of Fair Birth).

At some time during these proceedings the women indulged in an exchange of obscenities (*aischrologia*), literally the "speaking of shameful things." The ritual received special sanction from the fact that husbands were compelled by law to underwrite its costs. In this oddly mixed festival, fertility and freedom from the customary restrictions of the childbearing role were promoted at the same time. Men were strictly barred from the proceedings, and were evidently reluctant to reveal any detail known to them. Aristophanes' amusing comedy *The Thesmophoriazusai* brings the celebrating women right onto the stage, but we learn almost nothing about the cult practices from the play.

What the wives governed during those three days on the foothills of the Acropolis was a "city of women," in which they dispensed with men, just as men normally expelled women from the public life of the polis. There is today what appears to be a vestige of the Thesmophoria in several Greek villages, where, during one day of the year, the men stay home and cook and tend to the children, while the women go out and work in the fields.

## Of Pigs and Procreation

The association of the pig with the female reproductive mechanism in the Thesmophoria deserves a further comment. The sow is a familiar symbol of human fecundity, perhaps because she bears and suckles large litters, or perhaps because her rotund shape suggests abundance. A number of Greek artifacts produced in southern Italy depict a woman in the childbearing position, with her legs pulled up and spread apart, seated atop a pig (Figure 294). This scheme is not intended as erotic or obscene; it celebrates birth. In Attic usage, however, it acquired overtones of contempt. In the Classical Greek language the word for pig, *choiros*, also denotes the female sex organs, particularly the vagina—a circumstance especially dear to the comic playwrights. Suidas' *Lexicon* cites a proverbial saying derived from a comedy. The line is about the city that was famous as the seat of Greek prostitution: "Since you are a Corinthian, it seems you are going to sell your pig (cunt)" (s.v. *choiros*).

294. Woman in birthing position on a sow (South Italian).

On a higher level of art, Aristophanes squeezes the last drop of humor out of the pun in a scene of ferocious Swiftian satire in *The Acharnians* (730–835). During the war with Sparta, the Dorian town of Megara, surrounded by Attic territory, was cut off from the Athenian market and the Megarians were starving. A character named Dikaiopolis (Just City), a peasant from the rural village of Acharnai, decides to make his own peace and opens a private marketplace for the Megarians. A farmer takes his two little daughters there to sell them, but, because as humans they are worthless, he puts them in a sack and passes them off as pigs, "mystery pigs"—that is, destined for sacrifice. A protracted negotiation ensues, with a barrage of untranslatable *double-entendres* on the two meanings of the word *choiros*, while Dikaiopolis fingers the merchandise and anticipates the pleasure he will have in five years, when his "piglets" will have grown into real cunts. A deal is made for some salt and garlic, and the Megarian happily rushes home, wishing he could sell his wife and his mother as profitably (816–17).

The Greek word for wild sow, *kapraina*, also denoted a "lustful" woman, which to the Greek mind was the equivalent of "lewd" woman. One author of Old Comedy, Hermippus, staged a drama entitled *Women Bread Sellers*, in which he evidently made fun of women in various money-making pursuits and, as was common, equated wage earning with prostitution. In a fragment someone addresses a character as "Foul creature, every man's whore, wild sow (lewd woman)" (Fr. 10).

A certain condescending endearment was apparently contained in the word *choiros* as a personal name for non-citizen women, because it and some of its derivatives appear in inscriptions on vases as hetaera names. Such names as Choiris, Choirina, Choiridion translate roughly as Cunty, Cuntina, and Cuntlet.

The depth of this pig-womb symbolism can be seen in *The Eumenides* by Aeschylus, in which Orestes is pursued by the Furies, who perhaps personify his remorse over the murder of his mother. Eventually Orestes is cleansed of the pollution of matricide with "pig-slaying purifications" (283). Orestes, who had destroyed the genitals that had produced him, atoned for his act by offering a symbolic womb to the gods. In fourth-century vase painting Orestes is frequently depicted as seeking refuge from the pursuing Furies at the Omphalos, or Navel of the Earth, at Delphi, crawling as it were back into the womb, as hinted by Aeschylus in *The Eumenides* (40).

Pig sacrifices were made to a number of goddesses, but, significantly, not to Aphrodite (Ar. *Acharn* 793), since she was the patron of pleasurable, not of fruitful, sex. Although men also sometimes sacrificed piglets, the practice is most often associated with women, and numerous artifacts from all parts of Greece depict female figures with piglets. In Figure 295 a woman is holding an offering of cakes in one hand and a sacrificial piglet in the other.

Athenian myth and folklore gave a hateful twist to this very widespread symbolic equation of the sow and motherhood. One of the labors of the Dorian ethnic hero Heracles was the slaying of the Erymanthian boar, the boar, like the bull being a traditional symbol of masculinity. As noted before, his Attic counterpart, Theseus, assumed a number of the aspects of Heracles and several of his labors. In the case of the pig killing, however, a change of sex took place: Theseus did not kill a boar but Phaia, the Crommyan sow. Plutarch (*Thes.* 9) adds, as a bit of embroidery, the information that some people considered Phaia in reality a "female brigand, a murderous and unbridled woman." In Figure 41 we saw a detail of Theseus killing the sow. The animal there is richly endowed with

295. Woman with offering basket
and sacrificial piglet.

dugs, and its femaleness is evidently an important aspect of the new variant.

### The "Parliament of Women" During the Skira Festival

In the Thesmophoria a reversal of sex roles took place in combination with other features; in another Athenian ritual it was the dominant element. During one day of the festival called Skira, one of the many festivals surrounding the great annual panathenaic festivals, the women left their homes and organized an *ecclesia*, a political assembly or parliament. Much of our information about this ritual comes from Aristophanes' play *The Parliament of Women*, because for once this playwright did not invent a "fantastic idea" but used one that was readymade in the customs of the city; as a result, this work is less witty than his others. In Aristophanes' comedy the women go to the assembly disguised as men, in long cloaks and coarse shoes; they have tanned their faces and glued on artificial beards, and they carry walking sticks. These details are probably authentic. A number of vase paintings depict women attired as men, and some of these may allude to the Skira ritual. Figure 296 shows what appears to be a woman with an artificial beard, frolicking with a man with a wineskin, possibly in some revelry connected with the festival. To be president of the one-day parliament was an honor for a woman. What kind of mock politicking took place in the *ecclesia* during the Skira festival we do not know—though the ineffectual protests uttered by the women in Aristophanes' play are probably not too unrealistic—but the Skira celebration soon turned to more manly business, such as the bull-slaying rite (*bouphonia*), and the women were hustled back to their houses.

### The Mad Sex Life of Satyrs and Maenads

Less is known and more has been written about the ritualistic madness referred to as Maenadism than about any other aspect of Greek cult life (the word "maenad" means "raving woman"). The period of its greatest intensity coincided with the era of the sharpest sexual polarization in Athens, the earlier part of the fifth century B.C. This was also the age in which the ritual took on a more or less standard form, which was later imitated and domesticated wherever Greek influence penetrated the Mediterranean world. Unfortunately, we have almost no documentation for the seminal phase of the ritual other than artifacts, mainly vase paintings. Our earliest written source on ritualized madness is *The Bacchae*, the tragedy by Euripides which was produced posthumously in Athens in 406 B.C. In this play the god Dionysus, disguised as his own disciple, arrives with a band of female followers in Thebes, where King Pentheus refuses to acknowledge him. Dionysus drives the female members of Pentheus' house mad, and they tear the young king apart, thinking he is a lion. Abandoning the discretion of most earlier tragedy, in which bloody scenes are kept offstage and merely related by an uninvolved minor character, Pentheus' mother, Agave, comes on brandishing the severed head of her son on her wand (*thyrsus*) and exulting in her victory over the "lion." Dionysus then lifts the veil of madness from Agave's eyes and she realizes her error.

Critics agree that Euripides plays with authentic elements from actual rites involving madness or ecstasy. They are, however, uncertain as to what the playwright is trying to say in the tragedy. Was he denouncing the religion of Dionysus, or *all* religion, as barbaric and irrational? Was he branding opposition to an established cult as sacreligious? Or was he promoting a toned-down, tempered version of the wild rites for the benefit of simple folk who need emotional release?

If Euripides did indeed view the madness rituals as emotional therapy for ordinary people and a useful social institution, he was prophetic, for in the Hellenistic era the Dionysiac religion became a middle-class institution, highly organized, with elaborate initiation procedures and a complicated hierarchy of officials.

We have much information on this later form of Maenadism, especially from Asia Minor (modern Turkey) and southern Italy. But these latter-day raving madwomen were faking it. As the Hellenistic historian Diodorus Siculus described the Maenadism of his time, they were "imitating the Maenads who, according to legend, used to run with the god" (4, 3, 2). Women were the dominant sex in these later rites. When the Dionysus rituals, or Bacchanalia, spread from southern Italy to Rome in the second century B.C., the Romans clamped down on them, probably essentially because they were foreign, and especially curtailed their male membership. They ordained that the cult's priesthood should be

296. Transvestite ritual. Woman with false beard?

exclusively female and that women should outnumber men in all gatherings. By this time both the satyrs and the rituals of sexual antagonism which, as we will see, were essential to the religion in the fifth century B.C., had all but vanished from the cult proceedings.

What exactly was the Maenadism which these latter-day Bacchants imitated? Only the fifth-century vase paintings can tell us. A major difficulty, however, in interpreting scenes with Maenads and satyrs is uncertainty as to whether they represent fantasy, reality, or something in between. We have no record of specific persons participating in the rituals in the fifth century: the earliest "historical" Maenad was Olympias, the mother of Alexander the Great, who lived in the fourth century B.C.

Most Maenads of the fifth century B.C. were ladies of a certain class: the dress they wore under their cultic accouterments was expensive. A typical Maenad is shown in the lovely picture in Figure 297. She holds a live young panther in her left hand and a thyrsus in her right. The panther refers to the ritual of laceration (*sparagmos*), in which women tore a live wild animal apart, an enactment of aggression. The thyrsus, a fennel stalk topped by a pine cone, is the characteristic wand of the Dionysiac cult, and is wielded by Maenads, often in hostile fashion, as well as by satyrs and by the god himself. The lady in our illustration has a hide tied around her neck, and on her head she wears a live snake twined through her hair. More often Maenads are depicted with a snake coiled around one arm, a detail referred to as "snake handling" (Figure 298). In the latter scene two Maenads consort with Dionysus, who carries a wine cup and wears a woman's robes. On the far right part of a satyr may be seen. He has a snub-nosed face and a tail and that perennial satyr's attribute, a huge erect penis, which, of course, to the Greeks was a sign not of manhood but of bestiality. A deerskin hangs over his shoulder. The satyr's costume, unlike that of the Maenads, is a disguise; the simian face is a mask, and the tail and penis are tied on.

One of the epithets of the god Dionysus was "he who drives women mad" (*gynaimanes*), and this title points to the curious circumstance that, in the Dionysiac rituals, only the women go crazy, while the men merely act out a part. The Maenads, in their most unrestrained behavior, act like persons in an ecstatic trance: they throw back their heads; raise their arms in wild gestures; and maul animals, mostly young ones, in the cruelest fashion, and brandish their severed limbs. They let snakes entwine their arms, and they ululate and make a noise with clappers and tympana (Figure 299).

On the nature and social function of ecstatic cults, much light has been thrown by anthropologists. I. M. Lewis, in his classic study, has examined such rituals among peoples ranging from the Haitians to Moslem Arabic tribes of North Africa, and has concluded that the rituals regularly serve to provide a licensed and controllable outlet for the pent-up hostilities and frustrations of suppressed classes of the population. The behavior of fifth-century Greek mad women on vases is in keeping with these findings, but their staged interaction with the satyrs seems to be a unique feature of the Athenian cult.

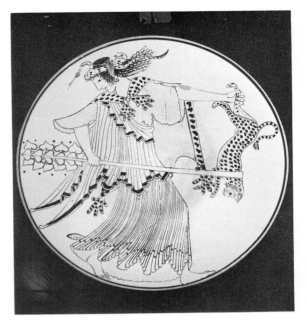

297. A Maenad of high fashion.

298. Dionysus and Maenads.

The satyrs are theatrical impersonations of man's "basal primate urges"—sex, hunger, and self-preservation. They behave in the most phallic manner, but only in jest. In Figure 300 two men in satyr costume, one with a simulated erection and one without, dance around a phallus with huge testicles, presumably made of stone. The eye of the phallus seems to look at them with approval. The background is filled in with Dionysus' vines. In the encounter with Maenads, the satyrs' function is mainly to molest, but not rape, their female companions, and in turn to suffer violence from the women, who attack them in self-defense.

Paradoxically, the Maenadic rites of sex antagonism may have developed out of an earlier Dionysiac ritual in which men and women danced together and practiced group copulation. A group of vases from the sixth century B.C. referred to as Chalkidian, though probably produced in Attica, depict men and women in choruses and men copulating with both men and women. Penetration is usually from the rear in these rites, and probably intended to be anal. Figure 301 shows such a ritual dance, and Figure 302, a scene of copulation. The men are masked and decked out in satyr garb, but the women are not in any way identified as Maenads. We do not know either the occasion or the significance of these acts, but it is interesting that, despite the prone position and anal penetration of the women, which we take to denote submission, no hostility between male and female is indicated. In fact, in Figure 302 the woman on the left turns to the satyr behind her with an affectionate gesture.

In vase paintings from the late sixth and the fifth centuries, however, different patterns prevail. Now satyrs masturbate and play sex games with each other—how they maintain their constant erection with this kind of behavior the paintings do not explain—but their pursuit of women rarely ends in consummation. They are infrequently depicted as actually copulating with women, and when so, the woman is not specifically identified as a Maenad and the occasions do not appear to be ritual. Figures 303 and 304 show men in satyr garb copulating with women without any identifying attributes; they are apparently amenable to the entertainment and so presumably they are hetaerai. In Figure 305 a satyr clutching his genitals is negotiating the consummation of his desire with a woman who holds out a hand for money. She, too, must be a professional prostitute.

299. Ranting Maenads.

300. Satyrs dancing around
a phallus.

301. Ritual dance of satyrs
and women.

302.  Ritual group sex.

303.  Satyr engaging in anal copulation.

304. Satyr copulating with hetaera.

305. Man in satyr garb negotiating
sex with a hetaera.

In his relations with Maenads, on the other hand, the satyr's never-spent randiness is not reciprocated. In constant sexual pursuit of the Maenads, he tries to molest them in whatever way the circumstances encourage. In the ritual dances he sneaks up on them from behind; when their hands are engaged he fondles their sexual parts, and when they have fallen asleep he reaches under their skirts. Almost invariably these efforts lead nowhere. Figure 306 shows a charming study of a satyr plotting sexual mischief against a Maenad (not shown) who is featured on the reverse; he is about to pounce on his victim. The scene on the outside of the cup by Makron in Figure 307 hints at gang rape, but it is not shown consummated. One satyr pulls back the head of the Maenad, the other spreads her legs apart.

Figures 308 and 309 depict two groupings of similar composition, except that in these cases the potential victim is clearly sleeping. The woman in Figure 308 is identified as a Maenad by her thyrsus. The sleeper in Figure 309 is naked and wears the pointed cap often donned by hetaerai; possibly she belongs to a lower class of participants in these rituals.

The repetitiousness of the motif of the sleeping Maenad makes it probable that these anonymous characters are acting out some mythological tale. If so, it can be only one story, that of Dionysus approaching the sleeping Ariadne on the island of Naxos after her abandonment by the treacherous Theseus. Dionysus awakens Ariadne to new sexual experiences and makes her his permanent consort.

The satyrs are mortal manifestations of the god himself: they represent the elementary drives and the more mundane pleasures of drinking, sex, and joyous abandon. These form the underbelly of the Dionysiac rituals, from which developed the satyr play, essentially myth transformed into a picaresque tale. When they feel up their sleeping Maenad companions, the satyrs are acting out the first mating of Dionysus with Ariadne. The assumption of a "sacred tale" behind the bawdy behavior of the satyrs helps to explain why they do not consummate their desires. Hugo von Hoffmansthal was surely not aware of the ritual of the molestation of sleeping Maenads when he wrote the libretto for Richard Strauss' opera *Ariadne auf Naxos*. Yet he could hardly have captured better the intertwining of sacred and scurrilous elements that characterized the Dionysiac religion.

That actual copulation was not part of the normal proceedings seems indicated by a legend about fourth-century Maenads preserved in Plutarch (*Mul. Virt.* 13). A band of Maenads roaming the countryside in a ritual event called "mountain wandering" (*oreibasia*) lose their way and, exhausted, fall asleep in the center of the town of Amphissa. The local women form a wall around the sleeping Maenads to protect them against sexual molestation by soldiers and later give them safe escort out of town.

When awake, the Maenads fight back. The thyrsus they wield is not just a ceremonial implement; it is a phallic weapon, a counterpart of the tridents, thunderbolts, and scepters with which the gods habitually threaten their sex objects when they go on rampages of rape (see the illustrations in Chapter 2). Like the male weapons, the thyrsus is often aimed at groin level, as in the cup by Makron in Figure 310.

The phallic component of Maenadic behavior can be documented in yet another way. A drinking cup by the painter Epiktetus, which recently appeared on the art market in Basel, juxtaposes, in the outside decoration, Maenads and Heracles (Figure 311). The half of the rim which is well preserved shows Maenads in a conventional revel, without satyrs in this case. The group includes a "snake handler" and a woman carrying a young deer, surely about to be ritually torn apart. The other half of the rim, of which parts are missing, shows Heracles in one of his monster-slaying roles. He is fighting the Centaurs, who are hurling large stones at him; as often, the Centaurs have satyr-like faces, signifying their barbarism. Thus, the Maenadic performance, including its ritualized aggression, is here presented as the counterpart of male phallic behavior in myth.

The vexing question remains: did Athenian men and women really act out these rituals of violence, lust, and antagonism? Pausanias (A.D. second century) reports that every other year a contingent of Athenian women went to Delphi, doing Maenadic dances all along the way, and there joined their Delphic sisters for rituals on Mount Parnassus (10, 4). Again, no satyrs seem to have been involved. For Maenadic customs in Athens during the fifth century B.C., we have no solid evidence. Yet it is hardly conceivable that the Attic vase paintings reflect only fantasy. Too many of them include elements that indicate organized ceremonies.

Figure 312 reproduces a wine krater, decorated with a scene of ecstatic women and girls. One woman plays the double flute, the

306. Satyr plotting mischief against a Maenad.

307. Two satyrs molesting
a reclining Maenad.

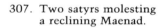

308. Satyr preparing to rape
a sleeping Maenad.

309. Satyr sneaking up on a sleeping Maenad.

310.
Maenad aiming thyrsus
at satyr's testicles.

311. Raving Maenads juxtaposed
with Heracles killing
Centaurs.

other beats a tympanon. The adult women who are not making music are "snake handling." The presence of the little girls surely points to an actual ritual occasion, and not one of imagination. An even more revealing scene is shown in Figure 313. On the left a Maenad is brandishing the severed leg of an animal, which she evidently has just lopped off with the sword in her right hand. That the scene alludes to a mimetic performance is indicated by the youthful flute player on the right, who is wearing the traditional long robe of the musicians in the theater. Except for the blood flowing from it, one might have taken the animal limb for a stage prop.

In the strange vase painting in Figure 314, a woman wearing an artificial phallus carries out a dance before the enthroned Dionysus. Since this picture has no analogies, its exact meaning is not known. However, the dancer's costume—tight shorts with a sewn-on phallus—is known specifically as the garb of the satyrs who perform on the stage, in the satyr play. The painting, therefore, confirms that women, while barred from the public stage, did participate in some theatrical activities in the rituals of Dionysus. Some of the vases showing women with artificial phalluses, which we saw in Chapter 3, probably derive from rites of this nature. The striking painting which appears as the frontispiece, depicting a nude woman in a forceful stride, with a huge phallus under her arm, I take to be a caricature of a Dionysiac ritual in which women acted out phallic aggression against the male.

## The Matrimonial Side of Maenadic Sex Rituals

The fifth-century vase paintings prove that the Dionysiac ritual had another bearing on the sex life of Athenians: it not only dramatized antagonism but, surprisingly, it also promoted a domestic, conjugal side of sexuality—how successfully we cannot say. This aspect of the early cult of Dionysus has not been recognized, perhaps because it is not reflected in *The Bacchae* by Euripides or in other literary sources.

In one of the more bizarre rituals surrounding the Anthesteria festival at Athens, the wife of the king ruler (*archon basileus*), an office which was a vestige of the former monarchy, was led to the central cult building of the god, the Cowherd's Den (*Boukoleion*), perhaps also her husband's official residence, where she was to mate

312. Girls learning how to become Maenads.

313. Woman acting out a Maenadic ritual to flute music.

314. Woman in phallic satyr apron dancing for Dionysus.

with the god. What form this copulation took has been the subject of somewhat lascivious speculations. Did she mate with her own husband disguised as the god, with a satyr, or only in fantasy? In any case, the ritual, called Sacred Wedding (*hieros gamos*), offered one of the very few Attic celebrations of conjugal sex. The ceremony is represented, or at least alluded to, in several vase paintings. Figure 315 shows a man wearing theatrical boots, in a satyr mask but without the phallus, leading the *basilinna* (as the wife was called) to the sanctuary. In Figure 316 we see Dionysus himself arriving: his divine status is indicated by his supernatural height. He is preceded by a young attendant, wearing an ivy chaplet and carrying a wine pitcher. A satyr with large but relaxed genitals sits on the steps of the *Boukoleion*. The *basilinna* awaits the god's arrival in the semi-opened door, the recurrent symbol for conjugal sex.

Dionysus even has a family life of sorts, though it is not prominent in his myths. Figure 317 shows a family group of Dionysus, his wife, Ariadne, and their son, Oenopion; the woman behind the god is an attendant, perhaps added for symmetry. Dionysus is enthroned on a chair covered with animal fur, holding a thyrsus in his left hand. He dandles the boy, whose name means "little wine drinker," on his knees. The lovely mother is making conversation, as her gesticulating right hand indicates. Thus, the cult of Dionysus had a pronounced dual aspect: it provided rituals of mad hysteria in which sexual hostilities and pent-up frustration were released, and, at the same time, it promoted a resolution of antagonism in harmonious family life.

With this background in Dionysiac symbolism, we can read the "program" of a number of multiple scenes on individual vases which otherwise might seem unconnected. The narrow neck amphora in Figure 318 depicts a formidable, matronly Maenad. More Athena than Ariadne, she has a snake in her left hand and an animal skin over her shoulder. In front of her a crouching satyr is molesting her sexually, but it is clear that he will get nowhere. He is puny in relation to the woman and she is resolutely grabbing him by the hair. On the neck of the amphora a slender young hetaera is tying her sandal; she is a pert figure, often reproduced to characterize the Greek prostitute. The import of this scene is "The sexual aggressiveness in the ritual is play-acting; for the release of his libido the satyr has a hetaera waiting."

315.
Dionysiac official leads
the *basilinna* to the
sanctuary.

316. The "sacred wedding": Dionysus arrives
at the *boukoleion*, where the *basilinna*
awaits him.

317.
The happy family: Dionysus, Ariadne,
the child Oenopion, and a nurse.

A unique juxtaposition of ritual and domestic sex relations governs the decoration of the jug in Figures 319 and 320. On one side of the vessel (Figure 319) a satyr is carrying off a Maenad. His erect penis, which points at her pubic area, leaves no doubt as to his intention. In this case the rather smug-looking Maenad does not seem to object very vehemently; she is mainly concerned with not being dropped. On the other side (Figure 320) we see a pair, probably the same two persons, in ordinary clothes, but with the grapes and ivy of Dionysus still surrounding them. The folding stool with garments loosely piled on it shows that we are now inside a home. The pair is exchanging an affectionate embrace. Again we have ritual play-acting of sex conflict opposite a private relationship, only this time the real sex is conjugal.

The cup in Figures 321 and 322 develops yet another variant of the conjugal theme. In Figure 321 Ariadne pours wine into Dionysus' drinking cup, the kantharos characteristic of the Dionysiac cult. On the other side a peaceable Maenad and a nonphallic satyr face each other calmly. One assumes they are husband and wife, experiencing their relationship as a mortal version of the Sacred Wedding of Dionysus and Ariadne. In Figure 323, a cup tondo by the Penthesileia Painter, the artist jokes on the tame character of some of these rituals. The slight satyr on the left, sporting a huge erection, pursues a Maenad in the standard tripping pose. His victim, however, remains serene and the satyr is losing his nerve, intimidated by her kantharos, the foot of which is aimed at his extended penis.

This matrimonial side of Dionysiac ritual and imagery provides the answer for a phenomenon that has puzzled scholars. Women dressed as Maenads sometimes appear on the white-ground oil flasks (lekythoi) which were fabricated for funerary purposes and are decorated with sepulchral motifs. In Figure 324 a woman wearing a furry skin over her robe sits on a stone or chair, also covered with fur; she is holding a thyrsus, at a grave monument. For additional Dionysiac effect the thyrsus is decorated with ivy. Whether she is the deceased or a survivor is not clear, but her Dionysiac garb surely celebrates her function as the good wife, as do the attributes of textile making on similar flasks.

The Dionysiac religion was to become the most successful and the most widely practiced pagan ritual of the Greco-Roman world. It flourished until the end of Classical antiquity. In its later phases the matrimonial aspects came to overshadow its function as a

318. Sturdy Maenad manhandling satyr

319. Satyr abducting nonresisting Maenad.

320. Same as 319, reverse: domestic bliss after the ritual.

321. Ariadne serves
Dionysus wine.

322. Same as 321, reverse:
a tame satyr-Maenad pair.
Husband and wife?

323. A confident Maenad.

mechanism for the relief of sex antagonism. We cannot survey this development here; however, as a small but amusing indication of this change of emphasis, Figure 325 shows a small Attic wine pitcher (chous) from the middle of the fourth century B.C. In Chapter 12 I showed several of these pitchers, made for boy participants in the Anthesteria festival, and noted that in the fifth century they tended to be decorated with themes relating to male-supremacist practices. Here, a century later, we are in a different social climate. The boys in this scene are enacting the wedding procession of the god Dionysus and his ceremonial bride, the wife of the king ruler. The god is already seated in the cart, wine cup in hand; his "bride" is just about to mount, looking back at the other participants in the ritual. This playful celebration of conjugal values in the Anthesteria festival would have been unthinkable on *choes* from the fifth century B.C.

## Female Aggression and the Rituals of Dionysus

Greek myth and legend abound in tales of female aggression

324.
Resting Maenad on
a funerary vase.

325.
Boys acting out the wedding procession
of Dionysus and the *basilinna*.

against the male. We have encountered a number of these already and will consider more of them in the following chapter. Everywhere in the world of mythological fantasy we encounter wives slaughtering husbands, mothers murdering sons. Dionysus himself was dismembered by raving women in one of his many myths, a tale which may be reflected in the Maenadic ritual of the laceration of live animals.

In the broader Dionysiac context, the archetypal myth of female aggression appears to have been the tale of the Thracian women, who lacerated the legendary musician-poet and cult figure Orpheus. This myth is frequently depicted on Attic vases, for example in Figure 326. In Figure 327 we see yet another instance of mythological aggression by women, this one echoing the pictorial motif of gods pursuing mortals with phallic weapons. The vase painting represents a woman in a rather obscure myth on the life of Heracles; she is a servant of Proteus, the "old man of the sea," and she is attacking the macho hero, who is depicted on the reverse.

Herodotus recounts several quasi-historical stories of Maenad-like behavior. From the history of Athens during the rule of the Peisistratids, he recalls the following naïve legend: After an Athenian fleet had been destroyed at the island of Aegina, the sole survivor of the calamity returned to Athens with the bad news. The widows of the victims grabbed the unfortunate man and stabbed him to death with the brooch pins of their gowns, each one of them asking him where her husband was.

> The Athenians thought that this deed of the women was even worse than the fate of the men. But, since they had no other way of punishing the women, they made them change the style of their dress . . . so that they would no longer require brooch pins. (5, 87)

Such myths and legends are the extension of male fear of female aggression. Given the conditions of repression, the psychic energy for such deeds may well have been pent up in women's souls. The Dionysiac rituals evidently allowed both men and women to discharge these hostilities, but they also pointed toward a reconciliation of the sexes.

326. Woman attacking Orpheus.

327.
Angry woman on the attack
(against Heracles, who is on
the other side).

# *16*

## Love, Not War: Protest in the Arts and on the Streets

> . . . no one, either then or later, has been able to tell the truth as to who had performed this deed.
> —Thucydides (6, 60)

> . . . and a lust to sail befell all of them.
> —Thucydides (6, 24)

> Women always tend to be more squeamish when it comes to war.
> —Art Buchwald, *The Washington Post*, December 3, 1982

Chapter 1 related the almost incredible events of the years 416 and 415, which precipitated the decline of Athens and ushered in an era of antimilitarism, liberalization, and feminism. The year 416 saw the punitive action against the island of Melos, including the slaughter of its adult male population and the enslavement of its women and children, by an Athenian expeditionary force. In the spring of the following year Euripides, in his tragedy *The Trojan Women*, perhaps the most powerful antiwar play ever produced, voiced a protest against this brutal deed, dramatizing the plight of the innocent after the sack of a city. Astonishingly, he also warned against disaster which often follows arrogant and cruel behavior. At about the same time the deliberations on the Sicilian campaign took place, with Alcibiades fanning the imperialist ambitions of Athens, and in midsummer the expeditionary force was launched, with great pomp and fanfare. One event put a damper on the exuberant spirits of the Athenians: very shortly before the sailing of the fleet, a band of unidentified persons knocked off the penises of hundreds of stele statues of the god Hermes. At approximately the time this sacrilege took place, the women of Athens were celebrating the festival of the Adonia, of which the antipatriarchal tendencies were noted in Chapter 1. What was the relationship between these different events, and most of all, who was responsible for this strange act of genital aggression? I shall try here to unravel this mystery, which through the ages has puzzled scholars as much as it did the Athenians themselves.

## The City of Athens as a Tragic Heroine

The historian Thucydides, whose account is the principal source for the events sketched here, tended to portray his native city as a typical tragic character, fallen victim to the vice of *hubris*, "overweening pride," perhaps better defined more loosely as "failure to recognize the limitations of the human condition." In his view, Athens was a character reminiscent of Creon in Sophocles' *Antigone*, a man who becomes intoxicated with the authority of his position to the point of inviting disaster. Thucydides praised the genius and virtues of Athens lavishly, notably in the famous funeral oration put in the mouth of Pericles, but he judged that Athens was incapable of "prudence in time of prosperity" (8, 24, 4, by implication). As events unfold in his history, the stage is carefully set for the great city's fall from pride. Some of the details reported by the author should perhaps be seen as stage clues; he notes, for instance, that during an earlier debate about an expedition against Sicily most of the members of the Athenian assembly had no idea of the size of the island or of the numbers and nationalities of its inhabitants (6, 1, 1)—an observation stressing the folly of the enterprise.

The author was a wealthy aristocrat and a former general, but had been exiled or forced to flee because an expedition that he commanded had failed to accomplish its mission, and under Athenian law he might have had to face trial and possible execution. Ambivalent notes of sorrow for his mother city and of personal bitterness lie under the surface of his account. Thucydides, then, was not present in Athens during the fateful summer of 415. Indeed, we have no idea where he spent his years of exile, or how he gathered his data. Nevertheless, as his narrative reveals, he was very sensitive to the irrational mood that prevailed in Athens at that time. By means of his customary technique of concocting set speeches—in this case, one by the general Nikias against the expedition and one by Alcibiades in favor—he dramatized the conflict between reason and greed. The sensible Nikias speaks of prudence, compromise, and regard for peace; Alcibiades, acting out of selfish motives of avarice and ambition, sways his audience by painting vistas of conquest, wealth, and power.

The signs of counter-cultural undercurrents, on the other hand, seem to have escaped the historian. He reports the "mutilation of the herms" as a freak event, as if it were unrelated to the expedition, and the coincidence with the Adonia is not mentioned by him at all, but is known from other authors.

## The Bright and Happy Expedition

In 415 the war between Athens and Sparta, called by Athenians the Peloponnesian War, was in its seventeenth year. The first years of the war had been hard on Athens. It had adopted the strategy of pulling in its indefensible rural population behind the great walls protecting the city and its harbor, allowing the enemy to ravage the cultivated countryside, but maintaining a safe outlet to the sea, where Athens had unquestionable superiority. This essentially sound strategy produced an unanticipated effect. As a result of unsanitary conditions in the overcrowded city, a plague of an unidentified type broke out, to which Pericles and an estimated fourth of the population succumbed. Thucydides also contracted the disease but recovered. Despite some further setbacks for the Athenians, the "spartanizing" and latterly peace-oriented Nikias managed to engineer a one-year truce in 423 and a favorable peace treaty, the Peace of Nikias, in 421. Athens soon recovered and began to tamper with the conditions of the peace treaty, at the prompting of belligerent politicians such as Alcibiades.

In the spring of 415 a delegation arrived from the Sicilian town of Egesta (or Segesta), a non-Greek polis, but allied with Athens, who pleaded for military aid against a quarrelsome neighbor, Selinus. The Segestan ambassadors brought money, as well as the promise of more treasure awaiting the Athenian forces in Sicily, a fund that later turned out to be nonexistent. Trivial in itself, this proposal fanned Athenian imperial ambitions of long standing. After a debate that was prolonged by the peace party, the assembly voted to send an army to Sicily. Events then moved at rapid speed, because the season was already far advanced; ancient warfare, until the time of

Alexander the Great, was largely conducted during the summer months and brought to a standstill before the onset of winter. Thucydides describes the festive mood that hung over Athens as the fleet was made ready for sailing in the harbor of Piraeus. On the day set for the departure, the entire male population of Athens and its environs rushed down to the piers at dawn to observe the spectacle of this "remarkable, even unbelievable undertaking" (6, 30, 2). This fleet, only the first contingent of the ultimate expeditionary force, was "the costliest and best equipped ever to be dispatched by one single Greek polis" (6, 31, 1). The historian, of course, wrote with wry hindsight, knowing the disastrous outcome of the expedition. The sailing of the Athenian fleet calls to mind the joyous departure of the German armies for the Western front in the First World War, with their exaltation of the "bright and happy war" (*der frischfröhliche Krieg*).

## Alcibiades: The Personification of Phallicism

The glamorous young Alcibiades played a key role in the events of 415, and he may be considered the very embodiment of the Athenian phallic ideal. Wealthy, handsome, and eloquent, renowned for his success at horse racing as well as for his sexual exploits, he was every inch what the Athenians called a *kalos kagathos*, literally a "beautiful and good man," the ideal of the privileged, accomplished citizen. He was also ambitious, manipulative, and without any discernible scruples. It was Alcibiades' wife, Hipparete, it will be remembered, who dared to lodge a complaint against him for bringing hetaerai into their living quarters. Alcibiades forcefully took Hipparete back home and she died shortly afterwards. The accounts of his life abound in tales of heterosexual and homosexual love affairs. From Plato's *Symposium* Alcibiades is known for his attempt, represented by Plato as unsuccessful, to seduce Socrates. Because of the latter's satyr-like appearance, Plato depicts Alcibiades as desiring Socrates for his wisdom rather than for erotic gratification. The comedy playwright Pherecrates said of this golden youth, "Although not a man, Alcibiades, so it seems, is now the husband of all wives" (Fr. 155), a comment evidently widely quoted, because it was later paraphrased in Rome in a scurrilous critique of Julius Caesar: "He was the husband of all wives and the wife of all husbands" (Suet. 1, 52).

The lengthy speech of persuasion that Thucydides attributes to Alcibiades is remarkable for its glorification of war and conquest. According to the historian, Alcibiades not only dangled in front of his audience the prospect of empire over Sicily (and, indeed, over all of Hellas), but he also exalted war for its own sake:

> . . . the city, while it is at peace, will wear itself out in its own concerns, and the knowledge of all things will go stale, but while it is at war, it will always grow in experience and preserve the habit of defending itself, not by words but by deeds. (6, 18, 6)

Alcibiades was appointed as one of the three commanders of the expeditionary force. The other two were Lamachus and Nikias, the latter an unfortunate choice in view of his opposition to the campaign.

According to Thucydides, at least, Alcibiades was never implicated in the scandal of the "mutilation of the herms," and there is no reason to believe that he participated in the act. He was, however, accused of unrelated "profanations," and after the fleet had left, the Athenians sent out the state trireme *Salaminia*, a fast vessel kept in readiness for emergency missions, to arrest him. Alcibiades jumped ship and crossed over to Athens' enemies, the Spartans.

## The Herms of Athens, or the Phallic Presence in Everyday Life

Despite the omnipresence of the phallus as an object and as an image in Athenian culture, it is likely that for the ordinary citizen of either sex the herms in the street constituted the most familiar phallic presence in his or her life. A herm, it will be recalled, was, at least originally, a statue of the god Hermes, consisting of a stone slab topped by a sculpted head and with testicles and an erect penis about midway down. The penis in most cases protruded from the slab and must have been extremely susceptible to damage. Such images stood in front of private houses and in courtyards, and they marked the boundaries of public and sacred precincts. A number of these statues stood in the Agora area, in a section referred to as The Herms.

The illustrations in Chapter 1 demonstrated the phallic nature of these statues and also their vulnerability to disfigurement. A few more representations of herms will bear evidence of their familiarity in everyday life. Figure 328 illustrates the role these statues played in the domestic atmosphere of the Athenians. Near a home altar stands a herm whose penis someone has decorated with a wreath of flowers. The inscription reads "Glaukon is beautiful." Glaukon, of course, is not the herm, but some male beauty to whom this vase painting was dedicated. In Figure 329 an older man and a woman, surely husband and wife, have his and her herms, which they caress lovingly. In Figure 330 the statue is drawn into the fantasy world of the Dionysiac cult. Partially humanized, the figure has limbs and the body is covered with a furry garment. He holds Hermes' herald

329. His and Hers herms. "His"
is located outside.

328.
The cult of the domestic herm:
a garlanded penis near a home
altar.

staff in the left hand and a drinking cup in the right; he seems to be toasting the master and the mistress of the house, who are dressed up as a very tame satyr-and-Maenad pair.

The Pan Painter, with his delightful flair for phallic imagery with a humorous twist, has given us the most charming pictures of herms. Figure 331 is the vase after which this painter is named. It shows Hermes' son, Pan, a randy mountain spirit, half-goat and half-man, running away from a herm which has a penis reaching up to the level of its face. Pan is in lusty pursuit of a young shepherd boy; he is no match in genital dimensions for his father, but there is little doubt that he will consummate his desire.

Few fragments of actual herms from the fifth century have been found. The portrait head of Hermes in Figure 332, unearthed in the Athenian Agora, is certainly one of them. Its nose is damaged, which has led archaeologists to believe that it may have been a victim of the mutilation of 415. That may well be the case, but, in view of the characteristic shape of the herm, it is unreasonable to suppose that the nose could have been the prime target of the vandals.

Thucydides reports simply that "meanwhile"—that is, during the preparations for the sailing—most of the numerous stone herms of Athens literally "had their fronts cut up all around" during one night (6, 27, 1). The Greek word used by the author for "front" is *prosopon*—literally, "that which meets the eye"—a word which can mean facade, mask, character, but also "face." Despite his delicate phrasing, face is surely not what Thucydides had in mind. In Aristophanes' *Lysistrata,* some men come on stage with huge erections, the result of the sex strike which their wives have inflicted on them. The chorus warns them, "If you are smart, you will cover up with your shirt, so that the herm choppers won't catch sight of you" (1093–94).

In a fragment from a comedy by Phrynichus, a character addresses either Hermes himself or his effigy, saying, "Dearest Hermes, don't you fall, too, and get yourself castrated, providing cause for slander" (Fr. 58).

## Who Did It?

Despite the intensive investigation of the symbolic castrations, no one has come up with a convincing identification of the culprits.

The account of events in Andocides' *On the Mysteries* is too obviously fabricated to take seriously. The Athenian authorities reacted sharply to the discovery. It does not seem to have occurred to anybody to take the mutilation as a harmless prank carried too far: it was seen as a subversive act, indicative of plots to overthrow the government. Hermes, after all, was the god of travel, and the sacrilege must have cast an ominous spell over the preparations for the expedition.

After offering rewards for the detection of the herm choppers, the magistrates took a fateful next step. Unable to solve the crime, they solicited information on any *other* acts of sacrilege that might have been committed and extended immunity from charges to any informant. After this offer accusations began to fly thick and fast, but they mainly concerned "profanation of the mysteries"—the sacrilegious enactment in a private home of certain secret rituals of the Eleusinian mysteries.

By inviting charges of this kind, the authorities set the stage for a veritable witch hunt, for "profanation of the mysteries" and actions that could be considered as such were going on in Athens all the time, in public and in private. Aeschylus had once been indicted for revealing details of the Eleusinian rites in his tragedies. In defense, he had explained that he had only "said what came into his head"—in other words, that the revelations had been unconscious. After he was acquitted, his words became a ready excuse in Athens.

The initiation rites, with their arcane proceedings and sexual symbolism, also lent themselves to satire. The comedies of Aristophanes, especially *Clouds, Birds*, and *Frogs*, are full of hilarious burlesques of the goings-on at Eleusis. The head bird of "Cloudcuckooland" in *Birds*, for example, is the hoopoo (*epops*), majestic though molting, which character, hooting jokes on religious rituals, alludes to the *epoptia*, literally "vision," the highest grade of initiation in the Eleusinian mysteries. The line between permissible and sacrilegious allusion apparently was a subtle one. Aristophanes, however, knew how to stay clear of it, because he was never prosecuted for profanation. Earlier we saw the affinity between the comedy of the stage and the revels at parties, and there can be little doubt that parodies of the mysteries were popular at the latter too. Isocrates' fragmentary speech *The Team of Horses* (16), written for the younger Alcibiades, contains a defense of the speaker's father,

330.
The herm as a member
of the family.

331.
Phallic humor: Pan, son
of Hermes, chasing a
shepherd boy.

by now some years dead. The son, of course, denies his father's alleged misdeed, but at the same time implies that "doing the mysteries" at dinner parties was a not uncommon pastime (6). Only in an emotionally charged atmosphere could such acts suddenly be declared capital crimes. During the crisis which followed the mutilation, numerous prominent citizens were charged with one sacrilege or another. We know the names of seventy persons implicated in the scandals, but surely there were more. Most of those charged were either executed, or, like Alcibiades, they fled before being apprehended. The estates of the fugitives were confiscated and sold

332. A mutilated herm head
from the Agora.

at auction. A fragmentary inscription from the period gives a list of personal belongings so sold.

Who were the perpetrators of this peculiar demonstration, and what was their purpose? The notion of a prank on the part of young men who had not anticipated such a fierce reaction must be discarded. In order to work on hundreds of statues and yet remain undetected, the herm choppers must have been well organized. And why would young men hack away at a public symbol of their own virility? Most modern historians assume that the act was a form of political protest on the part of a segment of the population opposing the expedition. But why should they not have voiced their protest in the assembly, especially since their view was already represented through the respected figure of Nikias? The slaves and the aliens in the city are unlikely candidates, as they did not have a major stake in the welfare of the city, and they could expect fierce retribution if caught. This leaves only one possibility—namely, the women of Athens. If this speculation seems far-fetched, it should be remembered that the Adonia was being celebrated about this time, which gave the women temporary freedom of movement. We know that they roamed around the city at night during the fateful events, because a woman named Agariste testified that she saw Alcibiades desecrate the mysteries at the house of Charmides, and she identified several other male participants as well. In any case, the herms in front of private houses would have been easily accessible to the celebrating women.

Even apart from the Adonia, it is likely that the women of Athens had more freedom than usual. The frantic preparations for the expedition must have engaged a large proportion of the men and caused a relaxation of the normal restrictions. Although the women did not attend the theater, they cannot have failed to hear about Euripides' *Trojan Women* and to remember afresh the fate of the wives and children of Melos. If defeated, the city of Athens could expect the same treatment from her Dorian enemies. That the Spartans would in fact spare the city and its people could not be foreseen in 415.

Although the Adonia released antimachismo feelings in Athenian women, it was surely the rituals of Dionysus—also known in Athens as Sabazius—which provided the model for the castration of the herms. Figure 333 shows another instance of a Maenad attacking a satyr in the groin with her ritual weapon, the thyrsus.

333. Detail of Maenad attacking the
genitals of a satyr in a ritual.

It was but one step from the enacted aggression against the genitals of satyrs in the controlled setting of cultic proceedings to the castration of the phallic stone symbols, at the prompting of fear and outrage. Among the many evil omens which were later said to have accompanied the expedition, there was one strange echo of the castration riot. According to Plutarch, an unidentified man leaped onto the Altar of the Twelve Gods in the Agora and there cut off his genitals with a stone (*Nic.* 13, 2).

It is, of course, improbable, if my speculation is correct, that in time the truth would not have leaked out. The hypothesis that the women were responsible provides the most likely explanation for the fact that this historical mystery remained unsolved: the truth was too shocking to acknowledge. By the time suspicions about the identity of the culprits began to filter through, so many heads had rolled that it would have been impossible to point the finger at that theoretically nonexistent class, the citizen women.

## Aristophanes and Women's Protests

Now let us look again at the plays of Aristophanes, in the light of this hypothesis. There can be no argument that through the medium of comedy and satire the playwright had long screamed out for peace. *The Acharnians*, which included the bitter-funny piglet episode described in Chapter 15, and *The Peace* had both been produced before the Sicilian expedition. *Birds*, also a fantasy about desire for peace, probably dates from 414, and so must have been written during the Sicilian war. By October of 413 the expeditionary force had received the *coup de grâce* from its allied Dorian opponents. Thucydides is sparing with figures, and those he does provide may be rough estimates, but they are telling nevertheless. Only eight days before the final carnage—the "Battle at the River Assinarus," south of Syracuse—the main Athenian force, including allies, and, perhaps non-combatants, still numbered 40,000 (7, 75, 5). After the slaughter at the river and the surrender or capture of all troops under Athenian command, the majority of the 7,000 survivors were sent as prisoners to the Sicilian stone quarries, where they were kept in excruciating conditions for seventy days; indeed, the Athenians and their close allies among them were never released from this death camp (7, 87). In the end most of the captives were sold into slavery. Some did escape, either from the battlefields or from captivity. Plutarch's romantic report that a number of Athenian fugitives received shelter and assistance from the native population in exchange for recitals of passages from Euripides' latest plays (*Nikias* 29) is surely apocryphal, but some survivors did make it back to Athens. As Thucydides says vaguely, "Few of the many returned home" (7, 87, 6).

After this debacle, Aristophanes produced three comedies on female rebellion: *Lysistrata* and *Thesmophoriazusai* in 411, and *The Parliament of Women* much later, in 392 or 391. All of these role-reversal plays, strikingly enough, represent women not rebelling within the confines of family life, as tragedy often does, but taking over men's roles in society and demanding an influence in politics and government. To be sure, in *Lysistrata* the women go on a sex strike, which is something of a paradox since their main complaint is the absence of their men as a result of the war. But they also occupy the Acropolis and take control of the state treasury in the Parthenon.

When Aristophanes produced *Lysistrata* in the spring of 411, the wounds of Athens were still raw. There can hardly have been a member of the audience who was not mourning a loss in the family. Most must also have harbored a gradually diminishing hope that their missing relatives might still be alive in captivity somewhere. Could the expedition have been a joking matter at this point? Yet the comedy, as we have already seen, abounds in allusions not only

to the expedition itself, but also to the castration of the herms and
to the Adonia. In fact, *Lysistrata* provides the most contemporary
evidence for the approximate coincidence of the Adonia with these
other events.

During the first scenes of the play the women are plotting their
strategy and bantering with a chorus of men who are too old to
take part in the war. On comes the "magistrate." He delivers the
following words, which I translate as literally as possible. Demostratos was a militant politician who favored all-out commitment
to the expedition. Several sources report that he intervened in the
debate, evidently briefly, but at a critical moment (Thuc. 6, 25, 1,
without naming him; Plut. *Alc.* 18, 2 and *Nik.* 12, 4). The island of
Zakynthos, located on the way to Sicily, was an Athenian ally.

> What! Did the wantonness of the women break out again
> And the beating of cymbals and the continuous orgies of
>      [Dionysus] Sabazius,
> And that accursed Adonis ritual on the roofs,
> Which I myself heard once when I sat in the assembly.
> And that fellow Demostratos—may he come to grief—
> Was saying we should sail to Sicily, meanwhile his wife danced
> And wailed "Alas Adonis," but Demostratos
> Says we must recruit an army on Zakynthos
> And she, half-soused, the woman on the roof,
> Says: "Beat your breast for Adonis." And he was restrained
>      [others: "pressed on"],
> That foul creature, hateful to the gods, with his bilious wife
>      [an untranslatable play on Demostratos' family name]
> Those are the acts of uncontrollable behavior we can expect
>      from women. (387–98)

Oddly, the "magistrate" is represented as still favoring the expedition, even though by now it has ended in disaster. The bitterness
of this conceit lies in the fact that he is a *proboulos*, one of the
Committee of Ten created to govern Athens during the crisis over
the expedition; in other words, he owed his position of authority
to the fateful undertaking. Although the wry-comical scene evoked,
with the "magistrate," Demostratos and other hawkish politicians
clamoring for war, while the shrill dirges of the rebelling women
on the rooftops penetrate the assembly, is not to be taken as history,
it surely alludes to some form of female protest. Moreover it reflects
the playwright's uncanny awareness that much outward aggression

ultimately is not aimed at the foreign antagonist, but at preserving a power base at home.

What is more, later in the same year Aristophanes again produced a comedy, *Thesmophoriazusai*, in which women aim to take control of the city government and clamor for peace. Politics and sex had always been the basic ingredients of Aristophanic comedy, and peace had always been his aim, but never before had his messages found female mouthpieces.

Aristophanes also wrote a play entitled *Danaïds*, of which the chorus must have been composed of those archetypes of female rebellion, the husband-murdering daughters of Danaüs. Since the Danaïds were punished by having to pour water into a leaking vat, the comedy may have mocked the launching of the second Sicilian contingent in the year 414 (Edmonds, on fragment 245). We have no other basis for dating this comedy, but it appears to have been yet another post-expedition play with elements of female rebellion.

I can see no other explanation for Aristophanes' sudden preoccupation with female protest than that he, and at least a part of the audience, knew or suspected that the castration of the herms had been perpetrated by women, a suspicion which by now could not possibly find overt expression. The mutilation was an act of impotent rage, and the women, their sense of independence fanned by the counter-cultural ritual of the Adonia, might well have rebelled at the prospect of renewed war and the inevitable slaughter being planned by their men.

## Was There a "Make Love, Not War" Movement in Classical Athens?

The unavoidability of war was apparently never questioned by the Greeks. Even so enlightened an author as Plato seems never to have contemplated a world without constant armed conflicts. The glorification of war, however, is another matter. In the Homeric poems the battlefield is a place of glory: here alone the heroes can reap the immortality of being remembered (*arete*). The reader is spared no detail of its horrors, but these are told in a matter-of-fact manner. The *Iliad* is the goriest piece of literature in the Western tradition. Consider this passage:

> . . . the brazen spearhead smashed its way clean through below the brain
> in an upward stroke, and the white bones splintered, and the teeth were

shaken out with the stroke and both eyes filled up with blood, and gaping he blew a spray of blood through the nostrils. (16, 346–49; trans. R. Lattimore)

In the most nauseating ·scene of all, the Greek warrior Peneleos taunts the Trojans with the detached eye of an opponent, which is stuck to the tip of his spear (14, 493–505). Achilleus rejects the blood-and-glory ethic, but only in the *Odyssey,* where he is a celebrated but very dead ghost in the underworld. In a famous passage in this poem he says,

> Let me hear no smooth talk of death from you,
> Odysseus, light of councils.
> Better, I say, to break sod as a farm hand
> For some poor country man, in iron rations,
> Than lord it over all the exhausted dead.
> (11, 488–91; trans. R. Fitzgerald)

On the losing side, King Priam does not reject the martial ethos whereby old men have ever persuaded young men to die for them, until almost all his friends are dead and Troy is doomed. Even then, he states that peculiarly Greek part of the ethic which considers the mutilated corpse of a young warrior "beautiful." (*Iliad* 22, 73)

The early lyric and iambic poets, it seems, could glorify heroism on the battlefield or reject it, as the occasion demanded. Generally earthier than the writers, the pictorial artists were the first to develop an ethic of antiheroism. The vase painters of Athens occupied a much lower place on the socioeconomic ladder than the tragedians and historians. It is thought that not a few of them were foreign residents, and some even may have been slaves or freedmen. Under the militaristic, expansionist regime that governed Athens at the height of her power, they evidently stayed closer to the undercurrents of antimilitarism, which must always have been present.

Figures 334, 335, and 336 reproduce a unique artifact, a large pointed amphora of terra cotta, found on the island of Mykonos. It dates from about 670 B.C., a good hundred years after the assumed time of the composition of the Homeric poems. It shows scenes from the sack of Troy, but in a version not closely parallel to that of Homer. On the neck we see the Trojan horse, which is naïvely depicted as striding, although its hooves are set on wheels (Figure 334). The heads of the hidden Greeks, visible to us through windows in the horse's rump, are to be read as concealed from the unsuspecting Trojans, who are gathering around the horse and preparing to drag it into the city. The relief on the neck foreshadows

334. The Trojan horse on a seventh-century amphora.

the approaching destruction of Troy. The body of the vase shows scenes from the actual sack, involving the capture of women and the slaughter of children, most of them apparently anonymous (Figure 335). An orgy of child slaughter is depicted on this curious monument. Only one of the preserved scenes can securely be connected with a mythological episode, the so-called recovery of Helen. According to a well-known Trojan story, Menelaos, after the capture of Troy, went in pursuit of his unfaithful wife with the intent of killing her, but after he caught sight of her, particularly of her abundant bosom, he was overwhelmed by desire and decided to take her home after all. On the Mykonos vase, the telling detail which identifies the pair as Helen and Menelaos is the richly decorated robe of Helen, which is folded over her head, symbolizing luxury and sex appeal (Figure 336). If we look at the total composition of the decoration, its message becomes clear: it points to the treacherous ruse of the Trojan horse, which had more effect on the outcome of the war than manly valor on the battlefield; to the suffering of the innocent; and to the ironic circumstance that the very woman who was responsible for the slaughter is the only one for whom the story takes a happy turn.

In Attic culture of the earlier fifth century B.C., well before

335. Same as 334: the sack of Troy deglorified.

Euripides, the tradition of using the legends of the Trojan War as a means to express an antiheroic vision of life was continued, but again only by the figurative artists. One mythological motif may even have been invented by the painters, inasmuch as we do not know it from any literary source: it is the incident from the sack of Troy in which Neoptolemos, the son of Achilleus, kills the aged king of Troy, Priam, at an altar, using the body of the king's grandson, Astyanax, as the weapon of execution. The story may, of course, have been told in one of the lost poems of the Trojan cycle. In fifth-century vase paintings illustrating the *ilioupersis*, or sack of Troy, this is a fairly common episode. Physically this action is highly improbable, but it is laden with antimilitaristic pathos. The "hero," in the prime of life, uses his military victory to wipe out the defenseless old and the very young in one swoop. The Brygos Painter, from whose hand we have already seen the ferocious rendering of men maltreating middle-aged prostitutes, was among those who used the motif. In Figure 337 we see details from his

336. Same as 334, detail: Helen pleads with Menelaos to spare her.

sack of Troy on the outside of a drinking cup, with Neoptolemos about to bear down on Priam with the apparently still living body of the little boy.

The antiheroic message is even clearer in an early-fifth-century sack of Troy by the Altamura Painter (Figures 338 and 339). This vessel is a so-called kalyx krater, with handles at the bottom of the container; as a result the decoration can go all the way around the vase. The composition, however, is symmetrical. Around the center of one side (Figure 338) are arranged scenes depicting the demise of three generations of the house of Priam. On the left is the rape of Cassandra by Ajax; he is dragging her away from the Temple of Athena. Her complete nudity dramatizes her sexual defenselessness. On the right we have again the motif of Neoptolemos killing old Priam with the body of his grandson. The artist has pulled these two episodes from the sack of Troy together, by making Cassandra and Priam reach out toward each other. The other side of the vase (Figure 339) is dominated by the figure of the Trojan Prince Aeneas, carrying out his old father, Anchises, on his back, foreshadowing the celebration of "pious Aeneas" many centuries later by Vergil. Aeneas is preceded by a youthful warrior, perhaps a son, and followed by his wife. Behind her, over the handle, are two fighting men, a Trojan and a Greek, who separate the Trojan from the Greek part of the scheme. The Trojan is the defender, because he is just drawing his sword, which can be seen in the illustration. In other words, the Trojan soldier is protecting the rear of the fleeing party. Especially striking is the contrast between the wife's firm stride and confident posture and, on the other side, the wretched plight of Cassandra. The antithesis of the overall scheme is unmistakable. On one side the flower of Greek manhood engages in the rape and slaughter of the defenseless; on the other side youthful male strength is applied to a labor of piety and compassion, the protection of the old and the weak against violence.

It is believed that long before the Romans did so, the Etruscans adopted Aeneas as their mythological ancestor, and that some of the sympathetic Greek portrayals of the Trojan prince may have been produced for export to Etruria. Accommodation to the tastes of foreign customers, however, could hardly explain the intricate, as it were rhetorical, antimilitaristic scheme of the Boston krater. It clearly communicates a message of protest to Greeks.

337. The sack of Troy: Neoptolemus attacks Priam with the body of his grandson Astyanax.

338. The sack of Troy: the demise of Cassandra, Priam, and Astyanax.

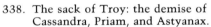

339. Same as 338, reverse: Aeneas leaves Troy, carrying his old father.

## Feminist Doctrine

Wartime and frontier conditions regularly have an emancipating effect on the female population: until the affairs of a society return to normal, women have to step in and take over tasks from which they are barred in peace time. The horrendous losses of male lives suffered by Athens in the Peloponnesian War and especially in the Sicilian expedition must have brought about a drastic, if temporary, change in the male-female ratio, and driven many women from the loom into the public labor market. Demographic data for the period are wanting, and I know of no evidence that women did take over functions previously performed by their men, but a certain feminism was in the air.

The most influential thinker of late-fifth-century Athens, Socrates, was a friend of women. Although later legend embroidered on his supposedly difficult relationship with his wife, Xanthippe, the sources close to his own time could not conceal the fact that Socrates had cordial and respectful dealings with priestesses and courtesans, including the fabled Aspasia. What is more, Socrates' adoring disciple Plato developed into the Western world's first feminist. This is the more remarkable because Plato never married and, as far as we know, never had any sexual liaison with a woman; hence we must assume that he was homosexual by inclination rather than, as in the case of normal Athenian men, bisexual by cultural tradition. Astonishingly, in Book V of *The Republic*, Plato advocates that women be given the same education as men, and access to all functions and professions (452a). Although in his view women are generically inferior to men, individual differences often cancel out that disadvantage, and it is uneconomical to waste their talents.

The Stoic school of philosophy was founded in the early Hellenistic age, and it incorporated many Platonic notions. It fostered the emancipation of women, and the Stoic philosopher Epiktetus, who lived in the first century, reports that Plato's *Republic* was often in the hands of liberated Roman ladies. The school must even have developed a doctrine of the equality of the sexes, because it is reflected in the writings of the Roman Stoic Seneca and also in the discourses of Musonius Rufus, another Roman Stoic of the first century. Whereas Seneca pays mere lip service to women's equality, Musonius Rufus developed a coherent doctrine of sexual ethics, based on the assumption of equality of male and female in virtue and educability. The case of Musonius Rufus illustrates the antifeminist bias which has always prevailed in historical scholarship. Whatever one thinks of Musonius' philosophy, his discourses offer the only ancient statement of a doctrine of the equality of the sexes. Yet this text is extremely difficult to find. The only English translation of Musonius Rufus (by Cora E. Lutz, 1947) is absent from most public and university libraries. The original Greek version is mostly buried in obscure anthologies. As a result, Musonius and his views are regularly overlooked by students of sex relations in antiquity. Yet, to quote one of the rare comments on this remarkable figure,

> . . . Musonius elaborates a perfect philosophy of equality in nature, education and virtues between sexes and outlines the ideal marital relationship between the partners. (Ghougassian, 1977, 96)

## The Aftermath of the Sicilian Expedition

After the debacle of 413, the war with Sparta dragged on for another nine years, until the decisive defeat of the Athenians at sea in the battle of Aegospotami of 404 B.C. Athens was never to regain her empire or her previous prominence among the Greek states. After his defection, Alcibiades spent the remaining years of the war engaging in the most checkered political manipulations. While in league with the Spartans, he inflicted great harm on his home state. Later he allied himself with the perennial Greek enemy, Persia. Miraculously, he was reinstated in command of a fleet by Athens; then he again sought refuge in Persia, and finally he was murdered there at the instigation of the regime of The Thirty Tyrants, a dictatorial junta which took control of Athens for a short period just preceding the surrender. The extreme phallicism that had brought Athens to glory and defeat in less than a century had spent itself, and its most prominent symbol died with it.

# Epilogue

Although her empire was lost, the city of Athens and the state of Attica recovered remarkably well from the crushing defeats in the Peloponnesian War, because of the generosity of the Spartan victors: they spared the city and extracted only moderate concessions from it. The character of Attic culture, however, underwent drastic changes. By the turn of the century Athens had started on what Classicist Moses Hadas called "a decline from the heroic to the bourgeois." She had lost most of her creative drive; as Aristophanes might have put it, the Attic genius had lost its penis, or virility. In the fourth century Athens was no longer the principal hub of painting and sculpture; other centers, notably Sicyon (the port of Corinth), began to rival it. The art of vase painting declined, both in quality and in the numbers produced, so that, for the second part of the Classical age, we no longer have this rich source of documentation for social life and mores.

New tragedies were still composed, but the dramatic festivals more and more centered on revivals of the fifth-century repertoire. The obscene and satirical Old Comedy was defunct and new genres of drama developed, the Middle Comedy of the early fourth century and the New Comedy of the late Classical age, both essentially a comedy of manners. Of Middle Comedy only fragments survive, but of New Comedy we have texts or major portions of five plays, in addition to fragments. Together these literary remains yield a picture of a comfortable middle-class society in which women have considerably more freedom of movement than they had in the fifth century B.C., and more dignity and authority within the household. In Figure 188 we saw an illustration of an Attic Middle Comedy in which a husband and his wife are taking a snack together, a small but telling detail of a changed domestic life. It is not to be thought, however, that the doctrinaire feminism of Socrates and Plato resulted in fundamental changes in Attic society. The Classical world was to experience new periods of phallicism.

## Later Waves of Phallicism

Plato's own pupil Aristotle was one of the fiercest misogynists of all times, obsessed with the need to prove that women play no genetic part in reproduction. Aristotle's misogyny was embraced by some of his more influential students. The last major lawmaker of Athens was Demetrius of Phaleron, who held autocratic sway over the city from about 318 to 308. A disciple of Aristotle's Lyceum, he sponsored a large body of new laws under the influence of Aristotle's successor Theophrastus. Among Demetrius' measures was the reinstatement (or the creation) of the Women's Police (*gynaikonomoi*). A fragment of a contemporary comedy, *Kekryphalos* (Headdress) by Menander, reveals that one of the functions of the Women's Police at this time was the curtailing of "luxury" in the home. If we may take the information of the fragment at face value, the cooks, or caterers, hired for weddings and other family ceremonies were used as spies by these officials:

> At the headquarters of the Women's Police I learned that according to some new law, a list is kept of all cooks who cater at wedding parties, in order to find out whether anyone entertains more invited guests than the law allows. (Ath. 6, 245, b–c)

Demetrius of Phaleron was succeeded by another Demetrius, this one with the ominous surname of Poliorketes (Besieger of Cities), who, according to accounts of his career, lived up to the phallic implications of that epithet. This Besieger embodies, as it were, the last paroxysm of traditional Attic phallicism. The so-called Elgin Throne is thought to have been manufactured for him. The back of the throne is decorated with patriotic themes in sculpted relief, which include, not surprisingly, the charter myth of the Attic state: a Greek, probably Theseus, killing a fallen Amazon (Figure 340).

340. Throne of the "Besieger of Cities" (detail): Greek slaughtering an Amazon.

## Alexander "the Great"

Aristotle's male chauvinism probably had its greatest effect on his best-known pupil, Alexander III, King of Macedonia, whom the world insists on calling "the Great." Aristotle was Alexander's tutor before the young prince ascended to the throne at the age of twenty, and the philosopher wrote treatises on politics and the art of governing for him. The Greeks were ambivalent about their Macedonian neighbors, sometimes considering them "barbarians" and sometimes expressing a sense of kinship with them. Alexander was enamored of Greek (and especially Athenian) culture and absorbed its values with the full ardor of a bastard trying to prove himself legitimate. The entire notion of the conquest of Persia, which had already been contemplated by earlier Macedonian kings, was motivated essentially by a desire to fulfill that "manifest destiny" of the Greeks, the final victory of West over East.

History has sung nearly unanimous praises of Alexander, although in the ancient sources there is also a hostile biographical strand in which the conqueror is represented as a raving madman. Currently Alexander's reputation is enjoying a new apotheosis, under the influence of modern Greek nationalism, and because of spectacular archaeological finds in various parts of Macedonia. Alexander's own capital at Pella, near Saloniki, has long been identified, and partially excavated. The most interesting artifacts found there are a number of fine pebble mosaics, which decorated the floors of the king's palace. The mosaics cannot be precisely dated, but reflect "Alexandrian" style. It will hardly come as a surprise that their motifs are largely of a phallic nature. The spearing, slashing, and clubbing to death of defenseless animals was a special favorite, although a scene of Amazon slaughter has also been found. Figures 341 and 342 show two of these hunting scenes, in which the lives of the hunters do not seem to be in imminent danger. The candor with which the artists have depicted the hunt as slaughter rather than as contest of man and beast is, indeed, surprising. Hunting was one of the king's two most cherished pastimes, the other being the symposium.

The most important Macedonian site excavated is located near modern Vergina, in the far north of what is Greece today. It has now been determined beyond a doubt that this site is identical with that of Aigai, the seat of the Macedonian monarchy before Pella. The identification of the most important tomb discovered there as that of Philip II, Alexander's father, is not unanimous, but there can be no doubt that the tomb finds derive from the approximate age of Alexander. Figure 343 shows a minor, but unmistakable, portrait of Alexander from a silver urn found at Vergina. The conqueror is depicted in the persona of the most brawny of all the Greek mythological heroes, Heracles. His head, with the wild eyes characteristic of his traditional portrait, protrudes from the jaws of Heracles' Nemean lion's skin.

In having himself portrayed in this heroic manner, Alexander set a trend for later rulers. One of the more comical artifacts from the age of the Roman Empire shows the Emperor Commodus, the son of Marcus Aurelius, similarly glorified (Figure 344). The portrait, which dates from about A.D. 190, shows the weak face of this debauched ruler, with his hairdo of mechanically drilled curly hair framed by the lion's jaws and legs. Commodus wields Heracles' traditional monster-slaying weapon, the stone-filled club, looking as though he is headed for a fancy costume party.

## The Alexander Mosaic: The Great Anti-Phallic Statement

The most important of the representations of Alexander, and perhaps the most skillful and most interesting of all Classical artifacts, does not glorify the king's martial and aggressive qualities. I speak, of course, of the Alexander mosaic, found in the Villa of the Faun at Pompeii, now one of the glories of the Archaeological Museum of Naples.

This fascinating monument is a fitting item with which to conclude this gallop through the iconography of glorified aggression,

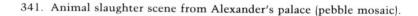

341. Animal slaughter scene from Alexander's palace (pebble mosaic).

342. The killing of a stag. Mosaic from Alexander's palace.

because, contrary to general belief, it is one of the great antiphallicist statements of all times (Figure 345). It has, however, been interpreted as just the opposite, because of the admiration of violence and aggression in our own culture.

The scene represents a confrontation of Alexander and the Persian king Darius III on a battlefield. In other words, it dramatizes the eternal conflict between Greek and barbarian; it is the Mycenaean Greeks against Troy, the Classical Greeks against Persia, and Alexander's campaigns rolled into one, and it epitomizes the entire motivation of Alexander's enterprise. But the picture is telling us something else. In this rendering, the "barbarian" is Alexander, and the hero is the kindly, aging Persian king.

Despite a great deal of authentic detail in clothes, arms, and equipment, it is not clear which one of the three historical clashes between Alexander and the Persians is represented here—the battle at the Granicus, that at Issus, or the decisive one at Gaugamela.

343. Alexander the Great as Heracles, inside the lion's skin.

344. The effete Emperor Commodus dressed up as Heracles.

The exact incident shown here has no parallel in any of the battle accounts. Alexander is depicted on the left, on horseback. In agreement with his well-documented recklessness he is bareheaded; his plumed helmet is partially visible on the ground. His long Macedonian lance, which had been aimed at the Persian king on the right, has instead just pierced one of the latter's aides, who is collapsing, pathetically clutching Alexander's weapon, the point of which is protruding from his back. King Darius stands in his chariot, which has just wheeled in flight. He is turning around toward the battle scene, stretching out his right hand in a gesture of helpless sympathy toward the dying aide who has just saved his life; his left hand rests on the now useless bow, symbol of Persian armed power. Alexander's disregard for his own safety in battle, his ambition to kill his royal opponent in person, and Darius' flight from the battlefield in a chariot—these and many other elements of the scene are paralleled in one or more of the various battle reports. The incident of the self-sacrificing aide, however, is not. In the accounts of the battle of Issus, to be sure, it is related that Darius' brother Oxathres threw himself in front of the king's chariot, but not that he had to pay for this act of devotion with his life (Quintus Curtius 3, 11, 8). Oxathres did, in fact, survive, because he is mentioned in connection with subsequent events. Alexander never caught up with Darius, who in the end was killed by his own lieutenants.

The artist has depicted the most telling moment in the encounter in order to dramatize both the sacrifice of the young Persian noble and king Darius' gesture of compassion for him, but it requires

345. The Alexander mosaic: aggression and compassion.

careful looking to sort out the details of the killing. Alexander is on horseback, whereas the Persian king stands inside his chariot. Even while bending slightly over its edge, making his futile gesture toward his dying aide, Darius is still higher than his attacker. Alexander thrusts his lance from below with an almost outstretched arm. Originally the weapon must have been aimed upwards, at Darius' chest or head, but the noble Persian youth is dragging it with him to the ground in death—not as a result of his own wound, which is still a second too recent, but because he had been hit at the very moment his horse was collapsing under him from a wound of its own. The horse is expiring on the ground, a pathetic heap of broken and scrambled legs. Its rider is shown in the act of alighting from it to the ground. In other words, if Alexander had thrust his weapon only the briefest moment later, he would have missed the young Persian noble and hit his target, the great king himself. How could Alexander have missed his mark? This, too, the artist has made clear. The right hand of the victim, clutching the fatal spear, had only a second before been on the hilt of his sword, which is shown, slightly protruding from its sheath, behind him. In other words, the Persian aide had just arrived on the scene to hurl himself between Alexander's famous horse, Bucephalus, and Darius' chariot, and had not yet had the time to draw his weapon.

The carnage in the scene is indescribable. Alexander rides rough-shod over the bodies of fallen soldiers. A victim caught under the wheels of Darius' fleeing chariot is actually being cut in two (Andreae, 1961). And the frightened, wounded, and dying horses, masterfully drawn by the artist, are equally pathetic.

The dying aide and his crumpled horse occupy a position close to the axis of the composition. The elevated figure of Darius protruding into the space over the heads of the troops, is the prime focal point of the entire scene. The Alexander figure on the far left of the scene is only peripheral, and despite the conventional bulging eyes and maniacal expression, is a lesser element in the design. Like Andromache in Euripides' *Trojan Women*, this artist is saying:

> O Greeks who have invented barbarian evils,
> Why kill this boy who is guilty of nothing? (764–65)

There is, in fact, among the legends surrounding the Trojan War, one which is so closely analogous to the events here depicted that it must have been consciously evoked by the artist. In a once famous myth, told in the lost epic poem *Aithiopis,* still outstanding at the time the mosaic was produced, the aging Greek hero Nestor foolhardily ventures onto the battlefield outside of Troy, even though he is too fragile to defend himself. He is attacked by the African warrior Memnon, an ally of the Trojans, but saved by his son Antilochos. The latter throws himself between attacker and target and is killed in his father's stead. Accordingly the son is remembered until late antiquity by the epithet "Fatherlover" (*Philopator*). No illustration of this story is extant, but we do have a description of an alleged painting on the subject in a late Greek author (Philostr. *Imag.* 2, 7, 1). In the voluminous scholarly literature on the Alexander mosaic there is no mention of the Antilochos story. To an ancient viewer of the work, however, steeped as he was in Trojan stories, the allusion must have been obvious.

In view of the fact that Alexander considered himself a reincarnation of the principal Homeric hero, Achilleus, and made a veritable pilgrimage to the site of Troy when he first reached Asia, the subtle and bitter reversal of values in the mosaic would have infuriated him.

Who painted the original of the Alexander mosaic, and who had an interest in seeing the conqueror depicted in so deglorifying a fashion? By sheer accident the literary sources in Greek and Latin from later ages have left us a few clues, which make it possible to piece together the extraordinary history of the work.

When in the year 334 B.C., at the age of twenty-two, Alexander embarked on his campaigns in the East, he left his father's long-time aide in war and politics, Antipater, in charge of Macedonia. Antipater had a son, Cassander, who was only slightly, perhaps two years, older than Alexander, and not dissimilar in inclinations from the king. Both were reckless, ambitious, talented, aggressive, and both were infatuated with the myths and legends of the Trojan War. Cassander joined the king's campaign in Asia in 324, and all our historical sources agree about the immediate animosity which arose between the two young men. Plutarch gives the most colorful account of their strained relationship. When Cassander, upon his arrival in Alexander's headquarters, saw the barbarians genuflect before the king, he broke out in loud laughter, whereupon the king rebuked him personally, "knocking his head against the wall" (*Life of Alexander* 74, 1–2). During another clash Cassander took a stand against Alexander in defense of his father, Antipater, against whom charges had been brought by some of his subjects. In the end, according to Plutarch, Cassander became so obsessed with fear of Alexander that, long after the latter's death, on seeing a portrait statue of him at Delphi, he was seized by a fit of panic (*ibid.* 3–4). The historical reports that Cassander killed Alexander, or was part of a conspiracy to do so, are almost certainly false, but he did murder the king's mother, widow, and son after Alexander's death.

After Alexander's demise, Cassander spent most of his remaining life in fierce struggles with some of Alexander's successors, the Diadochoi, about the hegemony over Macedonia and Greece. He gained power over Macedonia in 316, and managed to stave off rivals until his death in 297 B.C. During the later years of his life he became closely associated with Aristotle's Peripatetic school of philosophy, which by then had turned against Alexander's policies and memory, and was promoting hostile accounts of the conqueror's life and accomplishments. It was Cassander, so like Alexander, and so terrified of him, who sponsored the painting of which the Alexander mosaic is a copy. Pliny the Elder tells us that Cassander, after he had become king of Macedonia, commissioned a painting representing a "battle of Alexander and Darius," from a painter by the name of Philoxenos of Eretria, which became this artist's most famous work, "surpassed by none," as Pliny says of it (*NH* 35, 110). Philoxenos was the product of the fourth-century Theban school of painting, which, as literary allusions and descriptions reveal, was known for its highly dramatic style. This background explains the ambivalence of the painting. Cassander owed whatever claims he had to the Macedonian throne to his and his father's past associations with Alexander, and he could ill afford to erase the conqueror's memory. Yet the old animosity obviously lingered. Cassander was steeped in Trojan lore; he was even said to have copied the entire Homeric poems in his own hand. He must have recognized the echo of the Antilochos story. Perhaps he even suggested it to the painter.

How did the artist of the Pompeiian mosaic know the famous battle scene? For this, too, history has an answer. Macedonian Hellenism suffered its *coup de grâce* in the year 168 B.C., at the battle of Pydna, in which the last Macedonian king, Perseus, was defeated by the Roman armies. The commander of the Roman legions, M. Aemilius Paullus, sacked the royal palace at Pella and, as the Roman conquerors were wont to do, had great quantities of booty, especially works of art, shipped to Rome, keeping only Perseus' library for himself. The writings of Pliny, who died in the eruption of Mount Vesuvius which buried Pompeii in A.D. 79, reveal that in his time numerous Greek works looted during the conquest of Greece were on display in Rome and other Italian cities. Surely the "battle of Alexander and Darius" which he admired so much was among them. His brief reference to the painting does not reveal whether Pliny or any of his compatriots were aware of its antimilitaristic implications. Considering the glorification of military might by the Romans themselves, they probably saw the work, as do most modern observers, as a monument to the courage and accomplishments of Alexander, the Great Conqueror.

# Notes

*page*    **Introduction**

4  Chesler: *Women and Madness*, New York, 1972, 284.
5  "Draconian" laws: Aristotle, *AthPol.* 52,1.
7  "customary gentleness": Aristotle, *AthPol.* 12,4.
7  interrogations: Demosthenes 47,12.
8  "planking": Gernet, 254–55; Flacelière, 241.

**1. Military Expeditions, Protest, Lament, and Scandal**

20  My Lai: Edward M. Opton, Jr., "It never happened and besides they deserved it," in Nevitt Sanford and Craig Comstock, eds., *Sanctions for Evil*, New York, 1972.
28  prose romances: Longus, *Daphnis and Chloë*; Achilles Tatius, *Cleitophon and Leucippe*; Heliodorus, *Aithiopika*.
28  Heracles and virgins: Athenaeus 556 f.

**2. Attic Mythology: Barren Goddesses, Male Wombs, and the Cult of Rape**

38  virago: Firmicus Maternus, *Err. prof. rel.* 16,1.
42  enthroned goddess: Erich Neumann, *The Great Mother*, 98 f.
57  fragment about Heracles: Fr. Adesp. 402 N.
58  Theseus and Helen: Isocrates, *Helen* 18–19.
61  *Theseid:* Aristotle, *Poet.* 1451a,20.

**3. The Phallus and the Box: The World Seen in the Shapes of Human Genitals**

68  *posthion:* cf. Henderson, *The Maculate Muse*, 109.
68  the small penis is more fertile: Aristotle, *Gen.An.* 718a, 23–26.
77–78  curse tablets and voodoo dolls: K. Preisendanz, "Pluchtafel (Defixion)," *Reallexikon für Antike und Christentum* 8 (1978) 1–29; D. R. Jordan, "New Archaeological Evidence for the Practice of Magic in Classical Athens," *Acts of the XIIth International Congress of Classical Archaeology*, Athens, 1984.

*page*

78  sanctuary of Aphrodite: Broneer, 1933, 342 f., and 1935, 118 f.
88  Solon on women: Fragments 210 and 463, ed. Martina.
90  no mother's name: Rice and Stambaugh, p. 143 = $IG^2$ II,1237.
97  no outside windows: Aristotle, *AthPol.* 49,2.

### 4. Bearing Children, Watching the House

101  Hipparete: Plutarch, *Alc.* 8, 3–4.
102  a "living piece of property": Aristotle, *Pol.* 1253b 33.
104  literacy of women: Harvey, 621–23.
104  compulsory schooling for boys: Plato, *Kri.* 50d.
112  inscription from Eleusis: $SIG^2$ II, 587,183.
116  comedy fragment about the *olisbos:* Fr. Adesp. 5a J. M. Edmonds = POxy 212a2.
128  Lycurgus: cited by Stobaeus, *Flor.* 68,35.

### 5. Brides of Death, in More Ways Than One

131  the first menstrual flow: Aristotle, *Hist.An.* 581b 2.
132  the "bridal chamber of the earth" Aeschylus, *Pers.* 624; Euripides, *HF* 107.
135  Delphic oracles: Thompson, 1978, 102 and n. 33.
137  Thompson on the Leokorion: 101–2.
146  kinglets: Plutarch, *VitAges.* 2,3.
146  letter from Egypt: Lefkowitz and Fant, p. 91 = POxy 744.

### 6. The Athenian Prostitute: A Good Buy in the Agora

156  Roman brothels: Horace, *Sat.* 1,2,30; Seneca, *Controv.* 1,2; Juvenal, 6, 122–30.
160  *kottabos* in Old Comedy: Plato, Comicus Fr. 46.
165  "plodding heifers": Eupolis, Fr. 169.

### 7. The Whore with the Golden Heart, the Happy Hooker, and Other Fictions

187  Lysias and the Eleusinian mysteries: Pseudo-Demosthenes, *Against Neaera* 21.
192  Ovid on Menander: "*fabula iucundi nulla est sine amore Menandri,*" *Trist.* 2,369.
198  the comedians and Aspasia: Plutarch, *Per.* 24,6.
201–2  translations from Aristophanes by Jack Lindsay.

### 8. Two Kinds of Women: The Splitting of the Female Psyche

208  prostitution tax: Aeschines, 1,119.
208  Solon on selling daughters: Plutarch, *Sol.* 23a.
210  floorplans of houses in Olynthus by Roland Martin.
215  banquet of the dead: Its scheme was probably derived from that of votive tablets to minor divinities ("heroes"), who are often depicted as banqueting.

### 9. The Sex Appeal of Female Toil

231  Anacreon: Fr. 97, J. M. Edmonds.
236  wells filled in: Shear 4–6.

*page*

246  male weavers: Plato, *Rep.* 370d,3.
246  male textile shops: Xenophon, *Mem.* 2,7,6.
260  a money purse used for a cash transaction. On a red-figure lekythos in Boston, Fogg Museum, 1977.216.2236, a woman, probably a housekeeper, pays for an eel and a sponge out of a purse.

### 11. The Boy Beautiful: Replacing a Woman or Replacing a Son?

285  masturbating boy: See Boardman, 1975, p. 33, who wonders why the boy is punished.
289  curse of Laius: Of Aeschylus' Oedipus trilogy, *Seven Against Thebes* survives, but it contains no reference to Laius' crime.
291  singeing of pubic hair: Scholion to Aristophanes, *Nub.* 1083; Dover, 1978, 140.

### 12. Learning to Be a Man, Learning to Be a Woman

300  Corsican saying: Marise Choisy, *Psychoanalysis of the Prostitute*, New York, 1961, 45.
303  Plutarch on the *oschophoria: Thes.* 23.
303  Theseus worship: Brelich; Zeitlin.
305  bull's penis: G. van Hoorn, under no. 983.
308  Pandrosos as wool worker: Photius, s.v. "protonion," Burkert, 1966, 11.
310  Arrhephoroi House: Burkert, 1966, 4 f.
312  Kallisto on the Acropolis: Pausanias 1,25,1; 10,31,10; Trendall, 1977.
312  "sacred races": Kahil, 1978, 80.
316  Amymone at Brauron: Kahil, 1963, 18–19.
318  dedications of garments: Coulton, "Brauron" in *The Princeton Encyclopedia of Classical Sites*, 1976. Most of the inscriptions from Brauron are unpublished.

### 13. Sex Among the Barbarians

322  Rule of the Thirty: Aristotle, *AthPol.* 35,2.
324  Spartan women: Vidal-Nacquet, 1970, 73.
327  Herodotus as a model for other authors: Pembroke, 1967, 6; 11.
327  *Dissoi Logoi* on the Macedonians: Diehls-Kranz, *Fragmente der Vorsokratiker*, 5th ed., 90,11,408.
328  Plato's principle of promiscuous mating upheld by the early Stoics: Diog. Laert. 7,131.

### 14. Classical Tragedy: Weaving Men's Dream of Sexual Strife

332  Psychological interpretations of tragedy: See Caldwell, Devereux, Simon, Slater, and Zeitlin.
346  "laughterless stone": *SIG*[2] II, 587,183.

### 15. Sex Antagonism and Women's Rituals

352  Lucian on hetaerai: *Dial. mer.* 2,1.
355  hetaera names on vases: Beazley, 1935.
357  Skira festival: Burkert, 349 f.

*page*

358 Dionysiac hierarchies: Henrichs, 1978.
359 Roman cults of Dionysus: *CIL*² 581; Henrichs, 1978, 135.
360 Olympias as Maenad: Plutarch, *Alex.* 2,6–9.

**16. Love, Not War: Protest in the Arts and on the Streets**

383 "bright and happy expedition." For a discussion of the sources and the problems of their interpretation, see Dover in Gomme, Andrewes, and Dover, 1970, 264–88.
390 auction of confiscated property: *IG* 1², 327; 332; Gomme, Andrewes, and Dover, 268.
391 Agariste on Alcibiades: Andocides, 1,16.
394 the mutilation of the herms coinciding with the Adonia: Plutarch, *Alc.* 18,2–3; *Nic.* 13,7.

# Bibliography

### Introduction

Arthur, Marylin B., "Review: Classics," *Signs* 2 (1976–77):382–403.

Austin, M. M., and P. Vidal-Nacquet, *Economic and Social History of Ancient Greece: An Introduction*, Leiden, 1977.

Bachofen, J. J., *Mutterrecht und Urreligion: Eine Auswahl*, ed. Rudolf Marx, Leipzig, 1939.

Beazley, J. D., *Attic Black-Figure Vase-Painters*, Oxford, 1956.

———, *Attic Red-Figure Vase-Painters*, 2nd ed., Oxford, 1963.

———, *Paralipomena: Additions to Attic Black-Figure Vase-Painting and to Attic Red-Figure Vase-Painting*, 2nd ed., Oxford, 1971.

Brandt, Paul (Hans Licht, pseud.), *Sittengeschichte Griechenlands*, 2 vols., Dresden/Zurich, 1925–26.

Broude, Norma, and Mary D. Garrard (eds.), *Feminism and Art History*, New York, 1982.

Bullough, Vern L., *The Subordinate Sex: A History of Attitudes Towards Women*, Urbana, Ill., 1973, ch. 3.

Cameron, Averil, and Amelie Kuhrt, eds., *Images of Women in Antiquity*, London, 1983.

*Cité des images, La*, Institut d'archéologie et d'histoire, Lausanne, 1984.

Cole, Susan (ed.), *Male and Female in Greek Cult*, Cologne, 1984.

Dover, K. J., *Greek Homosexuality*, Cambridge, Mass., 1978.

Finley, M. I., *Ancient Slavery and Modern Ideology*, New York, 1978.

Flacelière, Robert, *Daily Life in Ancient Greece*, trans. from the French by Peter Green, New York, 1966.

Foley, H., ed., *Reflections of Women in Antiquity*, London, 1982.

Gernet, L., "Sur l'Exécution capitale," *Revue des Etudes Grecques* 37 (1924):261–93.

Gomme, A. W., "The Position of Women in Athens in the Fifth and Fourth Centuries," *Classical Philology* 20 (1925):1–25.

Goodwater, Leanna, *Women in Antiquity: An Annotated Bibliography*, Metuchen, N.J., 1975.

Gould, John J., "Law, Custom and Myth: Aspects of the Social Position of Women in Classical Athens," *Journal of Hellenic Studies* (1980):38–59.

Guhl, Ernst Karl and W. Koner, *The Life of the Greeks and Romans Described from Antique Monuments*, trans. from the German, London, 1889.

Hopfner, Theodor, *Das Sexualleben der Griechen und Römer*, Prague, 1938.

Hyatt, Stephen (ed.), *The Greek Vase* (Papers of the 1979 Symposium), New York, 1983.

Kuenen-Janssens, L. J., "Some Notes upon the Competence of the Athenian Women to Conduct a Transaction," *Mnemosyne* 3, 9, 3 (1941):199–214.

Lacey, W. K., *The Family in Classical Greece*, Ithaca, N.Y., 1968.

Lambropoulou, Stavroula, "The Condition of Women in Ancient Greece," *Parousia* (1982):444–60.

Leipoldt, Johannes, *Die Frau in der antiken Welt und im Urchristentum*, Berlin, 1953.

Lissarrague, François, and Françoise Thelamon (eds.), *Image et céramique grecque* (Actes du Colloque de Rouen), Rouen, 1983.

Loraux, Nicole, *Les Enfants d'Athéna: Idées Athéniennes sur la citoyenneté et la division des sexes*, Paris, 1982.

Mahaffy, J. P., *Social Life in Greece from Homer to Menander*, London, 1894.

Moon, Warren G. (ed.), *Ancient Greek Art and Iconography*, Madison, Wis., 1983.

Mortley, Raoul, *Womanhood: The Feminine in Ancient Hellenism, Gnosticism, Christianity and Islam*, Sydney, 1981.

Neumann, Erich, *The Great Mother: An Analysis of the Archetype*, trans. from the German by Ralph Manheim, Princeton, N.J., 1956.

Nietzsche, Friedrich, "The Greek Woman," *Complete Works*, trans. by M. A. Mügge, vol. 2 (1911):21–26.

Paoli, Ugo Enrico, *La Donna greca nell'antichità*, Florence, 1953.

Peradotto, John, and John P. Sullivan (eds.), *Women in the Ancient World: The Arethusa Papers*, Albany, N.Y., 1984.

Pomeroy, Sarah, *Goddesses, Whores, Wives and Slaves: Women in Classical Antiquity*, New York, 1975.

Post, L. A. "Women's Place in Menander's Athens," *Transactions of the American Philological Association* 71 (1940):420–59.

Redfield, R., "The Women of Sparta," *Classical Journal* 73 (1977):141–61.

Richter, Donald, "The Position of Women in Classical Athens," *Classical Journal* 67 (1971):1–8.

Roton, Chevalier de (G. Notor, pseud.), *La Femme dans l'antiquité grecque*, Paris, 1901.

Savage, Charles Albert, *The Athenian Family: A Sociological and Legal Study*, Baltimore, 1907.

Schmidt, Joël, *Vie et mort des esclaves dans la Rome antique*, Paris, 1973.

Seltman, Charles, *Women in Antiquity*, London, 1956.

Semonides, *Females of the Species*, trans. and comm. by H. Lloyd-Jones, London, 1975.

Stone, Merlin, *Ancient Mirrors of Womanhood*, New York, 1979.

Sutton, Robert, "The Interaction Between Men and Women Portrayed on Attic Red-figure Pottery," Diss., The University of North Carolina, 1981.

Webster, T. B. L., *Potter and Patron in Classical Athens*, London, 1972.

Wickert-Micknat, G., *Die Frau* (Archaeologica Homerica, vol. 3), Göttingen, 1982.

Wiedemann, Thomas, *Greek and Roman Slavery*, Baltimore, 1981.

Wilkinsin, L. P., "Classical Approaches: Women's Liberation," *Encounter* (1978):25–36.

Wright, F. A., *Greek Social Life*, London, 1925.

## 1 and 16. Military Expeditions, Protest, Lament and Scandal. Love, Not War: Protest in the Arts and on the Streets

Allen Ruth, "The Mutilation of the Herms," Diss., The University of Cincinnati, n.d.

Atallah, W., *Adonis dans la littérature et l'art grecs*, Paris, 1966.

Bonnamour, Jacqueline, *Aristophane, les femmes et la cité*, Fontenay-aux-Roses, 1979.

Bruns, Ivo, "Frauenemanzipation in Athen," *Vorträge und Aufsätze*, Munich (1905):154–93.

Clement, Paul A., "The Recovery of Helen," *Hesperia* 27 (1958):47–72.

Croix, G. E. M. de Ste, *The Class Struggle in the Ancient World from the Archaic Age to the Arab Conquests*, Ithaca, N.Y., 1981.

Detienne, Marcel, *Les Jardins d'Adonis*, Paris, 1972. Trans. into English as *The Gardens of Adonis*.

Dover, K. J. *Greek Popular Morality in the Time of Plato and Aristotle*, Oxford, 1974.

Erbse, Hartmut, "Sokrates und die Frauen," *Gymnasium* 73 (1966):201–20.

Ervin, Miriam, "A Relief Pithos from Mykonos," *Archaiologikon Deltion* 18 A (1963):48–64.

Finley, M. I., *Politics in the Ancient World*, London, 1983.

Fortenbaugh, William, "On Plato's Feminism in Republic V," *Apeiron* 9 (1975):1–4.

Ghougassian, Joseph P., *Toward Women: A Study of the Origins of Western Attitudes Through Greco-Roman Philosophy*, San Diego, 1977.

Gomme, A. W., A. Andrewes, and K. J. Dover, *A Historical Commentary on Thucydides*, vol. IV, Oxford, 1970.

Greve, W., "De Adonide," Diss., Leipzig, 1877.

Grote, G., *A History of Greece*, 12 vols., New York, 1855.

Kagar, Donald. *The Peace of Nicias and the Sicilian Expedition*, Ithaca, N.Y. 1981.

Kahil, Lilly, *Les Enlèvements et le retour d'Hélène*, Paris, 1955.

Krenkel, Werner A., "Der Sexualtrieb: Seine Bewertung in Griechenland und Rom," *Wissenschaftliche Zeitschrift der Wilhelm-Pieck Universität Rostock* 27 (1978):165–80.

Lehmann, Phyllis, *Roman Wall Paintings from Boscoreale in the Metropolitan Museum of Art*, Cambridge, Mass., 1953.

Lintott, Andrew, *Violence, Civil Strife and Revolution in the Classical City*, Baltimore, 1981.

Manning, C. E., "Seneca and the Stoics on the Equality of the Sexes," *Mnemosyne* 26 (1973):170–77.

Marr, J. L., "Andocides' Part in the Mysteries and Hermae Affairs 415 B.C.," *Classical Quarterly* 21 (1971):326–41.

Moret, Jean-Marc, *L'Ilioupersis dans la céramique italiote: Les Mythes et leur expression figurée au IVe siècle*, 2 vols., Rome, 1975.

Schefold, Karl, *Frühgriechische Sagenbilder*, Munich, 1964.

Vogt, Joseph, *Von der Gleichwertigkeit der Geschlechter in der bürgerlichen Gesellschaft der Griechen*, Akademie der Wissenschaften und der Literatur in Mainz, 1960.

Wright, F. A., *Feminism in Greek Literature from Homer to Aristotle*, London, 1923.

## 2. Attic Mythology: Barren Goddesses, Male Wombs, and the Cult of Rape

Boardman, John, "Herakles, Peisistratos and Eleusis," *Journal of Hellenic Studies* 95 (1975):1–12.

———, "Herakles, Peisistratos and Sons," *Revue archéologique* 1 (1972): 57–72.

Bremmer, Jan, "Heroes, Rituals and the Trojan War," *Studi Storici-Religiosi* 2 (1978):5–38.

Brommer, Frank, *Athena Parthenos* (Opus Nobile—Meisterwerke der Antiken Kunst, 2), Bremen, 1957.

Broneer, O., "Excavations on the North Slope of the Acropolis in Athens, 1931–1932," *Hesperia* 2 (1933):329–416.

———, "Excavations on the North Slope of the Acropolis in Athens, 1933–1934," *Hesperia* 4 (1935):109–88.

Burkert, Walter, *Structure and History in Greek Mythology and Ritual*, Berkeley, Calif., 1979.

Carlier-Detienne, Jeannie, "Les Amazones font la guerre et l'amour," *Ethnographie* (1980–81):11–33.

Diepolder, Hans, *Der Penthesileia-Maler*, Leipzig, 1936.

Dodds, E. R., *The Sophistic Movement and the Failure of Greek Liberalism in the Ancient Concept of Progress*, Oxford, 1973.

Dugas, Charles, et Robert Flacelière, *Thésée*, Paris, 1958.

Henderson, Jeffrey, *The Maculate Muse: Obscene Language in Attic Comedy*, New Haven, Conn., 1975.

Herter, H., Pauly-Wissow, "Phallos," in *Realencyclopädie der klassischen Altertumswissenschaft*, vol. XIX (1938):1681–1748.

Hoffmann, H., *Sexual and Asexual Pursuit: A Structuralist Approach to Vase Painting*, London, 1977.

Kaempf-Dimitriadou, S., *Die Liebe der Götter in der attischen Kunst des 5. Jahrhunderts V. Christus*, Basel, 1979.

Kerényi, Karl, *Zeus und Hera: Urbild des Vaters, des Gatten und der Frau*, Leiden, 1972.

Kirk, G. S., *Myth, Its Meaning and Functions in Ancient and Other Cultures*, Cambridge, Mass., 1970.

Knox, Bernard M. W., "Literature," in *Athens Comes of Age: From Solon to Salamis*, ed. W. A. P. Childs, Princeton, N.J., 1978.

Merck, Mandy, "The Patriotic Amazonomachy and Ancient Athens," in *Tearing the Veil, Essays on Femininity*, ed. Susan Lipshitz, London, 1979.

Merkelbach, S., "Aglauros," *Zeitschrift für Papyrologie und Epigraphik* 9 (1972):277–83.

Neils, Jennifer, "The Loves of Theseus: An Early Cup of Oltos," *American Journal of Archeology* 85 (1981):177–79.

Neumann, Erich, *The Great Mother: An Analysis of the Archetype*, trans. from the German by Ralph Manheim, Princeton, N.J., 1956.

Schefold, Karl, *Götter und Heldensagen der Griechen in der spätarchaischen Kunst*, Munich, 1978.

Sourvinou-Inwood, C., *Theseus as Son and Stepson*, Leiden, 1979.

Vernant, J. P., *Mythe et société en Grèce ancienne*, Paris, 1974. Trans. as *Myth and Society in Ancient Greece* by J. Lloyd, 1979.

Wycherley, R. E., *The Stones of Athens*, Princeton, N.J., 1978.

### 3. The Phallus and the Box: The World Seen in the Shapes of Human Genitals

Broneer, O., "Excavations on the North Slope of the Acropolis in Athens, 1931–1932," *Hesperia* 2 (1933):329–416.

———, "Excavations on the North Slope of the Acropolis in Athens, 1933–1934," *Hesperia* 4 (1935):109–88.

Boardman, John, and Antonia Mulas, *Eros in Grecia*, Milan, 1975.

Burkert, Walter, *Structure and History in Greek Mythology and Ritual*, Berkeley, Calif., 1979.

Dover, K. J., *Greek Homosexuality*, Cambridge, Mass., 1978.

Gould, John J., "Law, Custom and Myth: Aspects of the Social Position of Women in Classical Athens," *Journal of Hellenic Studies* (1980):38–59.

Henderson, Jeffrey, *The Maculate Muse: Obscene Language in Attic Comedy*, New Haven, Conn., 1975.

Herter, H., "Phallos," in *Realenzyklopädie der klassischen Altertumswissenschaft*, vol. XIX (1938):1681–1748.

Marcadé, Jean, *Eros Kalos: Essay on Erotic Elements in Greek Art*, Geneva, 1965.

Rice, David G., and John E. Stambaugh, *Sources for the Study of Greek Religion*, Ann Arbor, Mich., 1979.

Schaps, David, "The Woman Least Mentioned: Etiquette and Women's Names," *Classical Quarterly* 27 (1977):323–30.

Vanggaard, Thorkil, *Phallos: A Symbol and Its History in the Male World,* trans. from the Danish, London, 1972.

Vermeule, Emily, "Some Erotica in Boston," *Antike Kunst* 12 (1969):9–15.

Vorberg, Gaston, *Ars erotica veterum,* Stuttgart, 1926.

———, *Die Erotik der Antike in Kleinkunst und Keramik,* Munich, 1931.

———, *Glossarium Eroticum,* Stuttgart, 1932.

Wycherley, R. E., *The Stones of Athens,* Princeton, N.J., 1978.

## 4. Bearing Children, Watching the House

Blümner, Hugo, *The Home Life of the Ancient Greeks,* trans. by Alice Zimmer, New York, 1910.

Caillemer, E., Daremberg, and Saglio, *Dictionnaire des antiquités grecques et romaines,* s.v. "divortium."

Chesler, Phyllis, *Women and Madness,* New York, 1972.

Erdman, Walter, "Die Ehe im alten Griechenland," *Münchener Beiträge zu Papyrusforschung und antiken Rechtgeschichte,* Heft 20 (1934).

Flacelière, Robert, *Daily Life in Greece at the Time of Pericles,* trans. by Peter Green, New York, 1965.

Gernet, L., *Droit et societé dans la Grèce ancienne,* Paris, 1955.

Götte, Erika, "Frauengemachbilder in der Vasenmalerei des fünften Jahrhunderts," Diss., Munich, 1977.

Graf, F., *Eleusis und die orphische Dichtung Athens in vorhellenistischer Zeit,* Berlin-New York, 1974.

Graham, J. Walter, "Houses of Classical Greece," *Phoenix* 28 (1974):45–54.

Gramsci, Antonio, "Necessità di una preparazione ideologica di massa," *Scritti Politici,* ed. P. Spriano, Rome (1967):600–603.

Harrison, A. R. W., *The Law of Athens: The Family and Property,* Oxford, 1968.

Harvey, F. D., "Literacy in Athenian Democracy," *Revue des études grecques* 79 (1966):621–23.

Henderson, Jeffrey, *The Maculate Muse: Obscene Language in Attic Comedy,* New Haven, Conn., 1975.

Lacey, W. K., *The Family in Classical Greece,* Ithaca, N.Y., 1968.

Lippold, Georg von, "Vaseninschriften," in *Festschrift Bernhard Schweitzer,* Mainz (1954):134–38.

Richardson, N., *The Homeric Hymn to Demeter,* Oxford, 1974.

Roberts, Sally, *The Attic Pyxis,* Chicago, 1978.

Rosenbaum, Julius, *Geschichte der Lustseuche im Altertum,* Berlin, 1904.

Savage, Charles Albert, *The Athenian Family: A Sociological and Legal Study,* Baltimore, 1907.

Schaps, David, "Women in Greek Inheritance Law," *Classical Quarterly* 25 (1975):53–57.

Schmitt, Pauline, "Athena Apatouria et la ceinture," *Annales E.S.C.* 32 (1977):1059–73.

Slater, Philip E., *The Glory of Hera*, Boston, 1968.
———, "The Greek Family in History and Myth," *Arethusa* 7 (1974):9–44.
Travlos, John, *A Pictorial Dictionary of Ancient Athens*, Athens, 1971.
Vernant, Jean-Pierre, *Mythe et société en Grèce ancienne*, Paris, 1974.
Webster, T. B. L., *Daily Life in Classical Athens*, London, 1969.
Wegner, Max, *Musik und Tanz* (Archaeologica Homerica III), Göttingen, 1968.
———, *Musikleben der Griechen*, Berlin, 1949.

## 5. Brides of Death, in More Ways Than One

Engels, Donald, "The Problem of Female Infanticide in the Greco-Roman World," *Classical Philology* 75 (1980):112–20.
Hillman, James, "First Adam, Then Eve: Fantasies of Female Inferiority in Changing Consciousness," *Eranos Jahrbuch* 38 (1969):349–412.
Kurtz, D. C., and John Boardman, *Greek Burial Customs*, Ithaca, N.Y., 1971.
Kurtz, D. C., *Athenian White Lekythoi*, Oxford, 1975.
Lefkowitz, Mary F., and Maureen Fant, *Women in Greece and Rome*, Toronto, 1977.
Parke, H. W., and D. E. W. Wormell, *The Delphic Oracle*, Oxford, 1956.
Phillips, E. D., *Aspects of Greek Medicine*, New York, 1973.
Richter, Gisela, M. A., "Family Groups on Attic Grave Monuments," in *Festschrift Bernhard Schweitzer*, Mainz (1954):256–59.
Riezler, W., *Weissgründige Attische Lekythen*, Berlin, 1914.
Rose, H. J., "The Bride of Hades," *Classical Philology* 20 (1925):238–42.
Soranus, *Gynecology*, trans. by P. Temkin, Baltimore, 1956.
Thompson, H., "Some Hero Shrines in Early Athens," *Athens Comes of Age: From Solon to Salamis*, ed. W. A. P. Childs, Princeton, N.J. (1978):96–107.

## 6. The Athenian Prostitute: A Good Buy in the Agora

Birt, T., *Frauen der Antike*, Leipzig, 1932.
Brendel, Otto J., "The Scope and Temperament of Erotic Art in the Greco-Roman World," in *Studies in Erotic Art*, ed. T. Bowie and C. Christianson, New York, 1970.
Bullough, Vern L. and Bonnie, *Prostitution: An Illustrated Social History*, New York, 1978.
Fehr, B., *Orientalische und Griechische Gelage*, Bonn, 1971.
Hauschild, Hans, "Die Gestalt der Hetaere in der griechischen Komödie," Diss., Leipzig, 1933.
Herter, Hans, "Die Soziologie der antiken Prostitution im Lichte des heidnischen und christlichen Schrifttums," *Jahrbuch für Antike und Christentum* 3 (1970):70–111.
Lacroix, Paul (Pierre Dufour, pseud.), *History of Prostitution*, trans. by Samuel Putnam I, Chicago, 1923.
Marks, M. C., "Heterosexual Coital Positions in Ancient Greece, Ancient

Rome and Modern North America as a Reflection of Social Attitudes," Diss., State University of New York at Buffalo, 1978.

Seltman, Charles, *Women in Antiquity*, London, 1956.

Stotz, Otto, "De lenonis in comoedia figura," Diss., Giessen, 1920.

Rosenbaum, Julius, *Geschichte der Lustseuche im Altertume*, Berlin, 1904.

Vickers, Michael, *Greek Symposia*, Joint Association of Classical Teachers, London, about 1982.

Vorberg, Gaston, *Die Erotik der Antike in Kleinkunst und Keramik*, Munich, 1921.

———, *Glossarium Eroticum*, Stuttgart, 1932 (repr. 1965).

Wycherley, R. E., *The Stones of Athens*, Princeton, N.J., 1978.

## 7. The Whore with the Golden Heart, the Happy Hooker, and Other Fictions

Hauschild, Hans, "Die Gestalt der Hetaere in der griechischen Komödie," Diss., Leipzig, 1933.

## 8. Two Kinds of Women: The Splitting of the Female Psyche

Boerner, "Gynaikonomoi," in *Realenzyklopädie der klassischen Altertums-wissenschaft*, vol. VII (1912):2089–90.

Bullough, Vern L. and Bonnie, *The Subordinate Sex: A History of Attitudes Towards Women*, Urbana, Ill., 1973.

Friedrich, Paul, *The Meaning of Aphrodite*, Chicago, 1978.

Garland, B. J., "Gynaikonomoi: An Investigation of Greek Censors of Women," Diss., Johns Hopkins University, 1981.

Graham, J. Walter, "Houses of Classical Athens," *Phoenix* 28 (1974):47–50.

Gramsci, Antonio, "Necessità di una preparazione ideologica di massa," *Scritti Politici*, ed. P. Spriano, Rome (1967):600–603.

Hopfner, Theodor, *Das Sexualleben der Griechen und Römer*, Prague, 1938.

Keuls, Eva, "The Hetaera and the Housewife: The Splitting of the Female Psyche in Greek Art," *Mededelingen van het Nederlands Historisch Instituut te Rome*, 1982.

Martin, Roland, *L'Urbanisme dans la Grèce antique*, Paris, 1956.

Metzger, Henri, *Les Représentations dans la céramique attique du IVième siècle*, Paris, 1951.

Raab, Irmgard, *Zu den Darstellungen des Parisurteils in der griechischen Kunst*, Frankfurt, 1972.

Robinson, David M., *The Hellenic House: A Study of the Houses Found at Olynthus*, Baltimore, 1938.

Simon, Erica, *Die Geburt der Aphrodite*, Mainz, 1959.

Slater, Philip E., "The Greek Family in History and Myth," *Arethusa* 7 (1974):9–44.

Young, Rodney S., "An Industrial District of Ancient Athens," *Hesperia* 20 (1951):135–288.

## 9. The Sex Appeal of Female Toil

Baldwin, Barry, "Germaine Greer and the Female Artists of Greece and Rome," *Echos du monde classique: Classical News and Views* 25 (1981):18–21.

Beazley, J. D., *Der Pan-Maler*, Mainz, 1974.

———, Review of *Corpus Vasorum, Athens National Museum* 1, *Journal of Hellenic Studies* 51 (1931):121.

Crome, Johann Friedrich, "Spinnende Hetairen?," *Gymnasium* 73 (1966): 245–47.

Diehl, Erika, *Die Hydria: Formgeschichte und Verwendung im Kult des Altertums*, Mainz, 1964.

Dunkley, B., List of fountain scenes in Attic vase painting, *Papers of the British School at Athens* 36 (1935–36):198–207.

Forbes, R. J., *Studies in Ancient Technology*, vol. IV, 2nd ed.: *The Fibres and Fabrics of Antiquity*, Leiden, 1964.

Glotz, Gustave, *Le Travail dans la Grèce ancienne*, Paris, 1920.

Götte, Erika, "Frauengemachbilder in der Vasenmalerei des fünften Jahrhunderts," Diss., Munich, 1977.

Herbig, Reinhard, "Verkannte Paare," in *Festschrift Bernard Schweitzer*, Mainz (1954):264–71.

Herfst, Pieter, "Le Travail de la femme dans la Grèce ancienne," Diss., Utrecht, 1922.

Hill, Dorothy Kent, "What the Women Did," *Classical Journal* 42 (1949): 202–3.

Keuls, Eva, "Attic Vase Painting and the Home Textile Industry," *Ancient Greek Painting and Iconography*, Madison, Wis., 1983.

———, *The Water Carriers in Hades: A Study of Catharsis Through Toil*, Amsterdam, 1974.

Michell, H., *The Economics of Ancient Greece*, Cambridge, 1940.

North, Helen, "The Mare, the Vixen and the Bee," *Illinois Classical Studies* II (1977):35–48.

Pomeroy, Sarah, "Supplementary Notes on Erinna," in *Zeitschrift für Papyrologie und Epigraphik* 32 (1978):17–22.

Richter, Gisela, *Red-Figure Athenian Vases in the Metropolitan Museum of Art*, New York, 1936.

Rodenwaldt, Gerhard, "Spinnene Hetären," *Archäologischer Anzeiger* (1932):7–22.

Schaps, David, *Economic Rights of Women in Ancient Greece*, Edinburgh, 1979.

Simon, Erika, *Die Götter der Griechen*, Munich, 1969.

Tucker, T. G., *Life in Ancient Greece*, New York, 1906.

Williams, R. T., "An Attic Red-Figured Kalathos," *Antike Kunst* 4 (1961): 27–29.

## 11. The Boy Beautiful: Replacing a Woman or Replacing a Son?

Bethe, R., "Die dorische Knabenliebe, Ihre Ethik und ihre Idee," *Rheinisches Museum* 62 (1907):438–75.

Blanckenhage, P. H. von, "Puerilia," in *Essays in Archaeology and the Humanities*, Festschrift Otto Brendel, ed. J. J. Pollitt, Mainz (1975): 37–41.

Brelich, Angelo, *Paides e Parthenoi*, Rome, 1969.

Bremmer, Jan, "An Enigmatic Indo-European Rite: Pederasty," *Arethusa* 13 (1980):279–95.

Bruns, Ivo, "Attische Liebestheorien," *Vorträge und Aufsätze*, Munich (1905):118–53.

Devereux, George, "Greek Pseudo-Homosexuality and the 'Greek Miracle,' " *Symbolae Osloenses* 42 (1968):69–92.

Dover, K. J., "Aristophanes' Speech in Plato's *Symposium*," *Journal of Hellenic Studies* 86 (1966):41–50.

———, "Eros and Nomos (Plato, *Symp.* 182a–185c)," *Bulletin of the Institute of Classical Studies* 11 (1966):41–50.

———, *Greek Homosexuality*, Cambridge, Mass., 1978.

Hartwig, Paul, *Die griechischen Meisterschalen der Blüthezeit des strengen rothfigürigen Stiles*, Stuttgart, 1893.

Krenkel, Werner A., "Männliche Prostitution in der Antike," *Altertum* 24 (1978):49–54.

Schauenburg, Konrad, "Erastes und Eromenos," *Archäologischer Anzeiger* (1965):850 ff.

———, "Eurymedon eimi," *Mitteilungen des Deutschen Archäologischen Instituts* (Athenische Abteilung) 86 (1975):97–122.

Schefold, Karl, "Chrysippos im Ostgiebel von Olympia," *Classica et Provincialia* (Festschrift E. Diez) (1978):1977–81.

Schapiro, H. A., "Courtship Scenes in Attic Vase Painting," *American Journal of Archaeology* 85 (1981):133–43.

Webster, T. B. L., *Potter and Patron in Classical Athens*, London, 1972.

Williams, F. E., *Papuans of the Trans-Fly*, 2nd ed., Oxford, 1969.


## 12. Learning to Be a Man, Learning to Be a Woman

Brelich, Angelo, *Paides e Parthenoi*, Rome, 1969.

Burkert, Walter, *Griechische Religion der archaischen und klassischen Epoche*, Berlin, 1977.

———, "Kekropidensage und Arrhephoria," *Hermes* 94 (1966):1–25.

Chirassi Colombo, Ileana, "Paides e gynaikes: note per una tassonomia del comportamento rituale nella cultura attica," *Quaderni Urbinati* NS 1 (1979):25–58.

Choisy, Marise, *Psychoanalysis of the Prostitute*, New York, 1961.

Cook, Arthur Bernhard, *Zeus: A Study in Ancient Religion,* vol. II, Cambridge, 1925.

Coulton, J. J., "Brauron" in *The Princeton Encyclopedia of Classical Sites,* Princeton, N.J. (1976):163–64.

Hoorn, G. van, *Choes and Anthesteria,* Leiden, 1951.

Jeanmaire, H., *Couroi et couretes,* Lille, 1939.

Kahil, Lilly, "L'Artemis de Brauron: Rites et Mystères," *Antike Kunst* 20 (1977):86–98.

———, "La Déesse Artemis: Mythologie et Iconographie," *Papers of the XL International Congress of Classical Archaeology,* London (1978):73–87.

———, "Quelques Vases du Sanctuaire d'Artemis à Brauron," *Antike Kunst,* Beiheft 1 (1963):5–29.

Kirk, G. S., *Myth: Its Meaning and Functions in Ancient and Other Cultures,* Cambridge, 1970.

Sale, W., "Callisto and the Virginity of Artemis," *Rheinisches Museum* 108 (1965):11–35.

———, "The Temple Legends of the Arkteia," *Rheinisches Museum* 118 (1975):265–84.

Stinton, T. C. W., "Iphigeneia and the Bears of Brauron," *Classical Quarterly* 26 (1976):11–13.

Trendall, Arthur Dale, "Callisto in Apulian Vase-Painting," *Antike Kunst* 20 (1977):99–101.

Sourvinou, Christina, "Aristophanes, *Lysistrata,* 641–647," *Classical Quarterly* 21 (1971):339–42.

Vidal-Nacquet, Pierre, *Le Chasseur noir: formes de pensée et formes de société dans le monde grec,* Paris, 1981.

Zeitlin, Froma, "Cultic Models of the Female: Rites of Dionysus and Demeter," *Arethusa* 15 (1982):129–57.

## 13. Sex Among the Barbarians

Bonfante, Larissa, "Etruscan Couples and Their Aristocratic Society," *Women's Studies* 8 (1981):157–87.

———, "Etruscan Women: A Question of Interpretation," *Archaeology* 26 (1973):242–49.

Cole, Thomas, *Democritus and the Sources of Greek Anthropology,* Leiden, 1967.

Compernolle, R. van, "Le Mythe de la 'gynécocratie-doulocratie' argienne," *Le Monde Grec* (Hommage Claire Préaux), ed. J. Bingen, Brussels (1975):355–64.

Dumézil, Georges, *Le Crime des Lemniennes,* Paris, 1924.

Heurgon, Jacques, *La Vie quotidienne chez les Etrusques,* Paris, 1961.

Norbeck, Edward, "African Rituals of Conflict," *American Anthropologist* 65 (1963):1254–79.

Pembroke, Simon, "Last of the Matriarchs: A Study of the Inscriptions of Lycia," *Journal of the Economic and Social History of the Orient* 8 (1965):217–47.

———, "Women in Charge: The Function of Alternatives in Early Greek Tradition and the Ancient Idea of Matriarchy," *Journal of the Warburg and Courtauld Institutes* 30 (1967):1–35.

Trüdinger, Karl, "Studien zur Geschichte der griechisch-römischen Ethnographie," Diss., Basel, 1918.

Vidal-Nacquet, Pierre, "Slavery and the Rule of Women in Tradition, Myth and Utopia" in *Myth, Religion and Society*, ed. R. L. Gordon, Cambridge, 1981.

## 14. Classical Tragedy: Weaving Men's Dream of Sexual Strife

Burkert, Walter, "Jason, Hypsipyle, and New Fire at Lemnos: A Study in Myth and Ritual," *Classical Quarterly* 65 (1971):1–15.

Caldwell, Richard S., "The Misogyny of Eteocles," *Arethusa* 6 (1973):197–231.

———, "Selected Bibliography on Psychoanalysis and Classical Studies," *Arethusa* 7 (1974):115–34.

Devereux, George, "The Self-Blinding of Oedipus in Sophocles' *Oidipous Tyrannos*," *Journal of Hellenic Studies* 93 (1973):36–49.

Fantham, Elaine, "Sex, Status and Survival in Hellenistic Athens: A Study of Women in New Comedy," *Phoenix* 29 (1975):44–74.

Keuls, Eva, "Aeschylus' *Niobe* and Apulian Funerary Symbolism," *Zeitschrift für Papyrologie und Epigraphik* 30 (1978):42–68.

———, *The Water Carriers in Hades: A Study of Catharsis Through Toil*, Amsterdam, 1974.

Kitto, H. D. F., *The Greeks*, Baltimore, 1951.

Reckford, Kenneth J., "Medea's First Exit," *Transactions of the American Philological Association* 99 (1968):329–59.

Sandbach, F. H., *The Comic Theatre of Greece and Rome*, London, 1977.

Shaw, M., "The Female Intruder: Women in Fifth-century Drama," *Classical Philology* 70 (1975):149–84.

Simon, Bennett, *Mind and Madness in Ancient Greece*, Ithaca, N.Y., 1978.

Slater, Philip E., *The Glory of Hera*, Boston, 1978.

Spranger, Peter P., *Historische Untersuchungen zu den Sklavenfiguren des Plautus und Terenz*, Schwäbisch-Gmünd, 1961.

Trendall, A. D., and T. B. L. Webster, *Illustrations of Greek Drama*, London, 1971.

Vernant, Jean-Pierre, and Pierre Vidal-Nacquet, *Mythe et tragédie en Grèce ancienne*, Paris, 1972.

Webster, T. B. L., "Menander: Production and Imagination," *Bulletin of the John Rylands Library*, 45, Manchester (1963):235–72.

———, *The Tragedies of Euripides*, London, 1967.

Zeitlin, Froma I., "The Dynamics of Misogyny: Myth and Mythmaking in the Oresteia," *Arethusa* 11 (1978):149–84.

## 15. Sex Antagonism and Women's Rituals

Arthur, Marylin, "An Interpretation of the Homeric Hymn to Demeter," *Arethusa* 10 (1977):7–47.

Beazley, J. D., "Some Inscriptions on Vases, III," *American Journal of Archaeology* 39 (1935):487.

Burkert, Walter, *Griechische Religion der archaischen und klassischen Epoche*, Berlin, 1977.

——, *Homo necans: Interpretationen altgriechischer Opferriten und Mythen*, Berlin, 1972.

Detienne, M., *Dionysus Slain*, trans. from the French, Baltimore, 1979.

Fuchs, W., "Sleeping Ariadne Type," in Wolfgang Herbig, *Führer durch die öffentlichen Sammlungen klassischer Altertümer in Rom*, 4th ed., vol. I (1963), no. 144.

Gluckman, Max, *Politics, Law and Ritual in Tribal Society*, Chicago, 1965.

——, *Rituals of Rebellion in South-East Africa*, Manchester, 1954.

Gordon, R. L., ed., *Myth, Religion and Society: Structuralist Essays by M. Detienne, J.-P. Vernant and P. Vidal-Nacquet*, Cambridge, 1981.

Graf, Fritz, *Eleusis und die orphische Dichtung Athens in vorhellenistischer Zeit*, Berlin, 1974.

Henrichs, Albert, "Changing Dionysiac Identities," in *Self-Definition in the Graeco-Roman World*, eds. B. F. Meyer and E. P. Sanders, London-Philadelphia (1982):137–60.

——, "Greek Maenadism from Olympias to Messalina," *Harvard Studies in Classical Philology* 82 (1978):121–60.

Jenkins, Ian, "Dressed to Kill," *Omnibus* (1983):29–32.

Kraemer, Ross, "Ecstacy and Possession," *Harvard Theological Review* 72 (1979):64 ff.

Lewis, I. M., *Ecstatic Religion: An Anthropological Study of Spirit Possession and Shamanism*, 1971.

McNally, Sheila, "The Maenad in Early Greek Art," *Arethusa* 11 (1978): 101–35.

Mannhard, Wilhelm, *Wald- und Feldkulte*, 2nd ed., Darmstadt, 1904–5 (repr. 1963).

Norbeck, Edward, "The Anthropological Study of Human Play," *Rice University Studies* 60 (1974):1–8.

Oranje, H., *The Bacchae of Euripides: The Play and the Audience*, Leiden, 1983.

Philippart, Hubert, *Iconographie des Bacchantes d'Euripide*, Paris, 1930.

Segal, C., *Dionysiac Poetics and Euripides' Bacchae*, Princeton, N.J., 1982.

——, "The Menace of Dionysus: Sex Roles and Reversals in Euripides' Bacchae," *Arethusa* 11 (1978):185–202.

Simon, Bennett, *Mind and Madness in Ancient Greece*, Ithaca, N.Y., 1978.

Weege, Fritz, *Der Tanz in der Antike*, Halle, 1926.

### Epilogue

Andreae, Bernard, *Das Alexandermosaik* (Opus Nobile, Heft 14), Bremen, 1959.

————, "Zermalmt vom Wagen des Grosskönigs," *Bonner Jahrbücher* 161 (1961):4 ff.

Badian, Ernst, ed., *Studies in Greek and Roman History*, Oxford, 1968.

Bieber, M., *Alexander the Great in Greek and Roman Art*, Chicago, 1964.

Fox, Robert Lane, *The Search for Alexander*, New York, 1980.

Fuhrmann, Heinrich, *Philoxenos von Eretria: Archäologische Untersuchungen über zwei Alexandermosaike*, Göttingen, 1931.

Hölscher, Tonio, *Griechische Historienbilder des 5. und 4. Jahrhunderts vor Christus*, Würzburg, 1973.

Keuls, Eva, "The Brink of Death in Classical Greek Painting," *Mededelingen van het Nederlands Historisch Instituut te Rome*, 1982.

# Sources of Illustrations

*Frontispiece.* East Berlin 3206, krater by the Pan Painter.
1. Boston 95.48, squat lekythos.
2. Louvre Br. 1715, inv. MNC 623, bronze lid from Corinth, about 350 B.C.
3. Florence 81948, hydria by the Meidias Painter, ARV 1312,1. Courtesy Soprintendenza alle Antichità, Firenze.
4. East Berlin 3248, fourth-century lekythos, ARV 1482,5.
5. Leningrad 928 (inv. 2024), lekythos, ARV 1482,6.
6. New York, Metropolitan Museum, right wall of cubiculum from Boscoreale. Courtesy The Metropolitan Museum of Art, Rogers Fund, 1903.
7. Castle Ashby collection, Etruscan mirror.
8. Copenhagen 119, cup by Epiktetos, ARV 75,59. Courtesy The National Museum, Copenhagen.
9. Louvre C 10793, fragment of a pelike by the Pan Painter, ARV 555,92.
10. West Berlin 2172, pelike by the Perseus Painter.
11. Rome, Conservatori Museum, amphora, ABV 134,19.
12. Madrid 10961, amphora by the Sappho Painter, ABV 508. Photo courtesy Museo Arqueologico Nacional.
13. Munich 2648, kylix by Douris, ARV 441,185.
14. Munich 2301, amphora by the Andocides Painter, ARV 4,9.
15. Bari 6228, oenochoe.
16. Athena from Varvakion (after Frank Brommer, *Athena Parthenos*, Fig. 2).
17. West Berlin F 2159, amphora by the Andocides Painter, ARV 3,1 (detail).
18. Baltimore 54.766, statuette of Athena, 450 B.C.
19. Richmond 60.23, amphora, PARA 56,48 ter.
20. Boston 95.39, lekythos by the Alchimachos Painter, ARV 533,58. Photo courtesy Museum of Fine Arts, Boston, Catherine Page Perkins Fund.
21. Munich 2413, stamnos by Hermonax, ARV 495,1.
22. New York 31.11.11, column krater by the Lydos Painter, ABV 108.5. Photo The Metropolitan Museum of Art, Fletcher Fund, 1931.
23. Munich 2361, pelike by the Kleophon Painter, ARV 1145,36.
24. Basel, Market, amphora in the style of the Antimenes Painter.
25. Brussels A718, kantharos by Douris, ARV 445,256.
26. Morgantina, Sicily, fragment of a krater.
27. London B 210, amphora by Exekias, ABV 144,7.
28. Munich 2688, cup by the Penthesileia Painter, ARV 879,1.

29. Same as 28 (detail).
30. New York 06.1021.149, column krater attributed to the Orchard Painter, ARV 523,2. Photo courtesy The Metropolitan Museum of Art, Rogers Fund, 1906.
31. Boston 95.36, kantharos, ARV 381,182. Courtesy Museum of Fine Arts, Boston, Catherine Page Perkins Fund.
32. Same as 21, reverse.
33. Tarquinia RC 7456, bell krater by the Berlin Painter, ARV 206,126 (detail).
34a,b. London E 313, Nolan amphora by the Berlin Painter, ARV 202,87.
35. Boston 1972.850, kalyx krater by the Niobid Painter. Courtesy Museum of Fine Arts, Boston, Mary S. and Edward J. Holmes Fund.
36. Same as 35, reverse.
37. West Berlin F 2279, cup by Peithinos, ARV 115,2.
38. Munich 2689, cup by the Penthesileia Painter, ARV 879,2.
39. Madrid 11265, cup by Aison, ARV 1174,1.
40. Paris, Louvre G 71, cup by the Euergides Painter, ARV 89,21.
41a,b. Rome, Villa Giulia 20760, cup by Scythes, ARV 83,14.
42. Ferrara T 749, volute krater by the Boreas Painter, ARV 536,1.
43. Taranto 4545, lekythos in the style of the Pan Painter, ARV 560,5.
44. Geneva MF 238, kalyx krater by the Geneva Painter, ARV 615,1.
45. Frankfurt, Städel Museum, cup by the Brygos Painter or his circle, ARV 386.
46. Same as 45.
47. Same as 45, tondo.
48. New York 3711.19, chous. Courtesy The Metropolitan Museum of Art, Fletcher Fund, 1937.
49. Athens 9683, pelike by the Pan Painter, ARV 554,82.
50. West Berlin 2180, kalyx krater by Euphronius, ARV 13–14,1.
51. Toledo, Ohio, 64.126, cup.
52. Brussels R 259, cup by the Scheurleer Painter, ARV 169,7.
53. Caltanisetta 20371, column krater by the Harrow Painter, PARA 334,39 bis (detail).
54. Berlin 2278, cup by the Sosias Painter, ARV 21,1.
55. Boston 00.356, cup, Cairo group, ARV 741. Courtesy Museum of Fine Arts, Boston, H. L. Pierce Fund.
56. Philadelphia 90547.52, cup by the Penthesileia Painter.
57. Vienna 1773, skyphos by the Lewis Painter, ARV 972,2.
58. Harvard University, Fogg Museum of Art 1960.342, hydria.
59. Athens, Acropolis Museum, sherd from the Acropolis (after Botha, *Die antiken Vasen von der Akropolis in Athen*, vol. II, pl. 83, #1073).
60. Athens, National Museum 22, fifth-century bronze statuette.
61. Olympia, bronze statuette of satyr.
62. Berlin 2320, oenochoe, by the Painter of Berlin 2268, ARV 157,84.
63. Boston 08.31 c, skyphos. Courtesy Museum of Fine Arts, Boston, Gift of E. P. Warren.
64. Basel, Market, cup by the Akestorides Painter, PARA 417.
65. Boston 08.31 d, fragment of a kylix by Oltos. Courtesy Museum of Fine Arts, Boston, gift of E. P. Warren.
66. The phalluses of Delos.
67. Athens, Kerameikos Museum, leaden doll from Kerameikos tomb no. 40.
68. Basel, Market 1975, sixth-century column krater.
69. Munich 8934, kotyle.
70. Madison, Wisconsin, neck amphora, in the Medea group.
71. Florence 3897, cup. Courtesy Soprintendenza alle Antichità, Firenze.

72. Once Castellani collection, cup (after Vorberg, *Glossarium Eroticum* 409).
73. Leningrad 14611, cup fragment by Epiktetos, ARV 75,60.
74. Boston 08.30 a, cup, from the circle of the Nikosthenes Painter.
75. Once Berlin, cup by Oltos, ARV 66,121.
76. Syracuse 20065, pelike, ARV 238,5.
77. Paris, Petit Palais 307, amphora by Painter of the Flying Angel, ARV 279,2.
78. Rome, Villa Giulia 50404, kylix, ARV 1565,1.
79. Athens, National Museum A 2579, stamnos in Six's technique.
80. London E 815, kylix by the Nikosthenes Painter, ARV 125,15.
81. Taranto, Apulian pelike, by the Truro Painter.
82. London E 307, Nolan amphora.
83. Stuttgart V 84, "Chalcidian" amphora.
84. Naples 3232, hydria, ARV 1032,6.
85. The entrance to the Acropolis.
86. The Stoa of Attalus.
87. Private houses of Athens (reconstruction by J. E. Jones, after Wycherley, *The Stones of Athens*, Fig. 68).
88. Brussels A 891, ARV 771,2.
89. Munich S. L. 475, lekythos, ARV 1365,2.
90. London E 190, hydria, near the Niobid Painter, ARV 611,36.
91. Munich 2798, white-ground lekythos, ARV 1022,138.
92a,b. New York 56.11.1, lekythos by the Amasis Painter, ABV 154,57. Courtesy The Metropolitan Museum of Art, purchase 1956, Walter C. Baker Gift.
93a,b. New York 31.11.10, lekythos by the Amasis Painter, PARA 66. Courtesy The Metropolitan Museum of Art, Fletcher Fund, 1931.
94. Dallas, private collection, pyxis.
95. Brussels A 890, cup, workshop of Sotades, ARV 771,1.
96. London E 219, hydria, by the Painter of Munich 2528, ARV 1258,3.
97. Dallas, private collection (same as 94).
98. Once Berlin 4282, lost cup, ARV 644,134.
99. New York 08.258.17, white-ground lekythos, ARV 999,181. Courtesy The Metropolitan Museum of Art, Rogers Fund, 1908.
100a,b,c. Durham, England, kalathos.
101. Paris, Louvre CA 587, pyxis, ARV 1094,104.
102. Boston 03.802, loutrophoros. Courtesy Museum of Fine Arts, Boston, Francis Bartlett Collection.
103. Taranto, fragment of an Apulian vase (Gnathia technique).
104a,b. West Berlin 2406, lebes gamikos, ARV 1225.
105. Athens, National Museum 1963, lekythos by the Achilleus Painter.
106. New York 17.130.15, hydria by the Orpheus Painter, ARV 1104,16. Courtesy The Metropolitan Museum of Art, Rogers Fund, 1917.
107. London E 372, pelike by the Erichthonius Painter, ARV 1218,1.
108. Cambridge. Fitzwilliam Museum 3,1917, lekythos by the Painter of Cambridge 3, 1917.
109. London E 248, late Attic hydria.
110. Würzburg 521, kalyx krater, ARV 1046,7.
111. London E 215, hydria, by the Painter of London E 215, ARV 1082,1.
112. London E 192, hydria, ARV 548,54.
113. Athens, Kerameikos Museum, marble loutrophoros.
114. Malibu, California, J. Paul Getty Museum, marble lekythos (detail).
115. Munich 2797, white-ground lekythos by the Phiale Painter, ARV 1022,138.
116. London F 159, Apulian volute krater.

117. The Athenian agora in 150 A.D. (reconstructed, after Homer Thompson, *Athens Comes of Age*, p. 107).
118. Athens, Kerameikos Museum, fifth-century tomb stele.
119. Leiden 1903.12.1, tomb stele.
120. Houston, fourth-century Attic tomb stele.
121. Athens 1913, lekythos by the Timokrates Painter, ARV 744,A5.
122. London 1905.7-10.10, lekythos by the Bosanquet Painter (fragment), ARV 1227,10.
123. West Berlin F 2443, lekythos by the Achilleus Painter, ARV 995,118.
124. Attic relief (after Phillips, *Greek Medicine*, Fig. 3), private collection.
125. Vatican 350, amphora by Exekias, ABV 140,1.
126. New York, The Cloisters, fifteenth-century wood carving.
127. Paris, Louvre CA 453, loutrophoros by the Kleophrades Painter, ARV 184,22.
128. Athens 1170, loutrophoros by the Painter of Volonia, 228, ARV 512,13.
129. Athens 723, grave stele of Polyxena.
130. Athens 992, Corinthian cup.
131. Tarquinia, pelike, ARV 224,7.
132. Rome, Villa Giulia 27254, cup.
133. Munich 2421, hydria by Phintias, ARV 22,7.
134. Shoulder of 133.
135. Munich 1432, "Tyrrhenian" amphora.
136. Detail of 135.
137. London E 38, cup by Epiktetus, ARV 72,16.
138. Budapest, private collection, krater by the Telos Painter (fourth century), ARV 1426,27.
139. Naples R. P. 27669, kantharos by Epiktetos.
140. Basel, Market 1977, cup by the Curtis Painter.
141. Toledo, Ohio, 72.55, cup by Makron.
142. Same as 141, other side.
143. Basel Kä 415, cup.
144. Same as 143, other side of rim.
145. Tarquinia, cup by the Triptolemos Painter, ARV 367,94.
146. London E 68, cup by the Brygos Painter, ARV 371,24.
147. Munich 8991, omphalus cup in Six's technique.
148. Basel, Market 1977, cup.
149. Berlin 3757, cup, ARV 404,11.
150. Naples S. A. 5, cup, ARV 32,4.
151. Tarquinia, cup by Apollodorus, PARA 333,9 bis.
152. Würzburg 479, cup by the Brygos Painter, ARV 372,32.
153. West Berlin 2289, cup by Douris, ARV 435,95.
154. Louvre G 156, skyphos by the Brygos Painter, ARV 380,172.
155. Harvard 60.346, column krater, ARV 563,8.
156. Tarquinia, cup by the Briseis Painter, ARV 408,36.
157. London E 44, cup by the Panaitius Painter, ARV 318-19.
158. Oxford 1967,305, cup by the Briseis Painter.
159. Tarquinia, pelike, ARV 224,7 (reverse of 131).
160. Athens, Kerameikos Museum 1063, askos.
161. Munich, private collection, Attic black-figure lekythos, ABV 469,71.
162. Munich, private collection, cup by the Wedding Painter, ARV 923,29.
163. Würzburg 530, kalpis.
164. Once Munich, Arndt collection, cup by the Antiphon Painter, ARV 339,55.
165. Basel BS 440, cup by Onesimos, ARV 326,86 bis.
166. Louvre G 13, cup by the Pedieus Painter, ARV 86,$\alpha$.

167. Florence 3912, cup by the Brygos Painter. Courtesy Soprintendenza alle Antichità, Firenze.
168. Same as 167, detail.
169. Same as 167, detail.
170. Same as 167, other side of rim (fragmentary).
171. Würzburg 479, cup by the Brygos Painter, ARV 372,32.
172. London E 44, cup by Onesimos, ARV 318-19.
173. West Berlin F 2414, oenochoe by the Shuvalov Painter, ARV 1208,41.
174. West Berlin 2269, cup by the Kiss Painter, ARV 177,1.
175. Chicago 1911.456, hydria by the Leningrad Painter, ARV 572,88. Courtesy Art Institute of Chicago.
176. Same as 175, detail. Courtesy Art Institute of Chicago.
177. Late Roman mosaic in Mytilene (island of Lesbos), detail.
178. Schwerin 708, skyphos by the Pistoxenos Painter, ARV 862,30.
179. Same as 178, reverse.
180. Rome, Capitoline Museum, third-century B.C. statue of drunk old woman.
181a,b. New York 07.286.36, white-ground pyxis by the Penthesileia Painter, ARV 890,173. Courtesy The Metropolitan Museum of Art, Rogers Fund, 1907.
182. Same as 181.
183. Floorplan of a fifth-century Athenian House (after R. S. Young, *Hesperia* 20 [1951], Fig. 11).
184. Floorplans of fifth-century houses in Olynthus (after Roland Martin, *L'Urbanisme grec* 228, Fig. 42).
185. Brussels A 717, stamnos by Smikros, ARV 20,1.
186. London E 769, pyxis, circle of the Brygos Painter, ARV 410,63.
187. London 1910,6-15.3, oenochoe.
188. Milan, Moretti Collection, Apulian bell krater (Trendall and Webster, *Illustrations of Greek Drama*, IV,13).
189. Athens 1501, marble funerary relief.
190. Thebes Museum, tombstone of Melanos.
191. Rome, Terme Museum, "Ludovisi Throne," center panel.
192. Same as 191, left panel.
193. Same as 191, right panel.
194. Paestum Museum, east wall of the "Tomb of the Diver" (detail).
195. Würzburg 479, cup by the Brygos Painter, ARV 372,32, outside.
196. West Berlin F 2279, cup by Peithinos, ARV 115,2, outside detail.
197. Same as 196, outside detail.
198. Ferrara 9351, cup, ARV 880,12.
199. Same as 198, other side.
200. Same as 198, tondo by Penthesileia Painter.
201. Chicago 1889.27, cup by the Penthesileia Painter, ARV 884,77. Courtesy Art Institute of Chicago.
202. Same as 201, other side. Courtesy Art Institute of Chicago.
203. Same as 201, tondo. Courtesy Art Institute of Chicago.
204. Toledo, Ohio, 72.55, cup by Makron, tondo.
205. Adolphseck 41, pelike by the Pig Painter, ARV 566,6.
206. Same as 205, reverse.
207. Parthenon frieze, Acropolis Museum.
208. Rome, Villa Giulia 47457, hydria, ABV 393.
209. Vatican 426, hydria, ABV 266,2.
210. Naples S. A. 12. (H.), hydria, ABV 334,3.
211. Vatican 417, hydria, ABV 384,26.
212. Vatican 427, hydria, ABV 397,31.

213. Detroit 63.13, hydria by the Pig Painter, PARA 389,40. Courtesy The Detroit Institute of Art, Founders Society Purchase.
214. Tübingen 1343, krater.
215. Leningrad, Stephani 613, hydria, ARV 34,16.
216. New York 17.230.35, lekythos by the Phiale Painter, ARV 1020,100. Courtesy The Metropolitan Museum of Art, Rogers Fund, 1917.
217. Taranto 124520, Apulian pelike.
218. Same as 217, reverse.
219. Munich S. L. 476, hydria, ARV 1083,2.
220. Athens 12890, lekythos, ARV 641,93.
221. Oxford 539, amphoriskos, ARV 1248,10.
222. New York 26.60.78, lekythos by the Sabouroff Painter, ARV 844,151. Courtesy The Metropolitan Museum of Art, Fletcher Fund, 1926.
223. Chiusi 63.564, skyphos, ARV 1300,2.
224. Athens 1584, pyxis in the style of the Panaitius Painter.
225a,b. Same as 224.
226. Houston, Museum of Fine Arts (Annette Finnigan Collection) 34-131, white-ground lekythos by the Bowdoin Painter.
227. Washington, Smithsonian Museum, Apulian hydria.
228. Cleveland CMA 70.16, amphora attributed to the Painter of Berlin, 1899. Courtesy The Cleveland Museum of Art, Andrew R. and Martha Holden Jennings Fund.
229. Syracuse, Italiot terra cotta relief.
230. London, British Museum, tetradrachma from Asia Minor.
231. Taranto, Apulian terra cotta loom weight (after BCH 32 [1908], pl. VII,3).
232. West Berlin 2289, cup by Douris, ARV 435,95.
233. Florence 3918, cup by the Stieglitz Painter, ARV 827,7. Courtesy Soprintendenza alle Antichità, Firenze.
234. Athens 1629, kneecover (epinetron) by the Eritrea Painter, ARV 1250,34.
235a,b. Baltimore 48.233, alabastron, ABV 585,1.
236. Vatican 16554, hydria, ARV 252,47.
237. West Berlin 31426, cup by the Euaion Painter, ARV 795,100.
238. East Berlin 2254, alabastron by the Pan Painter, ARV 557,123.
239. Maplewood, New Jersey, Noble Collection, hydria by the Harrow Painter, ARV 276,70.
240. Baltimore, Johns Hopkins University, cup by Phintias, ARV 24,14.
241. Rhodes, Collection of the Knights of Malta 12887, pelike, ARV 1116,40.
242. Altenburg, Germany, Lindenau Museum 271, skyphos, ARV 823,31.
243. Baltimore 48,70, column krater by the Walters Painter, ARV 278,1.
244. Heidelberg 64/5, kalpis by the Nausikaa Painter.
245. Munich 1468, amphora, ABV 315,3.
246. Nicosia C 440, amphora, ABV 109,28.
247. Würzburg HA 47, amphora by the Phrynos Painter, ABV 169,5.
248. Swiss private collection, cup by Socles, PARA 72,2.
249. London W 39, amphora, ABV 297,16.
250. Same as 249, reverse.
251. Paris, Cabinet des Médailles 206, belly amphora by Sakonides.
252. Boston 08.292, skyphos. Courtesy Museum of Fine Arts, Boston, Gift of E. P. Warren and Fiske Warren.
253. Same as 252, reverse.
254. Oxford 1967.304, cup, ARV 378,137.
255. Villa Giulia, pelike by Euphronius, ARV 15,11.

256. Boston 01.651, eye cup by the Amasis Painter, ABV 157,86. Courtesy Museum of Fine Arts, Boston.
257. Boston 10.184, Nolan Amphora by the Pan Painter, ARV 553,39. Courtesy Museum of Fine Arts, Boston, James Fund and Special Contribution.
258. Olympia, terra cotta statuary group of about 470 B.C. (perhaps Corinthian work).
259. Basel, Market 1980, terra cotta statuette from Myrina, second century B.C.
260. West Berlin 1968.12, Apulian bell krater, (Trendall and Webster, *Illustrations of Greek Drama*, III,3,16).
261. Private collection, oenochoe (after Schauenburg, 1975).
262. West Berlin 1964.4, cup from the circle of the Nikosthenes Painter.
263. London F 65, bell krater by the Dinos Painter, ARV 1154.
264. Basel, Market 1977, pelike by the Eucharides Painter.
265. Same as 264, reverse.
266. New York 52.11.4, cup by Douris, ARV 437,114. Courtesy The Metropolitan Museum of Art, Rogers Fund, 1952.
267. London E 536, chous.
268. Paris, Louvre CA 2912, chous from Athens.
269. Private collection, chous (after *Antike Kunst* [1977], pl. 4,3).
270. Tübingen 1397, chous.
271. Boston 01.8085, chous, influence of the Dinos Painter. Courtesy Museum of Fine Arts, Boston, H. L. Pierce Fund.
272. East Berlin F 2658, chous, Manner of the Meidias Painter, ARV 1318,1.
273. Vienna 1043, chous by the Painter of the Louvre Centauromachy, ARV 1094,103.
274. Fresco from the Villa of the Mysteries at Pompeii.
275. Malibu, California, J. Paul Getty Museum, 72.AE 128, Apulian oenochoe.
276. Private collection, Apulian fragment.
277. Private collection, fragments of an Attic krateriskos.
278. Brauron Museum, Attic fragment.
279. Private collection, Attic sherds from Brauron.
280. Brauron Museum, Attic fragment.
281. Piazza Armerina, Sicily, bikini girl mosaic (detail).
282. Brauron Museum, Attic sherd.
283. Brauron Museum, fragmentary Attic cup.
284. Brauron Museum, portrait heads of girls.
285. Brauron Museum, children's statues.
286. Brauron Museum, fragment of black-figure epinetron.
287. East Berlin 2301, cup by the Brygos Painter, ARV 378,129.
288. London F 149, Paestan bell krater by Python.
289. Chicago 1905.345, donkey-head rhyton by Douris. Courtesy Art Institute of Chicago.
290. Policoro, Museo Nazionale della Siritide, early Lucanian pelike by the Policoro Painter (Trendall and Webster, *Illustrations of Greek Drama*, III,3,14).
291. Taranto 8935, Apulian amphora (shoulder detail).
292. Paris, Cabinet des Médailles 4892, relief lekythos.
293. London E 140, skyphos by Makron, ARV 459,3.
294. West Berlin, Apulian terra cotta figure (after Cook, *Zeus*, II, Fig. 79).
295. Athens 1695, lekythos, ARV 1204,2 (detail).
296. Munich 2647, cup by Douris, ARV 438,132.
297. Munich 2645, cup by the Brygos Painter, ARV 371,15.
298. Munich 2344, pointed amphora by the Kleophrades Painter, ARV 182,6.
299. West Berlin F 2290, cup by Hieron and Makron, ARV 462,48.

300. Athens 9690, lekythos by the Painter of Athens 9690.
301. Basel Kä 417, Chalcidian amphora.
302. West Berlin, "Tyrrhenian" lekythos.
303. Würzburg L 164, cup by Phineus, rim detail.
304. Würzburg 492, cup, ARV 1512,18.
305. London E 382, pelike, ARV 632.
306. Copenhagen 1943, skyphos by the Zephyros Painter, ARV 976,3. Courtesy National Museum, Copenhagen.
307. Boston 01.8072, cup by Makron, ARV 461,36.
308. Rouen 25, hydria by the Kleophrades Painter, ARV 188,61 (shoulder detail).
309. West Berlin 3232, cup by the Epidromos Painter, ARV 117,2.
310. Munich 2654, cup by Makron, ARV 462,47.
311. Basel, Market, cup by Epiktetus.
312. Ferrara T 128, volute krater by Polygnotus, ARV 1052,25; 1680.
313. West Berlin 3223, pelike, ARV 586,47.
314. Corinth, cup by the "Q" Painter, ARV 1519,3.
315. Private collection, skyphos by Polygnotus (after Erika Simon, *Die Götter der Griechen*, Fig. 269).
316. Tarquinia RC 4197, kalyx krater by Polygnotus, ARV 1057,96; PARA 445,96.
317. Ferrara T 311, bell krater by the Altamura Painter, ARV 593,41.
318. Louvre G 2, amphora by Oltos, ARV 53,2.
319. London W 40, pelike by the Acheloos Painter, ABV 384,20.
320. Same as 319, reverse.
321. Chiusi 1830, skyphos by the Lewis Painter, ARV 975,36. Courtesy Soprintendenza alle Antichità, Firenze.
322. Same as 321, reverse.
323. Louvre G 448, cup by the Penthesileia Painter, ARV 880,5.
324. Heidelberg 59/9, white-ground lekythos.
325. New York 24.97.34. fourth-century chous. Courtesy The Metropolitan Museum of Art, Fletcher Fund, 1924.
326. Munich 2330, neck amphora by the Phiale Painter, ARV 1014,2.
327. Munich 8762, pelike by Myson, ARV 1638, 2 bis.
328. Boston 68.168, Nolan amphora by the Nikon Painter, PARA 402.
329. Bologna 206, column krater by the Boreas Painter, ARV 537,12. Courtesy Museo Civico Archeologico, Bologna.
330. Syracuse 22934, kalyx krater, ARV 1050,4.
331. Boston 10.185, bell krater by the Pan Painter, ARV 550,1. Courtesy Museum of Fine Arts, Boston, James Fund.
332. Athens, Agora Museum, head of herm from about 415 B.C.
333. Munich 2344, pointed amphora by the Kleophrades Painter (detail).
334. Mykonos, relief amphora from about 670 B.C. (neck detail).
335. Same as 334.
336. Same as 334, detail.
337. Louvre G 152, cup by the Brygos Painter, ARV 369,1.
338. Boston 59.176, kalyx krater by the Altamura Painter, ARV 590,11. Courtesy Museum of Fine Arts, Boston, William Francis Warden Fund.
339. Same as 338, reverse.
340. Malibu, California, J. Paul Getty Museum, "Elgin Throne" (detail).
341. Pella Museum, mosaic from Alexander's palace.
342. Same as 341.
343. Salonike, silver urn from tomb II at Vergina, detail of handle.
344. Rome, Capitoline Museum, bust of Commodus as Heracles.
345. Naples, Archaeological Museum, The Alexander Mosaic.

# Index

*Acharnians* (Aristophanes), 120, 198, 354, 392
Achilleus, 45, 54, 70, 130, 149, 218, 255, 287, 289, 320, 339, 399
Achilleus Painter, 120
Acropolis, 62, 78, 94, 135, 312, 352, 353, 393
Adonia festival, 17, 23, 28, 30, 32, 382, 383, 391, 394, 395
Adonis, 17, 23–27
  as male sex symbol, 28
Aegeus, 58
Aegisthus, 338
Aeneas, 62, 400
*Aeneid* (Vergil), 62
Aeschines, 209, 291, 296, 297
Aeschylus, 8, 52, 92, 129, 150, 233, 235, 287, 331, 333, 335, 336, 338, 339, 344, 345, 346, 355, 388
Aethra, 58, 64, 258
*Against Androtion* (Demosthenes), 296, 297
*Against Aristogiton* (Demosthenes), 272
*Against Athenogenes* (Hyperides), 196
*Against Neaera*, 99, 156, 267
*Against the Stepmother* (Antiphon), 9, 91, 269, 322
*Against Timarchus* (Aeschines), 209, 296, 297
*Against Timocrates* (Demosthenes), 114
Agamemnon, 132, 136, 233, 323, 333, 338
*Agamemnon* (Aeschylus), 235, 333
Agathon, 291, 297, 333
Agave, 358
Aglauros, 64, 135, 308, 309
Agora, 44, 95, 137, 160, 385, 387, 392
Aison, 58
*Aithiopis*, 44, 45, 413

Ajax, 339
*Ajax* (Sophocles), 150
Alabastron, 120, 123
Alcestis, 253
Alcibiades, 32, 174, 271, 381, 383–385, 388
Alciphron, 137
Alexander Mosaic, 408–415
Alexander the Great, 359, 384, 406–408
  campaigns, 409–415
Alexis of Thurii, 200
Alke, 196, 197
Alkmene, 51, 341
Altamura Painter, 400
Altar of the Twelve Gods, 392
Amasis Painter, 245
Amazonomachia, 34, 39, 44, 45, 47, 264
Amazons, 3, 65, 320, 323, 324
  girdle of the Amazon Hippolyte, 56
  motif of rebellion, 4
Amphion, 343, 346
Amphitryon, 341
*Amphitryon* (Plautus), 341
Amymone, 240, 258, 316, 340
*Amymone* (Aeschylus), 340
Anacreon, 231
Anchises, 400
Andocides, 104, 388
Andromache, 21, 22, 45, 412
Andromeda, 57
*Andrones*, 162, 163
Androtion, 114, 296, 297
*Animal Farm* (Orwell), 18
Anthesteria Festival, 371, 373, 378
Antigone, 150, 324, 332, 334
Antigone (prostitute), 196
*Antigone* (Sophocles), 146, 150
Antilochos, 413

Anti-militarism, 9
Antiope, 60, 324, 339, 343
*Antiope* (Euripides), 341, 343
Antipater, 413
Antiphon, 9, 91, 128, 269, 322
Antisthenes, 210
Apelles, 195
Aphobos, 91
Aphrodite, 23, 26, 78, 205, 206, 255, 327, 355
Aphrodite Hetaera, 205, 217, 224
Aphrodite in the Garden, 308
Aphrodite Ourania, 217
Aphrodite Pandemos, 205
Apollo, 55, 70, 149, 340, 341, 345, 346
Apollonius, 327
Apuleius, 6
Arachne, 234, 235, 250
*Arbitration, The* (Menander), 192, 343
Archaeological Museum, Naples, 408
Archaeology, 334
Archidamas, 146
Architecture, 329
  colonnade, 94, 95
  inner and outer space, 93–97
  private dwellings, 95, 97
  temple, 94
Ares, 43, 255
*Arguments and Counter-Arguments*, 327
Ariadne, 58, 60, 61, 366, 373
*Ariadne auf Naxos* (Strauss), 367
Aristarchus, 232
Aristogeiton, 194
Aristophanes, 11, 68, 86, 89, 157, 162, 191, 196, 201, 231, 232, 238, 289, 293, 346
  plays of, 8, 23, 25, 30, 87, 99, 109, 116, 120, 198, 201, 231, 238, 291, 305, 331, 332, 333, 353, 354, 357, 387, 388, 392–395
Aristotle, 7, 68, 124, 144–147, 208, 209, 230, 322, 324, 348, 405, 406
*Arrhephoroi*, 308
Artayctes, 8
Artemis, 55, 136, 205, 346
  cult of, 310, 312, 316, 318, 320
Artifacts
  sources for rape stories, 50
  study of, 3, 12
Artists, conditions affecting, 3
Aryballos, 120
Asclepius, 79, 82
*Asinaria* (Plautus), 188
Aspasia, 198, 199, 268, 272, 402
Astyanax, 21, 22, 339, 399
Athena, 21, 52, 58, 61, 123, 205, 234, 235, 308, 316, 341, 351, 373

Athena *(cont.)*
  birth, 40, 41
  cult of, 306–310
  defeminization, 42
  Hephaestus and, 40–42
  Heracles and, 36
  Odysseus and, 35
  Parthenon image of, 38, 39
Athena Ergane, 42, 248, 250, 306
Athena of the Workshop. *See* Athena Ergane
Athena Parthenos, 45, 62, 306
Athena Polias, 306, 308
Athenaeus, 187, 194, 197, 198
"Athenian," the, 128
*Athenian Constitution, The*, 230
Athenian home, the
  men's part, 162, 210–213
  women's part, 110, 118, 119, 122, 124, 210–213
Athens, 404
  architecture, 93–97, 329
  creative genius, 329
  cultic life, 302
  describing phallocracy in, 2
  female social rites, 305, 306
  fifth-century phallocracy, 12
  in 416 B.C., 17–19
  herms of, 30–32, 385
  invasion of Sicily by, 16, 20, 23, 31, 381, 383, 384, 402, 403
  late-fourth-century family habits, 215
  literature, 329, 330
  love vs. war movement, 395–402
  male viewpoint of history, 301
  Melos and, 17–19, 20, 23, 381
  moral climate, 11
  pederasty in, 287–291
  phallic domination, 5, 6
  poetry, 329, 330
  polarization of the sexes, 301
  scandal of the Hermes statues, 16, 17, 30, 32
  sculpture, 329
  sexual politics, 17
Atossa, 92
Atreus, 132, 135
Attica, 306
Atunis, 26
Augustus, Emperor of Rome, 235

Babylonians, 327
*Bacchae, The* (Euripides), 351, 358, 371
Bacchanalia, 358
Bachofen, J. J., 65, 66
Berlin Painter, 51
Bethe, E., 276
*Birds* (Aristophanes), 388, 393

Black magic, 77, 78
Boardman, John, 36, 76
Boreas, 52
Boscoreale bedroom, 26
Brandt, Paul, 9, 10, 11, 205
Brauron, 312, 314, 316, 318, 320
"Brides of Hades," 131, 132
Bronze Age, 333, 334
Brothels, 5, 154, 156, 158
Brothel tax, 195
Brygos Painter, 51, 168, 174, 181, 182, 188, 218, 399
Bucephalus, 412
Burkert, Walter, 308
Busiris, King, 68

Cadmos, 255
Callias, 92
Calypso, 230
Candaules, King, 92
Carians, 326
Cassander, 413, 414
Cassandra, 21, 332, 333, 339, 400
Cecrops, King, 64, 135, 308, 341
Censorship, 3, 339
Centaurs, 367
Chabrias, 157
Chaerestrate, 90
Charisius, 343
Chesler, Phyllis, 4, 112
Children, 72, 73
Children's Police, 209
Chrysippus, 289, 291
Cimon, 92
Circe, 230, 323
Circumcision, 68
Civilization, phallic rule in Western, 1
Classicists, 10. *See also* Scholars, classical
Cleisthenes, 291
*Clouds* (Aristophanes), 388
Clytemnestra, 233, 323, 332, 334, 337, 338
Comedy, 332, 343, 344, 354, 387, 404, 405
Commodus, Emperor of Rome, 408
Concubinage, 187. *See also* Concubine
Concubine (*pallake*), 268, 327
  free, 271–273
  slave, 269
*Constitution of Athens* (Aristotle), 208
Copulation, 42, 352, 353, 362, 373
  intercrural, 274, 299
Corinth, 36, 155, 156, 196
Courtesan, 194–198
Cowherd's Den, 371
Creon, 146, 382
Creusa, 341

Cybele, 44
Cynosarges (gymnasium), 272

*Damar*, 6
Danaë, 51, 340
Danaïd myth, 324, 338
*Danaïds* (Aristophanes), 395
Danaid trilogy, 338, 340, 344
Danaüs, 323
Darius, King, 335, 410–412
Death, 129, 130, 316
  in childbirth, 138–144, 204
  preparation and burial, 149–152
Defeminization, 42, 64, 351
*Defense Against Simon* (Lysias), 298
Defloration, 114, 268
Deianeira, 57, 234, 340
Deinomenos, 312
*Deipnosophistai* (Athenaeus), 187
Delian League, 8, 18, 33, 92
Delphi, 312
Demeter, 64, 112, 129, 147, 205, 206, 346. *See also* Earth Mother
  at Eleusis, 351, 352
Demetrius of Phaleron, 405
Demetrius Poliorketes, 405
Democracy, 333
Democritus, 104
Demosthenes, 90, 91, 102, 103, 106, 114, 157, 160, 182, 231, 271, 272, 291, 296, 297, 322
Demostratos, 394
Detienne, Marcel, 25
Devereux, George, 285
Dido, 62
Dikaiopolis, 120, 354
Dildo, 82–86, 116, 117
Diodorus Siculus, 358
Dionysiac religion, 78, 358–362, 371, 373, 375, 378, 379, 391
Dionysus, 41, 42, 58, 129, 165, 349, 351, 358, 366, 371, 373, 378, 379
Dirce, 343
Douris, 36, 174, 252, 253, 296, 342
Dover, Sir Kenneth, 1, 68, 76, 274, 296
Draconian law, 5, 100

Earth Mother, 124, 129, 351. *See also* Demeter
Earth Mother cults, 44, 64
*Ecclesia*, 357
Egesta, 383
Egyptians, 326
Eleusis, 348, 351, 352, 388
Eleusinian initiation rituals, 64, 352
Eleusinian mysteries, 32, 388
Elgin Throne, 405
Elpinike, 92, 93

Empedocles, 145
Engels, Donald, 147
Enkelados, 36
Eos, 52, 147
Ephoros, 324
Epiktetus, 367, 402
Erastes, 275, 285
Erechtheum, 52
Erechtheus, 52, 138
Erechtheus (Euripides), 138
Erection, permanent, 75–78
Erichthonius, 123, 135, 306, 308, 309
Eromenos, 275
Eros, 121, 206
Erotic art, 75
Eteocles, 336
Etruscans, 26, 28, 325, 400
Euktemon, 196, 197
Eumenides (Aeschylus), 8, 331, 355
Euphiletus, 91
Euphronius, 68
Eupolis, 196
Euripides, 16, 17, 20–23, 135, 136, 138,
    140, 231, 289, 314, 331, 335, 339,
    340, 341, 343, 344, 350, 351, 358,
    391, 393, 412
Europa, 51, 149, 339
Eurytos, King, 36
Execution, methods of, 8
Exekias, 45, 147

Fellatio, 85, 86, 174, 180, 181, 182, 293
Female
    death, 129, 130, 149–152, 310, 316
    infanticide, 110, 146, 147, 204
    labor, 99, 108, 124, 229–264
    male domination, 6
    mental attitude, 124–128
    rebellion, 65, 126, 127, 323, 337,
        379, 392–395
    rituals, 302, 305, 306, 349–379
    sex life, 9–11, 30, 82, 85, 86, 107,
        145, 146, 310
    status, 6, 30, 87, 98–100, 108–110,
        116, 204
Feminism, 9, 402, 403, 405
Festivals
    Adonia, 17, 23, 28, 30, 32, 382, 383,
        391, 394, 395
    Anthesteria, 303, 371, 372, 378
    Carrying of the Grape Clusters, 302,
        303
    panathenaic, 306
    of the Pitchers, 303, 305
    Skira, 357
For Phormio (Demosthenes), 102, 271
Frogs (Aristophanes), 289, 346, 388

Galen, 120, 144
Ganymede, 43, 51, 223, 285–287
Garden of Adonis, 25, 26
Ge (earth), 55, 149
Geneva Painter, 62
Genitals, 30. See also Phallus
    female, 30
    idolization of male, 66
    large male, 68
    oiling of male, 120
Glaukon, 386
Glory of Hera, The (Slater), 111
Gluckman, Max, 350
Glykera, 199
Gomme, A. W., 10, 11
Gorgon Medusa, 323
Gorgons, 323
Gould, John J., 90
Gramsci, A., 103
Graus, 90
Greater Dionysia festival, 43, 78
Great Mother, The (Neumann), 66
Greek Woman, The (Nietzsche), 9
Grote, G., 31
Gyges, 92
Gymnasia, 302
Gynaikonitis, 243, 244
Gyne, 90
Gynecocracy
    fear of, 321, 322
    in myth, 323–325
Gynecology (Soranus), 142
Gynophobia, 4, 322

Hadas, Moses, 404
Hades, 129
Hadrian, Emperor of Rome, 274
Harmodius, 194
Harmonia, 254
Harpokration, 320
Harrison, A. R. W., 101
Hebe, 43, 285
Hector, 21, 89
Hecuba, 21
Helen of Troy, 21, 58, 89, 206, 334,
    397
Henderson, J., 120
Hephaestus, 40–42, 70, 78, 123, 135,
    306
    craftsman god, 248
    Hera and, 42–44
Hera, 42, 43, 116, 205, 206, 224, 339
Heracles, 24, 30, 68, 135, 230, 234,
    272, 351, 367, 379, 407, 408
    feats of, 36, 45, 59, 60
    killing the Erymanthian boar, 355
    women and, 56, 57

Hermes, 16, 17, 30, 31, 50, 132, 206, 381, 385–387, 388
Hermippus, 354
Herms, 78, 386
  mutilation of, 16, 17, 30, 32, 381, 382, 385, 387–394
Herodotus, 92, 179, 229, 326, 327, 379
Herse, 64, 308, 309
Hesiod, 230
Hesione, 57
Hesychius, 121
Hetaerai, 90, 99, 101, 120, 130, 162, 163, 325, 362, 366
  aging, 200–202
  daily life of, 158, 160
  humiliation and abuse of, 174–182
  name "hetaera," 194
  names, 355
  primping, 170
  spinning by, 258–260
  as stage heroines, 191–194
  witty, 199, 200
Hipparchus, 194
Hipparete, 384
"Hippocratic texts," 144
Hippolyte, 4, 56
*Hippolytus* (Euripides), 140, 314
Historians, art, 3
*History* (Herodotus), 326
Hoffmansthal, Hugo von, 366
Holofernes, 323
Homer, 35, 44, 323, 329, 396
*Homeric Hymn to Demeter*, 112
Homoeroticism
  male, 179, 274
Homosexuality, 1, 9, 34, 194, 204, 384
  censure of adults, 291–296
  copulation, 42, 274
  Dorian Greeks, 275
  as escape from the female, 275
  female, 85, 86
  love gift, 82
  pederastic, 275
  rape, 49
  sanctioned and glorified, 275
  seduction of boys, 296–298
  true male, 277
*Horse and the Maiden, The*, 209
Hyakinthos, 77
Hyperides, 88, 196
Hypermestra, 324
Hypsipyle, 324

Iakchos (Triptolemos), 64, 351
Iason, 234
*Idylls* (Theocritus), 26
Illegitimacy, 106, 110
*Iliad* (Homer), 44, 89, 334, 395, 396

Infanticide, female, 110, 146, 147
Infibulation, 68, 69
Interaction, male/female, 332–336
Io, 339
Iocasta, 289, 334, 336
Iole, 340
Ion, 341
*Ion* (Euripides), 340
Iphigeneia, 132, 135, 136, 316, 339
*Iphigeneia in Aulis* (Euripides), 135, 316
*Iphigeneia in Tauris* (Euripides), 135, 316
Isaeus, 91, 322
Ischomachus, 91, 99, 101, 103, 104, 109, 214, 245
Isocrates, 47, 116, 272

Judgment of Paris, 206
Judith, 323

Kaempf-Dimitriadou, S., 52
Kalais, 52
Kallisto, 168, 312, 316
Kiss Painter, 191
Kitto, H. D. F., 331
Kore. *See* Persephone/Kore
Korone, 60
*Kottabos*, 160, 164
*Kynodesme*, 68, 69

*La Bonne Soupe* (Marceau), 271
Lagisca, 272
Laius, 289, 291
Lamachus, 385
Lamprocles, 111, 147
Lapiths, 40
Lattimore, Richmond, 21, 22
Law
  Attic, 322
  Draconian, 5, 100
  marital, 101–103
  prostitutes and, 206–208
  respectable women and, 208, 209
  treatment of criminals under, 8
*Laws* (Plato), 117, 128, 299, 328
Leaena, 194
Leagros, 285
Leda, 51
Lemnians, 324, 338
Leokorion, 137, 138
Leos, 137
Lesbos, 86
Leto, 55, 149, 346
Lewis, I. M., 360
*Lexicon* (Photius), 68
*Lexicon* (Suidas), 353, 354

*Libation Bearers, The* (Aeschylus), 233, 338
Licht, Hans. *See* Brandt, Paul
*Life of Cimon* (Plutarch), 92
*Life of Pericles* (Plutarch), 198
*Life of Solon* (Plutarch), 114
Literature, 329, 330
Livia, 235
*Love of the Gods in Attic Art of the Fifth Century* B.C., *The* (Kaempf-Dimitriadou), 52
Lucretia, 256, 258
Ludovisi throne, 217
Lycurgus, 88, 128
Lynceus, 324
Lysias, 91, 100, 128, 187, 208, 212, 270, 272, 298
*Lysistrata* (Aristophanes), 23, 25, 30, 87, 116, 231, 238, 305, 387, 393

Macedonians, 327
Maenadism, 358, 379
Maenads, 350, 351, 391
  sex life of, 357–379
Makron, 167, 223, 351, 366
Male
  child education of, 302
  dominance of, 6, 34, 44, 47–55, 344
  genital narcissism, 67–75
  motherhood, 34, 40
  outnumbers female, 204, 205
  weavers, 246
  wife vs. hetaera, 212, 215, 217, 223, 224
  work ethics of, 229–231
  youthful experimentation, 267, 268
M. Aemilius Paullus, 414
Marcadé, Jean, 76
Marceau, Félicien, 271
Marcus Aurelius, 408
Marriage, 130, 131
  attic form of, 328
  bride's indoctrination, 103–106
  common-law, 187
  dowry, 100, 101
  monogamous, 117, 299
  premature, 103, 104
  reparatory, 344
  role of wife, 100
  sex in, 99, 106–108, 114–122
  wedding, 106–108
Marital law, 101–103
Masturbation, 85
Medea, 58, 135, 138, 234, 335, 344
Medusa head, 39
Megara, 36, 57, 354
Melian dialogue, 19, 22

Melos, 17–19, 23, 381
  women of Athens and, 19, 20
Memnon, 147, 413
*Memoirs of Socrates* (Xenophon), 99, 111, 197, 232
Menander, 103, 104, 188, 191, 192, 194, 199, 273, 343, 344, 405
Menecles, 322
Menelaos, 58, 397
*Menexenus* (Plato), 198
*Men of Athens* (Warner), 6
Menopause, 88
Messenians, 325
Menstruation, 82, 243
Metaneira, 187
Metroön, 44
Metropolitan Museum of Art, 26, 106, 147, 148
Midwives, 142
Miltiades, 92
Minotaur of Crete, 58, 303
Minyas, 135
Misogyny, 9, 130, 405
Monotheism, 112
Monuments, 215, 217, 235
Money pouch, 260–265
Moschion, 344
Mossynoeci, 327
Motherhood, 306
  joys of, 110–112
  male, 34, 40
  premature, 103
  sorrows of, 346
Mount Olympus, 43, 52, 78, 285
Mount Parnassus, 367
Music, 104, 106, 208
Musonius Rufus, 402, 403
*Mutterrecht* (Mother Right) (Bachofen), 65
Mycenaeans, 334
*Myrmidons, The* (Aeschylus), 287
Myrrha, 25
Myrtle, 30
Myrtle berry, 30
Myrto, 272
Mythemes, patriarchal, 62–64
Mythology, 33, 334
  Amazonomachia, 34, 39, 44, 45, 47, 264
  glorification of sexual violence, 57
  gynecocracy, 66, 321–325
  mass murder, 336–339
  motifs on black-figure vase paintings, 36
  mourning mothers, 147–149
  tales of male supremacy, 34
  Trojan cycle, 149

Names, significance of, 88–93
Nasamones, 327
*Natural History* (Pliny), 142
Neaera, 156–158, 182, 187, 196, 199, 208, 268, 272
Neoptolemos, 399, 400
Nessos, 340
*Net Draggers, The* (Aeschylus), 340
Neumann, Erich, 43, 66, 124
Nicarete, 157, 165, 187, 196, 259
Nietzsche, Friedrich, 9, 350
Nikias, 382, 383, 385, 391
"Nine Springs Fountain," 236
Niobe, 112, 147, 345, 346
*Niobe* (Aeschylus), 345, 346
Notor, Gabriel, 154
Nudity, 68, 88

Odysseus, 22, 36
  Athena and, 35
*Odyssey* (Homer), 35, 44, 323, 334, 396
*Oeconomicus* (Xenophon), 99, 231
Oedipus, 87, 289, 324, 336
*Oedipus at Colonus* (Sophocles), 324
Oenopion, 373
*Olisbos.* See Dildo
Olympias, 142, 359
Olympus, gods of, 36
Omphale, Queen, 36
Onesimos, 190
*Onomasticon* (Pollux), 114
*On the Conservation of Health* (Galen), 120, 144
*On the Diseases of Women* ("Hippocrates"), 144
*On the Estate of Philoktemon* (Isaeus), 196
*On the Guardianship of Aphobos* (Demosthenes), 102
*On the Inheritance of Menecles* (Isaeus), 322
*On the Murder of Eratosthenes* (Lysias), 91, 100, 208, 212, 272
*On the Mysteries* (Andocides), 388
*On the Wound* (Lysias), 270
*On Women* (Semonides), 230
Oreithyia, 52
Orestes, 233, 234, 323, 338, 355
Orpheus, 379
Orwell, George, 18
Ovid, 234
Oxathres, 411

Painting, art of Western, 329
*Palaestrai,* 302
Pamphila, 343

Pan, 387
Pandora, 40
Pandrosos, 308
*Panegyricus (Praise of Athens)* (Isocrates), 47
Pan Painter, 387
Paris, 21, 89, 206
*Parliament of Women, The* (Aristophanes), 99, 201, 357, 393
Partheniai, 325
Parthenon, 38, 45, 306
Patroclus, 149, 287, 289
Pausanias, 367
*Peace, The* (Aristophanes), 330, 331, 393
Peace of Nikias, 383
Pederasty, 275, 287–291
Peirithoos, 58
Peisistratids, 379
Peisistratus, 33, 235
Peithinos, 54, 218, 282
Peleus, 54, 218, 255
Peloponnesian War, 11, 18, 88, 272, 332, 334, 383, 402, 404
Pelops, 132, 289, 291
Peneleos, 396
Penelope, 245
Penthesileia, 44, 45, 130, 320, 339
Penthesileia Painter, 45, 46, 54, 55, 70, 149, 206, 218, 286, 287
Pentheus, King, 358
Peplos, 306, 308, 310
Pericles, 8, 40, 88, 198, 199, 272, 335, 382
Persephone, 64, 129, 132, 346
Persephone/Kore, 112, 147
Perseus, 323, 340, 414
Persian invasion, 335
Persians, 327, 335
*Persians* (Aeschylus), 92, 335
*Phaedo* (Plato), 79
Phaia, 355
Phallic bronzes, 75
Phallicism. *See also* Phallus
  Alcibiades and, 384, 385
  later waves of, 405
  in literature, 79
Phallocracy, 1–3, 86, 87. *See also* Rape
  apologies for, 9
  justification, 4
  modern problem, 12
  origins, 12
*Phallophoria,* 78
"Phallos," 66
Phallus, 2. *See also* Herms; Phallicism
  in Athens' public life, 30

Phallus (cont.)
  on Delos, 77
  processions, 78
  public cult, 78, 79
  symbolic, 50
Phano, 272
Pherekrates, 116, 130, 384
Phidias, 38
Philemon, 158
Philetaeros, 215
Philip II, 407
Philoctetes (Sophocles), 336
Philoxene, 298
Philoxenos, 414
Phokylides, 231
Photius, 68
Phryne, 197
Phrynichus, 335, 387
Phrynion, 157, 158, 182, 272
Piazza Armerina, 314
Pietà, 147
Pig Painter, 238
Pindar, 156
Piraeus, 153, 155
Pistoxenos Painter, 201
"Planking," 8
Plato, 8, 11, 67, 79, 85, 103, 117, 198,
    210, 230, 246, 278, 285, 289, 299,
    312, 328, 348, 384, 395, 402, 405
Plato (playwright), 162, 163
Plautus, 188, 341
Plays. See Theater
Pliny the Elder, 142, 144, 215, 414, 415
Ploutos, 201
Plutarch, 92, 114, 138, 146, 191, 198,
    209, 303, 355, 392, 393, 413
Pluto, 129
Poems, Homeric, 334
Poetics (Aristotle), 322
Poetry, 329, 330
Poison, 322
Pollux, 114, 238
Polygamy, 327
Polygnotus, 93, 312
Polynices, 336
Polyxena, 339
Pomeroy, Sarah, 11, 245
Pornoboskoi, 196
Poseidippus, 146
Poseidon, 50, 64, 240, 258, 340
Pottery, painted, 2, 3, 118
  black-figure style, 117, 272
  homosexual scenes, 277–285
  meaning of, 3
  motifs, 36
  phallic Attic vase, 76
  portrayal of children, 72, 73

Pottery (cont.)
  red-figure technique, 70, 117, 243,
    277
  water-carrying on vases, 235–240
Praxiteles, 195, 197, 215
Praxithea, 138
Precepts for Conjugal Life (Plutarch),
    191
Priam, 21, 206, 339, 396, 399, 400
Procne, 135
Procreation, male vs. female, 145
Prometheus Bound (Aeschylus), 339
Prostitution, 187, 272, 327. See also
    Hetaerai
  affectionate prostitutes, 188–191
  the courtesan, 194–198
  female, 153–155
  game of kottabos, 160
  hetaerai primping, 170
  homosexual, 277
  humiliation and abuse, 174–182
  male, 153, 296
  negative image, 200–202
  propensity for, 298, 299
  prostitutes on stage, 191–194
  revelry (komos), 170, 174
  social and moral sanction, 205, 267
  the symposium and, 160–169
Proteus, 379
Pseudolus (Plautus), 188
Pseudo-Xenephon, 230

Rape, 34, 47–55, 64, 116
  drive for revenge, 276
  marriage by, 52, 54
  motif in plays, 339
  "reparatory marriage," 344
  at the well, 235–240
Realenzyklopaedie der klassischen
    Altertumswissenschaft, 66
Relationships
  extra-marital, 267
  mother/daughter, 112
  mother/son, 111
  pederastic, 117
Religion. See Rituals
Republic, The (Plato), 117, 328, 402
Rites. See Rituals
Rituals
  cult of Demeter, 351
  Dionysiac, 78, 358, 359, 360, 362,
    368, 371, 373, 375, 378
  female indoctrination, 305, 306
  initiation, 301, 302
  as release, 301, 302
  religious, 350
  Sacred Wedding, 373

Rituals *(cont.)*
  significance of, 300, 301, 349, 350
  social structure and, 349
  Thesmophoria, 352, 353, 357
  transvestite, 303
"Roll-out-platform," 333
Rule of the Thirty, 322

Sacred Wedding ritual, 373
Sacrifice, human, 132, 135, 137, 138
Sandbach, F. H., 331
Sandys, Sir John, 156
Sarpedon, 149
Satyros, 197
Satyrs, 341, 360, 391
  sex life of, 357, 362, 366, 373, 375
Scholars, classical, 9–11
Script, "Linear B," 334
Sculpture, 329
Selinus, 383
Semele, 41, 51, 339
Semonides, 230
*Seven Against Thebes* (Aeschylus), 129,
  150, 336
Sex
  anal, 276, 277, 291, 293, 299
  double standard, 5, 6, 344
  Greek, 2
  Greek bisexual promiscuity, 51
  male antagonism, 145
  male ideas of female, 82
  marital and spinning, 252–258
  marriage, 106–108, 114–122
  in vase painting, 240–247
Sextus Tarquinius, 256, 258
*Sexual Life in Ancient Greece* (Brandt),
  9, 10
*Shield, The* (Menander), 103
Sicilian campaign, 16, 20, 23, 31, 381,
  383, 384, 402
  aftermath of, 403
Simon, Dr. Bennett, 348, 349
Skira festival, 357
Skiron, 60
Slater, Philip, 111
Slavery, 6, 7, 20. *See also* Slaves
Slaves, 20
  condition of, 7
  "gulp preventer," 7
  sexual condition, 7
  similarity to woman's position, 6
  torture of, 7
Society, male domination of, 1
Socrates, 8, 101, 104, 111, 147, 198,
  232, 328, 384, 402, 405
  last words, 79, 82
  Theodote and, 197

Sodomy, 179
Solon, 5, 33, 88, 114, 206, 208, 209,
  284
Sophocles, 36, 57, 89, 112, 146, 150,
  272, 324, 326, 336, 338, 340, 344
Soranus, 142, 144
Sorcery, 322
Sosias Painter, 70
Sparta, 68, 92, 138, 146, 324, 325, 334,
  339, 354, 383
  marriage in, 103
  moral climate of, 11
  Peloponnesian War, 11, 18, 23
Spinning, 252, 258–260
Stephanus, 68, 157, 158
Stoa of Attalus, 95
Stoa Poikile (Painted Porch), 45
Stoicism, 402
Strabo, 47, 155
Strauss, Richard, 367
Suidas, 353, 354
Susarion, 271
Symbolism, 129
  of boxes and chests, 122, 123
  of bridal shoes, 121, 122
  Dionysiac, 373, 375
  marriage/death, 130
  of a money pouch, 179, 260–265
  of pigs, 352–356
  of a seated woman, 123, 124
  symbols of domestic virtues, 247, 248
Symposium, 160–165
  cup, 165–169, 180, 217–224
  revelry (*komos*), 170, 174
*Symposium, The* (Plato), 85, 162, 174,
  299, 384
*Symposium, The* (Xenophon), 117

Tantalus, 132, 135, 346
  tortures of, 7
Taras, 324, 330
*Team of Horses, The* (Isocrates), 388
Teiresias, 116
Telemachus, 245
Temple of Nike, 94
Temple of Theseus, 45
*Tereus* (Sophocles), 98, 344
Textiles, 232, 233
  production of in vase painting, 240–
  247
Theater, 330, 340–343
  lost plays, 339
  Middle Comedy, 404, 405
  New Comedy, 343, 344, 404
  Old Comedy, 343, 355, 404
  stage settings, 332, 333
Thebes, 334, 336, 343, 358

Theocritus, 26
Theodote, 197
Theodotus, 298
Theophrastus, 405
Theopompus, 138, 325
*Thesaurus* (Stephanus), 68
*Theseid*, 61
Theseus, 4, 24, 45, 52, 56, 64, 73, 230, 258, 303, 324, 405
  Athens' national hero, 57–62
  killing the sow Phaia, 355
Thesmophoria, 352, 353, 357
*Thesmophoriazusai* (Aristophanes), 8, 109, 291, 332, 333, 353, 393, 395
Thetis, 54, 149, 218, 254
Thoas, 324
Tholos, 95
Thompson, Homer, 137, 138
Thracians, 326, 327
Thucydides, 17, 19, 20, 31, 334, 382, 384, 385, 387, 393
Thyestes, 135
Timarchus, 298
Tityus, 55, 149
Toledo Museum of Art, 223
Tomb, 129, 217, 218
Tomb of the Diver, 217, 218
Torture, 7, 8
Tragedy, 330
  emotional relief in, 348
  subject matter, 334
Trausi, 326
Trojan War, 16, 21, 22, 33, 44, 287, 335, 396, 397, 399, 400, 413
*Trojan Women, The* (Euripides), 16, 17, 20–23, 381, 391, 412
Trygaios, 331

*Vagina dentata*, 126, 205
Vase painting. *See* Pottery, painted
Vergil, 62, 400
Vermeule, Emily, 76
Villa of the Faun, 408
Villa of the Mysteries, 310
Viola, Franca, 344
Vitruvius, 210
Vorberg, Gaston, 76

Water carrying, 232, 233
Whore. *See* Hetaerai; Prostitution

Wife vs. hetaera, 212, 215, 217, 223, 224
Williams, F. E., 276
*Woman of Samos, The* (Menander), 191, 192, 201, 273, 344
Womb, 82, 129
  male, 41
Women
  art and music, 104, 106
  death, 129, 130, 149–152, 310, 316
  defeminization, 42, 64, 351
  education, 104
  house quarters for, 110, 118, 119, 122, 124, 210–213
  killing men, 337–339
  labor, 99, 108, 124, 229–264
  male fear of, 3–6
  marriage, 100–108
  of Melos vs. Athenian, 19, 20
  mental attitude, 20–23, 124–128
  motherhood, 103, 110–112, 306, 346
  in mythology, 323
  names, 88–93, 152
  rebellion of, 65, 126, 127, 323, 337–338, 379, 392–395
  rituals, 302, 305, 306, 349–379
  sex life, 9–11, 30, 82, 85, 86, 107, 145, 146, 310
  status, 6, 30, 87, 98, 99, 100, 108–110, 116, 204
  theater attendance by, 330–332
*Women and Madness* (Chesler), 112
*Women Bread Sellers* (Hermippus), 355
*Women of Trachis, The* (Sophocles), 36, 57, 340
Women's Police, 5, 209, 405

Xanthippe, 111, 147, 272, 402
Xenophon, 11, 91, 99, 101, 117, 147, 197, 212, 231, 232, 245, 327
Xenophon (Corinth), 156
Xerxes, King, 92, 335

Zetes, 52
Zethos, 343
Zeus, 22, 40–42, 89, 112, 116, 149, 339, 346
  Ganymede and, 43, 51, 223, 285–287
  master rapist, 50, 51, 340, 341, 343
Zobia, 272